W9-CYT-414

LOST GENERATION?

OR

LEFT GENERATION!

Confronting the Youth Crisis in Black America

by

REV. CLARENCE LUMUMBA JAMES, SR
"The Black Man's Preacher"

© 2004 by Rev. Clarence Lumumba James, Sr.
First Edition

All rights reserved. No part of this book shall be
reproduced, stored in a retrieval system, or transmitted
by any means without written permission by the author.
The only exception is brief quotations.

Published by Youth Leadership Development
Programs, Inc.
P.O. Box 30250
Elkins Park, PA 19027
215-924-4432
www.revcljsr.org

If you see a turtle sitting on a fence post, he had help.
African American Proverb

To my greatest teachers

My father: Arkansas born, West Side of Chicago-raised, Mr. Jesse Joseph Jerome James, Jr. Big, tall, coal-black, baldheaded, broad-shouldered, muscle-bound, soft-spoken, former master sergeant in the army, former hard-hitting professional heavyweight fighting, blues-crooning, original black gangster, numbers banking, two-gun-carrying, wife-loving, child-raising, two and half job working, community protecting Jesse James. The greatest man that I have ever known.

My mother, Mrs. Mayme Louise Graves James Howell, affectionately known to her family as "Sister". A mother from the old school. Loving wife, dedicated mother, master cook, seamstress, quilter, storyteller and family historian.

My grandmother, Mrs. Josephine Booker, who we knew lovingly as "Lil' Mama". I was her favorite. And she was mine.

The nuns and priests at St. Charles Borromeo and Holy Trinity Catholic Grammar schools on the West Side who designed special curricula to meet my precocious intellectual drive. Especially to Father John Marren and Sister Edna.

Mr. Lerone Bennett. A member of the great Morehouse College class of 1948. Scholar, writer, visionary, analyst, and historian who writes with the lyricism of a poet and the drama of a novelist. Until, at fourteen years of age when I picked up his magnum opus, <u>Before</u> <u>The</u> <u>Mayflower</u>, I did not know that any black person had ever written a book or that any black person had ever done anything worth writing a book about. His writing gave birth to my lifelong journey up the pathway of an African Christian identity.

Dr. Dorothy Taylor Clarke, my favorite high school teacher. The most brilliant and beautiful teacher who ever graced the halls of John Marshall High School. She walked like a queen and taught like an angel.

Mr. John Vanderhiden, my debate coach at Marshall. A man who knew intimately and shared passionately the powers of logic and argumentation. He did the greatest thing any teacher can do for his students: He loved us.

Rev. William Briggs, pastor of the Warren Avenue Congregational Church and organizer of the East Garfield Park Community Organization (EGPCO)who introduced me and the Youth Group at Warren Ave. to the Civil Rights Movement and thereby changed forever the course of my life.

Dr. Colia Liddel Lafayette Clarke: "Mama Colia" My chief godmother. A Mississippi girl in whose veins flows the blood of Africa and Native America. Civil Rights activist, strategist and visionary. Possessor of a spiritual strength so powerful that it continually and unselfconsciously overflows and overwhelms. A Renaissance woman: Scholar, professor, singer of the old songs of our people, actress, historian, writer. She

4

opened her house, heart and mind to me when I was most in need of shelter, love, and learning.

Dr. Martin Luther King, Jr. my leader, my teacher, my role model, my exemplar in the ministry. He taught us how to live and how to die. "See how many minor men worry themselves into nameless graves while every now and then some truly great soul forgets himself into immortality."

Rev. James Bevel, whom Dr. King would introduce as "that marvelous young prophet". Who walked with courage and grace, as have so many prophets before him, the thin line between genius and insanity.

Mr. Eugene Heytow, Harvard Man, University of Chicago lawyer, businessman, banker, philosopher, philanthropist, humanitarian. My Jewish godfather, who recruited me to Harvard College, and taught me not only the banking business but so much about the deepest aspects of life.

The Reverend Dr. Vernon Johns. The man who set the standard for prophetic preaching, excellence in scholarship, independence of thought, extraordinary boldness, fearless activism. He came out of Farmville, VA in Prince Edwards County with a self-taught fluency in Hebrew, Greek, Latin and German and in one semester became the most outstanding student at Oberlin College. Former president of the historic and esteemed Virginia Seminary and College in Lynchburg, VA Immediate predecessor to Dr. King as pastor of the Dexter Ave. Baptist Church in Montgomery, AL. Bennie Mays and Mordecai Johnson agreed that he was the most brilliant black preacher of the twentieth century. I never met him, but his legendary exploits as recited in awed voices by black preachers whose favorite hero he was, have fired my theological and activist imagination since I was seventeen years old.

Dr. Robert H. Brisbane, my major professor, advisor, mentor, and protector from my own youthful foibles, the legendary chairman of the political science department at Morehouse College during its Golden Age. Who for forty years held Morehouse men spellbound during his lectures while never looking at a note.

Rev. Paul Jakes, Sr., founder and pastor of Old St. Paul M. B. Church on the West Side. He saw something in me that did not appear to the natural eye, believed in me, trusted me, baptized me, licensed me to preach, ordained me over the objections of the catechizer, married me, and blessed my babies. "No matter how far the river flows it never forgets its source."

Rev. James Horton, pastor of the Kingdom Missionary Baptist Church. A pillar of strength. The strongest of men physically, spiritually, intellectually and emotionally. The catechizer at my ordination, who looked beyond my youthful faults and perceived a more promising maturity. A powerful preacher, teacher, leader, counselor. He was a walking textbook of pastoring black people.

The Reverend Dr. Shelvin Jerome Hall, from the hard lands of East Texas. Forever my pastor. Valedictorian of Bishop College Class of 1948. My chiefest advisor. The wisest among ten thousand. Brilliant, acerbic, a wit sharper than a razor blade, always cuts to the bone, eloquent, a gospel preacher of the first magnitude, civil rights leader, visionary, community builder. African-centered scholar before there was African American Studies. Never failed to stand out no matter how large the crowd.

Dr. Edmund Ilogu, Acting Chairman of the Department of Religion at the University of Nigeria in Nsukka. Visiting professor at the University of Chicago Divinity School. Scholar, seer, intellectual warrior. I watched in amazement as he humbled the greatest and proudest European scholars with the simplest truths of Mother Africa.

The Reverend Doctor Isaac Singleton. For 43 years pastor of the Mt. Zion Baptist Church in Joliet, IL My "Uncle Ike" and his wonderful wife my "Aunt Pearl". A true son of the fertile soul and salubrious climate of Louisiana. A powerful preacher, productive pastor, a man's man and a leader of men, civil rights activist, a fearless advocate for our people, a builder of buildings and a shaper of the characters of boys and girls. He inspired and instructed me in my first pastorates when I was young, inexperienced and unlearned in the ways of the Black Church. He opened doors for me when I had no prospects. He has remained a leaning post for me and a supporter of my ministry in these my days of maturity.

The Reverend Derwood Hunter, husband of Carolyn, father of Jada, Tiffany and Kia, godfather to my baby girl, Cemere. A true Son of Virginia Union. Renowned pulpiteer. Pastored Bethel Baptist Church in Rockford, IL and in Miami, FL. Also the historic Ebeneezer Baptist Church on the South Side of Chicago. Was chaplain at Florida Memorial College in Miami, FL. A strong and proud black man. My elder brother, my greatest friend in the ministry, who shared my secrets and took my confidences with him to the grave.

The Reverend Doctor Hezekiah Brady, Sr. "THE OLD

7

EAGLE" Originally of Natchez, Mississippi. A black theologian before the term "black theology" was coined. For many years pastor of the Christian Hope Baptist Church on the South Side of Chicago. Tall, lean, independent, fierce and powerful. He taught us by example the economic power of the black church by developing millions of dollars worth of businesses and employing scores of people from Christian Hope.

The Reverend Doctor Henry Mitchell, my "Pop". Mentor of my doctoral studies. A "Lincoln man" from her glory days when Morehouse called herself "The Lincoln of the South". The Dean of homileticians. Chief producer of black holders of doctoral degrees in theological studies. First chairman of an African American Studies department at the graduate theological level. World renowned author, international evangelist, raconteur. He actually has been everywhere, met everybody, seen everything and lived to tell about it in his own inimitable fashion.

Mr. Warren Settles Whatley, Sr. of Orchard Hills, GA. A Morehouse Man of the old school, class of 1939. Lovingly known as "Pops" to the men who worked and learned under him. A co-founder with his brothers Plemon, Sr. and Charles of Whatley Brothers Construction Company of Atlanta, GA Scion of a great family of builders with construction skills handed down from the generations of their fathers and grandfathers going all the way through to slavery to our homeland in Africa. A builder, philosopher, social critic, storyteller, teacher of youth. My major professor when I earned my "associate of arts degree" in basic construction from the school of hard knocks.

The Reverend Doctor Oscar J. Underwood AKA _Dr. OJU_. We have trod similar paths and shared similar visions. One of the greatest black educators of this dispensation. Former Teacher of the Year in the state of Indiana. A gospel preacher extraordinaire. Founder and Pastor of the Cornerstone Worship Center. Founder and president of the Cornerstone College Preparatory School both in Ft. Wayne, IN. I marvel at his ability and determination to "reach the unreachable and teach the unteachable".

Dr. Ayesha Imani, AKA Umayma (Lil' Mama) a sister from North Philly, a true daughter of the Garvey Movement (UNIA).The epitome of Pan-African Womanhood. A veteran teacher of some twenty five years in the Philadelphia Public Schools. Multi-talented, scholar-activist, African Christian theologian, historian, writer, poet, administrator, workshop leader, trainer of teachers and parents, R&B singer, African dancer. I continually stand in awe of her ability to disarm and defeat the self destructive urges of the most unruly students armed only with the irresistible weapon of her unconditional love.

The Reverend Doctor Jean Barber. Pastor, prophetess, queen, a gospel preacher of the first rank. My big sister in the ministry. My confidante, counselor and advisor. A southern girl from the old school who came up the rough side of the mountain and reached the top with grit, grace, power and elegance. Confucius looked around the curvature of time and saw her as his example when he penned the words: "She who knows and knows that she knows is a wise woman, follow her."

TABLE OF CONTENTS

INTRODUCTION

This book was written primarily for parents, preachers, and teachers, the elders of our people in general, young people in particular and any and everyone who are involved in the sacred task of raising children. From an African insistence on understanding the wholeness of life we cannot easily compartmentalize human society into neat categories of those who are involved and interested in the lives of young people and those who are not. Everybody must be concerned about everybody else in the human community. There are, for instance adults, that don't have children of their own but that doesn't mean that they are not involved in the lives of children whether the young people are their nieces and nephews, members of their churches or the neighbor children on the block where they live. Some people who have all girls may want to conclude that they don't have to concern themselves with raising boys except that their daughters will date, court and marry somebody's sons and those young men will be the fathers of their grandchildren. The same thing goes for families that have all boys and no girls.

The term and concept of fatherhood should not be narrowly defined as those who have either physically fertilized an egg nor should motherhood be limited to those women who have carried a baby in their own wombs. Neither ought parenthood be limited to those who exercise legal guardianship over a child. Parenthood is not just matter of biology or of legal status. Parenthood is a spiritual office. There are men who are unable to produce active and vital sperm and thus will never be anyone's genetic father. But because they are imbued with the spirit of fatherhood people call them "Daddy", "Pops", "Father", "Godfather" everywhere they go and they are described by young people as being : "just like my father". The same rule holds for motherhood. There are women whose wombs are barren so that they will never experience pregnancy or birth a child into this world. But they are caretakers and caregivers for every child that wanders within the orbit of their lives and they are called "Mama", "Moms", "Mother" everywhere they set foot. All preachers and teachers are by definition surrogate parents. African traditional values say that anytime an older person interacts with a younger person they must treat the younger person as their child. In their relationships with older people they must treat the elder as they would their own parent. It is only in their activity within the peer group that there is a certain relaxation of the responsibilities owed from youngster to elder. But even then they must treat their peers with same care and concern they would their own brothers and sisters.

The purpose of this book is to excite thinking about the current dilemma in the lives of our young people and thereby generate the kinds of dialogue among old and young, parents and children, teachers and preachers that will bring about necessary positive change in the life of the African American community. A major part of the problem with our young people is that they are no longer raised in a coherent fashion. In traditional African life all segments of the community stayed in constant contact and offered young people a single standard of what constituted acceptable behavior. It is one of the most popular but unstated goals of young people to find elders who will disagree with the strictures placed upon them by authority figures like parents, preachers, teachers and coaches and thus justify and facilitate their misbehavior. The fear of every parent is the irresponsible, childlike elder in the family or community who will entertain their children's delinquent behavior, allowing them to smoke, drink, and curse, have sex or use drugs. By coherence I mean the active ties that existed in the Black communities of the South and North prior to the 1960's when the parent, teacher and preacher were in constant contact and agreement in terms of the ethics and morals of childrearing and in insistence on common standards of behavior. Those ties have been broken by the alienation of urban existence where often people don't know even their next-door neighbors. In the old days a child's walking around the corner out of their parents sight did not mean escaping from adult supervision. Every adult had both responsibility for and authority over the conduct of all children.

I identify myself as a member of the last generation of black youth raised in the ten-thousand plus year of tradition of African childrearing. I was raised in the old way, some would say in the old school whose philosophy was established in African pre-history and survived capture, the Middle Passage, chattel slavery, lynch law, mob rule, chain gang, share-cropping, tenant farming, and every other vestige of American Apartheid. My late father is Mr. Jesse Joseph Jerome James, Jr. whose roots are in Mississippi on his father's side and Arkansas on his mother's. My mother is the former Mayme Louise Graves of Arkansas and Louisiana, known to her people as "Sister". There are six of us, my big brother, Jesse Joseph Jerome James, III, "Jo-Jo", and my baby brother, Ricardo, "Black Panther Rico" and three sisters, Darthula "Dot", Debra "Debbie" and Denise "DeeCee" were all born and raised on the West Side of Chicago thus making us city folk. However, the African American proverb says" It ain't where you're raised, its how your raised, that counts."

Because we were raised by country people our moral values and standards of behavior did not differ much from those of our cousins Down South. My father, without a college education, and my mother with two years of high school raised six children all of whom completed high school and attended some college. Four of us are college graduates, two with graduate degrees. My father worked two full-time jobs so that my mother could stay at home be there for the family. I remember only one time in my entire childhood coming home from school and not finding my mother there. My mother was celebrated in our neighborhood as a cook and a seamstress so that her staying at home was not the bored idleness of suburban housewives but an essential contribution to a household economy that was productive and not just a unit of captive consumerism, buying everything and producing nothing.

This book is also in a sense, a reflection on my thirty-four years as a Baptist preacher with a ministry profoundly committed to the development of young people of African descent. I have served young people for all of these years in ministry beginning in the latter part of my adolescence as a leader of my age group. I have six children of my own, four boys and two girls and eleven grandchildren, seven girls and four boys. I have some fifteen young preachers who recognize me as their father-in-the-ministry and upwards of a hundred more young people who call me their godfather. I have taught in grammar schools, high schools, colleges, and universities, both undergraduate and graduate courses, primarily courses in religion and African American studies.

As Director of Recruitment and Assistant Director of Admissions at my alma mater Morehouse College from 1985 to 1988 I was responsible for some 80 percent of the school's physical recruitment efforts. During that period I traversed the length and breadth of the United States visiting high schools seeking out serious, talented young black men and convincing them to choose Morehouse over white schools like Harvard, Yale, the University of Chicago, Stanford, etc. I was able to bring some of the most brilliant young minds to Morehouse because I could present to prospective students the pros and cons of white and black college life, having started college at Central YMCA Community College in downtown Chicago then transferring to Harvard for two years before completing my undergraduate studies at Morehouse.

I accomplished all these academic achievements without having graduated from high school. When I talk to young people about the importance of education I do not do so from the privileged advantage of having been an academic superstar all my scholastic life. I did not take the fast track or the easy road to academic success. I was seldom the teacher's pet. During my last two years at Marshall High School I flunked every class my last three semesters. Yet at the same time I was president of the Negro History Club, captain of the debate team and had the highest SAT scores in my class. My academic failures were due to the emotional traumas of a difficult adolescence and my participation in the Civil Rights Movement. Dr. Martin Luther King, Jr. heard me give a speech representing high school youth at a civil rights rally at a local Westside church and was impressed enough with my presentation to send an SCLC staff member to bring to me to meet him. As a result I was appointed the founding president of the Student Union for Better Education, an SCLC sponsored youth organization. For the next two years I led a student staff of some thirteen high schools that fanned out across the city organizing black high school students. We engaged in numerous acts of direct action and civil disobedience including marches, demonstrations, sit-ins and boycotts. As a result of these activities I was expelled from high school on my 18th birthday.

I am therefore intimately acquainted with the lives of our young people from a number of perspectives and experiences. If some of my writing seems harshly critical I have earned the right to address young people in such a manner because I have paid my dues. I don't write as one who stands on the sidelines gazing at our young people through the eyes of detachment and unconcern. I have coached them in basketball, brought them out of the projects to the countryside and taught them how to grow vegetable gardens, tutored them to pass GED tests, gone to their schools and confronted and chastised principals, teachers, and counselors for mistreating them. Driven long hours on highways to take them on college visitations, brokered their admissions to college when they lacked high school diplomas, housed them in my home and fed them at my table when their parents had banned them from their own, defended them in court when their own lawyers were ineffective and uncaring, and preached their funerals. I have negotiated truces among warring gangs like the Disciples, the Vice Lords, the Egyptian Cobras and the Latin Kings in Stateville Prison.

My journey as a minister to youth began during the last years of my teenage hood. I was in the liminal stage of seeking and searching for myself and for my role in life and society. This is the eternal task of teenagers, to break with their prior role as their father's sons and their mother's daughters, carbon copies of their parents and discover the purpose for which they were sent into the world. It is in the discovery and fulfillment of that purpose that our true identity is found. While I was in the midst of this intensely emotional and philosophical struggle Dr. Martin Luther King, Jr. came to Chicago at the invitation of the local leaders of the Coordinating Council of Community Organizations a city-wide umbrella group of local organizations whose principal struggle up until that time was the reform of the public school system. Dr. King taught my generation three paramount lessons of life. Firstly, that as young people we were important. Important enough that he sought us out and aggressively recruited us to be participants and leaders in the movement. Secondly, that we were responsible for defining ourselves. As human beings what distinguished us from all other earthly creatures was our divinely given power of self-definition.

17

Thirdly, and most importantly, that we must dedicate our lives to the pursuit of a noble goal in order to lift ourselves above the level of mere animal existence. He taught us that the purpose of humanity must be higher than the mere satisfaction of physical needs. The discovery of, commitment to and struggle towards a higher purpose is what elevates us above the animal.

My generation came into adulthood in the fires of the Civil Rights/Black Power movements. In her outstanding novel, The Wrestling Match, Nigerian author Buchi Emecheta explains that every African generation comes to manhood and womanhood in a unique fashion. Wrestling was the arena that the elders used to introduce the young characters in the novel to their new roles as adults. We crossed over organizing, agitating, analyzing, demonstrating, protesting, speaking out, and standing up. For some of us those fires seared so deeply that we are forever moved and marked by its light and heat. There are people who accuse me personally and any number of my peers of being as they put it- "stuck in the sixties". They pronounce these words contemptuously as harsh criticism. They seem not to understand that there are classic periods in the history of any people that bear never forgetting or forsaking. I'm proud to be not only stuck in the sixties but to have the sixties stuck in me. There is an element of timelessness about greatness. Some things don't go out of style. Some things don't rust out, wear out, or lose their value because they may no longer be appreciated by the followers of fads and those devoted only to all things popular. Telling us that we're stuck in the sixties is like accusing us of trying to sail like Paul Cuffe, build like Benjamin Banneker, rebel like Nat Turner, liberate like Harriet Tubman, orate like Frederick Douglass, analyze like W.E.B. DuBois, fight like Jack Johnson, organize like Marcus Garvey, pitch like Satchel Paige, sing like Paul Robeson, write like Zora Neale Hurston, run like Jesse Owens, humorize like Moms Mabley, litigate like

Thurgood Marshall, educate like Benjamin Elijah Mays, play basketball like Wilt Chamberlain, sermonize like Vernon Johns, agitate like Martin Luther King, Jr., instigate like Malcolm X.

It may be meant as criticism but it goes into my heart as the highest of compliments for it means that someone recognizes that there are those of us who continue to hold up the blood-stained banner of unremitting struggle. It means there remains, as ever, a faithful few who have never taken their eyes off the prize of freedom and liberation for our people. These sacred duties were passed on to us in utter confidence in our faithfulness by our freedom-fighting ancestors. The struggle for the liberation of our people is a 400 year-plus, protracted, trans-generational warfare handed down from parent to child, and grandparent to grandchild. The spiritual: **We Are Climbing Jacob's Ladder** alludes to this in the line "Every round goes higher and higher." Read "round" in this sense to mean "generation".

There are verses of freedom songs that express these sentiments also:

My father was a freedom fighter
And I'm his freedom son
I promised my Pop
I wouldn't get no rest
Until every battle was won

We are soldiers in the army
We got to fight although we have to die
We got to hold up the bloodstained banner
We got to hold it up until we die

My mother was a soldier
She kept her hands
On the gospel plow
One day she got old

She couldn't fight anymore
But she stood there and fought anyhow

I write with an abiding sense of hope for and faith in this current generation's ability to rise to the highest level of their possibilities. But I also understand the meaning of the African proverb that says "Unless you admit to your disease you cannot find a cure". And the similar African American expression: "If you don't face it you can't fix it". My writing will therefore seem to some extremely critical. But it is the criticism of a father and a coach who demands more from his children and team members than they think they have to give. To that extent this book is written with the purpose in mind that young people will read it and make a better choice for their lives than is offered them by the world as it is.

Every generation of people while in their youth begins the great task of defining themselves as a collective. The enduring glory of our history as a people in this land is that we have produced generation after generation that completed this task with genius, courage, and artistic creativity. Now we have birthed and raised a generation in a time of trouble so great that we seem as a people to have lost our way. Every past generation was able to recognize the challenges and obstacles that lie before them in the roadways of life and then intelligently organize responses to remove the obstacles and meet the challenges. Through the lenses of hindsight we can now accurately recognize how each of the past generations met the challenges and confronted the problems of their times. From the generation that survived the indescribable, incomprehensible horrors of the Middle Passage, to those generations that suffered in the hellholes of chattel slavery yet in the end defied, deflected, defeated and then destroyed the monster in whose belly they lived, to the triumphant generation that smashed the chains of slavery in the Civil War and then went on to build a new African society that they described as a "nation within a nation", to that group of our forebears that trekked North in the Great Migration and while doing so dismantled the humiliating structures of de jure segregation and American Apartheid. But today we are unclear just what the problems are that confront and assail us; just what it is that's holding us down and pushing us back.

Slavery was our finest hour. To understand what strategies, tactics, instruments, tools, and weapons our ancestors used to defeat slavery cannot help but inform us as to what kinds of approaches we need to use today to deal with slavery's child—racism.. If our grandfathers defeated a much more dangerous enemy that we face today why would we not ask them how they did it? In labeling our ancestors victims of slavery rather than victors over it we not only discredit their memories and deny the true power of their lives, but worse, we prevent ourselves from taking advantage of the lessons that their histories have to teach us and we give white people too much credit. The breakdown of black culture did not begin with the Middle Passage, Slavery, sharecropping, tenant farming, lynch law, or even with the Great Migration. It was in the sixties, as we greedily and unreflectively grabbed at the false premises and promises of integration, that we lost our way.

As parent, preacher, teacher and counselor I have watched an entire generation being raised without the foundation of ancient truths to stand on. That is not to say that there are no positive examples of well-raised, forward-moving black youth in this generation. There are in fact hundreds of thousands if not millions. But I understand my task as a minister of the gospel to direct my foremost attention to "the least of these". When I address an audience of young people my primary concern is not to commend those that have done well, as important as it is to do that. The reason that they will have achieved academically and socially is because they have been receiving support at home and probably also in church.

The majority of my remarks are made to encourage those who are not achieving at the level of their real potential. If there is one young person in trouble it is the responsibility of a Christian community to direct its energy and resources toward the rescue of that one person. We are instructed by Jesus in the parable of The Good Shepherd that if ninety-and nine sheep are safe in the fold and one sheep lost, the good shepherd will leave the ninety and nine to search for and rescue the one. Or again when Jesus was criticized by the prim and proper middle-class folk for spending so much of his time amongst the low-class sinner folk, the drinkers and gamblers, thieves, and prostitutes ,he answered them: "It is they that are sick that need a physician not they that that are well". My mission as a Christian minister is to serve those in need, not just be a cheerleader to those who are doing well. One of the chief responsibilities Jesus challenges us to fulfill is to heal the sick, whether that sickness is physical, mental, emotional, spiritual, social, familial, marital, professional or academic.

We have always had to fight a war on two fronts in such a way that our history in this country can accurately be described as being caught "between a rock and a hard place". The rock is the centuries-old stone of white racism which has killed tens of millions of our people and ground entire generations into the dust of chattel slavery, lynch law, chain gang, and mob rule. But the hard place is our own families and communities when racism's demon-spawned, deformed, monstrous offspring "self-hatred " eats away at our spirit and flesh from the inside. If we must prioritize and choose one to invest more energy in defending ourselves against, the choice must be targeting self-hatred as our most dangerous foe. No matter how powerful an enemy, how damaging a blow or how crushing a defeat a people can rise again out the ashes of a thousand calamities if they have the wherewithal within their own spirits to do so. But when a people are disarmed because they don't even know who they are, all is lost.

The ancient Chinese philosopher Sun Tzu said in his classic text: The Art of War: "If a people go out on the battlefield and know their enemy and themselves the odds are that they will win the battle. If they don't know their enemy but at least know themselves they have a fifty-fifty chance. But if they don't know their enemy or themselves they have no chance at all". He never imagined that there would ever be a people that would actually know their enemy but not know themselves. Such a situation is unthinkable. But that is where too many of us are. Too many of us have accepted the white supremacists presuppositions of integration and neglected to study and strengthen ourselves as we chase after the pipe-dream of losing ourselves and becoming like someone else.

While I am conversant with and will seriously discuss the effects of white racism on our condition as a people and on the state of this particular generation I know that the solution to our dilemma lies within us. It's not how white folks treat us that is critical. It's how we treat each other. It's not how white folks talk to us that's crucial its how we talk to ourselves. It's not the names that white people call us that are most injurious and disturbing, it's the names we call ourselves. If we are right then we cannot long stay defeated or repressed. On the other hand if we are not right we cannot win even when everything seems to be going our way. The pillars of our success are set in the rock bed strata of our own culture, values, families, neighborhoods, and institutions.

Some people will call this approach blaming the victim. They will argue they we can't do any better because of the horrendous weight of the multiple oppressions that are laid so brutally upon us. These are the people who are convinced that crime is always the child of poverty. But these folk most not know about slavery in which our African ancestors, though suffering from incredible poverty, would not steal from each other. Or they are unfamiliar with the rules that countless generations were raised under in which our parents told us if we brought home anything explaining that we "found it": "Take it back to where you found it because whoever lost it is coming there looking for it." Our ancestors courageously and ingeniously carved out for themselves a moral universe in which poverty was not an excuse for criminality.

Years ago I interviewed for a job as executive director of a community center in the black community of a mid-sized Midwestern, industrial town. As I laid out what some of my rules of conduct would be regarding behavior such as, "no fussing, no cussing, no fighting, not smoking, no drugs", the only white member of the interviewing committee, a white male fairly shouted in consternation and exasperation: "You can't do that. These kids are from the ghetto!" Like so many white and black people who don't know who we are, he equated being black with moral failure, the ghetto with dysfunctionality and being poor with being pitiful. He had a low expectation of black youth. I explained that I played ball with the young brothers at the black center where all the misbehavior took place and at the white YMCA. The same young men, who engaged in all kinds of misbehavior at the black center where standards were lowered because they were black and expected to be incapable of better behavior, when they were at the YMCA comported themselves perfectly in line with the rules of that place. Our young people are being ruined by an epidemic of lowered expectation on the part of liberal white people and their unknowledgeable black counterparts. We can understand the white peoples' failure to know how to challenge our youth to be at their best. But when black elders allow our children to fail it is because of laziness, cowardice or a combination of both.

In the fall of 1999 I left Lincoln University, whose beautiful tree-lined campus is nestled in the wonderfully quiet rural environs of the rolling hills of Chester County, Pennsylvania and relocated to the ghetto of North Philadelphia. One night a group of teenagers occupied the

24

porch of the row house next to ours and began talking and cursing so loudly that I could hardly hear my television. I went out and told them that they needed to quiet down and stop the cursing. One skinny fifteen year old jumped at me and declared that he wasn't cursing, so I quoted him a proverb. I said: "If you weren't cursing then I'm not talking to you. If the shoe fit wear it, if it don't fit don't force it". His friends pulled him away and they either quieted down or left. But the very next night as I parked in front of my home listening to the heartbreaking news of Wilt Chamberlain's unexpected and premature demise, I noticed three of the teenagers from the night before walking down the street towards me. I went on to my door and just as I was about to put the key in the lock I felt something hit me in the back of the head. As I turned around I *saw* one of the boys leap off the porch and take off running at full speed. In the days of my youth I might not have caught him, but I would certainly have tried; but at fifty-one I was not about to try to sprint with a high schooler. It turned out that he had hit me in the back of my head with an egg. What was incredible about it was that it was obviously in retaliation for the previous night's correction.

My short term-concern was whether or not I would need to arm myself against children who would physically attack an elder. But the larger question is: "What happens to a generation that will not be taught, that resents instruction, resists correction and assaults those who have the nerve to try to teach them"? It was as clear to me then as it is now that young people can only learn how to live in this world through the instruction of their elders. In the absence of that instruction there is literally no hope for them. The very idea only exists in the demonic realm of the unthinkable. Can anyone imagine a young lion that will not allow the old lion to teach it to hunt? Would anyone like to suggest what would happen to a young monkey that refused to listen to an old monkey show them what plants were edible and which were poisonous? What does common sense tell us about what would happen to a young goose that refused to follow the formation during its long distance southern sojourn to escape the deadly winters of the North? Whoever heard of a young eagle fighting the old eagle because it tried to teach how to fly?

Correction, instruction, education are keys to the enlargement of life's possibilities. Without them one is consigned to the scrapheap of perpetual failure. If they will not receive instruction and correction from their elders who care about them, then who will teach them? Somebody surely will. Everyone must learn how to operate and cooperate in this world, how to get along and make a way for themselves. No one is born knowing how to function as an adult. Those who are unable to accomplish this task are popularly known as outlaws, renegades and eventually jailbirds. The only other option for such individuals is an early death. The old people are still right: "If you live fast, you die young". If they do not learn from us there is a group of people responsible for reaching them. They are called the police. If our children cannot be reached, taught, instructed, trained, corrected in homes, churches, or schools then it is inevitable that they will become subject to the attention, tactics and treatment of law enforcement. The proof of this assertion lies in the fact that today there are more black males in jail than in college. We will spend an entire chapter later on talking in greater detail about just what that means.

While I am appalled at the state of African American youth I still entertain and enjoy a tremendous faith in their future prospects. This specific faith derives from a general belief in the Divine Order of the universe. I am convinced, as have been our people since time immemorial, that God is still in charge of His creation. I understand that man has a plan, the forces of evil have a counter plan, but God has a Master Plan. Any generation that individually and collectively engages in the spiritual quest and inquiry to discover their place within that Master Plan will overcome the inevitable vicissitudes of earthly existence. Our strength as a people has always been predicated upon our spiritual genius which keeps us in touch with that Incomprehensible Power who is eternal, all-powerful, all-knowing, all-loving, transcendent and ineffable. We have not been destroyed by our experience in this country because we never surrendered our high moral standards and lowered ourselves to the wickedness and perversity of those that brought us here.

PROLOGUE: *THE EAGLE AND THE CHICKEN*

(This is my version of an ancient African tale later to become a part of African American folklore. It is primarily found in the sermons of black preachers. I first heard it in a sermon by Rev. Hezekiah Brady, Sr., then pastor of the Christian Hope Baptist Church on the South Side of Chicago. He told the story at the Abyssinian Baptist Church of Rockford in Rockford, Il in the early 1980's.)

There was an eagle one day who lost an egg. The egg was found by a little mother hen who took the eagle egg home with her to the chicken coop and sat on it with all the loving patience of a soon-to-be mother. After many days the little eaglet hatched out of the egg. On that very day of his arrival into this world he was by every measurement, definition and estimation of the word- an eagle. He was an eagle genetically, an eagle genealogically, an eagle anatomically and an eagle physiologically. But he was born in chicken circumstances and raised up in a chicken environment; therefore he grew up believing that he was a chicken. He grew up playing chicken games, thinking chicken thoughts, dreaming chicken dreams, walking a chicken walk, talking chicken talk and entertaining for his eagle future chicken ambitions. When the counselor at the chicken high school asked him what he wanted to be when he grew up, his greatest ambition was to some day hop, skip and jump up on a fence post and cock-a-doodle-do for day like he saw the roosters do.

Now, the chickens that he lived among got together and waged a behind-his back, destructive, psychological

28

warfare against him. Because they knew who he really was. They got together when he wasn't around and said to one another: "If he ever finds out that he's an eagle, us chickens are in trouble! So they did every thing that they could to make him ashamed of his eagle self. They were determined to rob him of his eagle self-esteem. They laughed at him, called him names and pointed fingers of scorn at him. They made him the butt of their jokes and the target of their ridicule. They made fun of his eagle features. They called his large, powerful, curvaceous, intimidating eagle beak ugly and said that he was deformed. When in fact they were just jealous because they had little-bitty, thin, chicken lips. They poked fun at his razor sharp, steel strong, eagle talons but it was because they had weak, puny, pitiful chicken feet. After so many years of being bombarded with negative messages about himself that little lost bird began to feel ashamed of his own self. He even considered making an appointment with a cosmetic surgeon and having his talons reduced and half of his beak cut off so he could look more like and fit in better with the chickens.

One day while the lost bird was playing in the barnyard, he saw the dark contours of a mighty shadow float across the ground like some great ship swims across the restless bosom of yonder's mighty oceans. For the first time in his life he looked up, higher than the chicken coop, higher than the fence post, higher than the line of trees that ringed his chicken environment. And he saw, framed against the sun-drenched afternoon sky, the regal form of an adult eagle in full flight, with all the power, beauty, grace, rhythm and majesty of that very king of the air. It seemed as if his mighty wings filled the sky, blotted out the sun and stretched from horizon to horizon. When that little lost eagle beheld the fantastic sight of that adult bird his mind was blown. He was so startled that he exclaimed to himself deep down in the innermost recesses of his heart of hearts: "Boy, I sho' wish I could be like that"! But then he remembered that they told him at the chicken high school that his I.Q. was too low and his SAT scores weren't high enough for him to entertain exalted ambitions for his future. So he dropped his head in sorrow and despair.

But that adult eagle with the accuracy of his long-range, binocular vision saw that lost bird and with the wisdom that comes from many years he perceived his dilemma. He then swooped down from his stratospheric height, landed next to that little lost bird, walked up to him, looked him in the eye, and said: "Boy , you ain't no chicken. You a eagle! Your mighty talons were not meant to grub and scrub along the lowlands of the earth for worms and caterpillars but to grab hold to the craggy sides of fierce mountains of mighty achievements. Boy, did you hear what I said. You ain't no chicken, you a eagle. Your eagle eyes were never meant to be limited to the narrow confines of the barnyard but to seek out to the distant panoramic horizons of your own unfulfilled potential. Boy, spread your wings and be caught up in the wafting winds of your own immeasurable genius."

The moral of his story is
For those that don't know
We are not a chicken people.
We are a race of eagles.

So even if you have to attend
Some chicken schools,
And even if you have
Some chicken teachers,
Who make you read chicken books,
And even if you have to work
On some chicken jobs
Under some chicken supervisors
Who give you chicken assignments
And pay you chicken money

Don't do chicken work
And don't bring home no
Chicken grades
'Cause you ain't no chicken
You a eagle!

There is a generation that curseth their father and doth not bless their mother. Proverbs 30:11

There are no bad children. There are only irresponsible parents. African Proverb

I. The Current State of African American Youth

For thousands of years African people have raised their children in a unique configuration based on the peer group. Each generation has its own name, and other identifying characteristics such as music, dance, clothing and hair styles. Each generation comes to manhood and womanhood as a group and then is given its place in the government of the village, city and nation. Their roles are clearly defined for them. There is a time for them to be children with a minimum of responsibilities. There is a transitional period when they begin to spend more and more time with their elders as they are being prepared for the realities of adulthood. They are, toward the end of this period, given final formal training in sacred secluded spaces and then brought back into the village where their transition into adulthood is celebrated by the entire town or village. Upon ascendance into adulthood they are required to fulfill certain roles in society particularly that of married couples and parents.

For Africans marriage and child-rearing is not an individual choice but a moral obligation owed to the community of the living, the dead and the unborn. When their children are grown they will make another transition into being elders where they will become the source of wisdom needed to maintain traditions, withstand calamities, adjudicate conflicts, and envision and prepare a brighter tomorrow. As such they are the chief judges and wisest counselors, master teachers, high priests, and most accomplished healers for the community. These societies are organized in such a fashion that the generations rise together as a collective. Upon reaching a certain age an entire generation of administrators will be retired, promoted to active emeritus status so that the next generation can have their opportunity to fulfill those functions. This makes for an orderly transition of power without loss of status so that one generation will not feel the need to wage war against the other in order to have their place in the sun. They did not suffer the all-too familiar American and even African American phenomena of an individual hanging onto power so long that younger people became frustrated with the thought that they would never have the opportunity to bring forth their gifts.

Children were structured into age grades in which each older group of children functioned as supervisors for the younger groups. Interestingly enough, it is in gang structures that I've observed the closest continuation of these practices, though they are now also to be seen in athletic competition. When I was growing up on the West Side of Chicago in the fifties and sixties the two most powerful and popular gangs were the Vice Lords and the Egyptian Cobras. They were organized into age grades that ran from pee-wees, to midgets, to juniors, seniors, and at the top "old-heads", while the board of directors or council of the elders were known as The Main Twenty-one.

This African sense of generational identification was still being expressed by my parents' generation. My mother and her female friends and relatives would always describe their children as being the "mate" to another child or children. Children born in the same year were age-mates. I was always described as being the mate to my cousin Lorenzo. He was the second son of my mother's maternal Uncle Son (Mr. Albert Jones and his wife Aunt Julia in Little Rock, Arkansas) Lorenzo was my second cousin as were his two brothers and nine sisters but the description that was most important for the female elders was that he was "the mate to Clarence".

Every generation of people of African descent raised in this country has made an historical mark while yet in their youth. In the contributions that they made to history they also earned the name by which they would be known. All the generations in slavery are seen as one. However, it is important to understand that the average age in the slave community was twenty-two. The protracted resistance to slavery and the final victory over it was the product of young people. We often tend to think of the enslaved generations as mostly older people. The fact is that the brutalities of slavery ensured that the bonds people did not live long lives. The slave master watched carefully for the time when an individual reached "the point of diminishing return", when they began to consume more than they produced. At the point that they were no longer producing a profit for the slave master they would often be driven off the plantation into the wilderness in the same way many people today drive a dog into the woods and kick them out of the car when feeding them becomes too expensive, or caring for them too bothersome. The glory of the younger slaves is that they would take care of the abandoned ones as best they could, building them homes, however rude and primitive and bringing them food, clothing and medicines. They provided for them with their own meager resources while risking punishment if caught.

The next generation started out as the Civil War generation who as soldiers in the Union Army served as the spearhead of the Union's final assault against the Confederate rebellion. After breaking the back of Confederacy and ending slavery by force of arms they became the Reconstruction Generation who built "a nation within a nation". There was the turn of the century generation who started the Great Migration and who fought in World War I. There is the generation of the twenties

34

who might also be called the "Red Summer Generation" because they fought back against white race rioters and lynch mobbers until both phenomena ceased being a popular form of entertainment for white America. Or they can be called the Garvey generation. It was from amongst them that Mighty Marcus Moziah Garvey called together the six million world-wide that constituted the most populous and powerful black organization of this century. Or they can be called the Harlem Renaissance Generation.

Then there was the Depression generation. Some one once proclaimed that "When White America sneezes Black America gets pneumonia." It might then be logically extended that while the Depression was the flu for white America it was tuberculosis for us. That generation survived the Depression and went on to fight World War II. Its soldiers returned from making the world "safe for democracy" to fight a more important war to make democracy safe for black people. That was the generation of my parents.

This book centers on the generation of my children, which I indicate in the title are called by some the Lost Generation and others the Left Generation. White folks call theirs Generation X. Some people call ours and many of them call themselves the Hip-Hop Generation. My generation has two names. We started out in the fifties and sixties as the Civil Rights/Black Power generation. It was our commitment and sacrifices that brought about the great changes in American society from the mid-fifties to the early seventies. We were involved in direct action and civil disobedience campaigns such as bus boycotts, the freedom rides, sit-ins, demonstrations, and marches. We went to jail by the tens of thousands. Thousands were beaten by police and racist white civilians. Hundreds were killed.

We began the Black Power Movement. When I shake hands with young men today many of them look at me funny because I give what I know to be the "Black Power handshake". They look at me curiously as if to say: "Why you trying to act young"? Because of historical illiteracy in our own community they don't know that that is not a young black man's handshake, not their invention. That handshake came on the scene in 1966, my last year in high school, the year the Stokely Carmichael (now Kwame Ture) and Willie Ricks (now Mukasa) began the cry for "Black Power" when the James Meredith March Against Fear reached Grenada, Mississippi. We started wearing natural hair styles and African clothes as we searched for a Pan-African identity. We organized tenant unions and negotiated contracts with white slum landlords. We fought the fight for the Black Studies departments that exist now on hundreds of white college campuses, creating not only a newly recognized field of study but also providing teaching positions for thousands of black professors and administrators. We opposed the War on Vietnam, burning our draft cards, refusing induction into the armed services, living out Dr. King's preachments against the war and following the example of Muhammad Ali. We engaged in urban guerrilla warfare, as unsuccessful and counterproductive as it was. We fought back against police brutality and urban racism by putting our bodies on the line against superior firepower. We demanded community control of schools, another series of battles that we lost and are still paying the cost for today.

However, time, circumstance and the choices many of us made in the seventies caused us to be given a different name, one we share with many of our white peers. That name is the Me Generation. In the seventies the energy of the movement waned after the assassinations of Imam El Hajj Malik El Shabbazz (Malcolm X), Dr. King, Fred Hampton, Mark Clark, Bunchie Carter, John Huggins and all of the other multiple persecutions of the FBI-led Counter Intelligence Program (Cointelpro). This collaboration among FBI, CIA, Army, Navy, Air Force intelligence and state and local police literally broke the back of movement leadership. In conjunction with the blunting of the spearhead of the movement was the popular notion that all the victories had virtually been won and that we were in fact finally and fully as free as any other Americans. This mistaken notion was supported by the numbers of high profile instances of black people living in previously all-white neighborhoods, particularly suburbs, even though they usually remained "the only ones on the block". Attendance at white colleges in massive numbers began to replace the two or three in a class that had been the norm for most of the twentieth century.

In sports we were finally able to play for the previously segregated colleges of the South, even for Bear Bryant at the University of Alabama and Adolph Rupp at the University Kentucky. In the northern schools the rule in the Big Ten basketball had been, for black starters "two at home, three on the road and four when you get behind". That custom was changed so much until some teams had all-black starting fives and in football we even began to see black quarterbacks. During this period of surface integration and seeming freedom many of our generation began to integrate their mentalities, world-views, philosophies and moral standards.

Intensive exposure to white society wrought a change in perception which for too many of us demanded that we dispense with our parents' old-fashioned notions of behavior which were an embarrassment to us when we were around white people. Many black parents surrendered to the pressure from their white neighbors and co-workers not to be so strict on their children. We began to allow our children to blur the lines between the child and adult status. We started allowing our children to call grown people by their first names. Many black adults with child-like minds did not want to be called Mr. or Miss because it reminded them that they were "old". These adults were unthinkingly surrendering to the youth worship of white society.

From the most ancient of days African people looked forward to each passing phase of life as they climbed the ladder of maturity that ultimately carried them out of time into eternity. Black women and even men began to hide their ages. In traditional Black society, age, along with gender, is a foremost marker of identity, place, role, function, authority and responsibility. There were even those who resented and resisted being addressed as Sir and Ma'am. We no longer were comfortable with exercising absolute authority over our children. We let them argue with us like they saw their white friends argue with their parents.

Black children by ancient custom were not allowed to listen to and participate in what my parent's generation called "grown people's conversation". In those days children were not allowed to "look in grown people' mouth while they talking". In other words the adults realized that there were conversations among grown people that involved information that children should not be made privy to. When the conversation got to that level either the children were told to leave the room or the adults began speaking in coded language. They would use such phraseology as: "You know that little Jones' girl broke her leg". We would hear every word but not understand what they meant because we had seen Nita Girl just that morning and both of her legs were fine. We even began to see Black children throwing temper tantrums in public as they loudly protested their parent's refusal to obey their commands to buy them this or that trinket that they saw on TV.

Many black parents felt powerless to correct their children who followed the advice of police and social workers on TV who told them that if their parents struck them to call a certain number and have them arrested. I personally have listened to scores of accounts by black parents of being arrested, convicted, fined and even jailed for physically correcting their children according to the best traditions of African and African American childrearing.

We even began to avail ourselves of white authority figures in the social services industry to determine who our

38

children would live with when there was a disruption in the family. The role that had been played by the elders of the family since slavery was now being handed over to twenty and thirty-something white female social workers who had no understanding or appreciation of how our families operated.

Until the 1970's the elders of the family had absolute authority over child placement in our families. If a child was being neglected or ill-treated those elders would order the parents to surrender the child to their decision as to who they would live with. Back then a black child as young as five years old could be put on a train with a shoe-box of fried chicken to eat and a note pinned to their clothing indicating who the child was and where they were headed. Every adult on that train would exercise supervision over, care for and protection of that child until he or she arrived at their destination. That is the practical meaning of the African proverb; "It takes a whole village to raise a child". When children began engaging in delinquent behavior they were often sent Down South back into the environs in which were found the wellsprings of our values. Those generations knew how to rehabilitate their wayward youth.

White social workers had their own scales of measurement based on family income, value and size of home, type of neighborhood, job title or education by which they would determine where a child would be placed. They had no understanding of the spiritual, moral, social, familial traditions which had worked for us for thousands of years. Not to mention that they didn't love our children.

The Lost/Left Generation can be located in time as those children born in the 1970's and 1980's. This cohort is also known as the Hip-Hop Generation because rap music and its attendant phenomenon such as break-dancing, scratching, human beat box and graffiti made their debut during this same time period. I also extend the label to the children of this group, that is the generation of my grandchildren, those born in the 1990's and the first decade of the new millennium.

The Lost Generation did not conceive, carry, birth, or raise itself. It is the product of its parents. The African proverb says: "There are no bad children, only irresponsible parents". Another says "The way that the twig is bent is the way that the tree will grow". My parents used to tell us: "The actions of the child reflect upon the parent." This book therefore is not an attack upon these young people. In fact it is just the opposite—a critique of their parents, my own generation. Therefore it is inner-directed. Those who bear responsibility for the current condition of black youth it is my generation, the generation of their parents, the Me Generation.

Divorce has had tremendously negative impact on this generation. The "Me Generation" can also be described as the "Divorced Generation" and its children called the "The Children of Divorce". Of the many the popular movements among white people that we have embraced, among the most unfortunate is divorce. Heretofore our families and marriages by nature and necessity were stronger than those of white people. Marriage for us was in the tradition of African people. It was not an individual choice but a social obligation for the strength of the family and the health of the community. Marriage was a debt owed by present generations to past generations paid forward to future generations. In other words the debt owed one's parents for getting married and sacrificially providing the best possible environment for us to grow up pin is repaid by doing the same thing for our children. What we owe to the past we pay to the future.

I heard this logic expressed in a story told by a preacher who had run out of money while in college. The administrator, also a preacher, paid the boys fees enabling him to continue his education. As he expressed his thanks to the older man he said: "How can I ever repay you?" The administrator said: "One day a young man or young woman will come to you with the same problem. Do for them what has been done for you. Pass it on to the next generation.

In the movie <u>The</u> <u>Five</u> <u>Heartbeats</u>, which to me is the cinematic anthem of my generation, there is a most poignant and instructive scene regarding this very topic. The bass singer in the group came to confess to the rest of the fellows that his long time sweetheart was pregnant. He was in a dilemma because the group was still in the struggling stage of its career and money was short. He told that an older, unsavory, unethical business associate had offered him money for an abortion. His "boys" after hearing the story took their meager monies and gave it to the brother to use to get married. When marriage is supported, encouraged, even mandated by the most significant people in one's life it is delivered beyond the narrow confines of mere whim and becomes a matter of moral obligation.

Some years ago an article appeared in Jet magazine entitled "Shotgun Marriages Last Longer". The results of a survey showed that people who got married because they "had to" had more enduring marriages than people who got married because they "wanted to". The article went on to explain that when marriage is seen as a moral and social obligation that is supported by the sanction of the elders it carries tremendous weight. A shotgun wedding is not an individual affair caused only by the militant actions of the aggrieved father of the bride. It is the expression of the will of the community at large with the father, grandfather, uncle, older brother or cousin, godfather or whichever male responsible male relative acting as final enforcer. Not only the girl's father and mother but the boy's parents, all the other elders on both sides, preachers, schoolteachers, coaches, counselors, the lady who runs the drycleaners and the man who owns the barber shop and finally and most tellingly the boy's peers also uphold the ancient way that builds communities. When people feel that marriage is an ought, the fulfillment of a divine mandate, an act of

41

obedience to the will of God, and a way of honoring all the people that they love and respect it is approached differently than as if it were just another optional item on life's menu of choices. The people who see marriage as a moral obligation are also slow to leave it. Their marriages are more enduring.

At the end of the article a prominent Black female leader was quoted as responding that: "People shouldn't get married because they have to. They should get married because they want to ". She missed the whole point of the article. As long as people feel they have to and ought to be married they tend to stay longer in it and work harder at it. It's just the opposite when people feel that marriage is just a matter of what one "wants". Our wants change from year to year, month to month, day to day and for some folks hour by hour if not minute by minute. Imagine if people only went to work when they wanted to. Everybody will experience times, even seasons, when they no longer want to be married. If that "want to" always had the final word in the matter we would have even fewer successful marriages than we do already. Marriages are for children more than for anyone else. But it also brings health, stability and security to the married couple and is the basic building block of human society. The mutual support and dependability of a marriage cannot be matched by any other social configuration yet known to humankind. Children need constant care that ought not be interrupted by one of the parents deciding that they don't "want to" anymore.

Part of the sexual revolution was the proliferation and popularization of divorce until it has become almost coequal to marriage as an American institution. During the height of the Me Generation (the 1970's) psychologists and marriage counselors popularized the approach that couples should not stay in an unhappy marriage. According to them it was bad for the children to see their parents in disagreement, constantly arguing, and being unhappy with one another. Their conclusion was that divorce was a better alternative to an "unhappy" marriage. Twenty years after the devastating consequences of divorce were made clear the same psychologists and sociologists collectively exclaimed: "Oops, we made a mistake!" Now they conclude with the unerring accuracy of hindsight that actually it would have been better for the children to see their parents remain committed to each other and their children while they worked out their problems. But by then the popularity of divorce had already introduced a new phenomenon to the social scene and caused a sea change in the family landscape of this nation. It gave us fatherlessness.

We have yet to fully comprehend the entire consequences of, not just a distinct minority of fatherless children, but an entire generation in which a full eighty percent of its children are born to and raised by single mothers. What we do know is that fatherless children are more likely to die by miscarriage or stillbirth, be born premature, develop more slowly both physically and intellectually in infancy and early childhood, fall behind academically, engage in delinquent behavior like gang membership, drug use, premature sexual activity, become singe parents themselves, and most devastatingly of all, wind up in jail or an early grave.

We don't leave the most important matters of life to mere individual choice. Children are not free to decide if they want to go to school. Young men are not left to decide individually whether they will defend their country in time of war. They are drafted. Our old people believed that it was more important to draft young people to be husbands and wives and fathers and mothers than any other roles in life. We have no problems with drafting young men and women to play sports like basketball, tennis, boxing, football, or baseball. Why should we object to the kind of drafting that our old people did to keep the family intact and provide the optimal set of circumstances for children to be raised in? Because that's exactly what shotgun marriages were. They were the old folks engaging in a form of social engineering to ensure that men and women would rise to the occasion of filling the one indispensable role in the lives of children: that of parent.

Marriage is also the civilizing dynamic in the lives of young men. Young single men are the most volatile, violent, disruptive, dangerous and deadly element in any human society. Young men tend to run in gangs and have sex in trains. Marriage harnesses their energy and channels it into the productive area of responsibility for others. The reason that girls are more mature than boys their age is because maturity is the by-product of responsibility. Girls began practicing responsibility for others at an early age. The little girl's favorite toy is her doll. What doe she do with that doll? She takes care of it. She feeds it, bathes it, dresses it, combs its hair, coos to it, and takes it on walks in its miniature stroller. As teen-agers one of the most popular part-time jobs for girls is that of baby-sitter. By time a girl reaches the first stages of womanhood in her late teens and early twenties she has already spent a lifetime practicing the duties of responsibility for others and receiving its consequence- maturity.

Most boys, on the other hand, do not become responsible for anybody else until marriage. As little boys, if they have the masculine equivalent of their sister's doll it is an action figure like G.I. Joe. Do the little boys wash, clean, change diapers and put cute outfits on G.I. Joe? No! They put him in harm's way. The psychology of single men is a risk-taking, thrill-seeking approach to life fed by the absence of a need to consider anybody else in their short-sighted, ego-centric decision-making. The reason that the military draft typically ends at age twenty-six is to limit it as much as possible to single men. There is an instructive scene in the popular movie, Top Gun, when a top-flight fighter pilot tearfully gives his resignation to his commanding officer explaining that he had "lost his edge" (his fearlessness) in battle because he began to consider what his death would mean to his wife and newborn child. Marriage matures men because it directs their concern and commitments to the needs of others and not just to their individual consciousness.

This current generation of Black youth is in a state of crisis bordering on catastrophe. Just how bad things are for our teenagers is reflected in the name we have given them: The Lost Generation. Some people have given them the name Hip-Hop Generation which identifies them in terms of styles of music, dance, hairstyles and clothing. I consider the term Lost Generation as addressing the question of their long-term prognosis in the deeper issues of life. They are referred to as the Lost Generation because they are the first generation of people of African descent raised in the United States whose pathway leads backward and downward rather than upward and onward. This generation has more opportunities for education but will take less advantage of them. Many of them, especially males, but increasingly females also, have embraced an anti-intellectual approach to the very idea of education. They pride themselves on academic mediocrity, look with scorn upon true scholars and curse them with names like "nerds".

Most of the children of this generation have never experienced the finest tradition of Black family life because so many of them refuse to get married. They bear the vast majority of their children out of wedlock. They are babies making babies who will, to a significant degree, either neglect and abuse their children or abandon them for someone else to raise. Child abuse of every kind from passive neglect to active and aggressive verbal, emotional, physical, and sexual abuse is rampant. Incidents of children being molested, tortured, raped and murdered by their parents or other caretakers are the subject of news stories daily.

A criminal mentality is so rampant amongst them that

approximately half the males are caught up in the so-called "criminal justice" system. More black males in this generation go to jail than to college. Rather than trying to avoid jail, these young men see incarceration as a rite of passage into manhood. Hardcore and gangster rap, their most popular forms of music, lead them in celebrating dope-dealing, robbery, pimping, violence, sexual outlawry, rape and murder as though these criminal activities represent the core values of their lives. Our daughters are addressed by their brothers and refer to themselves as "bitches"and "ho's". The only absolute value for them is "getting paid". Anything done for money is not only acceptable but admirable, no matter how immoral or criminal it is.

They have little respect for their elders and are a threat to physically attack an older person, male or female, if one attempts to correct or discipline them. Violence against schoolteachers has reached such epidemic proportions that hundreds of thousands of veteran teachers have fled their profession in fear and triggered a tragic teacher shortage in black grammar and high schools. Alcoholism and other forms of drug abuse are rampant as they are targeted by liquor companies and drug dealers for conspicuous consumption of these dangerous and addictive poisons. Their promiscuous sexual behavior including homosexuality and bisexuality, has brought them an epidemic of venereal diseases such as gonorrhea, syphilis, chlamydia, herpes, human papiloma virus (HPV) and most devastating of them all, AIDS, which is now the largest killer of young black males, while almost 70% of women with AIDS are black females.

We cannot afford to have a Lost Generation. If one generation is lost three generations are put at risk. Every generation has the responsibility of taking care of three generations: firstly, itself; secondly, its children; and thirdly, its elders when the infirmities of old age prevent them from taking care of themselves. A Lost Generation

46

means one that is unable to take care of themselves, their children or their elders. The reality of this condition has yet to hit us because it is only in middle age that a generation's true nature is found out. Jesus said: "Ye shall know a tree by its fruit." Luke 6:44KJV The fruit of a people are its children. The fruit of humanity ripens in middle age when people have reached spiritual, intellectual, emotional and financial maturity. It is at that time when a generation is required to fulfill its threefold task.

I thought that I was grown when I was twenty years old and made more money working part-time than my Daddy was making working two jobs. It was only after I had a family of my own to be responsible for that I realized that I had used my "mo'" money to take care only of myself while my Daddy was the true adult because he was using his "less" money to take care of a household of eight people.

Most young people in their late teens and early twenties believe that they are grown because they can take care of themselves. That's not enough. Any dog will take care of himself. Any old mongrel, mutt, alley dog of dubious parentage, will dig a hole to lay its head in and find a bone to gnaw on. Adult human beings are not people who meet the minimalist standards of canine adulthood but those who take care not only of themselves but also are responsible for and accountable to other people who are dependent upon them.

Right now the Lost Generation's weaknesses are being covered by the financial strength of their parents who are still in their most productive years and are able to take care of all three generations. However, we can see the handwriting on the wall in the numbers of children of the Lost Generation who have returned to their parents' home as adults. When they return many of them come back with their own children after experiencing failure in marriages, in schools and on jobs. They are known to sociologists as "adult children" or "grown kids". They have not been able to match their parents' success in their twenties and are not willing to go through the hardships that their parents went through to get to where they are. Many of their parents raised them with the idea that "I don't want my child to go through what I went through". These parents have forgotten the wisdom of the generations that raised them: "You got to go through something to get to something". For a dramatic and scholarly presentation of this phenomenon read Mary Pattillo-Mckoy's book: *Black Picket Fences*, one of the most significant and insightful sociological studies of the black community since E. Franklin Frazier's *Black Bourgeoisie.*

They have ill-equipped their children for success because they have given them no appetite for the kinds of sacrifice, hard work, suffering, "taking low", "giving up their rights for other people's wrongs", "coming up the rough side of the mountain", and "bearing their burdens in the heat of the day", that laid the foundation for their own accomplishments and successes. These children want to start off where their parents ended up. They don't realize that the fine clothes, the big cars, the nice houses came about from twenty and more years of self-imposed discipline, hard work, struggle and sacrifice. The members of the Lost Generation want it all now without having to sweat, strain and suffer for it. They want to take the elevator to success. They have been raised to believe that they are entitled as their birthright to the luxuries and privileges that their parents worked so hard to obtain. As I heard one old preacher put it "They done 'rived before they left."

An old preacher in Atlanta told me once how the young brothers on his job made fun of him because he was such a jack-of-all trades around the workplace. They would laugh at him and say: "Old man you just do everything around here don't you?" He told them in return: "Ya'll just don't understand the reason why. Ya'll that don't do but one job, it's easy to get rid of ya'll and get one somebody else to take your place. But me, they can't afford to get rid of me because they'd have to hire six men to do all that I do". An uneducated barely literate man, he was operating out of the African-American philosophy of survival that instructed our ancestors to be super-achievers that knew how to make themselves indispensable to guarantee a means of generating income to support their families.

Many members of the Lost Generation are living in their parents' homes, forcing their parents to care for them and their children. Or they are living off their parents, who are paying a substantial portion of their budgets or at least bailing them out of their regular shortfalls. But the parental generation is now approaching retirement age. When this super-responsible older generation reaches the real helplessness and infirmity of their final years and must be taken care of by their children, when the grandchildren are in the last days of teenage hood and the early days of adulthood and need support with the daunting costs of college educations and new families, the Lost Generation will find itself unable to help the declining generation of grandparents or the rising generations of their own children and grandchildren. Then we will reap the bitter harvest of a crop not well-raised. The dependent generations will collapse unto weakened unsupportive structures of the Lost Generations and we will face calamities of unthinkable proportions.

Past generations built families that could handle the unthinkable horrors of slavery. This present generation of black families can hardly deal with the relative luxuries of freedom. *The old people did more with less. This current generation does less with more.*

Though Lost Generation is a dramatically accurate name for them, I don't call them the Lost Generation. I call them the Left Generation. If I gave some trusted adult friend of mine permission to take some of my children to the mall and they returned hours later without my children explaining to me: "Your kids got lost at the mall." My reply would be "No, my kids didn't get lost at the mall. They got left at the mall. You go back to the mall and find my children and bring them home"!

We have a generation that has been left in the wilderness of contemporary American culture by uncaring irresponsible adults. They have not been properly taught the best traditions of our people. Therefore they are cut off from the ways of success and are practicing the habits of hopelessness as they wander down the low way to destruction. They have been left by parents so busy chasing the American Dream of individual success, conspicuous consumption and personal fulfillment that they have left their children to be raised by the TV, also known as the Boob Tube and the Idiot Box because of its lack of standards of morality, intellect and common sense.

Left by teachers who only wanted to teach the best and the brightest of students, those whose futures were already assured by the positive homes in which they were raised. Teachers who did not want to engage in the glorious historical struggle of black educators to "teach the unteachable and reach the unreachable". Left by teachers whose integration into white-led unions have made them place their priorities more on salaries and working conditions than student performance.

Left by churches that made their priority building buildings rather than building people. These are churches that have ten and twenty times if not a hundred times more money in their building fund than in their scholarship fund.

Left by leaders who failed to recruit, embrace, prepare, and establish successors; men and women who died without anyone having been made ready to take their place and ensure the ongoing progress of their missions and their institutions.

Left by a so-called "criminal justice" system that is more interested in locking our children up than in straightening them out. A system that not only disproportionately suspects, stops, searches, harasses, arrests, prosecutes, convicts and incarcerates our young people but once they lock them up rather than educate and rehabilitate instead punishes, tortures, brutalizes, rapes, enrages, further addicts and finally kills them.

Left by a media industry that instead of using the awesome hypnotic imagery of the silver screen, the overwhelming influence of vivacious and outrageously talented personalities and the mesmerizing power of amplified music to lift our young people to higher heights use their persuasive powers over our children to cater to their lowest selves and consign them to dangerous depths of unrestrained degeneracy and demonism.

Our old people taught us that when you lose something the way you go about finding it is to first of all remember when and where you were the last time you had it. We must go back into our collective racial and cultural memories and recall when the last time Black youth were with us was. When Black children were among the most positive, industrious, studious, energetic, inquisitive, enthusiastic, happy, cheerful, respectful, imaginative, obedient, helpful, delightful children that anybody could ever want to be around. If so, we will go back to the sixties when the classic traditions of black family and community life were still strong. In those days we were together as a people, young and old alike striving toward the same goals, investing in the same vision of a better future.

The civil rights movement that characterized those years was not a youth movement or an adult movement. It was a trans-generational, community-wide campaign that had a powerful youth presence. Black youth were not on the margins of our social lives engaging in acts of protest against the standards of our community that had kept us strong as a people for tens of thousands of years. They were at the very center of the organizations, institutions and movements that were waging war against the multiple oppressions of American Apartheid.

The heroes of my generation were not foul-mouthed comedians, pimps, dope dealers, gang-bangers, criminals, convicts, child-molesters, Mafioso, mass-murderers, serial killers, and jailbirds. We revered the leaders of the movement as our role models. Dr. Martin Luther King, Jr., Rev. Adam Clayton Powell, Jr., Ella Baker, Diane Nash, Imam El Hajj Malik El Shabbazz, James Farmer, Septima Clark, Floyd McKissick, Rev. James Bevel, James Forman, Julian Bond, Stokely Carmichael now Kwame Ture, H. Rap Brown now Imam Jamil El-Amin, Fannie Lou Hamer, Huey P. Newton, Bobby Seale, are just some of the people after whom we modeled ourselves. As we looked up to them as our honored elders they reached out to us as their cherished youth. Every organization had an active youth component. Not just the national bodies that enjoyed tremendous prominence but even the smallest neighborhood associations actively addressed the needs and issues of young people. We, as young people, were sought after, recruited, instructed, put to work, given assignments and responsibilities. The key to these processes were mutual respect and affection. Grown people valued younger people for the energy and imagination we contributed. We honored older people for the wisdom, resources, know-how, and expertise that they so generously shared with us.

The black community back then still operated from ancient African values that insisted that everybody was important and had a divinely ordained place in the world. The African proverb says: "Everyone is a child of God. No one is a child of the earth". Children were raised to be respectful, respectable, polite, cooperative, obedient, hard-working, forward-thinking, family-centered, community-minded, and education-seeking. My parents would often explain: "The reason we raise ya'll the way we do (so insistent upon disciplined behavior) is so that if anything happens to us, nobody will mind taking ya'll into their home. Because don't nobody like a bad child". As young people we knew how to endear ourselves to our elders through proper conduct and deportment.

In the late sixties, the white community began experiencing what was called a "generation gap". It was, what we perceived then, a catastrophic alienation between white youth and their elders. So much so that one of the catch-phrases for white youth was: "Don't trust anybody over thirty." The anti-war movement, the hippie movement, the drug culture were activities of white youth that so opposed the conventions of ordinary society that these movements and the people involved in them were termed the "counter-culture". We in the Black community looked with amusement on the traumas played out in public between white youth and their elders. It was amusing to us because we believed such a thing could never happen to us. However, the generation gap for white people disappeared in the mid-seventies when it was time for the rebels to assume their adult roles in society. We often talked about how white people who were involved in the movement only had to clean up, shower, shave, get a haircut, put on a suit and tie and walk straight into the offices of corporate America and get a well-paying, decision-making job and loans for a house and a car.

We used to laugh at white folks for their generation gap because it seemed so ridiculous to us. We knew that this was something that could never occur among black people. Now we've been made to eat our arrogant words and swallow our derisive laughter since we are the ones suffering from a generation gap now. Generation gaps are for wealthy or at least well-off white people, whose children can give up their youthful rebelliousness when they decide to and not suffer any lasting effects from their days of frivolity, no matter how much it bordered on or even crossed the line into the criminal. Black people can't afford a generation gap. We need each other too much. There is too much to lose if our young people, ignoring and rejecting the wisdom of the elders, find themselves in dire straights that we don't always have the resources to get them out of. The world of white people waits for their wayward youth with welcoming arms full of forgiveness, restoration, scholarships and jobs. The same world looks at our youth with critical eyes searching for the one flaw in their record, reputation or character to use to disqualify, disappoint, and displace them.

Another contributory factor to the contemporary failing of the black family is the lack of elders in our homes and neighborhoods. The church, unfortunately and I'm sure unwittingly, played a prominent and indispensable but short-sighted role in cooperating with the federal government in the building of senior citizen complexes and displacing our older people out of our homes and neighborhoods and warehousing them into age-segregated facilities. The black extended family was almost always characterized by its multi-generational make-up. On any block in the black community would be found numerous homes in which lived great-grandparents, grandparents, great-uncles and great aunts, uncles, aunties, older brothers and sisters and senior cousins.

These old people served three critical roles in our homes and neighborhoods. First of all, they were the instructors of young married couples on how to successfully handle the stresses of their union which were constantly subjected to powerful forces of destruction. They also taught them how to raise their children and how to conduct relationships with friends and neighbors. Secondly, they were the baby-sitters. There was no need for the impersonal system of day care centers that has become institutionalized as a standard part of child- care responsibilities in our communities. Thirdly, they were the neighborhood watchers. Sitting on porches on every block they scanned the scene and took in everything that went on and faithfully reported their findings to the adults responsible for maintaining order. They stayed in touch with each other through the grapevines of communal communication that ran across backyard fences as they hung their wash to dry so that important information was regularly passed on from household to household. What they represented in the overall sense was wisdom. This is the quality that is most lacking in black neighborhoods where chaos, driven by youthful foolishness, abounds. The African proverb says: *"When an old person dies its like a library burning down"*.

I believe that one of the first steps that must be taken to restore the power of the black family and provide a positive alternative for the youth of today and tomorrow is a revitalization of the role of the elders in the family. My generation's parents are literally on their last legs, yet they carry within them individually and collectively knowledge and wisdom that are of immeasurable value. This generation survived some of the toughest times in our history in this land. They are full of know-how, stories, skills, experiences, songs, sayings, and practices that must be passed along to the younger generations. The African family is child-centered, adult-run and elder-ruled. It is the role of the elders as the keepers of our best traditions that is missing today. We cannot afford to have our families distorted into centers of youth-oriented values that mirror many of the worst aspects of Euro-American culture.

In one sense the elders are already playing an increasing role in childrearing as the number of grandparents, grandmothers in particular, increases daily. These intrepid, self-sacrificing elders' willingness to forego what should be the care-freeness of their golden years in order to take care of their grandchildren and even great-grandchildren has been a standard feature of African American community life since slavery. The challenges that the old people face today are made increasingly difficult by various factors in contemporary life that did not exist for past generations. Many of these grandparents must labor in relative isolation. The support systems of the extended family for the most part are not there to give them dependable assistance and particularly much needed breaks from the draining intensity of child-rearing. Also they face a type of child more unruly and disobedient than those of the past and therefore much more difficult to raise. There is no greater illustration of this fact than the murder of Dr. Betty Shabbazz by her own grandson when she took him into her home after his mother showed no signs of being able to handle him. Not to mention the dangerous presence in their own homes of the corrupting messages that children have access to with cable TV, personal CD players and internet access.

It is the middle-aged and older black male who is most in need of restoration to a place of responsibility and authority in the family. Many such men failed in their attempts to raise their own children whether by choice, by necessity or by circumstances beyond their control. In these, the latter days of their maturity, they can have an opportunity to make up for their past failures and errors. First of all we need to figure out how to bring these men into positions of responsibility. As a community we began to recognize in the late seventies a need to reestablish rites of passage for young people who were moving from adolescence into adulthood. Even though the steps we have taken are far from sufficient. (For instance most of these programs are centered more around celebration than preparation. Many of them last one weekend ending with a ceremony of conferment of adulthood, whereas in traditional Africa, manhood training begins at 10 or 11 and lasts at least six or seven years.)

There is an equally important passage which is the one when adults rise to the exalted status of elders. In Africa at the around the age of fifty, when one's own children are grown one is expected to ascend to the state of elderhood. This is accomplished not only in celebration of the anniversaries of one's birth, but more importantly through an educational process that prepares its students for the critical work of becoming in a sense members the boards of directors, the primary decision-makers the chief counselors, the appellate courts, the council of the elders for extended families and the entire community.

Most men in this culture suffer from a syndrome known as "mid-life crisis". When a man passes his peak of physical performance (when his sons begin beating him at his favorite sport) he must make a spiritual, emotional, psychological, intellectual and social adjustment to a new way of being in the world. We do not, as an African people, have an organized means of assisting men in this transition. Mullions of black men feel displaced and confused about their new role in life as older men past their physical primes, in possession of the invaluable wisdom of life's bittersweet experiences, but having with no organized way to pass this information on to new generations or share it with the world at large.

The life's lessons of too many older men are wasted when there is no way for them to pass them on to the generation of their grandchildren and great-grandchildren. Malidoma Patrice Some instructs us in his great work on African society, <u>Of Water And The Spirit</u>, that grandfathers are considered more important than fathers in the rearing and education of boys. Most fathers in the early lives of their first children are still in their twenties if not their late teens. They do not yet possess the powers of wisdom that can only come from experience. They are in fact, at that age, still learning to be fathers so that they are novices in a critical office. The mistakes that they will inevitably make due to lack of experience can have a life-long effect on the children they are rearing who are in the most sensitive formative stages of development. Therefore it is the grandfather who bears the greater responsibility and authority to rear the young. In fact his is a dual role. He must teach his how to be a father as well as impart invaluable lessons to his grandson..

We have to develop a way to bring older men into the state of being elders. It must be composed of at least three steps. Firstly, definition. We have to come together, in families, churches, schools, and community organizations and define for ourselves what it means to be an elder.

What are the functions of an elder? What are things one must know to be recognized and be able to function as an elder? Secondly, education. An organized means of transmitting to the men who are candidates for elderhood must be put in place. It does not have to be a formal institution with a building and budget and staff. But it must be for real, entirely serious and effective in carrying out its purpose. Lastly, celebration, when those men who have met the prerequisites in knowledge and performance are in a public ceremony introduced to their community as elders, men whose very presence call forth a more elevated level of behavior and performance,.

The same must be done for women. The grandmothers who are so courageously raising young children need to have the power that they carry extended beyond the narrow walls of their own homes and out into the wider community. There was a time when we could take it for granted that any and every grandmother was a positive personality. But I read a few years ago an article in an Atlanta newspaper that described a *twenty-three year old grandmother*. The grandmother had a daughter at the age of ten. The daughter also gave birth the age of ten, following her mother's example, as most little girls are wont to do. At the time the article was written the grandmother was twenty-three, her daughter was thirteen and the grandbaby was three.

Along with Pittillo-McCoy's <u>Black Picket Fences,</u> University of Pennsylvania sociology professor Dr, Elijah Anderson's <u>Code of</u> the Street is an equally important critique of what's happening to the black family and black community. Dr. Anderson in his chapter on grandmothers says that we now have a new kind of grandmother that he calls the "street grandmother". These are grandmothers young enough or in some instances just plain foolish enough to be running the same streets their wayward daughters are running. This behavior leaves us with a smaller and smaller pool of truly responsible grandmothers to be the pillars of the black family and the leaning post of the black community. We must therefore also prepare ways to increase the numbers of positive grandmothers.

Don't complain to God about making the tiger. Thank Him for not giving it wings. **African Proverb**

II WHY BLACK PEOPLE ARE CHRISTIANS

This work is written from an African Christian perspective. I know that this terminology demands explanation because this combination of words "African Christian" is an unfamiliar one to most eyes, ears and minds. The form of Christianity organized and practiced by people of African descent can accurately be described as African Christian just as the form of Christianity most white people practice can and is called European Christianity. It is no accident that there is the Roman Catholic Church, the Greek Orthodox Church, the Church of England (Anglican), the Russian Orthodox Church, the Armenian Evangelical Church, the United Free Church of Scotland, the Evangelical Formosan Church, and the Ethiopian Orthodox Tewahedo Church just to name a few. Individual Catholic parishes in the United States were historically all ethnic based so that there are Irish, Polish, Lithuanian, Italian and assorted other Catholics. We know that Lutherans derive from Germany, that the social and historical seat of Anglicans (Episcopalians) is England and that Presbyterians have their roots in Scotland.

Not just Christians but all religions come out of a particular historical, social, cultural, geographical and linguistic context. Roman Catholicism derives from Italy, its historical and geographical headquarters is the Vatican City in Rome, and its sacred language is Latin. Judaism comes from ancient Israel, modern-day Palestine. Its sacred city is Jerusalem. Its holy language is Hebrew. Islam comes from Saudi Arabia. Its historical and contemporary headquarters are in the holy cities of Mecca and Medina. Its sacred language is Arabic. One of the struggles in the history of all religions is how flexible they will be when they come into contact with and make converts among people from different cultural backgrounds. Will that religion insist that its new adherents totally adopt the entire social identity of the classic religion or will allow it people to express the values of their new faith within their own cultural dynamics. This was a question for the original Christians, many of whose leaders insisted that converts had to become Jews and be not just baptized but also circumcised. It is an issue with Islam with some converts believing that they must become Arabs in their dress, diet, and language in order to be true Muslims. European Christians tried mightily to ensure that black converts would also become Europeanized in order to be practice Christianity. However that was not to be the case.

Our ancestors who accepted the values and beliefs of Christianity insisted on expressing them through the powers of African culture. Our historical lands are down home in the South. Our sacred music is rhythm-based music that demands that we move by swinging and swaying and clapping hands and stomping feet while we are singing. We have the holy dance which is not found among European Christians at all. Our high holy moment in worship is when the Holy Spirit descends. Our sacred language is Black English. Though derided by white scholars, politicians, pundits and so-called educators it is the language that must be used when practicing Black Christianity. You cannot pray black prayers, sing the spirituals and gospel songs or preach black sermons without using Black English.

Most black practitioners of Christianity can accurately be called African Christians even though few black Christians would be comfortable with that terminology. The overwhelming majority of African Americans are what I call "unconscious Africans". We are for the most part unaware of the role that Africa continues to play in our everyday lives. This is one of the great tragedies of our experience in this country. We did not lose our identity in slavery. What we lost was the consciousness of who we were. Like someone with amnesia who cannot remember the particularities of their lives but those around them who even though they don't know them can tell them: "Well at least we know where you are from. The clothing you wear, the accent of your speech, the way you walk, all mark you as being from a certain place and member of a certain race."

Can anyone imagine a red-haired, freckle-faced man waving his shillelagh and declaring in a thick brogue: "I'm no Irishman and that's for sure"? That's the "we got a laugh to keep from crying" situation too many black people find themselves in when we gracefully, slipping and sliding with a diddy-bopping walk; big, wide African feet stuffed into painfully narrow European shoes; African noses that stretch from cheek to cheek; big, large, shapely, protruding, soft, succulent, juicy, delicious African lips; thick, strong, crinkly, kinky, nappy, wild, wooly hair; eating fried chicken smothered in hot sauce talking about: "I ain't no African"! The whole world takes one look at us and knows where we are from. We only try to deny it because we have been made to feel ashamed of our origins by the propaganda machinery of Euro-American media that popularly portrays Africa in Tarzan movies and cartoons as being the land of naked savages who in live in trees and run around hunting and eating each other. It is the shame that derives from ignorance of the truth about our own selves that leaves too many of us denying the obvious, unmistakable truth. But when we know the truth about Africa being the seat of civilization and the most ancient of cultures; the most beautiful and the wealthiest of lands; only then can we experience the liberating power of Jesus' dictum: *"Ye shall know the truth and the truth shall make you free."*

The organizational structures, the liturgical practices and

the theological beliefs of the black church come from Africa. When Europeans trace their journey back to the origins of their faith in the biblical lands they take the Northern route historically and culturally. They travel back across the Atlantic through the various nations of Europe, whether Ireland, England, France, Holland, Scandinavia, Germany. They must then go through Rome and Greece before they arrive at the Holy Land of biblical Israel. When we trace our path back to Jerusalem and Bethlehem we take the Southern route that begins in the South of this country where over 90% of the slave ships landed their human cargoes. Then we pass through the islands of the Caribbean whose original Native American populations were wiped out by the European conquerors' combination of mass murder and infectious diseases, through Jamaica, Haiti, Cuba, Antigua, Barbados, Grenada, and the Bahamas. Back across the Atlantic to our homelands among the unfamiliar names of our people that slavery tore us from, the Yoruba, the Hausa, the Ibo, the Efik, the Tiv, the Kru, the Mandinka, the Mende, the Soninke, the Ga, the Bambara, the Ashanti, the Fanti, the Dagara, the Ebira.

We must stop in the sacred cities of Ile-Ife, Timbuktu, and Kumasi. Travel the trade routes across the burning sands of the Sahara to Egypt, Nubia, the Sudan, and Ethiopia where Christianity was first accepted outside of Israel. The practices of the black church are African practices. The way we preach has no roots in any European culture. Our songs, from the spirituals to gospel, are derived from African melodies, harmonies and most importantly African polyrhythm. The ways we sing them, propelled by the awesome, emotive, artistic power of shouts, cries, groans, growls, soaring screams and deep-digging gutturals accompanied by swinging and swaying, hand-clapping, foot stomping and holy-dancing are all African.

The fact that our paramount ritual is the funeral is African. One of the most oft-stated sentiments at our funerals is some variation of: "Why do we have to wait for somebody to die for all of us to get together?" The answer is because we are Africans and the most importance rite of passage universally among African people is the funeral. It celebrates the transition from time into eternity, from this world if flesh into the world of the spirit. It surpasses in importance births, graduations, weddings, reunions and anniversaries.

Our reverence for our elders and ancestors is African. In traditional cultures children still bow, curtsy, genuflect kneel or even prostate themselves before their elders. Even slavery could not stop our ancestors from rendering due regard to their elders as Frederick Douglas so proudly describes in his autobiography. Even today those of us who have raised right would never think of addressing by elders by their first name except that we fix a "Mr." or a "Miss" in front of it. We were taught always to "put a handle on grown folks names. And we knew that you never outgrew those rules. We were taught that no matter how old you got you could never became the peer of your elder

Our conception and perception of time as being subject to the movement of the spirit rather than the mechanistic hands of a human engineered clock is African. African-Americans humorously and familiarly refer to our approach to time as CPT (Colored Peoples Time). People from the Caribbean call it Caribbean Time. Continental Africans refer to it as African Time. Whatever name it is given it is uniquely and peculiarly ours. European time mandates that they be "on time" to the exact minute even at the cost of pushing people aside so that we won't be late. Africans believe that time belongs to us, we don't belong to time . So we are always free to make time or take time to spend time with an individual we run into on our way to where we are going. African time insists that we get there "in time". As long as we arrive in time to kiss the bride, in time to eat some greens and cornbread, in time to hear the sermon.

When we arrive in Jerusalem in the time of Christ we are still in Africa. Just as racism in Euro-American scholarship and popular culture has removed Egypt from Africa so it has also dishonestly and inaccurately done so with the lands of the Bible by calling these places the "Middle East". It would be the same as someone claiming that England is East America or that Japan is North Australia. India and China are in the East, better known as Asia. Israel, Syria, Iran, Iraq, Kuwait, and Saudi Arabia are all just across the Red Sea from Egypt which is in Africa.

When Jesus had to escape from Herod's soldiers he went to Egypt. If he had been white he would have gone to Europe to hide, to Greece or Rome. The reason he went to Egypt was so he could mix and mingle with other black people that he resembled and not stand out in a crowd. The relationship between the Old Testament Hebrews and the Egyptians is an ancient one that began in friendship during the time of the Prophet Joseph, Pharaoh's dream-interpretor. It matured into the commingling of blood in intermarriage during their four hundred years of sojourn as strangers in that strange land. It was only temporarily interrupted by the escape led by Moses. For the rest of the thousand years of the Old Testament and New Testament Israel and Egypt continued to be family, friends and allies.

Over the past thirty years a new approach to biblical study has become popular among black Christians which centers around the task of "finding" black people in the Bible. This approach is wrong. You don't have to look for black people in the bible. We are everywhere. The biblical lands are the regions where African people have lived since the beginning of time. The Garden of Eden is set in Africa with one of its four bordering rivers being the Gihon, an ancient name for the Nile. You don't have to look for black people in the Bible. You have to look for white people. There was practically no European presence in the biblical lands until the Alexandrian invasion of around 300 BC.

The parallels between African Traditional religion (the faith of our people before the introduction of either Christianity or Islam) and Old Testament Judaism are dramatic and instructive. The religion of our forefathers, the most ancient of people, has such powerful similarities to Old Testament Hebraisms that it made it an easy process for them to accept Christianity as their religion. They recognized in Christianity the organizational genius to be used as the instrument by which disconnected and lost nations could be forged into one people while wandering in and struggling against the wilderness. They saw in it a spiritual and moral bulwark against the unending and vicious attacks of the heathen people that they were forced to live amongst.

Among the similarities between the Hebrews and African Traditional Religion are the following:

A holistic, non-dichotomous view of reality that instructed them that all of creation was holy. No division between the sacred and the secular, between the politics and morality. Knowledge of One God to be experienced through personal encounter and not just theological imagining and intellectual musing

Acknowledgment that God expressed the varieties of His divine power through the agency of spiritual beings-- by some called angels, archangels, seraphim, cherubim, thrones, powers, and divinities, by others ancestors, loa or orisha. .

Awe of creation,

Harmony with nature.

Seekers of peace,

Love of wisdom.

The preeminence of spiritual leadership over merely secular leadership(the authority of prophets and priests over kings and potentates).

The absolute requirement of ministry as a spiritual call and divine claim upon the life of the preacher not a professional or occupational decision.

The highest order of religious functionary is the prophet.

Every prophet is a priest but not every priest is a prophet.

Ecstatic worship, spirit possession and holy dancing.

Reverence for the ancestors, awareness of their continuing activity in the lives of the living.

Respect for elders.

Male circumcision,

Polygamy.

Children as the greatest measure of true wealth,

Recognition of the humanity of unborn children

Exogamy (marriage prohibited within the widely extended circle of the family—no marrying cousins)

Levirate marriage, a man must marry his brother's widow.

Casting out of demons,

My conclusion after considering all of these factors is that the ancient Hebrews were Africans, that Old Testament Judaism was an African Traditional Religion and that the Bible is an African document. Therefore Traditional African Religion becomes a precondition that prepared us to accept Christianity not a barrier against it or an objection to it. One of the classic stories that sums it all up is the one told all over Africa and slavery time America. The white people come preaching Jesus and at night when they are gone the African convene an ancient ceremony and call upon the ancestors to tell them whether or not Jesus is who the white folks claim he is. An ancestor possesses one of the elders and speaking through him says: "Jesus is for real; but ya'll better watch them white folks!"

When our enslaved ancestors chose Christianity for their religion it was an independent, intelligent choice based upon the spiritual principles, moral values, social practices, and ancient wisdom of the faith of their father's fathers and their mothers' mothers.' It was the religion of Apostle and Bishop Richard Allen, Deacon Denmark Vesey, Steward Gabriel Prosser, Theologian David Walker, Prophet Nat Turner, Missionary Harriet Tubman,

Evangelist Sojourner Truth, Rev. Frederick Douglass, and Bishop Henry McNeil Turner. I don't think that anybody can really believe that any of these awesome personalities could have been the victims of a plot to control their choice of religions.

There are those that call themselves Pan-Africanists and yet they hate and despise Black Christianity. They forget that the theology, philosophy and organization of Pan-Africanism was birthed out of the bowels of the church before our people ever came up out of bondage. They act as if they are not familiar with the proverb that says: "No matter how far the river flows it never forgets its source". It is to the church that we all return for sustenance, protection and revival in the time of trouble. As Egypt went back to its mother Ethiopia in the times of its troubles in the days of the Pharaohs so Black America comes back to the church in its hours of need. It is the only freestanding, fully independent institution that we have. It is free from white control, trains and certifies its own leadership, raises its own finances and sets its own agenda. Whatever deficiencies the Black Church has, they are like the failings of one's parents; they are understandable given that the parent is like the children only human. But one has to finally admit that the parent has done a good job bringing us thus far. If we would go forward in this world we must do so hand in hand with our elders; not condemning them or casting them off because we consider their limited understanding to be backward and unequal to our own modern way of thinking.

I caution all those detractors of the church to understand that the church is a spiritual, family-like, living organism that can only be changed from the inside out, never from the outside in. You cannot move the church by protesting and picketing it from the outside. You move it by hard work from the inside. Only members of the family have a place in its councils. That membership is never merely by blood but more surely by spirit. One earns and maintains

68

one's place in the family through service to the existence and furtherance of the cause of the family. There can be those of blood that have a lesser place in the family than those of spirit. Because the black church is by nature a democratic organization anybody can join and gain influence if they will show themselves to be faithful members. Through consistent dedicated service to the cause one can gain access to the councils of power in the church and lend a hand to make up for its deficiencies by helping it to move in the right directions.

The perspective I speak from therefore has three sources: the Bible, African Traditional Religion and Black Christianity, the faith of our fathers unbroken from slavery up until the generation that came to adulthood in the sixties, my own generation. I consider all of these sources as one in the agreement of their basic principles.

There are a number of white racist sociologists that operate from the deficit theory of African American culture and society. Using their own Eurocentric standards of measurement they conclude that there is something seriously wrong with us because we are not like them. They use two familiar arguments to stake their claim. One is that we are from Africa, a benighted land of savages and barbarians. Two that we are the products of American slavery and whatever little good sense we had slavery took that away so that we are a totally inferior people and every thing we do is flawed. In fact to them anything that is black is inferior by definition. This theory is not only found amongst white racists.

Black theorists who maintain that we lost our identity in slavery believe by logical conclusion in the same deficit approach to black culture and society. They insist that everything was taken from us in slavery and that the answer to what they see as our identity is not to go back to our most recent home in West Africa where we were stolen from but to travel intellectually all the way to Ancient Egypt in the days of the Pharaohs when according to them

African peoples reached the height of their power in human history. I do not denounce this approach because I am a student of ancient African history and recognize the unfathomable depths of the wisdom of the ancient Egyptian as one of the wellsprings of African genius. But I insist on not doing so at the expense of the ignoring or downplaying the contributions of our kidnapped ancestors. They too left a legacy that is still alive amongst us today.

A people are judged by how they respond to tragedy and calamity. Slavery was our finest hour. Out of the bare bones of our spiritual powers we constructed a new civilization in the midst of our enemies. While today majority black populations have not figured out how to take mere political control of American cities our ancestors were plotting and planning to, by force of arms, take total power over entire cities like Richmond and Charleston by force of arms. They built villages, towns, cities, hospitals, churches, denominations, businesses, factories, purchased over twenty million acres of land, made pacts with foreign governments, built systems of black, private, Christian kindergartens, high schools, boarding academies, colleges, universities, seminaries, schools of law and medicine. Until a generation rises up that outthinks, out builds, out imagines and outworks, the generations of the enslaved ones and their children they are not qualified to look with scorn upon their legacy.

While the Black Church may lack in its entirety the kind of direct and obvious African consciousness that many anti-Christian Pan-Africanists would like to see, it still has retained a sense of self that has kept it under black control and ownership despite years of attempted takeovers by various white interests. On the other hand, we see important national black businesses being sold to white people. We see many of our most gifted and accomplished artists trying so hard to cross over and achieve acceptance from and popularity with white people that they sacrifice the highest ideals of their people on the altar of personal success. Many of our leading civil rights organizations are afflicted by white influence and power in high places because of sponsorship and funding by corporate commercial interests. Too many black politicians are unable to take stands on principle because they are beholden to the party they belong to and dare not anger or alienate their white resources. None of our supposedly most powerful politicians will organize a third party and carve out their own philosophical ground. They would rather be clients for their white bosses who will instruct them how to think, speak, act and vote.

The power of the black church or lack thereof is not in its systems but in its people. Because it is a spiritual institution it can only be affected for good or for evil by the presence or absence, activity or passivity, dedication or dereliction of its membership. Neither stone and wood, nor the creedal systems of ecclesiological organizations, nor any architectural marvels are visited by, imbued with or inhabited by spirit. Flesh and blood are the dwelling places of spirit. How many times have we heard our elders declare by way of proverb: "The church is not the building. The church is in the hearts of the believers." Those who move, define, empower and direct the church are the people of the church.

The black church is the one essential center of African American culture. It is where the cultural practices of black American are most consistently and dynamically practiced not merely as a celebration of history but as a continuation of the living traditions of our people. If African culture can be distilled down to its essence I would suggest that it can be said to consist of three fundamental components: telling the story, making music and feeling the spirit. Our classical music is the spirituals. They are sung every Sunday not to mention Wednesday night prayer meetings ands Friday night praise services. European classic music only exists because wealthy patrons subsidize symphonic orchestras.

The most authentic expression of the African art of storytelling is found in the virtuosity of the black preacher. Nobody can tell the story like him. Nowhere else is the African dynamic of call and response more powerfully expressed than at the preaching hour in the church when preacher and people function as an organic entity. The poetic imagery, the emotional power, the fearless confrontation with controversial even dangerous issues, the unique musicality of voice, the practical wisdom, the call to action, the improvising, the poeticizing and the signifying are just some of the elements that cause the black preacher to be the standard for excellence in high speech not just in the black community but farther for the whole of America if not the entire world. The highest level of oratory is preaching and when a black person boasts: "I was preaching"! They are not talking about like Billy Graham. It is no accident that many of our most eloquent non-preacher leaders like Malcolm X, Harold Washington, Huey P. Newton, and Maynard Jackson are the children of preachers.

It is no accident that the church produces our artists, our leaders and is our central gathering place. It is the place that we experience the freedom to be our best selves. That best self is self in communion and community with the fullness of human life which is the spirits of the living, the dead and the unborn. African spirituality is communal. People come together in great numbers to invite, invoke and celebrate the presence of the holy in our lives. This is not to decry any individual spiritual practices by which people come into more or less private contact with the world of the spirit. It means that as an African people we practice communal celebration as the height of spiritual communication.

Furthermore it is the Black Church that has been the true Christian church in this country. The European forms of Christianity have yet to live out the true meaning of their declared beliefs. It is impossible to proclaim that one is a follower of Christ and believe in white supremacy, organize a system of chattel slavery, or concoct an economy based on monopoly capitalism. The very ways in which Europe and America have conducted themselves contradicts their preaching and pontificating. That's why our enslaved ancestors had no confidence in the so-called Christianity of the slave owners. They watched and noted the contradictions between how holy white folks tried to act on Sunday morning and how brutally and savagely they treated us all week long. They studied, analyzed and criticized this behavior through the penetrating lenses of their ancient African spirituality. The conclusion they came to is expressed in the spiritual: "Everybody talking about heaven ain't going there" and "None but the righteous shall see God." While Europeans proclaimed their Christianity in theologies, creeds and high-sounding philosophical formulations, Africans sang and danced their faith and lived it out in their everyday lives as they organized societies based upon the biblical principles of love, mercy, forgiveness, justice, generosity and hospitality unto the least of these.

The living truth of Black Christianity's faithfulness to the teachings of Jesus is an undeniable part of American lore. During the Depression when forlorn and hungry hobos rode the rails from town to town, when they arrived in a new town or village or city whose neighborhood would they go to beg for food? Would they go to the upper class white conclaves known universally as the "Gold Coast"? No! Because wealthy white people's mansions are secreted behind high walls and protected by armed men and vicious dogs. Would they then go to the working and middle-class neighborhoods of their own white people? No! These classes of white people are known to zealously and violently protect their homes with private arsenals of deadly weapons and are notorious for shooting strangers on sight. Their motto is: "A man's home is his castle". Even white hobos knew to seek out the areas where black people lived. They could be sure that if all we had was a pot of black-eye peas and a cast-iron skillet of cornbread and water to drink out of mason jars we would share what we had. No matter how little we had our belief system required of us to share.

White liberals and radicals, who come out of a powerful agnostic, atheistic, and anti-Christian tradition dating back to the European Enlightenment of the 18 and 19th centuries, have for generations been astounded and discomfited by the fact that in order to be involved in the cutting edge of social issues and progressive movements they had to come to and deal with Black Christians because we have been at the forefront of every movement for social justice in the history of this country. The struggle for black liberation from chattel slavery which was organized and engineered in the church is the wellspring for every progressive movement in this nation's history. The Black Church has been the headquarters and the black preachers the generals and line lieutenants from abolitionism, to women's rights, to various anti-war struggles, to multiple aspects of the Civil Rights and Black Power Movements.

Therefore I am unperturbed, unabashed, unashamed, unbowed, unmovable and unapologetic about my faith. It is the organizing principle and analytical tool by which I make sense of this world and the condition of my people. It has proven itself from slavery times to carry power by which our people have been able not only survive the worst atrocities of white racism but to defeat and destroy many of them. Through the prophetic lenses of this transcendent system of values and beliefs I can see answers to our continuing dilemmas as our ancestors did in their day.

In its essence what Christianity has enabled our people to do is having taught them how to carry invisible, unsearchable, undetectable power through a world organized to deny them power. It has been our source of comfort, our tool of construction and our weapon of indignation. Giving us comfort to preserve us from the insanity of hopelessness in our worst days, the tool of unquenchable, unalterable determination with which we built structures for our sustenance in hard times and the weapon of courage and boldness with which we smote our enemies in more propitious hours.

No one is a child of the earth. Everyone is a child of God.
African Proverb

III. THE BLACK CHURCH'S MINISTRY TO YOUTH

Church attendance is a primary determinant of a positive life for black youth. Black youth who are active in church are much less likely to drop out of school, get pregnant, go to jail, use drugs, join gangs, and run the street at night past curfew. Being in a community which gives constant positive reinforcement to uplifting values makes it much more possible for young people to excel. We spend a lot of time decrying peer pressure as a major contributing factor to teen-age problems. We often fail to recognize that there are two kinds of peer pressure- positive and negative. A group like the church youth organization provides young people with an environment filled with encouragement for doing right, like getting better grades, ambitions of going to college, determination to be sexually disciplined. It also provides access to elders whose consistent messages will be uplifting, encouraging and informative.

The church provides its youthful members with positive role models and surrogate parents. Children need Godparents because of the natural tension that occurs when there is a disagreement between what a child wants to do with their lives and what the parents want them to do. Parents are often ego-driven enough to demand that their children follow the script in life that they have written for them. Whether it's that they want their children to follow them into their profession and occupation, or because they want to live vicariously through the child's achievement in a field that they failed at in their own youth, or because

76

they have a dream of their "baby" achieving success in a particular area or that they just think that they know what is best for the child. But when the child has other ideas for himself or herself it can lead to major relational problems. It is not simply that the child resents being forced into an area alien to their own sense of themselves and what they should be doing with their lives. It is also because they are distressed by the disappointment in them expressed by their parents. No matter how cool or unmoved a teen-ager might be able to act like, in fact, it is a heartbreaking experience to be a disappointment to one's parents who are still the most important people in their lives.

One of the reasons that the peer group is so strong among teenagers is that during this developmental stage young people are in the midst of what might be a decade-long series of experiments trying to figure out who they are and what they want to be. They might change their minds from one day to the next. While the parents may be upset even angered because thy "no longer know who their child is", the members of the peer group who are all going through the same thing accept each other at face value along with their periodic transformations. A Godparent would be able to deal with a child without the tension of clashing expectations because they are not invested in the child's following in their footsteps as so many parents are.

But despite all the positive aspects of church life for our young people youth ministry is still the weakest department in the life of the black church. This is in comparison to what it could be and what it should be. We have no coherent approach to youth ministry. While there are outstanding individual youth ministries in every town these are, unfortunately, the exceptions to the rule. They are to be likened unto the exceptional successful black school in a system full of institutions that fail to educate black youth. Our challenge is the one that public schools refuse to face up to. That is to institutionalize the successes of the few and make them the standard for youth ministry throughout all black churches and denominations.

The white Christian community ministers to its youth through such organizations as the Youth for Christ, Young Life, Campus Crusade not to mention such secular organizations as the Boy Scout, Girls Scouts, Cub Scouts, Campfire Girls, Boys and Girls Clubs, etc. This is how they make up for any flaws in the individual family. These institutions stand at the ready to provide children from the worst homes with the kind of resources they need to successfully maneuver through the dangerous waters of modern life.

We have only a very few really dynamic and successful youth ministries scattered in various locales around the country. We have no central organizing philosophy or theological framework much less actual organizations and institutions with headquarters, staffs, recreational centers, and summer camps with which to provide our children with the advantages they need to live full, productive, and holistic.

The ministry of the black church ought to have a significant positive impact on the lives of the young people. The standards of behavior set by the church needs to be the community wide standard and the source of guidance for parents, teachers, counselors, coaches and any one involved in the lives of young people. The church ought to set a standard that leads to all the children in our community living more spiritually rich, socially progressive, intellectually and academically successful and materially prosperous lives. All young people in our communities ought to be touched and made better by the presence of the church in the wider community. The church's leaven ought to cause the entire black community to rise.

The practicality and relevance of black Christianity to the everyday lives of God's people is reflected in the ways in which the church enables its adult members to successfully address the paramount issues in their lives. These chief concerns are family and employment. The

78

freedom of the church allows it to organize holistic ministries with unrestricted license to speak to every area of the lives of our people. For young people the most important issues are school and relationships. Our young people must be successful academically because their school records are the best indicator of how they will perform in the adult world of employment. The relationships I'm talking about are with their parents, their peers and their boyfriends and girlfriends.

The ministry of the church to young people ought not to be limited to youth who are members of the church. I was born and raised a Catholic but enjoyed a consistent relationship with the Black church. My Boy Scout troop was headed by Rev. Turner and met often at the St. Michael Baptist Church in the 1800 block of 13th St. where he served as an associate minister. One of my most enduring memories of young teenage adventure was attending the annual church picnic of a neighborhood church and becoming lost in the woods of the forest preserve with a group of my neighborhood friends. The churches outreach to the youth of the entire community made a difference in our lives whether our names were on the membership rolls or not. Christian youth across the board ought to be leaders among their peers in all the aforementioned areas. Our young people ought to have an academic work ethic second to none. They ought to approach school with a joyous enthusiasm that indicates an irrepressible commitment to excellence. They ought to be as on fire to attend class and get their lesson out as they are to participate in a church play or to lead a song with the choir...

Our young people ought to have more respectful, honest, loving social relationships as the most dramatic proof of the efficacy of our faith. They should know how to relate to the most significant people in their lives. We should lead them through the maturation process and enable them to move successfully from one stage of life to another. As little children they were Daddy's little boy and Mama's little but as they move into adolescence their parents are replaced by their peers but the highest relationship is that of marriage. Since marriage begins with courtship our young people need to know how to properly engage in the activities and rituals of courtship. We ought to have a way of dating, courting and partying that is consistent with the high moral standards of our faith. The out-of-control social and sexual behavior of our youth is primarily due to parental and adult withdrawal form these processes. Modern parents have so little involvement in their children's lives that there are those who will actually leave home and allow teen-agers to have parties with no adult supervision.

We need to develop guidelines for peer relationships. Our children need to be taught how to be friends. They need to know what a friend is, how to choose a friend, how to treat a friend, how to make a friend and how to keep a friend. The horrific levels of violence among black males and increasingly among black females also are indicative of the fact that our young people know very little about how to properly relate to each other.

During my tenure as chaplain at Lincoln University there was a conflict between two male students from West Africa. Both men, one in his late twenties the other in his late thirties, were regular attendees and participants in the life of the Christian community on campus. One of them came to me and explained the situation and asked serve as a mediator and adjudicator. Knowing enough about African traditional culture to understand that these kinds of situations were typically handled by a group rather than an individual, I convened a council of the elders composed of a number of African professors and myself. It was my first experience in such an event and I learned much more than I had to contribute. The fellows each explained their point of view in turn without interrupting the other. The elders asked questions, deliberated among themselves and then issued a conclusion that included how the two men would conduct themselves toward one another from then on. The brothers humbly and obediently accepted the conclusions and recommendation of the older men and the incident was over, never to surface again during the reminder of their student days,

This is to be contrasted with an incident that occurred about the same time among African American students. A member of the freshmen class had a dispute with fraternity members that climaxed in what can only be called a gang-fight. At high noon in a crowded cafeteria, the two group threw metal chairs across the room at each other and then fought with knives, bottles and sticks through the cafeteria and out onto school grounds. I could not help but ask myself: "Why is it that our big boys and young men do not know how to submit themselves to their elders to settle their disputes before blood has to be shed?"

The same is true for courtship and dating. We have no community-wide, church-wide, not even family-wide rules about how the dating process operates. When I was growing up in the fifties and sixties there were universally respected rules concerning relationships among boys and girls who were engaged in dating. First of all the parents were in charge of the process. Every date and social visit began with the introduction of the young man to the parents. They would then subject him to an interrogation in the form of a battery of questions. His answers to those questions would determine whether he would be allowed to stay and visit and for how long, whether he would be allowed to take the girl out and what the curfew would be, or whether he would have to leave that house running. The tragic epidemic of unwed teenage mothers and uneducated, unemployed immature teenage fathers is due to teen-agers who are allowed to interact with one another without parental guidance. This tragic phenomenon of babies having babies is the primary cause of much of the social insanity rampant in our community.

Young people cannot successfully navigate the dangerous and confusing waters of adolescence without the guidance of their elders. The more leeway we have given our children to make their own decisions and depend on their own counsel the more trouble they have gotten themselves into.

The redoubtable black psychologist Dr. Amos Wilson, author of a number of significant books on the psychology of African American adolescents, instructed us about this in his definitive work entitled <u>Developmental Psychology of the Black Child.</u> He said that one of the most significant markers of future success among black youth is their access to and reliance on the counsel of their elders. That unsuccessful youth when they face a dilemma rely on the advice of their peers who of course are in the same boat and don't have any more knowledge or wisdom than those seeking their advice. On the other hand he explains that successful young people when seeking counsel venture outside the circle of the familiar and avail themselves of the information, expertise, experience and know-how of parents, preachers, teachers, deacons, counselors, coaches, the bible, librarians, encyclopedias, histories, classic and contemporary works of great literature.

Youth ministry in the black church is so weak for a number of reasons:

1. While there are individual congregations in every city that have outstanding youth ministries on the whole we have no coherent, denomination-wide, national, not to mention international, approach to youth ministry. There is no authoritative text, no universally accepted guide, and no general philosophy that informs our dealing with youth. We lack a set of specific goals in terms of their development and what we intend to produce at the end of the developmental process. All education (and youth ministry ought to primarily be Christian

Education) is a process that begins at the end. That is to say it is a process that begins with a vision of the end product. We do not have a clear vision of where we want our young people to be 10, 15, twenty, even fifty years from now. We hear too many of our parents and elders proclaiming: "I sho" hope my child go to college and do something with they life". This is a dangerous approach to preparing for the future. We don't hope that the gas don't get cut off. We pay the bill. Our ancestors did not just hope that slavery would end some day. They organized resistance against it for over three hundred years. When able they joined the Union Army by the hundreds of thousands and struck the death blow to the Confederacy and to slavery. After slavery they redefined themselves as builders of a "nation within a nation". They insisted on becoming doctors, scientists, school teachers, inventors, airplane pilots, lawyers, writers, factory owners, businesspeople, politicians and government officials. When they could see little hope of things getting better for them in the South they organized perhaps the greatest migration of all time and move North by the millions converting themselves from a Southern rural folk to a Northern urban population. We don't hope that the car don't throw a rod. We change the oil. We seem to have forgotten the industry, boldness, and visionary thinking of our ancestors as we allow ourselves to be mere victims of history rather than victors in history. We need to put structures in place to insure that our children will rise to the best of their possibilities and not become tragic statistics of a generation that did not fulfill its potential.

2. We do not require that our youth ministers be specially trained professionals. Less than 10% of

black churches have youth ministers. Of those that do the number who are paid is closer to 1%. Those who do have youth ministers generally appoint them to that office by default. They are appointed youth ministers because they are young and they have no church of their own. The idea that because someone is young they are thereby qualified to teach, train, and lead our youth is a remarkably resilient but biblically unsupportable idea. As Jesus put it:" ...if the blind lead the blind they both fall in a ditch". Mtt. 15:14KJV It is actually the shallowest kind of thinking to believe that just because someone is young enough to be conversant with the latest styles in language, clothing, hairdos, music and dance that they have something of substance to say to our young people. We would never use that kind of logic in our educational institutions. We don't choose people to teach or to coach or an administrator based on their youthfulness. It's not being able to speak the young people's language that qualifies one as a great teacher of youth but one who can teach young people new languages that will be vehicles for the uplifting and broadening their lives. It is being able to speak a language that engages and inspires our young people to strive toward their best selves. One of the greatest youth ministers of all time was Dr. Benjamin Elijah Mays, the most illustrious president of Morehouse College who led that great institution into and guided it through its golden years. He is as well known for being the chief mentor and father-in-the ministry to Dr. Martin Luther King, Jr. Dr. Mays remained a remarkably effective youth minister until his failing years in his eighties because he had a message of power, wisdom and transformation for young people.

3. Our Christian youth do not have centers in our churches which is their space. For recreation they have to go to the same places that the unchurched and unbelievers go and in those places they are subjected to the same negative influences of the children of the world. Our children need a space and a place of their own where they can participate in recreational and educational activities designed for their uplift. They need to be able to study, socialize, dance, and conversate in an environment where they will be under the caring and careful supervision of adult Christian leadership.

For churches that are too small to afford a paid youth minister of their own or recreational space for their youth they might consider joining together and pooling resources to put together a salary for a youth minister who would direct a joint youth program for all the churches . The same approach could work for a recreational space for young people. A number of churches whether in an ad hoc formation or along the traditional organizational lines such as a district association could cooperatively obtain properties that could serve as recreational space for their youthful members.

There is no course on ministry to black youth at any level of ministerial preparation whether college, bible college, or seminary except for a course I taught at Interdenominational Theological Center (ITC) in Atlanta back in the summer of 1993 entitled Youth Ministry to Black Teenagers. We must consider how we can be instrumental in training youth ministers. One approach is to sponsor seminars and workshops in youth ministry in various locales at different levels of outreach. They can be sponsored by local churches, district or state congresses or conventions, and even interdenominational ministerial associations. Our long-term goal must be to fund chairs in our seminaries to hire professors to be the resident experts in youth ministry.

4. The largest financial fund in 99% of black churches is

the building fund. Until the scholarship fund reaches parity with the building fund or even surpasses it we are planning for and financing the failure of future generations. People build buildings. But buildings cannot build people. When we major in building buildings and minor in building people we are ensuring the underdevelopment of our youth. There are fewer greater tragedies than great cathedrals built at the time of a particular church's golden age that because of the neglect to provide an effective ministry to the youth have now declined into cavernous sanctuaries almost empty of people. Too many formerly great churches are still living off their memories of oft-repeated glories of a storied past. Now they are full of elders in their last days. The cries of babies are not heard. There are no newly-married young couples. There no teenage boys there. The little children are there because they are being baby-sat by their grandparents. They conduct many funerals but few baptisms. These churches are dying because they invested in the building and not in their children. On the other hand there are lively active, populous congregations whose worship services are replete with hundreds if not thousands of young people. They constantly replenish and refresh the body of their membership by making themselves attractive to young people by demonstrating a real commitment to helping them live more progressive and productive lives.

You can't teach what you don't know and you can't lead where you don't go.

You got to see a man to be a man. African American Proverb

IV. THE DIFFERENCE BETWEEN A BOY AND A MAN

It takes a man to teach a boy how to be a man. Women cannot teach boys how to be men because, as the adage has it: "You can't teach what you don't know and you can't lead where you don't go." Perhaps never before in human history has a race of people depended upon its women to instruct its boys in manhood and lead them through the rites of passage that take them from boyhood to manhood. No group of women in the history of the world have ever brought their daughters to their fathers, their grandfathers, their uncles and said to them: "Teach these girls how to be women." The very idea is so ridiculous that it is beyond laughable it is unthinkable. How is it them that as a race we have allowed two generations of black males to be left to the ministrations of their mothers and grandmothers and then wonder why our boys and young men are in such a state of crisis and confusion?

The mainstream feminist attack on manhood as being not just an inferior gender but an inherently flawed and dangerous one that is the source of all that is problematic in human society has brought about a general devaluation of manhood. Not only a sense that men are less valuable than women but that manhood itself is some kind of artificial social construction that can be done away by the genius of the post-modern liberal imagination. The use of the term "macho" is a case in point. The word simply means masculine but it is used as a derogatory adjective to indicate that there is something wrong with a man being manly. On the other hand there is no comparable term that describes feminine women as having something wrong with them.

The contemporary cry for androgyny, for blurring and blending the sexes until there are no recognizable males or females just a hodge-podge of homosexual, bi-sexual, pansexual, transgendered creatures of their own perverse imagination threatens to destroy human society as we have known it since human beings first appeared on the earth. The greatest victims of this kind of thinking, that we are creatures of our own making, are men. Men are seen in this scenario as not only dangerous but unnecessary. Men are now challenged to be less like men and more like women. Men are identified in this school of thought as being the source of all that is wrong, evil and dysfunctional in the human community.

There are some things that should never be confused the one with the other. Such confusion of vital realities introduces chaos into the human community.

1. We should never confuse the divine with the demonic as do the devil-worshippers who have made Satan their god.

2. We should never confuse the temporary with the eternal as do those who live their lives as though there is no world other than this one.

3. We should never confuse the living with the dead. The old folk in church have a saying: "Anything dead ought to be buried".

4. We should never confuse the material with the spiritual as do people whose entire life is dedicated to the acquisition of material things. Jesus said: "A man's life does not consist of the number of things that he possesses".

5. We should never confuse the animal with the human as do the radical animal liberationists who view their pets as their children lavishing on beasts the kind of care denied to orphaned and abandoned children.

6. We should never confuse the married with the single as have too many people who got caught up in so-called love triangles and found themselves the victims of crimes of passion.

7. We should never confuse the male with the female. The fullness of life is found in the coming together of male and female for they were created to rightly fit with and balance one another.

8. One should never confuse a grown person with a child. It is an injustice to treat a child like a grown person. It is dangerous to treat a grown person like a child. The reason that there has no peace between black and white people during our five hundred year sojourn as strangers in a strange land is because too many white people insist on treating black men like boys and black women like girls.

Our contemporary confusion concerning manhood operates on two levels. Firstly, we don't understand the difference between men and women and secondly we don't understand the difference between boys and men.

There is a general misunderstanding in American culture concerning the difference between men and women. For hundreds of years as Christians we have understood sexual difference as the act of an all-wise God who in the beginning of the Bible instructs us in Genesis that He created us "male and female." For tens of thousands of years in Africa we understood the complementary roles of the sexes as being the cornerstone of human society. Contemporary Western re-imagining of gender to be a man-made construct has allowed us to devalue men and overvalue women. Matriarchy from this point of view is all good. Patriarchy is inherently evil. The maternal instinct is one of the most profound and noblest characteristics found in the human community and the exclusive province of the female of the species. Its counterpart the paternal instinct is thought not to even exist. Motherhood is deified and worshipped. Fatherhood is optional and non-essential. One never hears a man say: "My baby don't need no mama."

But the female declaration: "My baby don't need no daddy" has become almost a proverb.

We have already seen the effects of the premature conclusion on the part of social scientists that divorce was healthier for children than a challenging and difficult marriage. The divorce culture, like integration, was a social experiment. Those who cried out for integration in the sixties now realize their mistake and demand the reestablishment of black institutions. Those sociologists and psychiatrists that reasoned that divorce was a solution to marital and family difficulties now produce studies on the devastating effects of single parent homes, fatherless children and blended families and the way many American marriages are now described as serial monogamy—a series of monogamous marriages with people being married two, three, and more times with all of the physical and emotional displacement attendant to any form of transience.

American society in general and many black people in particular bought into the idea fostered by the mainstream feminist movement that women were like black people--an oppressed minority. White women jumped on the bandwagon of the black liberation struggle, incorporating the rhetoric of our demands for freedom. In the liberal atmosphere of the sixties, as a progressive community, we welcomed them with open arms. However, we are only now coming to understand that the true agenda of the feminists was for a negative freedom not a positive one. Black people from slavery times had fought for a positive freedom- the freedom to rise to our highest capacities. White woman and later homosexuals demanded a negative freedom. They wanted freedom from all moral restraints. Mainstream white feminists and many of their misguided black counterparts over time revealed their agenda to be one of freedom from having children, freedom from marriage-- which they defined as an oppressive institution and finally freedom from sex with men which they defined as by nature being rape. They identified all men as being

90

the enemy. They revealed themselves to be a lesbian movement which is why author, Daphne Patai, describes their operative philosophy as "heterophobia" in her book by that name.

Once it became obvious that the true agenda of mainstream feminism was lesbianism it lost popular acceptance in the wider society. This is most clearly observed in the defeat of the Equal Rights Amendment (ERA). But because they retained their prominence in two of the most essential and powerful American institutions, the academy and media, their ideas receive a level of exposure that is disproportionate to their true place in the culture as a whole.

Over the past twenty years feminism's coming out of the closet as man-hating lesbianism has generated a powerful response in the form of a number of popular and scholarly works that offer cogent and insightful criticism by authors male and female, black and white from a number of perspectives, from African to biblical, political, sociological, historical, literary, and psychological. Among my favorites in this genre are Father Songs edited by Gloria Wade-Gayles, Airing Dirty Laundry, Writin' is Fightin' and Reports from the Front all by Ishmael Reed; Anatomy of Female Power by Chinweizu; Africana Womanism by Clenora Hudson-Weems; Crisis in Black Sexual Politics and The Endangered Black Family both by Dr.'s Nathan and Julia Hare; Whatever Happened to Daddy's Little Girl by Jonetta Rose Barras; the aforementioned Heterophobia by Daphne Patai; Who Stole Feminism and The War Against Boys both by Christina Hoff Sommers; The Myth of Male Power by Warren Farrell; The Masculine Mystique by Andrew Kimbrell; Men We Cherish edited by Brooke Stephens; Abused Men: The Hidden Side of Domestic Violence by Phillip W. Cook; How Fathers Care for the Next Generation by John Snarey; Recovering Biblical Manhood and Womanhood by John Piper and Wayne Gruden; Feminism Is Not The Story Of My Life by

Elizabeth Fox-Genovese; Man and Woman in Christ by
Stephen B. Clark; Not Guilty: The Case In Defense of Men
by David Thomas; Men and Marriage by George Gilder;
The Father: His Role in Child Development by David B.
Lynn; Fatherless America by David Blankenhorn, and
Code of the Street by Elijah Anderson.

For a fictional treatment of these themes read the
remarkable Standing at the Scratch Line and its sequel
Echoes from a Long Ago Summer by Maya Angelou's son,
Guy Johnson and Always Outnumbered, Always
Outgunned by the esteemed Walter Mosley. These last
three I highly recommend for teenage-boys as the kinds of
books that they will enjoy so much that they can serve as
the inspiration for the development of a lifelong reading
habit. Men and boys love adventure stories and these books
are full of wonderful adventures experienced by awesomely
heroic, yet down-to-earth, true-to-life black and easily-
recognizable male characters.

But the damage has already been done to society's sense
of the value of men in general and husbands and fathers in
particular. Institutionally it means that in the divorce
culture mothers continue to receive custody of the children
in 98% of cases. Subsequent studies show that the less
access the father has to his children the less he pays in child
support. What we perceive from a shallow reading of this
phenomenon is "dead-beat dads". A deeper look exposes
us to the tragedies of fathers often denied access to their
children by the custodial mother for any number of reasons
ranging from the desire for revenge to the presence of a
new man in her life.

The truth is that husbands and fathers are essential to the
collective health of the entire family and to the individual
well-being of each of its members.

Men and women are different. Making that statement
places one in the difficult and ridiculous position of having
to prove the obvious. Author Alan Medinger in his book
Growth into Manhood lists a few of the differences

between men and women in terms of their bodies and brains:

Height: In the United States, men average five inches —about seven percent—taller than women

Legs: A man's legs are longer in proportion to his trunk than a woman's.

Muscle-to-fat ratio: At the same weight, a man averages less fat and more muscle than a woman. Men average 15 to 20 percent fat; women 20 to 25 percent. Men have up to 42 percent muscle; women 35 percent

Vocal cords: A man's are longer.

Jawbone: A man's tends to be square; a woman's rounded or pointed.

Senses: A woman has more acute senses of hearing, smell and taste.

Red blood cells: Proportionately a man has more than a woman, enabling him to carry more oxygen to the muscles.

Bone mass: Women have 30 percent less than men.

Upper-body strength: A man's typically is two or three times that of a woman.

Men's brains are more specialized than women's. This means that a woman can use an individual part of her brain for several purposes, whereas men tend to use an individual part of the brain for only one purpose.

Men tend to operate more out of the right side of their brain where visual and spatial abilities reside. Women tend to operate out of both sides of their brains more or less equally.

Men often have superior hand-eye coordination.

The areas of a woman's brain devoted to language comprehension and the spoken word are considerably larger than in men, 23.2 percent vs. 12.8 percent respectively..

Women's brains are more integrated than men's. This means a woman can draw quickly on more parts of her brain than a man. The testosterone food a seven-week –old boy experiences in the womb destroys a part of the corpus callosum, the bundles of nerves that carry information between the two hemispheres of the brain and integrate thinking.

Men excel more often in mathematics and abstract thinking. In an ongoing Johns Hopkins University talent search for youth with extraordinary mathematical skills, the ration of boys to girls at the highest levels of performance was 13 to 1.

In American universities, over 75 percent of the students planning to major in foreign language are women, while only 14 percent of those planning to major in engineering are women.

Where men and women suffer similar brain damage from a stroke or accident, women generally recover more quickly and more completely. They have a superior ability to use other parts of their brains to substitute for the damaged areas.

Reading and speech impediments are far more common among boys than girls. A boy's greater brain specialization handicaps him in being able to use alternative parts of his brain when one part doesn't function well.

Because we don't have a clear understanding of the difference between boys and men we have boys declaring themselves to be men and attempting to assume manly roles which are beyond their capacities and men acting like boys, neglecting the most positive contribution they have to make to human society.

Despite the irrefutable statistical evidence of the difficult lives children are forced to live when they have no fathers, we still play the paternal office cheap. Unquestionably, part of the reason is because the influences of androgynous thinking have robbed us of the common sense ability to recognize the unique contributions of men.

Many of our boys are confused about the proper role that men play in society. They hear many of their mothers say: "My baby don't need no daddy". They end up without a proper male role model in their lives and look to movies, rap songs, singers, actors, comedians and entertainers for their examples of what a man is and how a man functions in the world. What they get from these sources are cartoon characters, one dimensional caricatures of true manhood. Rambo, Batman, the Terminator, and various kung fu heroes. They see manhood from an immature perspective of the action hero who is constantly engaged in some form of exhilarating struggle.

While teaching a black history class at the Stateville Maximum Security Correctional Institution in Joliet IL, I noticed that many of my inmate students constantly referred to themselves by using such terms as "frontline soldiers" and "the revolutionary vanguard". It was obvious that they identified their manhood as being inseparable from unending warfare. One day I asked the question: "When a society is at war what percentage of the population serves on the front lines of combat"? The point of the question was to get them to consider that the vast majority of any population even of a country at war is engaged in the everyday activities of building and maintaining families, going to schools, growing food, manufacturing not only munitions and war materials but housing, clothing, and all the other everyday needs of regular society.

For far too many of our young men real manhood is a fantasy derived from songs, sports, movies, and video games. Without the presence of the father to provide them with a down-to-earth, inescapable, and unmistakable truth of manhood they are left to be victims of their own and other people's fantasies. This kind of manhood is often referred to as "hypermasculinity". It is concentrated on the physical, the short term, the exciting, thrill-seeking, and dare-devil behavior which are really the province of little boys pretending to be men.

These fatherless boys are also misogynistic to a large extent. One of the roles of the father in the home is to protect his son from the mother's natural female inclination to overprotect and even smother him. A mother's over protectiveness can rob a boy of his innate urge to be aggressive, take risks, and stand up under the physical consequences of making mistakes, such as falling down, being cut and bleeding, or breaking a limb. While women seek to hide their scars because they see them as marring their beauty; men and boys boast of theirs and proudly display them as trophies. In the absence of a husband mothers often take their sons to be their friends, companions, even confidantes. Boys are often resentful to the point of rage of being required to share emotional issues which they cannot begin to comprehend or make sense of. The mother who so attaches herself to a son also tries to keep him close to her past the point when his normal development demands that he break emotional ties with her and seek his true masculine identity in the world of men. Boys who run in gangs are also trying to escape from the smothering environment created by a mother who is too dependent on them emotionally because she doesn't have a husband to share those needs with and so substitutes her son.

Here are a few differences between boys and men:

Boys are students. Men are teachers
Boys are consumers. Men are producers.
Boys play with toys. Men work with tools.
Boys break things, Men make things.
Boys take things apart. Men put things together.
Boys ask questions. Men give answers.
Boys introduce chaos, men bring order.
Boys run in gangs. Men organized in teams.
Boys play house. Men build homes.
Boys shack up. Men get married.
Boys make babies. Men raise children.
A boy won't raise his own children. A man will raise his and somebody else's.
Boys invent excuses for failure. Men manufacture strategies for success.
Boys are self-centered. Men are other-directed.
Boys look for somebody to take care of them. Men look for somebody to take care of.
Boys want popularity. Men command respect.
Boys are presented centered. They are up on the latest.
Men are time-balanced. They are down with the greatest.
Men have knowledge of the past, understanding of the present and a vision for the future.

We need men. We need men to fulfill the two essential roles of males in all human societies-- to be husbands to our daughters and fathers to our grandchildren. But they have to be produced. Boys cannot teach themselves how to be men. When they are left to that alternative the result is gangs. There is no greater desire in the heart of a big boy than to finally achieve manhood and have it recognized by those most important to him personally and by society at large.

In traditional African societies and to a large extent in the historical family structures of black America there was a process by which boys were taught to be men. In traditional Africa the process was institutionalized and formalized in the everyday dynamics of society. A boy was aware at each stage of his life of his position in society and his distance from or closeness to achieving manhood. Formal schooling led him from one stage to the next and graduation ceremonies marked his successful passages. When he completed preparation he was introduced to society in grand public ceremonies and rituals and then accorded all of the responsibilities and privileges of his status.

In Black America the men of the community, meaning fathers, uncles, grandfathers, big brothers, older cousins, godfathers, pastors, teachers, coaches and counselors were responsible for teaching boys the ways of men. While there were few formal occasions to mark the achievement it was made clear by his treatment and acceptance of real men that a boy knew that he had crossed over from boyhood to manhood. Some of the markers included graduation from high school or college, successful completion of basic training in the armed forces, getting a job, moving into one's own living quarters, getting married, defeating a dangerous foe, and /or completing a hazardous assignment.

Boys face a different set of issues and problems in becoming men than girls do in achieving womanhood. On the Cosby Show years ago there was an episode in which the Claire Huxtable character, played by Felicia Rashad, announced to her TV husband Cliff Huxtable, played by Bill Cosby, that their baby girl, Rudi, had become a woman that day. Rudi was only twelve years old and her father, medical doctor Heathcliff Huxtable expressed dismay, confusion, consternation, indignation and just plain anger at his wife's, to him, frighteningly premature announcement of his daughter's womanhood. But the mother went on to explain that in her family when a daughter experienced her first menstrual period she was understood to have by that fact attained to the state of womanhood. She further explained that they celebrated the occasion with a ritual of their own design and the entire exercise was called "woman's day". There is no doubt that young females are admitted in many cases into the sorority of women when they obtain the ability to have children. Possessing the physical capacity to bring new life into the world is enough for girls to become women.

On the other hand, *no boy is recognized as a man just because he has wet dreams.* The ability to contribute to the reproduction of life brings no concurrent conferment of manhood upon boys as it does womanhood for girls. A male must be able not merely to be a sperm donor, he must be able to take care of, support, provide for and protect new life in order to be recognized as a man. And boys want to be men. Manhood is a taste in a boy's mouth from early childhood. Healthy boys imitate men as their heroes from the time they are able to walk. Once they become teenagers there are few things more important to them than being recognized as a man. It is still a deadly insult to call a black man "boy". Only within the intimacy of peer group of running partners is the word "boy" substituted for man.

But where do boys go to obtain such a needful thing when there are so few fathers in their homes to teach them how to be men?

There are four institutions in American society that purport to teach boys how to be men: the street, the prison, the military, and college. All of them fail in a major way in accomplishing this task. Yet because they all have reputations as man-making institutions boys flock to them in massive numbers. Yet at the end of their experiences they are often disappointed at still not being what they want to be and what we need them to be—real men...

So compelling is the call of the street to black boys and men that in any group of black men found any where school, church, family gatherings, the majority of the men present will have done some amount of "street time" as an important part of their quest for manhood.

Survival on the street is a test comparable to the African boy's development of survival skill in the rain forests, mountains and deserts of Africa. A black male who is able to successfully negotiate the considerable dangers of street life in urban America feels that even if nobody else agrees he feels within himself that he has become a man. However, the working definition for being a man according the code of the street is based on the amoral values of street life. Gaming, hustling, tricking, lying, stealing, faking, taking, being slick, running game, beating people out of their money, fussing, cussing, fighting, cutting, stabbing, shooting, loud talking, bad mouthing, getting high, handling your liquor, gambling, fronting, running many women, having many babies, breaking the law, going to jail, are all considered to be evidence of the attainment of manhood. None of these proficiencies will be found in the list of skills we look for in our prospective our sons-in-laws and the future fathers of our grandchildren.

Secondly, are the jails and prisons. Going to jail has come to be considered a rite of passage into manhood for almost two generations of black youth. Imprisonment is now a more common experience for young black males than going to college. Young brothers today eagerly go to jail, looking forward upon their release to a community-wide celebration or at least a block party and recognition by their "boys" that they are real men now. They don't have the analytical skill that would inform them of the serious long-term consequences of a stretch in jail. They can't think far ahead to see the most common challenges of ex-convicts included among which are unemployment, homelessness, difficulties in male-female relationships, estrangement from their children, loss of status among decent people, general suspicion, alienation from civilian society in the first months or even years of release and loss of the right to vote .

The fellows in my generation that I grew up with were not interested in going to jail. Not only because of the warnings of our parents and other elders. There was a vicious young brother in our neighborhood named Snake. Snake was tall, about six feet three inches, slim as a young tree, strong as new steel, and mean as his name, Snake. Snake went to jail and came back a year or so later more effeminate than his girlfriend. We looked at Snake in wide-eyed, scary wonderment and said to one another: "Whatever it was in jail that grabbed Snake and turned him out, we didn't want to meet him." Anything so twisted that it could see Snake as a girl and powerful that it could reduce him into acting like one, we had no desire to have any first hand experience with. If jail harbored individuals like that we wanted to stay out of jail.

This was the old school approach which is very much unlike the way things operate in prison today. In the old days the universal philosophy of black manhood held sway. That is the rule of "heart" as the defining characteristic of a real man. Back in those days even if a man were confronted by a group challenging his right to be their territory he had the right, universally respected among black men to demand a "fair one". That is a one- on-one fight with one member of the group. He could choose who he wanted. If he stood toe-to-toe and went blow-for-blow against his opponent, even if he lost, even if he didn't get in but one good punch. The fact that he had the "heart" to try, gave full and indisputable proof of his manhood.

This was the rule for homosexual seduction in prison in the old days. One man approached his quarry alone. If his intended victim fought off his approach with "heart" he was recognized as a man and from then on treated as such by the entire inmate population. Sometime in the 1970's this changed. Homosexual rape became a group activity in which victims were subjected to attacks by such overwhelming numbers of men that it was impossible for one individual to fight them off. The only protection from group rape was for the individual to become a member of a gang that would fight to protect him. The protecting group could be a criminal gang or a religious organization like the Nation of Islam. A major reason for the growth of Islam among inmates is that Muslims offer their members such protection. And the reason that Christian ministries are so weak in prison is that black Christian men have lost the capacity to be warriors. It's one of the most disturbing aspects of modern life that so many black Christian men will go overseas at the behest of Uncle Sam and wreak havoc among foreign peoples that have never done them any harm then come back to America and feel unqualified to raise their trained fists to protect a helpless brother.

Therefore the working of definition of manhood in the prison is someone with the physical force to protect the physical integrity of their anal cavity. This definition assigns the identity of homosexual only to the person who is penetrated. The penetrator is considered to be a man. What inmates seemed to miss, as do so many brothers on the street, is that both individuals involved in homosexual activity are, in fact, homosexuals. Prisons are, as we will discuss in greater detail in the chapter by that name, hothouses of homosexual activity and its most deadly by-product, AIDS. There is little question that the phenomenon of the "down-low brother" has much of its genesis in the prison system.

Prisons don't produce the kind of men that we need to build healthy relationships, families and communities. Most brothers coming out of prison are in need of serious long-term therapeutic experiences in order to be healed from the ravages to their psyches that result from living for years in a brutal and inhuman environment.

The third institution that we depend on to produce men is the armed forces. It is a universal experience among teenage boys to imagine that the army, navy, air force, and marines provide them with a reasonable alternative to life at home when they are tired of the limitations that adult authority imposes on their growing sense of a need for freedom and autonomy. The argument within their own minds and with their friends goes something like this: "Man, I'm tired of my parents telling me what to do. I'm tired of them telling me what time to get up , what time to come in, what time to go to bed, what clothes to where, how to wear my hair, what food to eat. Man, I'ma join the army!" Their adolescent response is, of course, humorous after the fact when viewed through the lenses of hindsight. But at the time young men make these statements they are deadly serious. Not only do they mistakenly imagine that leaving home and joining the service will liberate them from the oppression of hierarchical authority but they also believe that the discipline instilled in them in the service will serve to make them men. They are unable to see the fallacies and contradictions in their thought processes.

First of all, they haven't seen authority until they join the service. They call themselves trying to escape regimentation but what they do is jump out of the frying pan of parental authority into the fires of military domination. The rule in the military is best expressed in these lines from Alfred Lord Tennyson's classic poem "The Charge of the Light Brigade":

> Ours not to reason why
> Ours not to make reply
> Ours but to do or die.

Success in the military requires shutting down one's critical faculties. The individual soldier is to have no mind of his own. He is not to think. Rather like a machine he merely responds appropriately to specific stimuli. He obeys commands without thought, question or challenge. A soldier must also suspend his moral sensibilities. He must deny to his own self his sense of good and evil. He may well be ordered to do something that goes against the grain of everything he has been taught at home, in church, in school and in his community about right or wrong.

This is particularly difficult for black soldiers because America's wars are overwhelmingly fought against non-white people so that they are racist conflicts reflecting how black people are treated in this country. They are also usually wars of extermination. When Europeans fight wars against non-Europeans, against the people they refer to contemptuously as "natives", they conduct their military campaigns as wars of extermination (unless they need a particular population for slave labor). These are the most vicious, brutal, murderous, sick, evil, wicked, demonic forms of war which are directed more by the guidelines of mass murder than the rules of military science. Much of South Vietnam was a free-fire zone for American troops which meant they were to kill anything that moved-- men, women, children, and animals. The incident in the village of My Lai when over five hundred villagers were killed by U. S. troops, then buried in a mass grave, is a case in point. Another is the genocidal wars that almost wiped out the Native American Indian Nations.

The position of the black soldier is complicated by the fact that racism remains so strong at home so that while he's out forcing democracy on a foreign people overseas his mama is being beat up and his brother is being shot by white racist police at home. Even as I right black soldiers who have invaded Iraq supposedly to "impose democracy" on those people watch the news reports from home of the theft and hi-jacking of a presidential election based on illegally denying black citizens the right to vote. The inability to deal with these kinds of contradictions was the source of the horrendous emotional distress suffered by black soldiers then and now. While we have produced a generation that is inured to violence and seems to experience no distress at the most heinous acts of rape, murder even mutilations, historically this has not been the case with us as a people. African culture has from its beginnings been one of the most humane in the world. People raised from infancy to honor human life, to cherish children, respect woman and hold the elders in high regard cannot help but suffer tremendous psychic, emotional and spiritual tearing and twisting when they are required to murder such people in cold blood.

It is not forced discipline that makes a man. It is self-control. Discipline is for children. Parents impose discipline from the outside until it takes root on the inside and children internalize the discipline and begin to exercise self-control. This should happen before a child goes off to school or even to pre-school. A child should know how to follow orders before they walk or talk and how to control themselves without constant reminders by time they are potty-trained at 2 years old. Taking orders from superior officers is not a mark of manhood but a mark of retarded development. What soldiers find out is that they have to become men despite the service because the service robs them of the prerogatives of real adulthood which is to be free-thinking, free functioning, decision-making, autonomous moral beings.

Many of our young men come back from their stint in the service injured, wounded even twisted not so much in their bodies as in their minds. Particularly those who have seen combat. War by its very nature is destructive to the human personality. Human beings were put on earth to build not to destroy, to heal not to kill, to love not to hate.

The so-called objective science of psychology recognizes war's inevitable debilitation of the human personality in its studies of what happens to soldiers on the battlefield. In World War I it was called "shell shock". In World War II it was called "combat fatigue". The new name given it in Vietnam is the one still used today, Post Traumatic Stress Disorder (PTSD). It is standard military procedure to rotate all troops off of the front lines every six weeks before they become psychologically incapable of continuing to participate in combat. They know that 95% of all troops will break down within a certain amount of time. The five percent who are able to function on the battlefield without any symptoms of distress were already psychopaths before they enlisted.

When I was asked by the National Association of Black Veterans to deliver the keynote address at their annual convention they gave me the topic: "The Black Church and PTSD". I learned one of the great lessons of my ministerial life: that the black church has no ministry to one of the groups of men in the greatest need of healing.

The armed forces do not make men. They take our big boys and as often as not give them back to us in need of special care to heal the wounds that have been inflicted, for the most part, not on their bodies but on their minds, hearts and souls.

The fourth entity that we expect to turn boys into men is the colleges and universities that we send our high school graduates off to at the age of 18. They used to be called college men and college women. There is a reason that they are most often referred to as college boys and college girls today. College no longer produces men and women. They are in fact more likely to prolong adolescence.

Until the 1970's there were clear markers that determined the beginning and the end of adolescence in the black community. Teenagehood lasted from fourteen to eighteen. It basically consisted of the high school years. Until they began to attend high school girls were dressed in a manner that clearly indicated to the public at large, but males in particular, that they were innocent, sexually unconscious little girls and not teenagers striving and trying to be grown women. Girls were dressed and presented to the world in a manner that made their status as asexual creatures clear. Little black girls did not have their hair pressed or straightened. They wore their hair in braids adorned with ribbons. They did not wear stockings or high heel shoes. They wore no make-up or lipstick. Once they graduated from grammar school they began to dress like little women cosmetically preparing themselves to attract and receive the attentions of the males of the species.

And just as there were clear markers indicating the end of childhood and the beginning of adolescence there were also clear markers delineating the end of adolescence and the beginning of adulthood. In our last year in high school which also roughly corresponded to our eighteenth birthday our parents would constantly introduce the subject of our plans for the future with the words: "Have you decided where you going?' We were mandated to go somewhere other than their house. Go to college. Go the army. Go the Peace Corp. Go live with your uncle. They made it clear that their responsibility for taking care of us was completed when we reached the age of 18. By then we were supposed to be ready for the world. It was common for couples to get married right out of high school and any number, due to pregnancy got married while still in high school, some dropping out, and some finishing with the help of their parents. When we went to college we went as adults to practice and perfect our adult skills and proficiencies.

College today prolongs adolescence not only during the time that the students are on the campus but even after graduation. Historically, adulthood meant assuming the roles of spouses and parents. The first duty for newly confirmed men and women in traditional African society was to find a husband and a wife and begin the great task of preparing the next generation. This present cohort of college graduates will put off both marriage and child-rearing to an unheard of degree. They will have imbibed in college the pleasure principle that teaches them to seek first for success in the careers and the enjoyment of the freedom of their youth. Marriage and children are relegated to secondary consideration. So, rather than being young parents practicing the noblest of calling which is to continue the traditions of family life these young people are dedicated to the hedonistic principles of being "swinging singles". In other words they are basically behaving the same way at twenty five and even thirty or older that they did at fifteen and sixteen..

They don't understand that the greatest impetus for success in a career or graduate school is the presence of a family. It is having a higher principle to be dedicated to that motivates young people, particularly young men, to rise to a higher standard of productivity. Marriage matures men by giving them, for the first time in most of their lives, people to be responsible for and accountable to other than themselves. Employers prefer to hire married men because they have more confidence in their dedication to the job since they are living and working for people they love who are depending on them. The grand scheme of nature intends for us to have our children while we are young. The twenties are our most fertile years also our most energetic. We were meant to bear our babies when we had the energy to keep up with them.

College students today act more like the high school students of my youth.. An amazing number of parents contribute to this phenomenon in various ways. One is by not allowing their children to attend colleges more than an hour's drive from their home so that they can be readily available to handle any challenge that the students face. My rule is: *The further away from home young people attend college the sooner they grow up. The closer to home they remain the longer they stay a child.* Today we have parents arriving on college campuses for a student's disciplinary hearing with a lawyer in tow to insure that the student suffers no consequences for their misbehavior. Doing the same things they did for the child in grammar school and high school. Which is why, now in college, the child still doesn't know how to act right.

The students themselves call their parents constantly and nowadays assisted by the electronic umbilical cords of cell phones, pagers, beepers, email and instant messaging they are never more than a few key-strokes away from mother's comfort and protection. These young people, continuously smothered and coddled by their parents' over-protectiveness, are inevitably and unavoidably late in learning the first law of adulthood which is accepting responsibility for one's own behavior. College resembles high schools and college students rather than acting like young adults and professionals-in-training are just big overgrown adolescents loudly and obnoxiously proclaiming themselves to be adults when defying authority then calling their parents to rescue and defend them when its time to face the consequences of their misbehavior.

We see that none of the four institutions that we popularly rely upon to produce men adequately do the job. There does remain one unnamed institution besides the family that is best prepared to the do the job. That is the black church.

If the church were to rise to the challenge it could become the institute of manhood-training that we need it to be. In doing so it would solve its own manhood deficit problem. We already know that boys will go wherever they are confident they will be taught to be men. They go to the streets, prisons, military and the colleges. When we produce within the structures of the church the dynamics needed to teach boys to be men they will flock to the church like a gathering of young eagles and we won't have room enough to accommodate them all.

We must produce men not only because our daughters must have good husbands and our grandchildren need good fathers. Also because our society cannot move forward or even survive much longer without the crucial contribution of good men.

The male of the species represents two critical factors for the survival and progress of any body of people. These are: discipline and order. Without disciplined individuals chaos threatens any situation. It is the male of the species that is responsible for maintaining order. I know this reasoning flies in the face of feminist philosophy that has given us female police officers and female soldiers.

The greatest threats to family and community order are teenage boys and young single men in their twenties. These young males lack structured lives dedicated to any principle higher than their own self-interest and pleasure. They see themselves as men but lack the self-sacrificing commitment to serving others that constitutes true manhood. When these big boys in their homes get too big for their mothers to control it is the responsibility of the father or the father figures in the family to put them in check. If the men of the family cannot control them then the police must be called and there are few more dangerous situations for black men than to have the police called on them.

In too many instances black women have denied their husbands, fathers, brothers, uncles or male family friends the right and authority to discipline their sons. Not understanding the nature of the male mentality that respects the strength involved in the giving and taking of blows the mother fears that her son will be hurt if a grown man has to use his strength to restrain him. She doesn't understand that restraint is preventive. If a young man on a rampage cannot be restrained then he has to be violently subdued which, when the police do it, can result in his being rendered unconscious, beaten to death or shot, not to mention, in the long term, facing the very real probability of incarceration..

The first law of any and all laws is: *"No law has any meaning without enforcement"*. This law is universal for the animal world and for the human. Or another way is putting it: "Talk is cheap. Actions speak louder than words". The smallest child being told to go to bed or not to play with the knobs on the stove looks inquiringly into the face and eyes of the person giving the order. He or she is searching for signs of their resolve. If they show none the child goes about doing what they were doing knowing that the words of the would-be-authority figure are not backed up by the consequences of force. The speed of cars on streets and highways is not determined by speed limit signs but by the presence or absence of the police and state troopers who *enforce* the speed limit. The fewer police drivers see the faster they go. The more police they see the slower they go.

The use of force as a means of achieving objectives is an inescapable and undeniable reality. The question is: "Whose force will prevail?" The righteous must use force to prevent and end the crimes of the unrighteous. In the 1970's the All Africa Council of Churches coined a term to describe and endorse the use of violence by the African National Congress against the ultra-violent, serial-killing, mass-murdering, state-sponsored terrorist regime of Apartheid South Africa. They called such righteous use of force to free people from oppression "sanctified violence".

The question is not whether or not force is going to be applied but who will do the applying. Will it be fathers guided by their love for their children or racist police and prison guards who aggressively look for any opportunity to be violent with black males?

In refusing black men the authority to manhandle their sons when they deem it necessary black women are in agreement with the current laws of the land that deny parents the right to use corporal punishment on their children. This tactic has been one of the most destructive intrusions into black family life. Its result has been disorder in our homes, chaos in our classrooms and danger on the streets of our neighborhoods and wherever our young people gather in groups.

The two institutions most targeted for destruction in slavery were the black church and the black family. Slavery failed to destroy either of them despite the brutal

110

nature of its frontal assaults. But this new modern approach of subtle seduction to the values of European culture has accomplished in freedom what cold-blooded violence failed to produce in slavery. We have given away our most precious responsibility which is to raise the children God has blessed us with in the best way that we know how, in accordance with the traditions of our ancestors who raised entire generations of astounding human beings in the midst of all the horrors of slavery and segregation.

An entire industry in the social services arena has grown up around the issue of parenting. White so-called experts on child-rearing are teaching seminars and classes on parenting to tens of thousands of black professionals. I attended such a training session in which the lead instructor told a group of some seventy five black social workers, counselors and probation officers that: "We cannot control our children. We can only control their things. If they misbehave the only way we can exercise control is to take their things from them" I asked him: "If we can't control them how are we supposed to stop them from taking their things back?" He had no answer. If it wasn't so tragic, the idea of white people teaching us how to raise our children would be laughable. Their children are the most violence-prone, drug-ridden, sex-crazed, hateful, murderous, greedy, vulgar, disrespectful, destructive people on the face of the earth. How can they have the arrogance to suggest that they should teach us how to raise our children? And how can we have the stupidity to accept their suggestion?

The absolute authority of the elders in the African community was never based on the giving or withholding of things. This has continually been one of the great spiritual weaknesses of the European value system. Things are at the center of their lives. They live for things rather than for people. Holding money and privilege over their children's heads as a coercive means of control has been standard among the higher European classes for centuries.

But his approach has caused the murder of parents for the sake of inheritance a common feature in their social landscape.

Our parents did not exercise authority over us by bribing us or begging us. Their authority derived from their absolute confidence in the spiritual nature of their parenthood. They believed without question that they had a Divine appointment, that they had been especially chosen by the Creator to raise His children in accordance with His immutable and lofty standards of values and conduct. When we were bold enough to ask our parents: "Why"? Their reply was: "Because I said so"! That was the end of the discussion.

Now are faced with black parents who like their white counterparts boast that they want their children to express themselves and to say what is on their minds. They have forgotten that everything that comes into our mind's imagination is not to be given utterance. The inability to control evil thoughts is the doorway to disaster. These parents try to explain everything to their children. Our parents didn't try to explain everything to us for two main reasons, among any number of others. 1. They knew that the childish mind cannot attain to adult realities. Explaining something to a child that they can't comprehend is just an exercise in futility and makes the parents look as foolish as the child. 2. It gives children an option in terms of deciding what they will do. Intelligent adults know that children are not mature or responsible enough to make decisions for themselves. That's why they have parents.

I've heard children demand of their parents to answer the question "why?" in a tone of voice that indicated that if the parent did not give them a good enough reason the child was not going to obey the directive. Children should be allowed to ask "why?" only after they have complied with the parental demand and then the question should be asked humbly as a seeking after understanding rather than a demand for justification.

The issue of corporal punishment must become a plank in a new civil rights platform that seeks our reclaiming of our identity. We have allowed the incursion of white people and their self-serving philosophies into too much of our lives and the results have been disastrous. We have allowed them to take over the responsibility for placing orphaned children and the result is a foster care system that is an international scandal for the number of children placed in it that are molested, beaten, tortured, starved to death, killed or worst of all, that just disappear. We have handed over the responsibility for our children's education to them and our school systems are cesspools of failure preparing our young men not for jobs or higher education but for jails and prison. We allowed them to take over our children's moral instruction concerning sexuality and now we have seventy percent of our children being born out of wedlock and raised in single parent households. Instead of husbands and wives and mothers and fathers we have "my baby daddy" and "my baby mama".

The traditional childrearing practices of our people have been sufficient for tens of thousands of years in preparing each new generation to assume responsibility for the care of the family, the leadership of the race and the government of the nation. These practices included corporal punishment. Now we are told that we cannot strike our children but when our children get out of hand because we have not been able to teach them self-control at home they get shot down in the street.

We must take back control of the rearing of our children as a right of religious freedom and a mandate of our faith. The bible tells us in Proverbs: "He that spareth his rod hateth his son; but he that loveth him chasteneth him."13:24KJV "Foolishness is bound in the heart of a child; but the rod of correction will drive it far from him." 22:13KJV "Withhold not correction from the child: for if thou beatest him with the rod, he shall not die. Thou shall beat him with a rod, and shall deliver his soul from hell."

23:13-14KJV "The rod and reproof give wisdom: but a child left to himself bringeth his mother to shame".
29:15KJV The African proverb says: "The child that will not learn at home, life will teach him". Those of us with some experience know that life is a mean, vicious, rough, unfeeling, unsparing teacher. To discipline a child at home is an act of love that spares our children from the merciless brutalities of the police and prison.

In traditional African societies it was the glory of young men to see to the protection and well-being of their communities and villages. How is it that today these same young men are the greatest threat to the peace of the community? It is in the broken relationships between fathers and sons. Under the direction of the old man the young man is taught true manhood which involves being a provider for and protector of his family and community. In the absence of the wisdom of the old man young men are left to their own immature, shortsighted, foolish devices perversely imagining true manhood to be the caricatures they hear about on rap songs or see in movies like Scarface, Rambo, and the Predator.

The most mannerly and polite black men I've ever known were those locked up in prison. Because they knew that to get out of hand meant a brutal beating at the hand of a gang of conscienceless brutes who passéd for prison guards. I witnessed an inmate I knew by reputation as one of the most feared men on the streets of the West Side, come into a meeting with his hat in his hands and every sentence prefaced by "sir" and please and ended with "thank you". I thought to myself: "Why did he have to come to prison to learn to be polite and mannerable. I would rather my children learn these things at home."

We have forgotten as a people that the first line of defense against disorder in any family or community is the fathers of the community. The police are only to be called as the last resort because they so often bring with them greater disorder and more violence.

My father had a saying: "Either you get your whipping at home or you get it in the street. But if you don't know how to act, how to treat people, how to talk to people and how to conduct yourself somebody will whip your behind. If I do it here at home your mother is here to beg for your life when it look like I'm about to kill you and to bind up your wounds when I get through. But if they whip you in the street they will leave you bleeding somewhere lying in an alley".

Black males are the ones who suffer most from the church's lack of a powerful, positive, progressive youth ministry. All too often the person in charge of the youth group in the local church and larger denominational bodies such as district associations and state conventions are middle-age females. These are the very people that teenage males are trying to get away from because they are essentially their mothers. These big boys know intuitively if not consciously that they need men to teach them how to be men. They need to be taught by men that understand and appreciate the male psyche, particularly the fragile stage of development that constitutes the middle and final years of adolescence and the initial stages of young adulthood. Boys seeking such mentors and role models will find them wherever they can. They will seek them out on the streets if they cannot find them in church.

The rate of incarceration of black males has reached the proportions of an epidemic. White sociologists, psychologists and social workers try to convince us that there is an inherent strain of criminality lodged in the very core of the black male psyche. That he is a criminal by nature. History does not bear out this claim. In the Red Summer of 1919 a race riot in Chicago began after white bathers stoned a black teenage boy to death for crossing over the invisible line that separated by custom the black beach from the white beach. Almost two weeks of rioting took place in which over fifty people were killed. As has always been the case most of the fatalities were black people. The governor of Illinois appointed a commission to study and report on the causes of the riot. The study found that a major contributor to the continued orgy of violence was the participation of teenage gangs. They found numerous gangs amongst the working class white people based on ethnic identity and neighborhood. There were gangs of Irish, Polish, Hungarian, Jewish, Italian, Lithuanian youth and others too numerous to mention. *They did not find a single juvenile delinquent gang in Chicago's black community.* Our children have been known from Africa days to be among the best behaved children in the world.

The introduction and proliferation of gangs in the black community is a mid to late twentieth century phenomenon. Gangs emerged when black men began abandoning or being driven away from their families. Some deserting them because the anonymity of city life freed them from the social constraints and pressures that were the cornerstone of life in the smaller communities of the South. Many others were driven away by welfare rules that insisted that women could not receive welfare if there was a man in the house. This was never the case in white families. There is no evidence, either anecdotal or statistical, that indicates that white husbands and fathers were subjected to this family-destroying strategy. Welfare was created to save the white family and hold it together; but was used to destroy black families by tearing them apart

Boys need men to teach them how to be men. The great task of every boy is to complete the difficult journey from boyhood to manhood. That difficulty is distorted into something approaching impossibility when there are no men around to do the leading, guiding, teaching and directing. My single sentence definition of gangs is this: *"Gangs are groups of fatherless boys trying to each other what don't none of them know, which is how to be a man".*

The exponential increase of young black males going to jail coincides directly with the absence of black fathers. Boys raised by women are taught inevitably, if inadvertently, to see the world through feminine eyes. Black women are treated differently by racist society than are black men. Despite the new phenomenon of female boxers, women are not recognized as dangerous warriors anywhere in the world. This does not deny the extraordinary powers of such individual exceptions to the rule like Harriet Tubman, Sojourner Truth or Ida B. Wells. Yet the exception does not disprove the rule, it dramatizes it. Nobody is afraid of black women as a collective.

Black men on the other hand are universally recognized as being among the greatest warriors and most dangerous fighters in the history of the world. The white race across the board fears black men. Fear is just as dangerous to the person who is feared as it is to the person who is afraid. The African proverb says: "Fear is worse than a blow". A scared person will kill you. Most often when school children take weapons to school it's because they are afraid of bullies who have been terrorizing them.

Too many young black men watch their mothers behave emotionally, disrespectfully even threateningly toward men and mistakenly believe that they can get away with the same kinds of performance. They see their mothers cussing men out, hitting men, hollering at them, even policemen and they think they can act the same way. They don't understand that the same behavior that is overlooked and dispensed with in a woman will be met with maximum force when it is done by a male. The fear that white men, even and perhaps especially, white policemen experience when in our presence makes them dangerous to us. The all-white jury in Simi Valley that found the torturers of Rodney King not guilty was acting out their authentic sympathy for what they knew to be the real fear the policeman has of whom they all agree is the truly dangerous black male.

Our boys need men to teach them how to conduct themselves around people who are afraid of them. Scared people are a constant threat to attack, even kill, without warning or reason. When I was growing up the understanding of white people's fear of us was common knowledge. It was almost unheard of to get a "fair one", (a one on one fight) with the average white boy. They generally would not stand and fight a black male unless the odds were at least five to one in their favor. We must understand that when they see a black man they see Chaka Kwa Zulu, Kunta Kinte, Nat Turner, Jack Johnson, John Henry, Stagolee, Shine, Joe Louis, Sugar Ray Robinson, the Mau Mau, Sonny Liston, Muhammed Ali, Smokey Joe Frazier, Wilt Chamberlain, Jim Brown, Big Daddy Lipscomb, Malcolm X, The Black Panthers, Big George Foreman, Marvelous Marvin Hagler, Mighty Joe Young and King Kong all wrapped up into one frightening, terrifying, almost phantasmagoric creation of their most fearful racist imaginations.

My high-school classmate and much admired friend, John Dunn, AKA Ogun, AKA Blood tells a story instructive in this regard. He related how he was stopped by the police who threateningly demanded to know if he was armed. When he replied: "I'm well armed", they pulled out their own weapons and stepped back, pointed their pistols and prepared to fire. While yet startled by the boldness of the reply the police asked another question: "What kind of weapon do you have"? Ogun replied: "My mind"! The police were so stunned by the power of that assertion that they holstered their guns, got in their cars and drove off without another word. What happened is that they had run into a black man who they recognized as being better armed than all of them put together. They didn't comprehend much less possess the use of the mind as a dangerous weapon. Confronted by a black man armed with an intellect so sharp he could describe it as a weapon plus discipline, boldness, and courage, their only plausible

118

response was to get as far away from him as they could as soon as possible.

The understanding of real manhood among young black males is so poor that it would be funny it if it were not so tragic. I had an incident in which a young man cursed in my presence but tried to do so surreptitiously. When I found him out and challenged him he resisted my attempts to correct him by telling me: "I'm a man". His friend stood next to him exasperated at my insistence on correction and told him: "Man, you ain't got to put up with this. Call your mama". The young man with the foul mouth and lack of respect for his elders then echoed his friend and told me: "I'm a call my mama". I was so astounded that at that point I left the scene knowing I would inevitably bring it to its conclusion in the near future. But I had to think about what it meant for a six foot four inch 224 pound 21 year old male to try to intimidate me and protect himself by threatening to call his mama. I tried to remember how old I was the last time I invoked my mama as a threat to anybody, particularly somebody on the street. I probably would still have so threatened my siblings at home as late as twelve or thirteen. But I couldn't imagine even at seven or eight telling another boy who I was having a confrontation with in the street: "I'm a tell my mama".

The black church can reverse this trend of lost manhood if it will dedicate itself to becoming the institution responsible for producing future generations of black men.

The only thing worse than not knowing is not wanting to know. **African Proverb**

Get an education, 'cause they can't take that from you.
African American Proverb

V. ACADEMICS

Education begins at home. The first and most important teacher a child will ever have is the parent. The first and most important school a child will ever attend is the home. Beyond these two foundational rules there are two pillars that our children's educational future rests upon. The first is appreciation of the very idea of learning. The second is discipline so that the child can properly receive instruction. Children ought to leave the house headed off to school full of eagerness and enthusiasm. They ought to be on fire to learn. Education should be seen as one of the greatest and most satisfying adventures life has to offer. The homes our children are raised in must be designed for their academic success. Every home in order to be a successful school must also be a library, a museum, an art gallery, and a musical conservatory, at the very least.

I challenge each parent reading this to take an inventory of their home to determine how well or poorly it is equipped for the education of their children. Go through out every room in your home and count how many TV's, VCR's, DVD's, CD's, boom boxes, Nintendo's, play stations, basketballs, footballs, soccer balls, volleyballs, boxing gloves, jump ropes, tennis rackets, roller skates, and any number of other toys and entertainment vehicles that I have failed to list. Then go back again and count how many books, magazines, dictionaries, encyclopedias, thesauruses, atlases, concordances, computers with internet

120

access, chemistry sets, microscope sets, telescopes, construction kits, African-centered works of art, chess sets, scrabble sets, and short wave radio receivers your home has. If your home has more of the former and less of the latter, yours is a home designed and equipped for your child's social and athletic success but academic and professional failure.

Secondly, successful education begins with instilling discipline within the heart of the child. Nobody can be successful at anything without discipline. Discipline is simply the ability to focus on a goal without being victimized by the innumerable and inevitable distractions of life; whether these distractions are childish fantasies in the form of day-dreams or biological urges to use the bathroom, or other children's teasing attempts to recruit classmates into their playfulness. Temptations to diversion are always there threatening the order of the classroom.

Because we are a people at war, under siege and trying to live in the very midst of the enemy, we have to have more discipline rather than less. Anyone who knows anything about warfare knows that the most dangerous place to be in a war is behind enemy lines. Only the very best trained, most courageous and disciplined soldiers are assigned to duty behind enemy lines. We have survived and even prospered for four hundred years behind enemy lines, in the belly of the beast and in the lion's den because we were more disciplined than the people who held us captive in slavery and then tried to deny us progress in freedom.

We have problems with understanding the essential role of discipline except in the field of athletics. The athletic coach is still a hard man or tough woman on any and every high school campus. Every body knows that you don't play with the coach. We give coaches almost carte blanche license to be as physical as they have to be (short of acts of sadistic brutality) in order to instill discipline within our athletes so that they can achieve championship status. It is unthinkable for players to bend over in a huddle or sit on the bench laughing and talking with one another while the coach gives instructions and direction. Why won't we insist on the same kind of disciplined behavior in the classroom?

White people raise their children under the guiding rubric of "self-expression". They go through tremendous pains to stimulate their children to express themselves. African people raise their children under the rule of "self-control". Our culture is so dynamic that there is no lack of stimulation. If anything, people can get overloaded by the excess of stimuli. We don't have to teach our children to express themselves they are practically born expressing themselves. Many of them are expressing themselves in the womb. We have to teach our children to control themselves. When I was in seminary a white female student leaned over towards me in class and whispered:" Clarence, I'm forty-two years old and I'm just beginning to develop some style". I immediately thought about my oldest daughter, Cailisha, who was three months old. I thought about how she had been born with style and was already moving around vigorously in her crib trying to dance to her theme song, Stevie Wonder's "Isn't She Lovely".

There is one indispensable ingredient for the proper education of children which is most often tragically disregarded in our post-modern, scientific-based recipes for contemporary high-tech education. That ingredient is love. Children must have love in everything that is done to them and for them. We cannot accurately diagram the place in a child's psyche where love fits. We cannot measure with a spoon or cup the exact amount of love that needs to be mixed into a meal. But we do know on the practical side of things that children, like all human beings and most animals, must have love. Grown people need love too, but we have learned through the disappointments, heart breaks and hard knocks of life to live for substantial periods without it. We have grown calluses on our hearts and souls that enable us to withstand and work through the trauma

122

and hurt that result when one is not loved. But children need love every day and every hour. Nursing babies have been known to reject the milk of mothers who do not love them. Infants have been known to die from the "failure to thrive syndrome". This condition derives from the kind of neglect that is the result of infants never being picked up, cradled in loving arms, cooed to, played with, tickled, hugged and made much of.

Just as no parent should have custody of a child that they do not love; neither should any teacher be allowed to have a child in their classroom that they do not love. Living without love batters the psyches and distorts the personalities of little children, often leaving them in such a condition of distress that their acting out will cause them to be rejected by people around them who don't understand or recognize the reasons for the child's misbehavior. It is an act of abuse to leave a child in any loveless set of circumstances.

There is a story told in educational circles about a group of immigrant children at a public grammar school in an impoverished section of Baltimore. The children were surveyed in adulthood in order to determine if the predictions of lives of crime and time in jail for most of the boys of that school and neighborhood turned out to be correct. In most instances this was the case, but there was one group of boys from a particular teacher's class who did not fit the pattern, Somehow all of the boys from that class had managed to carve out relatively successful, undeniably positive lives for themselves. Since the one thing all these fellows had in common was their teacher, the researchers found her to ask what she had done to make such a difference in the lives of her charges. They expected her to explain some unique novel strategy of pedagogical sophistication or at least some innovative adaptation of some classic approach designed by one of the recognized geniuses in the field. Instead they listened astounded to the little gray-haired lady say simply: "I really can't explain it.

All I do know is: I loved those boys."

It would be as impossible to overstate and overestimate the power of love to do good as it would be difficult to understate and underestimate the power of the absence of love to do harm. As the saying goes: "The opposite of love is not hatred. It is indifference." No one who is indifferent to the present conditions and future prospects of children should ever have charge over them.

Ninety percent of emotional patterns have been established by the time a child is five years old. It is in the home that the child's attitude towards education, school, teachers, and learning is founded. It is in the home that children learn to love the very idea of learning, to revere knowledge, to respect teachers, to have a high regard for books and other learning materials, to have curious minds, active imaginations, and a bent for asking questions and solving problems. How a child will behave in the classroom is determined by their attitude. A child's teachability rests upon their attitude. No teacher, no matter how skilled, gifted, determined, and dedicated, can instruct a child who has not been prepared at home to receive instruction.

On the first day of school in kindergarten a child needs to walk through the classroom door having been taught at home how to sit down, be quiet, be still, pay attention, follow instructions, listen, think, ask questions, learn, remember and recite.

Moreover and more deeply the child needs to love education and see the experience as being one of the greatest adventures of life. Children need to be taught to love the very idea of learning at an early age and enjoy and remain committed to that love affair for the rest of their lives

Perhaps what I am trying to say will be clearer if we replace the word attitude with the word spirit. It is the sprit that we entertain in approaching or engaging or participating in any aspect of life that determines what we will put in and what we will take out of that encounter and

124

experience. Our young people are habituated to entertaining only the most positive and powerful spirits when engaging in those activities that the culture of the United States is most supportive of. When they get out on the dance floor, when they squat down on the starting line for the hundred yard dash, when they go into the boxing ring, when they approach the microphone to sing or rap they draw to themselves spirits of excellence, determination, and creativity. When they look for examples as to who to pattern themselves after in their physical and athletic behavior and they look to the greatest of all-time. They want to entertain the same spirits that drove and drive Jesse Owens, Althea Gibson, Marion Jones, Muhammad Ali, Michael Jordan, Beyonce, Kobe Bryant, Venus and Serena Williams.

As they approach the classroom door they should be drawing to themselves similar spirits of power, success, and productivity. They should be able to imagine what kind of spirit the generation of our ancestors who had freed themselves from chattel slavery enjoyed. These great people had been denied the opportunity not only to attend school; it was against the law for them to learn to read or write or even to be found in the possession of learning materials. If discovered reading or writing they would have a finger cut off of their hand, a hand sawn from their wrist, an ear torn from their head, a flaming white hot branding iron stuck to their faces or bodies. Can we imagine what they felt like when they were finally able to freely attend school? What feelings of gratitude, joy, enthusiasm and ecstasy must have run hot through their veins at their meeting that long grieved over, dreamed of, hoped for, and prayed about, hour of opportunity! Our children must be challenged to imagine what spirits were entertained by such people as W.E.B. DuBois, Frederick Douglas, Ida B. Wells, Mary McLeod Bethune, Paul Cuffee, Bishop Henry McNeil Turner, as they prepared to enter the classroom. We must pray as we send them off to school calling those same spirits down upon our children and teach our children how to carry and appreciate their power. One of the greatest honors we can pay to our ancestors is to share their appreciation for the opportunity to learn.

We teach our children which sprits to entertain by the spirits that we invite into our homes and lives. Because children are imitators they will reflect what they see and hear at home. The African proverb says: *"What a child says, they have heard at home"*. Are our homes full of the spirits of love, generosity, respect, dedication, courage, forgiveness, forbearance, inquisitiveness? Or are they full of the demonic spirits of anger, resentment, bitterness, depression, slothfulness, drunkenness, pettiness, lasciviousness, rebelliousness, vulgarity, envy, violence, selfishness?

The educational system in this country is not a failure when it comes to educating our children. It is a wonderful success at doing its job. Producing failure in black children is their job. Education is a process that begins not at the beginning but at the end. That is to say education is based upon a vision of the end product, a vision of the role and purpose that society has in mind for the person that it is attempting to educate. This society has a different role and purpose for black youth than for white young people.

They educate their children to succeed. They educate ours to fail. They educate their children to give orders. They educate ours to take the orders they are given even by people less intelligent than they are. They educate their children to believe in their superiority. They educate ours to be convinced of their inferiority. They educate their children to lead. They educate ours to follow. They educate their children to speak out; ours to be silent. They educate their children to sell; ours to buy. They educate their children to produce, ours to consume. They educate their children to rule, ours to be subservient. They educate their children to own, ours to rent. They educate their children to be aggressive, ours to be complacent. They educate their children to think globally, our children to think locally or, better yet, not to think at all. They educate their children to be critical, ours to be accepting. They educate their children to criticize and analyze, ours to be fascinated by things to that flash and shine without ever asking why. They educate their children to deal in substance, ours to deal in style. They educate their children to plan for the future, ours to live for the moment. They educate their children to invest, ours to borrow. They educate their children to work, ours to gamble. They educate their children to innovate, ours to imitate. They educate their children to make TV's and movies, our children to buy them and watch them.

All educational systems are based upon the vision of the finished product. The public schools of this country do not produce failures among black children at such a standardized massive outcome by accident. Just like General Motors does not produce Ford Cars by accident. They produce what they were designed and intended to produce. I have a standard rule for dealing with outcomes. "The first time it's an accident. The second time it's a coincidence. The third time it's a conspiracy." The academic failure of black youth is a centuries old conspiracy that began with denying the children in the slave community access to books, reading and learning.

They have three basic roles they are preparing black children to fulfill in their adult lives: cheap labor, captive consumers and cannon fodder. The capitalist system experiences its greatest periods of growth and profit when it can get the cheapest labor. The largest category of overhead, that is the costs of doing business before the business owner can experience a profit, is the cost of labor. The rule is so simple as to be inescapable: "The cheaper the labor, the higher the profit." Labor was cheapest during slavery. It was during the era of slavery that the profits of the capitalist system were so enormous that the standards of living in Europe and America went from being one of the lowest in the world to the very highest. Europeans left their native land traveling across treacherous and uncharted seas in fragile, rickety boats in search of the kinds of wealth and resources that did not exist in their own countries.

The period of exploration was followed by the era of slavery, colonization, genocide and the expropriation of foreign lands wherein the white invaders took the best and most fertile land for themselves. The same land that the people had previously raised food on they were forced to grow cash crops on like coffee, cotton, cocoa, indigo, sugar cane, rubber and tobacco. And we wonder why Africans are so poor and hungry in the midst of the natural wealth of their own nations?

Education for the slaves consisted of being taught to obey orders, plow a straight row, chop and kill the weeds surrounding the cotton plant without damaging the crop, do what they were told, and never talk back to or raise their hand at a white person no matter what was done to them or their loved ones. After slavery was ended by the victory of the black troops who served as the spearhead of the Union army they replaced slavery with sharecropping and tenant farming. It was critical for them not to give us our promised forty acres and a mule. People who have their own land are independent and don't have to work for anybody else because the three basic necessities of life, food, shelter and clothing, are provided for from the land. Lacking these necessities people have to work for somebody else. During this era black education was not much different from slavery. Those who ran the system wanted our children to receive just enough education to be good sharecroppers and tenant farmers.

Black men are not chronically unemployed because of laziness. This is one of the greatest and most oft-repeated and readily accepted lies of racist mythology. No one has worked harder than black people. We have for four hundred years worked the hardest, the longest, done the dirtiest and most dangerous work with the least of amount of reward and the greatest amount of injury, exploitation and abuse. One of the ways that capitalism holds wages down is by always maintaining a ready pool of surplus labor consisting of the chronically unemployed. When there are a lot of unemployed people, those who have jobs have no leverage to demand higher wages. When they attempt to do so the bosses and owners tell them: "I've got ten people waiting outside that will take your job today for half what I'm paying you." An old man told me years ago: *"When you have a skill people ask you what you charge. When you don't have a skill they tell you what they pay"*. This society uses its educational system to insure that our children have no marketable skills so that they have no leverage to obtain a job or when having a job to demand a higher wage or better working conditions and fringe benefits.

There are some nations such as Cuba that do not have unemployment at all. Social scientists in the West have recognized for well over a hundred years that the most dangerous element in any population is unemployed men. The welfare system in European was invented in mid-nineteenth century Germany by Otto von Bismarck, the Iron Duke, who was responsible for organizing the first unemployment insurance. Why would this ruthless warlord be interested in a soft-hearted, liberal policy like care for the unemployed? Because as a military genius he recognized the danger to society of desperate men who felt that they had no choice but to rob and steal to feed themselves and their families.

During the Great Depression the United States government spent hundreds of millions of dollars organizing make-work programs such as the Civilian Conservation Corps (CCC) and the Works Progress Administration (WPA). In both instances the government realized it was to the advantage of the welfare of the larger society not to have desperate men roaming the streets and highways living by the power of their fists or the proficiency of their weapons.

The response to the condition of black men has been different. The unemployment rate among young black males has remained comparable to those of white men during the Great Depression. However, racism has determined that this country would not spend the same kind of money and employ similar strategies to prevent unemployed black men from becoming a threat to the public order. Instead of instituting make work programs to provide black men with at least a paycheck and tasks to keep them busy the black male unemployment and subsequent crime rate become the springboard for one of the fastest growing industries in the United States—private security. This nation has opted to protect the rich man living on the top of hill with an army of poorly paid men who will protect them from the other poor people.

The second role that they prepare us for is captive consumers. "The poor pay more" is a proverb of every capitalist, racist society. You will not find "rent-to-own" businesses in middle-class white communities. Only in neighborhoods of poor people do you find these shops making enormous profits renting to people who can't afford to purchase their products outright and in the process charging them four and five times what they are worth on the retail market. Captive consumers are people who pay $150.00 for a pair of gym shoes that were manufactured in a sweat shop in Indonesia by workers being paid fifty cents an hour. These same shoes could be purchased on any street corner in Hong Kong for ten dollars and the seller would still have made a $7.00 profit because he bought them for $3.00 a pair wholesale because they are produced at a production cost of $1.50 per unit. We don't find currency exchanges in white neighborhoods. They have banks.

The television is the chief instrument, other than an inadequate education, for producing captive consumers. So important is TV in producing poor, uneducated people who provide tremendous profits for the cheap retail stores selling shoddy goods that are ubiquitous in black neighborhoods that the State of New York has legislated that TV's are essential domestic items and cannot be repossessed. You can go into the most impoverished neighborhood, into a housing project full of raggedy deteriorating buildings, most of which are boarded up and uninhabitable. Walk into an apartment whose inhabitants are so poor that they sit on milk crates for their furniture and eat their food with their fingers straight out the can. Yet they will be sitting there looking at a 32 inch, cable ready, 110 channel color TV with a VCR on top and a DVD on the bottom. The primary purpose of the television is to sell. Its role in our homes and lives is to convince people to buy stuff that ordinarily wouldn't even cross their minds that they wanted, much less needed. The power of the television is to capture and hold one's attention while filling his or her mind with ideas and thoughts that are not critically and analytically dealt with. The presence of the TV feeds the need to consume and drives the consumptive behavior of our people.

Too many of today's young people feel entitled to have what they want regardless of the cost. This is one of the most insidious features of contemporary life, working class people being sold on the idea that they can live an upper middle or even upper class lifestyle through credit. In the past what we could not afford we did without It was as simple as that. Our parents did not hesitate to put it just like this: "We can't afford it". That was usually the last word on the subject.

Long before we arrived on these shores African proverbs taught our people that debt was a form of slavery. After the end of chattel slavery hey experienced this debt slavery in sharecropping which was a system of enforced indebtedness that tied them to the land and to the landowner for almost a hundred until they fled the South during the Great Migration. In sharecropping they worked the white man's land for a share of the crop. (Land that was stolen from the Native American Indian nations). It might be written or agreed upon that the owner got sixty per cent and the workers forty, but it seldom worked like that. They were loaned housing, food, clothes, tools, seeds, a mule, and a plow that they must pay for at the harvest. At the end of the planting season when the crop was divvied up somehow or another no matter how hard they worked or how bountiful a harvest they produced they always ended up owing the owner. As a result they had to return the next year and work for him again trying to pay off the debt that somehow was never reduced. If they disputed the debt they were subject to physical intimidation if not lynching. Local statutes made leaving owing a debt a crime so if they tried to escape and were caught by the High Sheriff they could end up on the chain gang.

One of the reasons our people left the South despite their love of it rural environment, their romance with the land, the lazy meandering rivers, the exotic sweet-singing birds, the fragrant flowers like magnolia and honeysuckle, the glorious summers, the relatively mild winters, was to escape from the forced poverty of imposed credit and its inescapable debt.

Recognizing the inherently dangerous disabilities of debt our ancestors did all that they could to avoid it by striving for self-sufficiency. Self sufficiency is the enemy and the conqueror of debt. Dependency is debt's parent and child. Those past generations not only tried to avoid debt but every form of consumerism by producing most of what they needed themselves. They grew their own food, both animal and vegetable. They made their own clothes with wool from sheep they herded and cotton from the plants they grew. They build their own houses and made their own furniture. They only bought what they could not produce themselves. Shopping was a luxury for them. It was a matter of pride that they could produce most of what they needed. They possessed few store-bought items.

132

Shopping and consumerism driven by a level of mass psychology beyond most of our consciousness has driven us to the point where shopping and consumerism is no longer a rare luxury or even a seasonal recreational event. Shopping today has become necessary therapy for the depressed. "I don't feel so good. I'm so broken-hearted, lonely and depressed. I'm going to the mall and give white folks my hard-earned money so I can feel better".

While generations of our ancestors left their beloved environs of the South to escape systems of indebtedness present generations embrace credit as though it were the route to freedom. While our old folks were forced into positions of unfreedom, quasi-slavery and exploitation we voluntarily become contemporary, post-modern, urban suburban, high-tech, and state-of-the-art volunteer sharecroppers. We are not sharecropping for Mr. Charlie, Miss Ann, and Uncle Bubba. We are sharecropping for Lord & Taylor, Saks Fifth Avenue, Brooks Brothers, Visa, MasterCard, Discover, American Express, Tiffany's, Tommy Hilfiger, Gap, Old Navy, Gucci, Cadillac, Lexus, BMW, Rolex and unnamed others. We still work hard all year long, harder than anybody else because we still have to work twice as hard to get half as far. But when the year is over and we take stock of where we are we are still so loaded and overloaded by debt that we don't have discretionary funds to start our own businesses, send our children to college, invest in land and real estate. We end up agreeing with the brutally honest bumper sticker I saw once that said: "I owe, owe so off to work (for somebody else) I go."

Consumer credit with its interest rates as high as thirty percent and more is now the way the working class can assume an aspect of upper class life-style. But at what cost! The latest fad is for young people to have their weddings on one of the Caribbean Islands. Rich people throw their parties at exotic locations because if anybody they invite can't afford to come they will send a private jet for them or least provide them with a plane ticket. We have people requesting that working class individuals either go in debt or save their money for a year to spend a thousand dollars and more to attend a single social event. First of all this violates one of the oldest family laws which is that you don't price family members out of a family event. People should not have to meet a certain financial standard to participate in family affairs and attend family gatherings. The rich don't do that. As I said a few sentences ago they have their affairs in far away places because they can afford to make sure that whoever they invite will be able to attend even if it's at the inviter's expense. Past generations were not trying to lead upper class lives with working class incomes knowing that such a thing, though it might be accomplished temporarily, but only at the unacceptable cost of long-term if not life-long debt.

On many black college campuses today our children are introduced to captive consumerism as an aspect of college life. Credit card companies are given space at freshman registration to sign people up for "free" credit cards. Some students will graduate with a greater debt to credit card companies than for educational loans.

Companies are also allowed to place numerous "free" TV sets in cafeterias to be seen from every possible vantage point in the room with volumes set high enough to interfere with anybody's conversation. Students who ought to be using mealtimes to fellowship, get to know each other and engage in exciting intellectual exchanges instead sit through their meals silently being bombarded by commercials.

Cannon fodder is the third role that they envision for us. The day after the September 11 attacks on the World Trade Center in New York City and the Pentagon headquarters in Washington, D.C. there was an editorial on the third page of the Philadelphia Inquirer, written by one the chief executives of that great metropolitan daily newspaper, which began with the word in big bold print: REVENGE! Upon reading those audacious and intemperate words and understanding all that they meant I wished within my heart that I could find the writer and give him a ticket to Afghanistan and a pistol so that he could go there and personally seek and take his revenge. But I knew that he had no intention of going himself. He intended to send my son and the sons of other dark-skinned and poor and working class people to exact his revenge for him. The proverbial statements are true. "It's a rich man's war but a poor man's fight." "Old, rich, white men declare wars but young, poor and black men fight them." People join the armed forces and make their living by putting their lives on the line because they have no other options since they lack the kinds of educational preparation that will give them access to higher paying, less dangerous work.

Slavery was spiritual warfare fought for the hearts and souls, the values and principles of a people. Carter G. Woodson told us over a half-century ago in his classic Mis-Education of the Negro that the most effective way to make a slave was not by putting the chains on their ankles and wrists but on their hearts and souls.

American society was intent on enslaving the spirits of our ancestors by forcing them to bow down to the corrupt values of slave society. This was a demonic structure with the nature of a religion in which white people insisted that they were God and that they should be worshipped and obeyed by their black subjects whom they purported to own as their property. Just as they exalted themselves to superhuman status as gods they devalued us to the subhuman condition of lower animals. Their struggle was to bring us into agreement with their system so they would not have to worry about rebellion and resistance. The rewards that they offered us for our willing compliance were the pleasures of the flesh. They wanted to reduce us to the same amoral level on which they lived, rendering us people that would be satisfied with the shallow offerings of

135

alcohol, drugs, sex and violence to soothe our pains. If they could have reduced us to a race of alcoholics, pimps and prostitutes we could have had all the earthly pleasures we could stand.

But our ancestors understood the truly moral nature of the spiritual universe that they lived in and they would not sell the eternal birthright of their intended destiny for a mess of worldly pottage. Their African Traditional Religion agreed with the teaching of the bible that if they were true to the ways of righteousness in life that death would find a place for them among the ancestors for all of eternity. They were faithful unto death to standards of right living that kept them completely at odds with the boundless corruption of the slavery regime.

The genius of our kidnapped African ancestors was that they were able to educate their children based on a vision entirely contrary to the vision of the master. Those enslaved generations knew in their spirits that the day of jubilee and the hour of their deliverance would surely come. They testified of that steadfast unmovable belief in their songs.

They sang:

I'm so glad
Trouble don't last
Always.

They shouted:

One of these mornings
Won't be long
You'll look for me
But I'll be gone

They declared:

God's gon move

This wicked race.
He's gon raise up
A righteous nation
That will obey

Freedom was a living, palpable, inevitable reality for them. So they prepared their children for its coming, though that kind of education for liberation had to be done in secret.

The positive education of black youth has always been a subversive activity in America. Because we don't understand our history we engage in contemporary debates about whether or not private schools are good for our children. We forget that the first black schools and the most important ones, those in slavery, were much deeper than merely being private-- they were secret. Our enslaved ancestors had a vision separate from and more excellent than that of the slave masters. They understood life as having a divine origin and an eternal destiny. They knew that the body could be enslaved but not the soul long before the English poet, Richard Lovelace, penned the classic couplet:

Stone walls do not a prison make
Nor iron bars a cage

They conducted freedom schools in the midst of slavery. They knew who they were and what they were capable of. They had clear memories of the lives that they had led in Africa. They remembered the nations they ran, the cities they constructed, the wars of resistance they fought, the economies they ran, the markets that prospered, the arts that flourished. So in their spirits they harbored a continuing vision of their real capacities and possibilities. This truly transcendent sense of their real identity had to be hidden from the prying eyes of the slaveholder who would interpret any attempt on their part to define themselves or to entertain a definition of themselves different from his own as acts of rebellion punishable by summary execution. Based on that vision they prepared future generations for the hour of deliverance and for the year of jubilee.

The men were prepared to be warriors, ready for the day when they would be called, recruited, armed, trained, equipped and organized into massive military formations to make the final frontal attack on slavery. So it was that when the Union threw open the ranks of its army to the recruitment of black soldiers, 187,000 of the former slaves who had been reviled by white men North and South alike as fearful, child-like cowards formed the spearhead of the Union final offensive that broke the back of the slaveholders' rebellion and drove Johnny Reb into the seas of defeat. The women were prepared to take full control of their households and communities, to build institutions like churches and schools, to organize out of whole cloth household and community economies based on their independence, hard work, artistry and business sense.

The slave masters' educational system was an utter failure. Our kidnapped ancestors so successfully resisted their attempts to turn them into mental, spiritual and intellectual slaves that the freed people were the most productive generations in our history in this country. They had been prepared in slavery to handle freedom. So excellent was their education for freedom that within a few years of the end of the slavery they were running for office, conducting political campaigns, voting in elections, holding office, rewriting state constitutions, passing laws, governing states, building churches, purchasing land, owning farms, patenting inventions, building factories, establishing cities, founding colleges, establishing national and international denominations, publishing newspapers, writing books, and organizing state-wide systems of private Christian schools. By 1900 our people owned over 20 million acres of farmland. Today we own less than a million acres collectively. Ninety percent of all black colleges and universities were established before the start of the twentieth century. The generation of freed people was the most aggressive, productive, courageous, creative, free and far-thinking, long-term planning, and institution-building generation, that we have produced in our history in this country.

For instance, during slavery we were housed in huts, hovels, shacks and shanties. Within one generation a major portion of our people were living in frame and brick shotgun houses. This was an architectural style based on an ancient African design. These houses were not built by HUD, Section 8 or Habitat for Humanity. Out of their own resources our ancestors designed and built these houses for themselves. Black architects designed them; black factories made the bricks, black carpenters and bricklayers constructed the buildings. They had no doubts about their ability to build. They knew who they were they were. They knew that the white man brought them here from Africa to exploit their building skills. They constructed the palatial estates of their so-called owners during slavery. They partially designed and mostly built the brand new capital city of Washington D.C.

Back in those days and until the generation of my fathers black men were distinguished by their building skills that had been handed down the line of a thousand generations. The grandfathers taught the fathers and the fathers taught the sons how to build. In those days you could pick up any stray group of idle black men and have them build any kind of structure you wanted because they all had building skills. Today the average group of young black men couldn't build a lean-to in the woods to keep a torrential rainstorm off their heads.

It is the church that must once again, as it did in slavery, harbor the flame of resistance and nurture the vision of liberation. The spiritual community must be responsible for holding a more excellent vision for the futures of our youth and make moral demands upon the rest of black society to support that expectation of excellence. The well-established, long-entrenched, institutionalized racism of American society cherishes a vision of our young people as future jailbirds, dope addicts, prostitutes, criminals, and failures. Their ideas are propagated by their leading thinkers, taught in their most elite universities, popularized by their most successful newspapers and magazines, celebrated in their music, dramatized in their plays and movies and published in their most scholarly books. Take note for example how both black winners in this year's academy awards played the most degrading and demeaning of stereotypical roles, part of a continuum of the cinematic assassination of African moral character that goes back to the first and most racist film, Birth of a Nation.

The ideas of black inferiority and white superiority are so firmly established in the popular imagination that those who challenge its validity are most often portrayed as fools unable to accept a self-evident truth. However, we must remember that chattel slavery was also considered to be an unchallengeable reality. There must always be a source of a separate vision and that source ought to be the black church. It is the church that bears the responsibility for dealing in the higher and deeper truths of the spirit. We must see our children not merely through our own human eyes whose perceptions are so often distorted by the errors of human fault and mortal failure. We must be able to see ourselves and our children through the eyes of our Creator. Then and only then, are we able to imagine for ourselves and for unborn generations the kinds of exalted possibilities that the popular idea and common truth do not allow for. Today's preferred imagination consigns human beings to the negative status of accidents, mistakes, problems, unwanted, unneeded, surplus and superfluous flotsam and jetsam of modern miscalculation. The church must never let us forget that all life is of divine origin.

The scientific mind would convince us through the seemingly logical conclusions of Malthusian computation that that there are too many people in the world and that poor people constitute the majority of that surplus. We must continue to agree with our cousins among the Ebira people of West Africa who instruct us that there is no such thing as too many people because people are the height of creation and the only source of true wealth in this world. They say by way of proverb that: *"Children are the reward of life."* They tell us that if you can't have too much money, too many houses, too much land, too many jewels, too much gold, too many cars, too many clothes, too many horses, too many stocks and bonds and treasury notes then you can't have too many children. Because one single child is worth more than all the money, the gold, the diamonds, the silver, the jewelry, the cars, the houses, the land, horses, cattle , stocks, bonds, treasury notes, and investment portfolios in the entire universe.

Our young people are behind academically. The Reverend Doctor Benjamin Elijah Mays told us that when someone is behind in the race of life they must run faster to catch up. Our children have lower statistics of academic achievement than Europeans and Orientals. Their reading and math scores are lower. Their graduation rate is lower and their high school dropout rate is higher. Their entrance into college is lower and their rate of successful matriculation is lower still. Our young people read less, and watch TV and attend movies more than the children of other races. Failure in academics almost invariably leads to failure in the work world and the inability to handle the financial responsibilities of family life. In the Old Testament as in all of traditional African culture a father owed two things to his son: One, to teach him a trade so that he could make a living and two, to find him a wife. When we insure that a young person has been properly educated so that they are able to find a productive place in the world of work we also to a great extent insure that that person will not end up on the welfare rolls, out in the street robbing, stealing and selling drugs or being locked up in prison.

Our youth are tested and tracked. Tested with instruments that supposedly, in an objective fashion, measure not only the test-takers accumulated knowledge but further determines their potential and capacity for future learning. The best of our progressive educators tell us that these instruments are racist devices that are culturally biased. We have heard this term many times but let me attempt to define them in a practicable manner. It is as if you and a friend decided to give your children two days of intelligence testing. On the first day you design the test and compose all the questions on it. You base your questions on your house, where your children were born and raised but where your friend's children have never set foot. At the end of the first day of testing your children's' scores show that they are geniuses. Your friend's children's' score say that they are morons. The next day, however, your friend designs the test with all the questions based on the realities of life in his house where his children were born and raised and yours have never seen except in pictures. Now your friends' children score as geniuses and your children score as morons.

This is what their testing is to us and our children. They base their estimate of our intelligence on how well we know their culture. Then when our children don't do so well trying to answer questions about that which is beyond their own life's experience they declare them unteachable and consign them to the lowest rungs on the ladders of academia. We as parents and community leaders allow these practices to go, for the most part, unchecked. We uncritically accept the supposedly informed opinion of strangers that our children cannot measure up to theirs. They would never allow us to design a battery of tests, all of whose questions are based on the everyday realities or the oral histories of black people, make their children take our tests, and then determine their intelligence and their academic and employment opportunities on how poorly

142

they scored.

One of the worst mistakes we have made concerning our children's education was our demand for integrated schools. James Meredith, famous for being the first black student at the University of Mississippi, says that integration is a "social experiment". He explains that no people in the history of the world has every integrated themselves into another people thereby committing collective mass suicide through the surrender of their own identity while melding themselves into another people. Integration has always meant black out and white in. There is the tacit assumption of black inferiority and white supremacy at the very foundation of the theory of integration. The Supreme Court decision of 1954 came to a basically unchallenged racist assumption when it declared that any school that was all-black was by definition inferior. There might have been some fairness involved if they had come to the same conclusion about any school that was all-white. However that was not the case. The next logical step, of course, if all black institutions are inferior is to integrate black students into white schools. This attempt at integration has been an utter failure for any number of reasons but for the sake of argument let me cite just a couple.

The idea of the efficacy of integration was based on the often stated expectation that if our children were in the same classroom as the white students then they would get the same quality and quantity of education. It seemed logical to our parents at the time that the fact of physical proximity itself would be enough. My oldest son, Clarence Lumumba James, Jr., told me this story fifteen years after the fact, of his first day in kindergarten as the only black student in his class at a public school in Rockford, IL.

The white female teacher asked the class who knew their ABC's. A number of white boys jumped up immediately because they are taught at home to always project themselves to the forefront of anything intellectual.

143

My son reported that none of them could get past "E". After the last one finished he stood up and did the alphabet without a hitch or hesitation since he had been reading since he was three years old. The teacher responded by shouting at him in red-faced anger: "Who do you think you are. I guess you think you're so smart, huh!"

The psychodynamics of racism in classroom interaction are such that it is possible for white children to get a positive response for being wrong and a black child to receive a negative response for being right. The resulting sense of alienation can be so profound that many of our children will be so traumatized that they will suffer from episodes of disassociation of varying lengths throughout their educational experience. One former student told me that he had not a single memory of a classroom experience during his entire four years in a mostly white high school. These are the experiences of severely abused children who commonly suffer from gaps of memory of entire periods of their childhood.

One of the reasons our children are made to suffer so is because we have yet to put in place a strategy to protect them from racist teachers and administrators. I don't believe that it is possible for any black teacher that demonstrates the slightest possibility that he or she might hate white people or simply not entertain the highest expectations for white students to be allowed to teach at a white school. You will not read about a controversy in which a former Black Panther or a member of the Nation of Islam (or any other group that white people identify as racist) was hired to teach in a white school. If such a hiring did place it would only be done after that person had gone through extraordinary lengths to prove that they did not have a racist bone in their bodies. The administrators would not put up with the slightest possibility that their students might be exposed to a black teacher who had the mentality or philosophy to possibly abuse them. It is not an issue that would ever have to be dealt with by the parents.

White people insist, in their dealings with us, that we render unto them every possible iota of respect and courtesy not to mention expecting many of us to go overboard with fawning admiration of them and their culture. However, we have not and do not provide our children with the same protection from racist white teachers.

Most of the teachers in the public schools that we send our children to are working class white females. The major problem here is the unique combination of class and color. White teachers, once they earn their degrees and become active in their profession, have achieved middle-class status. Yet, they began their lives and were raised in working class homes and neighborhoods. The white working class has historically harbored a particularly violent attitude towards us that differs in degree from members of the white upper-middle and upper classes.

The white upper classes do not come into direct competition with us whether for housing, jobs, or sports. We don't compete against them for housing because so very few of us can afford to live in their gated communities and we are the continuing victims of redlining in the real estate industry which continues to practice discrimination in housing forty years after the signing of the open housing bill. We don't compete with them for jobs because the glass ceiling keeps us out of the senior vice-presidencies and CEO positions in Fortune 500 corporations. We don't compete with them in sports. They swim, golf, yacht, ski, play tennis and polo. They are therefore generally perceived as being more liberal than working class white people because the nature of their interaction with us is not so face-to-face and full of dangerous consequences. The middle and upper class whites are more likely to express their racism through the more subtle form of paternalism.

Working class white people, on the other hand, spend their entire lives trying to stay two blocks ahead of the ghetto. When the first black resident appears on the block, the house that they live in immediately loses fifty percent of its value. The presence of black neighbors is a financial and emotional disaster for them. They compete with us not only for housing, but also for jobs and in sports. The working class white man is, like the overwhelming majority of black men, seeking blue collar jobs which are already scarce due to the removal of factories to foreign lands in search of cheaper labor. He competes with us in sports. He plays baseball, football, and basketball just like we do. He even boxes. Therefore he understands us to be a threat to his material well-being and reacts to us with a violence that is legendary and has served as the basic rationale for such hate groups as the Klu Klux Klan, Nazi Party, the Aryan Brotherhoods and the numerous militia groups.

The ghetto does not expand into middle or upper-class neighborhoods. It is the neighborhoods of working class whites which are most devastated by the vicious practice of blockbusting whereby the housing industry composed of realtors, banks and insurance companies make obscene profits from the need of black people to have better housing and the desire of white people not to lose their hard-earned housing value by living in a neighborhood that is "going black". This face-to-face competition for the scarce resources allocated to the working classes by the wealthy ruling class leaves white working class people with a peculiar resentment, fear and hatred of black people. The white upper classes can be contemptuously amused with us from a distance because we represent no true threat to their financial or even physical well-being.

Black people have a long history of taking care of white people's children, from the time slavery time to the present. We can go into any middle-class white neighborhood today and find dozens of black women out traveling the streets with their white infant charges. It is a testimony to the profoundly enduring humanity of our people that there is little if any record of the maltreatment of white children by

146

their black caretakers. In other words we have proven over hundreds of years of bondage and domestic servitude that we can and do treat their children with love and respect.

Unfortunately, there is no equal reality on the other side of the racial divide. One of the classic expressions of white people's rampant lack of regard for our children came from the infamous, racist governor of 19th century North Carolina, "Pitchfork" Ben Tillman. When asked by a reporter why black children were lynched as well as black adults he replied: "Because nits make lice." When we hire white teachers to educate our children we are expecting these people to operate against their own perceived best interests. Since they are so aware that their children will be in competition with ours in a way that we have little consciousness of we are in effect asking them to prepare our children to beat out their children for life's scarce resources. That is a lot to ask of any people, much less a people terminally infected with by a history of hundreds of years of racism.

This does not mean that no white people are capable of properly educating black children. Just as it cannot mean that any teacher who is black is automatically a good teacher. It simply means that we must be more vigilant and diligent in protecting our children from any teacher that does not believe in their ability to learn and does not entertain the highest expectations for their futures. It is the responsibility of black parents, church leaders, and educators to develop and put in place a process that will test and measure teachers, administrators, counselors and anyone that has access to our children, for the presence of racism.

White society has accepted racism as being an inconvenient, leftover set of emotions that black people need to get used to having to deal with and wait patiently while it takes its gradual course of naturally subsiding over the passage of time. We as black people understand that racism is in fact a deadly emotional, mental, psychological, spiritual, and intellectual institutionalized illness that can cause horrendous harm to the people, particularly children, who are exposed to it. The effect that racism has on the character of the individual infected by it is the distortion of the personality into a delusional state that gives the racist personality an exalted sense of superiority and entitlement to treat other human beings as if they were less than human and not much better than animals.

I am not suggesting that our children must accept the fact that they just can't do any better. I am saying just the opposite. The only way that our children can compete is that they must return to the classic way of success for black people in this county which is: "to work twice as hard to get half as far." There is a way for our young people to excel in other people's schools and other people's culture. How do you learn about a place that you have never been? Through reading. Reading is transportation into the unknown. We must devise ways to increase our children's relationship to reading as the key to propelling them forward in the great contest of life. They do not have to remain consigned to the bottom of the academic ladder. No matter how formidable the racist strategies are that exist to keep them down they can overcome them. This is the glory of our history on these shores. We have been an overcoming people. Our ancestors defied and defeated much more powerful enemies than any our children face today.

In the system of academic tracking, the so-called slower students are segregated by supposed ability and potential from the allegedly faster and more advanced students. However study after study shows that being with slower student doesn't slow down the faster students; it speeds up the slower ones. Just like in athletics playing with a better player makes every player on the team better by challenging them to elevate their skills to a higher level of performance.

The lowest level of the educational tracking pyramid is

at the bottom where the students are variously labeled educable mentally handicapped (EMH), mildly mentally retarded, slow, or today's most popular rubric Attention Deficit Disorder (ADD) or hyperactive. These all are assigned to the class of students who are labeled special education. Most of the people in special education are black males. The majority of them will be on the drug Ritalin. The children in the upper and middle levels of the educational pyramid will be prepared for productive lives in society. Those at the top: the gifted, magnet, advanced placement students will be given all the resources and assistance they need to be admitted to colleges and prepare for top-level, well-paid, decision-making, executive positions. Those in the middle in the vocational tracks will at least receive the training they need to obtain and hold jobs that will pay them a living wage though they will struggle with the up and down cycles of inflation, recession and unemployment all of their lives.

But the ones at the bottom in special education are being prepared to spend most of their adult lives in jail because they will receive no preparation for living productive lives. Men, in order to express their manhood, will do so in one of three ways: They will make something, take something or break something. Men who have no skills or ability to make something will inevitably resort to the two negative options which will lead to jail or an early death on the street.

Finally, there is the problem of Ritalin. The prescriptions of this drug for school age children have multiplied exponentially over the past twenty years until it has become a national epidemic. Principals, teachers, counselors and administrators are being empowered to make medical diagnoses of hyperactivity in children which should logically and legally be the province of medical doctors and trained psychologists. Once again black males are the predominant recipients of these massive misdiagnoses. Many white teachers, particularly females, who are completely unfamiliar with black male culture are literally so frightened by the rambunctiousness of black male behavior and their own lack of adult authority to deal with it that they turn to the drug for a solution. We seem to forget in our acceptance of the drugging of literally millions of school-age children that drugs are drugs. Whether you get your drug from a doctor through the writing of a legal prescription of from Sweet Willie the street-corner dope dealer, drugs are drugs. People who are high lack the ability to focus and think clearly in order to complete rigorous intellectual tasks. While in a drug induced fog they do not develop the emotional maturity needed to cope with the regular challenges of everyday human interaction. The child who is on Ritalin throughout grammar school when he or she is suddenly removed upon the arrival of puberty and the onset of adolescence will find themselves behind both academically and socially with almost no devices in place to help them to catch up with their peers.

Once a child reaches adolescence the responsibility for receiving an education rests more upon them than upon the teachers. As adolescents students should have achieved enough ego strength and sense of identity to strive for what is best in life and in them. Teenagehood is that critical period when young people go through the process of individuation, separating themselves from the psychological, emotional and spiritual domination of their parents, striving to determine for themselves who they are and what they will do with their lives. At this point their choices become their own. They can be hardheaded and stubborn enough to decide that no one is going to force them to learn anything. They can decide that they are grown already and nobody can tell them anything. If they choose that state of mind they will be uneducable except in the school of hard knocks.

On the other hand if the teenage boy or girl decides that they love learning, revere wisdom and are determined to follow in the footsteps of the greatest examples that our ancestors have provided for them, nothing will stop them from attaining an education. Not the worst schools, not the most uncaring teachers, not the most corrupt administrations, not the most unconcerned of counselors. Once in high school years all education is self-education.

 "You can lead a horse to water but you can't make him drink.
You can send a kid to school but you can't make her think".

Good students will learn from the worst teachers. Bad students will not learn from the best teachers.

No matter how far the river flows, it never forgets its

VI. HIGHER EDUCATION

Higher education has been a way out of poverty and material deprivation for us for well over a hundred years. Ninety-five percent of Jews go to college. Are Jews therefore to be considered more intelligent than other groups in the American population? We know that is not the case because there are no superior or inferior races. The Jews came here as immigrants from Europe consigned to the bottom of the socio-economic ladder but two or three steps above black people, basically on the same level as the Italians and the Irish. The Jews after arriving here decided to redefine themselves from cheap labor, which is the role all the original immigrants have played and still fill in this society, into a race of professionals such doctors, lawyers, dentists, accountants, educators, scientists.

Jews do not have more native intelligence than any other group. *But they have more effectively allocated the resources in their communities for the maximum academic and professional development of their children.* They redefined themselves as a community of professionals. If they can do it anybody can. That's exactly what our ancestors did coming out of slavery. They redefined themselves as a people that valued education. They did not just build grammar schools and high schools. They built colleges and universities. In the midst of a people that tried to limit them to the most rudimentary pursuits in education, they insisted on seeing themselves as scholars of the first rank.

Most black students are still first generation college students. As a young minister determined to encourage and assist high school students in attaining a college education the greatest difficulty I continually faced was convincing them that they belonged in college. Too many of our high

152

school age youth do not see themselves as college material. Most of them do not have a college graduate in their family. Also to a large degree because racist teachers and especially racist counselors in their high schools work hard at convincing them that they are not college material. Almost every black college student and adult professional has at least one story about a teacher, counselor or administrator, usually white, but sometimes a class-conscious, color-struck black person, who tried to convince them that they did not belong in college and were not intellectually capable of obtaining higher education. Years later they are still pained by the memory of people that they looked up to and trusted as authority figures expressing their lack of confidence in them through contemptuous statements based on negative expectations.

First generation college students did not experience their parents' campus reminiscing as a part of their dinner-time conversations. College is a foreign, far-off and alien idea to them. The most effective way to overcome this ingrained sense of unworthiness is to take students on campus visitations so they experience the reality of college first hand. In order to be convinced that they belong on a college campus they must see themselves in college. By intermingling with college students they discover that college students are normal people just like them.

Doctors don't necessarily have more intelligence or ability than other people. What they have is higher ambitions and greater determination. It is where we project our aspirations and goals that determine where we end up. The world tries to put low ceilings on the ambitions of our young people. We have to help them to dream dreams of exalted accomplishments. We must encourage them to dream of climbing mountains when others would convince them to be satisfied with nightmares of clawing and crawling through valleys. The media representations would convince them they can't swim across a pool when they should be dreaming about sailing across oceans.

Our ability to rise from the horrors of slavery and show ourselves to be a great people was based upon our construction of powerful institutions that served as the pillars of our progress. The first institution was the black church.. The second was the black family. Immediately after slavery ended they built the third great institutional pillar of the black community, the schools. They built entire systems of black, private and Christian kindergartens, grammar schools, high schools, and at the top colleges, universities, seminaries and medical and law schools. As with the black church and the black family our schools were first of all spiritual institutions. For African people morality comes first. Our old people have a name for people not properly educated according to our standards. They call such people "educated fools". In the European mindset education centers around technology and commerce, consigning questions of spirituality and morality to the outer margins of what is important in life. Education for them is a question of hours, credits, majors and degrees. If one has these things they are accepted as truly educated and therefore automatically intelligent. Our tradition disagrees. It instructs us that no matter how much education one has, if one concludes that they are better than anybody else (they don't know how to treat people right) or that there is no God then they have become an "educated fool". The Bible says: "The fool hath said in his heart, there is no God". Ps 14:1KJV

The black colleges were spiritual institutions first. The making of black students was more of a spiritual phenomenon than an intellectual one. Morehouse men, for instance were made more in the chapel than in the classroom. Dr. Fred Lofton compiled a collection of sermons by Morehouse men who came up under the presidency of Dr. Benjamin Elijah Mays. The book is entitled God Our Help in Ages Past. In the chapter, "The Chapel Hour", Dr. Charles Epps, the long-time pastor of the Zion Baptist Church in Jersey City, New Jersey, testified that it was the chapel experience that transformed the lives of young men who had been traumatized, tortured, and distorted by the unending horrors and everyday humiliations of American apartheid. It was under the daily Holy Ghost inspired, soul-shaking, mind-waking, spirit-moving teaching and preaching of men and women such as Dr. Mays, Dr. William Holmes Borders("The Prophet of Wheat St"), Dr. Charles DuBois Hubert, Dr. George D. Kelsey and weekly exposure to such guest speakers as W.E.B. DuBois, Mary McLeod Bethune, Paul Robeson, Rev. Adam Clayton Powell, that those young men were liberated from a sense of inferiority to an understanding of and utter confidence in their unlimited possibilities.

Hear Dr. Epps testimony:

"The great moment in the history of my life at Morehouse College was the Chapel Hour. This was the time when great educators, statesmen, preachers, and a host of others distinguished characters and scholars, along with our own faculty members, would speak to the hearts and minds of the student body in particular and the college community in general. This was the hour where the black boy was able to realize his great potential by seeing and hearing great men and women of accomplishment. This venture alone contradicted a biased philosophy that the black race is inferior. Every chapel hour and every chapel speaker gave the men of Morehouse a sense of worth, the value of human personality, dignity, and faith in themselves and their God. It encouraged us to know that man has the ability to conquer any foe, to solve any problem, and to face any obstacle rationally and prayerfully.

The Chapel Hour at Morehouse was a time when God spoke to his children. Oh, when the man of God spoke to us, the backward boys from the peach orchards of Georgia, the coals mines of Alabama, the cotton fields of Mississippi, the tobacco fields of Virginia, the turpentine fields of North and South Carolina, the rice and sugar fields of Louisiana, and the ghettos of New York, Chicago, St. Louis, and Los

Angeles, we heard the voice of God speaking to us. This is what made the difference in many of our lives. The voice of God was heard which changed our lives and redirect our goals whether in the sciences or education or the arts- all to the glory of God.

As in all things truly black it is the spiritual experience that is paramount. Morehouse men were not made in the classroom they were made in the Chapel. They were finished and polished by the intellectual dynamics in the classroom but they were fired, forged and shaped by the spiritual experiences of the Chapel.

In direct opposition to racist thought and practice is the undeniable witness that it was the spiritual element in the lives of black colleges that gave them their power to enable our young people to experience transformation from the powerless to the powerful, from the looked down upon to the looked up to, from the left out to the invited in. However, today our schools have become increasingly secularized into unspiritual, non-religious, anti-Christian even amoral institutions as we strive as a people to integrate and become more like the people that we live amongst.

Black colleges are still the best places for our students to obtain higher education. Firstly, because they are uniquely ours. They were designed to serve us. They measure their failure and success upon how well or poorly we perform as students. We are their target audience. We are the clientele they were built to serve. Every group in this country has institutions of higher education that exist to serve their peculiar needs. But nobody talks about closing them. Harvard is for upper-class, old-money white people. Brandeis and Yeshiva are for the Jews. Brigham Young is for Mormons. Notre Dame, DePaul, Loyola and Georgetown are for Catholics. In all of these other schools the presence of our young people is secondary, tertiary, incidental, marginal, ancillary, auxiliary, tangential, peripheral, out of the question and beside the point. They really don't care whether we do well there or not. They don't measure their institutions' success or failure on how well we do. We are nowhere near the center of their concerns. If the failure rate of white, or Catholic or Jewish or Mormon students were anywhere near that of black students it would precipitate a crisis and bring about an institutional wide shake-up. Presidents' heads would roll. Boards of directors would be replaced wholesale. Chairmen of departments would lose their endowed appointments. Tenured faculty would be summarily dismissed. When the only people with a high failure, low retention rate at these schools are our own children it doesn't even rate a two paragraph article on back pages of the student newsletter. But at our schools our children are the reason for their existence, and the measurement and definition of their success or failure. If they don't serve them well the very existence of the institution is called into question and put at risk.

Secondly, at our schools our students have greater access to faculty, staff and administrators after hours. Jacqueline Fleming, in her insightful work entitled Blacks in College, says that the intellectual progress of college students is based to a significant extent on the amount of their access to professors and administrators outside the classroom. In order to invite our children to their homes, clubs, churches, after office hours, on weekends and during holidays, faculty members must be able to look at our children and see their own. They must be free of the racism that infects the overwhelming majority of white people in this country regardless of education or professional standing. It is in these informal venues that the formal, general and idealistic lessons written on blackboards are translated into tangible, relevant, practical lessons of everyday life. It is at the dinner table, around the fireplace in the den, in the car during long drives that the student has the opportunity to customize their education by bombarding the professor with questions and engage in lengthy and deep conversations that could never take place in classroom.

While I was at Harvard I had one occasion to schedule a meeting with one of my world-renowned professors. I had to set the date three months ahead and was given ten minutes of his precious time. On my first day at Morehouse College I spent over three hours relaxing in his office and talking about an unlimited range of subjects with the legendary Dr. Robert H. Brisbane, Lincoln U. graduate, Harvard Ph.D., chairman of the political science department, author of numerous published works of masterful scholarship and mentor to three generations of Morehouse men such as Dr. King, Lerone Bennett, Maynard Jackson, and Julian Bond, who went out and changed the world.

Finally, black colleges are the best places for the development of our new young leaders. What would a white school do with a young Martin Luther King, Jr., a new Frederick Douglass, a young black woman imbued with the fiery, unquenchably rebellious spirit of Fannie Lou Hamer? Would a young Kwame Ture be nurtured and celebrated on a white campus or would he become the target of repression by those who recognized his potential as a dangerous threat to their white supremacist way of life and would then do everything they could to crush his powers before they could come to full maturity? How do white professors typically respond to the piercing questions that arise from the challenging intellects of a young Ida B. Wells, a still-developing Mary McLeod Bethune, an adolescent Kwame Nkrumah, or an immature Nelson Mandela? The horrendous failure rate of black students, particularly males on white campuses tells us that something of the like has already been going on for the past thirty years.

Our students on black and white campuses today are still in need of the transforming message of the gospel. White racism has made a demonically ingenious move by

158

inserting itself into the mainstream of black youth culture in the guise of being a new creation of black authenticity. The incredibly negative message of so-called "gangster" and hard-core rap purports to give an entire generation a new, "keepin' it real" black identity. This music preaches a negative line of thought that demands that our young people accept and promote an identity of being, in its own words, "real niggas". According to this philosophy young people are wrong to try to better themselves by believing in the principles of uplift and engaging in the practices of positivism. Their message is that black people are defined by the self-destructive values of alley life. Fighting, cursing, killing, drinking, raping, gambling, all forms of criminal behavior, sexual promiscuity, disrespect for elders, refusal to accept correction, defiance of authority are their watchwords.

We see on some campuses the determined efforts of the students to distort the college surroundings into the familiar pathological environment of the worst parts of the projects. We see graffiti, trash, beer bottles, cigar butts, and discarded condoms scattered around in dormitory corridors and out in the open public spaces of flowered quadrangles and green lawns. We hear the profane lyrics of gangster rap music blasted across the campus out of dormitories windows and from passing cars. Gang fights, including drive-by shootings, have become a common occurrence on college campuses, both black and white as our young people take gang dynamics as the paradigm for their social organization and interaction. Almost daily there are newspaper reports of fights among athletic team members and members of fraternities. In the old days if you were in a gang at home you might not even tell anybody because you came to college to rise above that life-style. In those days athletes were never gang members because the gangs themselves respected athletics as an admirable path to a better life. Today we read of football players flashing gang signs at each other across the lines of scrimmage during college football games.

Many proponents of gangster rap and other negative aspects of hip-hop naively claim that it is a culture unto itself and others take it so far to declare that it their religion. These kinds of statements only reveal our failure to properly educate this generation so that would know that difference between a culture and a fad. A fad is the style of clothes one wears; a culture includes the farms that grow the cotton and the factories that manufacture the cloth. A fad is the entertainment delight of young people exercising their first freedom from childhood and adolescence, a culture involves the rearing of the next generation and care for the past ones. A fad is the latest word spoke in the slickest fashion by the newest stars. A culture has an educational system that preserves and imparts the greatest wisdom from ageless personalities. Fads fade after a season; culture endures for thousands of years. People outgrow fads as they mature. Culture is a cradle for babies and a walking stick for the advanced in age. Fads are the toys of children; culture is the enduring construct of the life's work of generation after generation. Fads are discarded when their novelty wears off. Cultures are living monuments of profound meaning. Fads are distractions; cultures are beacon lights of direction. Fads are flowers that blossom in the spring and summer of delight but die under the harsh cold of the challenge of the hard times of fall and winter. Culture is a tree that sends its roots down deep into the subterranean bosom of trans-generational soil then spreads its limbs so high and thick and strong that future generations can find shelter there from storms of life and fruit to feed its offspring.

So powerful is this trend to insist that to be authentically black means to be a criminal that I have witnessed the tragic sight of young people raised in strong positive households try to portray themselves as thugs and gangsters in order to be accepted by the group who holds respectable, responsible, intelligent behavior in utter contempt. Our

160

young people on college campuses are increasingly caught up in the deadly tentacles of a negative peer pressure that tries to force them into behavior that conforms to the lowest common denominator. These young people are in need of the power of edifying messages that will deliver them from the paralyzing destructive grip of the negative forces that many of them feel powerless to escape or defeat.

We are witnesses to the power of the spoken word backed by powerful rhythms to invade, inform, and mold the lives of our young people. They are hearing the words of Ice T, Too Short, Snoop Dog and Fifty Cent urging them to pimp their sisters. They listen to 2 Live Crew, Jay Z and DMX describe in graphic detail the pleasure of raping our daughters. They are mesmerized by Lil' Kim, Foxy Brown, Missy Elliot and Da' Brat mounting the auction blocks of their own perverse passions offering their bodies for sale to the highest bidder. They listen to NWA, Tupac Shakur and Biggie Smalls speak so eloquently, poetically and convincingly about the glories of the thug life. In one song the Notorious B.I.G celebrates defecating on a woman as part of having sex. R. Kelly celebrates unrestrained sex that includes the seduction, manipulation and exploitation of underage young girls and urinating in their faces. They pop their fingers, clap their hands and dance in celebration to notions of going to jail as a rite of passage into manhood. They listen to all of them describe the ghetto, the black community, the neighborhoods where people of African descent reside as though it was nothing but a cesspool of human corruption with no redeeming features.

The question for this generation must be the same that our ancestors asked when they were bombarded by slavery's negative messages that insisted that they were not even human beings and should be rejoicing that white folks rescued them from the barbarities of life in African and introduced them to the light of the gospel and the marvels of civilization. They raised the biblical question: "Is there any word from the Lord?" Jer. 37:17KJV They asked further: "Is there no balm in Gilead, is their no physician there?" Jer. 8:22KJV'

The answer came swiftly. There was a word from the Lord that contradicted the lies of slavery and told them the truth about themselves. It came in the form of the proverbs of Africa which contained the ancient wisdom of our people translated into a new language but losing none of their original power and profundity. It was on the lips of the elders as they counseled their children and grandchildren how to live in sanctified dignity in the midst of all the horrors of their daily lives. It was in the preaching of men and women who produced a body of sermons that were radical in their theology, dramatic in their presentation, spellbinding in their creativity, musical in their delivery, cuttingly accurate in their criticism of the moral failings of a racist society, empowering and convicting in their insistence that right would win out in the end

It was in the ineffable artistry of the spirituals, a body of music that constitutes along with jazz and blues the classical music of African people living in the United States of America. So timeless their power and practicality, so unchanged by the passing of the years their relevance and applicability to the challenges of life that they are sung in ten thousand worshipping congregations every Sunday morning. Preachers today still quote from them, often in the close of their sermons, when the greatest power of expression is insisted upon. As did Dr. King in his "I Have a Dream" sermon closing with the exultant words of the old spiritual;

Free at last
Free at last
Thank God almighty
We're free at last

It was in the prayers that the people prayed. Prayers that

were also works of art in that they were at the same time prayers, then poems, then chants, then songs. Prayers that brought down power from on high that energized them to go on another day, preparing the way for the generation of promise that would be the fulfillment of the prophesies of deliverance.

I went to the valley
I didn't go to stay

But my soul got happy
And I stayed all day

My head got wet with the midnight dew
The morning star was a witness too

My hand got stuck to the gospel plow
And I wouldn't give nothing for my journey now

Tell me
How did you feel?
When you come out the wilderness?
I felt brand new
When I come out the wilderness
I was leaning on the Lord!

Some Black colleges have become so increasingly secularized that the Christian message is barely heard in any formal gathering on campus. Some colleges even go so far as to demand that prayers not be offered in the name of Jesus. Their rationalization being that to do so would offend practitioners of other religions. The consequence of the enforced downplaying of Christianity on our campuses is a moral crisis that has resulted in unprecedented levels of chaos in the classrooms, dormitories and offices of many of our most cherished institutions. Christianity is being pushed further and further into the background on black college campuses. Chapel attendance is no longer mandatory at any black college as far as I know. Most state colleges no longer have a campus chaplain at all. On those campuses where the school does sponsor a chaplain he or she is often required not to pray or preach in the name of Jesus. Many of our professionals and educators justify the downgrading of Christianity with two arguments.

The first is the peculiarly European notion of the supposed necessity of the "separation of church and state". They do so without seeming to consider that this separation is not carved in stone but is an on-going debate. In fact the Bill of Rights to the Constitution does not say that religion cannot play a role in government. It says just the opposite: that the government can play no role in religion. It's not that religion should not establish a presence in politics but that politics cannot establish a presence in religion. The point is to keep religion free from the often amoral proclivities and corrupting pressures of politics so that it can play its proper role as a moral compass for the body politic.

The contemporary controversies over the display of the Ten Commandments in governmental space is a case in point. What makes the attempt to ban this Judeo-Christian document from courthouses and government office buildings so silly is that without the Ten Commandments there would be no rule of law as it is known throughout Europe and Euro-America. The entire European system of jurisprudence is based on the moral proscriptions of the Ten Commandments. Morality has always preceded legality. It is only in today's world, replete with its worship of all things modern and contempt for the old people and their old ways that we imagine that we can redo the moral structures of the universe and replace ancient precepts by popular fiat.

For us as a people our religion plays a much more significant role than it does among white people. African people have always recognized that that we live a spiritual

164

universe of God's creation and control in which the most crucial concerns of life are moral questions of good and evil. White people have twisted their minds to conceive that they can carve out spaces in God's world that belong to them, in which good and evil have no place. They have even shook their fists at heaven and declared that either there never was a God or if He ever did exist He died and left them in charge. For them the most pressing questions are of winning and losing, domination and subjugation or profit and loss. If we ever fully accept their approach then we will have truly lost our souls and with it all hope for fulfilling our ancestors' dreams and visions of true freedom.

We would be doing ourselves a disservice to sit on the sidelines of this great debate of questions of such immensity, as though our unique world view was irrelevant. One of the struggles of the civil rights movement concerned our demand for self-determination and self-definition. We have continually since we have been in this country fought to maintain the integrity of our own sense of self. Our ancestors refused to allow these people to rob them of their sense of who they were which was tied to their understanding of how the universe operated. No amount of indoctrination, propaganda, beating, torture, mutilation, and mass murder could convince them to bow down to the false gods, heathen concepts and demonic activities of people who claimed they were God and could decide what was right and wrong.

But today we seem to have lost the power of independent thought. After appearing on a local radio station in Atlanta to discuss educational issues I received a call from a listener who introduced himself as the president of the PTA at a local school. He invited me to address the school's student body and the parents. I readily accepted. A few days later I received another call from him in which he explained that he had to withdraw the invitation because administrators (probably white but possibly black) told him that for me to appear there would a violation of the separation of church and state. I tried to explain to the man that his invitation was not for me to preach a revival, that his original impetus came from my intelligent discussion of the critical issues that our young people face in trying to obtain a public school education. When that didn't work I ran off a list of black people that would not have been able to speak at a public school if this "law" had been recognized or accepted by our ancestors. On the list were the names of Bishop Richard Allen, Rev. Frederick Douglas, Bishop Henry McNeil Turner, Rev. A.D. Williams, Rev. Adam Clayton Powell, Jr., Rev. Dr. Mordecai Johnson, Rev. Dr. Benjamin Elijah Mays, Rev. Dr. Martin Luther King, Jr., and countless others of the past, and today such men as Rev. Dr. Floyd Flake, pastor of Allen Temple AME church in Jamaica, Queens and president of Wilberforce College in Ohio and Rev. Dr. Calvin Butts, pastor of the world-renowned Abyssinian Baptist Church of Harlem and president of the State University College at Old Westbury .

Because of our lack of a narrow definition of religion and any attempt to segregate moral and spiritual concerns from other aspects of life black men and women of a religious temperament have had full access to the entire institutional life of the black community. Black preachers have been teachers, college professors, business men and women, ambassadors to foreign lands, medical doctors, lawyers, state legislators, members of the House of Representative and the Senate, and in the case of Osagyfo Kwame Nkrumah, president of the sovereign nation of Ghana in West Africa.

It was the unlimited portfolio of black religious functionaries dramatized by their leadership role in the domestic black liberation struggle and on the international fields of peace and human rights that provided the inspiration for white ministers to become overtly involved in the political process beginning with liberals like Catholic priests and continuing with conservatives like the so-called Moral Majority and the Christian Coalition.

One of the most important struggles of the freedom movement during slavery concerned the slave owners' attempts to deny to the slaves the free practice of their faith. Today in freedom we surrender voluntarily that which all the brutalities of slavery could not take from us by force.

The black students attending college today are in need of spiritual transformation if they are ever to achieve the kind of morally responsible adulthood that is required for our race to have a healthy, positive future. We must carve out our own space in terms of our interpretation of what "separation of church and state" means. We know that this kind of "either or" dichotomous, oppositional thinking is not a part of our African and biblical world view. We also know that government does not define human beings, human beings define government. Our ancient, divinely-inspired bedrocks of morality must never be made subservient to the popularity-fed notions of legality. We must remember that human beings change according to the spirits of the age. Slavery was legal. The constitution of the United States endorsed it. White supremacy and black inferiority was the official, operative philosophy of the nation. The Dred Scott decision said it was so. Segregation was the law of the land. The Supreme Court mandated it in the Plessy vs. Ferguson decision. Our war here has always been one of rebellion against humanly instituted and legalized wickedness as we held up the banner of a higher law from a divine source.

Secondly, they argue that any expression of Christianity offends practitioners of other faiths. This kind of reasoning is disingenuous at best, dishonest at worst, and is once again an expression of the kind of opposition-based thinking that is foreign to us at our best. To ask a person to become less of who they are because it makes somebody else feel uncomfortable about their identity is truly racist thinking. We all have a right, even a responsibility, to be

167

fully ourselves. That approach is no different than concluding that someone is too black or too rhythmic or that their hair is too kinky. My being Christian is no threat to anybody else being whatever they are. Once again it is a case of us being told that we cannot be ourselves. Some of us understand that the essence of our African identity is firmly embedded in our spirituality and our belief system. Surrendering the practice of our faith would certainly sound the death knell on our struggle to be free to be who God calls us to be.

Many private colleges insist on robbing their chaplains of the real power of the unadulterated gospel by demanding that they practice a stripped-down version of Christianity that they call "ecumenism". In this form of religious "diversity" the name of Jesus cannot be mentioned because supposedly it offends someone else's religious sensibilities. Supposedly ecumenism is a form of "universal" religion that will somehow encompass everybody's religion and offend nobody's. This approach is based upon the worship of an imagined deity they call the "universal god". It is an invention of academia and a concession to some of the worst of teachings of the Nation of Islam.

The academicians are engaged in a frantic search for political correctness in religion while the Nation of Islam from its inception has made the destruction of black Christianity one of its major goals. Vicious attacks upon the character of individual black Christians, particularly preachers and denouncements of the efficacy of the Black church were cornerstones of the Nation of Islam's teaching during their heyday in the 1950's and 1960's. The greatest Muslim minister of this dispensation was Minister El Hajj Malik El Shabbazz (Malcolm X). In the final months of his ministry he made his peace with black Christianity, in the end honoring the church-led struggles for liberation. In doing so he paid homage to his own father who was a Garveyite Baptist preacher and a local leader of the Universal Negro Improvement Association.

The problem with ecumenism's so-called "universal god" is that he is a figment of the non-believers' imagination. He is a god that has no creed, no scriptures, no beliefs, no principles, no proverbs, no practices, no standards, no liturgy, no congregations, no pastors or prophets, no traditions, and no commandments. He is just a feel-good figment of the post-modern intellectual imagination. He is a god who accepts everybody and everything and is careful not to offend anyone by being critical of anything. This god is not the God of our ancestors whom we have known from time immemorial. He is not the God who guided our fore parents when they built the great civilizations of Mother Africa. He is not the Divine Creator known universally across the entire width and breadth of the African continent who established justice and mercy as the foundation of His measureless realm. He is not the God who traveled with our kidnapped ancestors across the Atlantic in the terrible holes of the slave ships. He is not the God our enslaved fore parents cried out to: "Father I stretch my hand to thee, no other help I know. If thou withdraw thyself from me, whither shall I go"? He is not the God of the spirituals, that awesome body of transcendent song, composed and sung as testimony to the goodness and faithfulness of God and to the primacy of his rule in the heavens and on earth. He is not the God of Paul Cuffee, Denmark Vesey, Nat Turner, Harriet Tubman, Frederick Douglas, Sojourner Truth, Henry McNeil Turner, Ida B. Wells, Marcus Garvey, Adam Clayton Powell and the countless other great heroes and heroines of our people. In other words he is a god we do not know. He is not our God and he cannot be made to replace Him who we do know from the testimony of our ancestors, from the teaching of our elders and from our own personal encounters.

When we send our children to college they are not adults. Despite the claims of popular lore and legal definition that young people are grown at eighteen, when they reach the campus they are in the final stages of adolescence, striving toward the beginnings of adulthood. In this post-adolescent, pre-adult stage they are still in need of the caring ministration of adults. Thrown into an alien atmosphere and surrounded by and having to live in intimate quarters with strangers, many of them often suffer from various physical symptoms of alienation and disorientation. As adolescents they are still subject to the dangerous effects of negative peer pressure. As freshmen particularly, female freshmen, they are the special targets of older students who plot and plan how to take advantage of their innocence, naiveté and lack of experience. We should be careful to provide a ministry for them that will give them succor in times of distress, provide for them a home away from home and a safe haven grounded in the timeless values of their familiar faith.

In those institutions that refuse to provide for our children's spiritual growth out of their own budgets and with their own resources it is incumbent upon our larger church bodies to do so. On white campuses various denominations, at their own expense, build, maintain and staff centers for their youth. The Catholics on state college campuses have Newman Centers, the Methodists have Wesleyan Centers, the white Baptists have Judson Centers where their student members find refuge and sanctuary from the threateningly irreligious aspects life of the campus. They have there a place of their own in which they can socialize with kindred spirits and avail themselves of the teaching and counseling resources provided by ministers specially prepared to address their needs. Only black denominations provide no resources for the spiritual care of our young people while they are away at college. Not to mention evangelical outreach to the unchurched and unsaved on those campuses. Then we wonder why our kids lose their Christian witness while on these campuses and some of them never regain their Christian walk. We send them to foreign environments infested with all sorts of contrary and perverse doctrines taught by mature, skilled, slick authority figures who attack our children's faith traditions. They are subjected to daily if not hourly attacks upon their most cherished values. Yet we leave them unarmed and unable to answer or defend their positions or to deal with critical challenges to the beliefs that they have held uncritically since childhood.

For instance they are criticized by Muslims who will tell them that Christianity is "the white man's religion" and that Islam is the original faith of African people. Our young people should have been taught in their homes and churches that Christianity was established in Egypt and Ethiopia six hundred years before the birth of the prophet Muhammad. Those that come to college unknowledgeable of critical areas of their faith need highly educated, specially prepared ministers who can handle the intellectual task of equipping them to understand, explain, defend and maintain their black Christian walk.

Those of our children who attend white colleges face a unique challenge in that they must be able to retain their sense of identity in the midst of an environment which constantly devalues them as individuals and their culture as a whole. The influx of black students on white campuses did not come about because the administrators of those schools finally discovered a generation of black students intelligent enough to handle the academic rigors of those institutions. The most knowledgeable of white people have known for centuries of the genius of the African people. They opened up their doors because of the pressures of the Civil Rights Movement. However, they also had a more sinister agenda in their decision to provide us with higher education. They knew that the leadership of the race for over a hundred years had primarily been prepared on black college campuses where the professors and administrators instilled in their students the African sense of collective responsibility. Those students were taught that individual success alone was not enough. The entire race must benefit from their exposure to higher education. Out of this ethos came the men and women whose motto was "uplift the race".

The Counter Intelligence Program (Cointelpro) which orchestrated the assassinations of Dr. King, Malcolm X, Fred Hampton, Mark Clark, the dismantling of SNCC, the serial killings of Black Panthers and finally the destruction of the Civil Rights Movement, had long term aspects to its attack on black progress. One of the stated goals of Cointelpro was the destruction of black leadership. This was accomplished through such activities as murder, jail and exile. At a lower level they destroyed marriages and destabilized families through the dissemination of false accusations of contrived infidelities to gullible husbands and wives.

The longer term approach was to recruit the best and the brightest, the cream of the crop of black high school students to attend white schools. Clearly the vast majority of black leaders attended black schools where they were inculcated with the communal value system of our people and a leadership philosophy based on service to the community. The white establishment believed that if they could bring these same young people who were destined to be our future leaders to their own institutions they could significantly effect what our leadership would look like ten, twenty, thirty years down the road. It turns out that they were right. The generations of students who attended white schools have not produced a leadership tradition that can in any way be positively compared with the generations that preceded them.

From 1955 to 1965 there was a distinct pattern of leadership preparation, emergence and productivity. Every five years almost like clockwork our community witnessed the emergence of new leadership cohorts that brought unique gifts to the scenes of local and national civil rights activity. In each instance these groups of young people in their late teens and early twenties introduced new tactics

172

and strategies and founded new national organizations.

In 1955 Dr. King's generation gave us direct action in general, bus boycotts in particular and a new organization called the Southern Christian Leadership Conference (SCLC). In 1960 black college students gave us sit-ins, freedom rides, voter registration and the Student Non-Violent Coordinating Committee (SNCC). In 1965 another generation of students and youthful community activists gave us the philosophy of Black Power and its attendant, derivative strategies and tactics of armed self-defense, black studies, Pan-Africanism, and opposition and resistance to the war in Vietnam. Their organization was a transformed SNCC (changing from Student Non-Violent Coordinating Committee to Student "National" Coordinating Committee in effect repudiating non-violence) and the Black Panther Party. Due to the ravages of Cointelpro the effective leadership of all three cohorts was wiped out.

We have failed to produce since the late sixties a new generation that even begins to approximate the accomplishments of these previous groups. Our major leaders today continue to be men and women of the late fifties and sixties. We have no new thoughts, novel approaches, and innovative strategies. Where we have a few new faces they deal in old ideas many of them long since discredited. We have lost two generations of promise sacrificed on the altar of integration to the false god of white supremacy.

The atmosphere of white campuses even to this day is one of alienation and isolation in which almost everything black is devalued and held in contempt. One of the most important concerns of black people is learning how to cope with racism. This is a constant topic on black campuses. Such a discussion is hard to come by within a white university classroom. If raised by a student, white or black, they will often be roundly attacked by most of the class who will be supported by the instructor in insisting that racism does not exist or that if it does, black racism is as prevalent and as dangerous as white racism.

One of the most dramatic indications of what white college education has done for us is what has become of the Harvard University African American Studies Department. I sat as a member of the working committee given the responsibility of establishing that department in the summer of 1969. It was a joint student–faculty committee composed of seven faculty members all white save one and six students. As students ranging in age from eighteen to twenty-one years we did the majority of the everyday administration of the office in the basement of University Hall in the center of Harvard yard. We interviewed and hired a secretary, established a budget, and along with the adult faculty members we designed a curriculum. As individuals we traveled across the country and consulted with black leaders and scholars such as Dr. St. Clair Drake and Rev. Jesse Jackson. We believed that we were building a department that would train future freedom fighters

In 1999 the Department sponsored a thirtieth year anniversary celebration that was a marvel of intellectual dishonesty and moral corruptness. It falsely presented a revisionist history of the founding of the department that was a celebration of Harvard altruism and liberalism not a commemoration of a successful student rebellion. The administration only agreed to the establishment of the department after a two week long strike and student boycott. Only after Harvard weathered a storm of protests by the black student organization (the Association of African and Afro-American Students at Harvard and Radcliffe) in conjunction with the mostly white Students for a Democratic Society (SDS) .

But at the so-called celebration it was only the establishmentarian type of Negro students who had played mostly quiescent roles during the demand for a department that were given recognition. These students' major strategy to force the administration to cede us a department was to put on three piece suits and hold a press conference because they had "friends at the New York Times". They were too naïve to understand that the people who owned the New York Times were the people who ran places like Harvard. The militant student leaders who organized and participated in the disruptive activities and events that forced the administration's hand were ignored and written out of history, replaced by a group of non-confrontational people who were willing to go along with the charade that the department was the result of white altruism not black struggle.

It was as if there was a commemoration of the end of segregation in Birmingham and Sheriff Bull Connor was feted as the engineer of the desegregation with no mention of Dr. Martin Luther, King, Jr., Rev. Fred Shuttlesworth, marches, fire hoses, jailings, beatings, shootings, the bombing of the 16th Street Baptist Church and the murder of four little black girls there attending Sunday school. Six former students were given specially minted W.E.B. DuBois medallions. (What a travesty and an act of sacrilege to invoke the name of a great truth-teller in the service of such a monstrous lie!) Leslie Francis (Skip) Griffin, the president of The Association of African and African American Students at Harvard and Radcliffe (Afro) who led us through that great time of challenge was left unrecognized while another student was introduced as the president of Afro during that period. This former student gleefully (no shame to his game) stood in someone else's place receiving honors he knew were not his and delivered the day's major address.

We believed that African American Studies departments would be havens of truth in the midst of institutions given to racist lies. Instead we find that the generations of black scholars and so-called leaders prepared in white institutions made deals betraying and corrupting the high ideals and lofty expectations that built those departments.

Just for the historical record the six black students who

sat on the committee that established the Afro-American Studies Department were L. F. (Skip) Griffin, Jr.; Loretta Hardge; Kathryn Bowser; Mark D. Smith; Myles Link and myself.

But far worse, in the spring of 2003 the same department sponsored a week-long conference on the works of gangster rapper Tupac Shakur. They invested tens of thousands of dollars and gathered some of the supposedly best minds of our people to study the raps of Mr. Shakur as though he were some major black leader whose words give direction to this and future generations. This same department has not invested that kind of time, money or energy studying Toussaint L'Ouverture, Paul Cuffee, Frederick Douglass, Ida B. Wells, Marcus Garvey, Mary McLeod Bethune, Adam Clayton Powell, Jr., Paul Robeson, Fannie Lou Hamer, Kwame Nkrumah, Martin Luther King, Jr. and other people who unquestionably made contributions to the progress of our people that have made them true immortals.

What has Mr. Shakur contributed to the uplift and benefit of our people other than being a popular entertainer whose recordings of black self-destructiveness are mostly bought by suburban white teenagers who love immersing themselves in lurid visions of black pathology? He was a self-proclaimed thug who advocated drug use and sale, rape of black women and the murder of his brothers. He had etched across his stomach the self declaration and definition "Thug for Life". Went to jail for gang rape in which by his own testimony he surrendered a women who was visiting him to his friends because as told her he "shared everything with his boys". He created a blood feud with his former friend and fellow gangster rapper Christopher Wallace AKA Biggie Smalls or the Notorious B.I.G by boasting in public and on record that he had had sex with Biggie's wife. His last act before his unsolved murder was running across a hotel lobby in Las Vegas with twenty or more of his fellow thugs from the Death Row

176

posse attacking a man who was alone; beating and stomping the man as he helplessly rolled on the ground. He didn't have enough heart to stand toe-to-toe and go blow-for-blow against the man by himself in a "fair one", in other words one-on-one, which is the classic black male measurement of true manhood.

Mr. Shakur started no organization, built no institution, promulgated no positive philosophy, wrote no books, built no schools, attacked no bastions of racism, headed no movement, married no wife and raised no children, but this supposedly leading institution of black intellectual excellence chose him to present to its students and the black community at large as an icon of black manhood. As the old folks would say: "Shame on you that you don't have enough sense to be ashamed of yourself"!

For black students who attend white colleges the Bible gives us instruction on how to deal with trying to obtain a true education in a hostile environment. The Old Testament book of Daniel is the story of Hebrew children kidnapped and held as hostages by a foreign power: the Babylonians. Subjected to the intention of the Babylonians to remake the Hebrews in their own image the heroes of the story, Daniel, Shadrach, Mesach and Abednego resisted the pressure to become intellectual and spiritual Babylonians and instead maintained their own identity as Hebrews.

Historically, when young people are forced to attend the schools of their enemies it is as hostages. When a student understands that he or she is being held hostage by their enemies they can clearly comprehend the true nature of the experience as an adversarial one and therefore the role that they must play in it as resistors and rebels. Too many of our young people mistakenly believe that the experience of being educated by white people is the greatest thing in the world and they fully give themselves over to it, allowing themselves to be remade in someone else's image to their detriment and to the detriment of the future of our people.

When one attends the school of an enemy to one's own

people and their way of life that person must be clear that they are not there to embrace or internalize the entire teaching of those people, especially, as regards morals. They go their as spies with the covert mission of using their closeness to their enemies to seek out the roots of evil in their intellectual system, analyze the inner workings of oppressive and exploitative structures and design instruments and weapons to defeat their strategies. Their challenge is to recognize what is worthy in those people's teaching and what is unworthy. As the old saying would have it to "eat the meat and throw away the bone". To be able to think critically and creatively enough to understand and comprehend what they have been taught that can benefit their people and what cannot be brought back home with them. The old folks had a saying when I was coming up: *"You don't bring home everything you find out in the alley. Some things you find in the alley, you leave in the alley"*

White schools were determined to instill within their black students their own sense of individual prosperity alone as the sole measurement of success in life. Teaching the imperative ethic of service to one's people was the guiding rule of black higher education. As one generation put it "lifting as we climb" Unfortunately white schools and black colleges that imitate them have done a good job of making the classic black leader an endangered species. We are becoming more and more like them everyday in putting individual accomplishment and personal wealth over service to God's people.

The white conservative churches upon witnessing the increasing secularization of their denominational colleges made two outstanding countermoves which we ought to find instructive. First, they took back control of the schools from those forces that they perceived as having left the pathways of Christian principles and morality. Secondly, they founded new schools which they could be confident would represent their values.

178

The increasing secularization of black colleges is one of the great tragedies of the latter half of the twentieth century. Like the ancient Hebrews in the time of the Judges too many of our people, after experiencing prosperity, decided that they would get rid of the old-fogy notions of spirituality and religiosity that were out of step with the practices of the people that they lived amongst. In the bible the Hebrews became ashamed of the fact that they were led by prophets and judges, men and women who derived their power of leadership from the spirit of God, who was concerned about divine considerations of Love, Truth, Wisdom, Justice, Mercy. They wanted instead to have kings like the people that were their neighbors, rulers who were militarily powerful and wealthy according to the shallow standards of the world. They felt ashamed not to be part of what was perceived and promoted as the prevailing motifs of the modern scene.

It is the same with our people in the last half of the twentieth century and the beginning years of the twenty-first century. The desire for integration has driven us to do everything we can to be like our neighbors. The people that we live amongst are oriented differently than we are. For them religion is a one hour, one day of the week experience. It is a mostly empty ritual because it has no effect on how they live their lives, how they treat each other and other people the rest of the time. They even maintain in their approach to life that spiritual and moral considerations should be separated from concerns of a more practical nature such as politics and economics. It is this separation that allows them to claim Christianity yet practice slavery, capitalism, and militarism. Unfortunately more and more of our schools have lost their original sense of mission and are becoming more and more like white schools in their approach to education in two critical areas-- administration and educational philosophy.

Until this generation of black college presidents the pinnacle of their careers was to ascend to the presidency of one of the leading private schools such as Fisk, Hampton, Lincoln, Morehouse, Bennett, Dillard, Edward Waters, or Wilberforce. As the old saying goes: "From there they would go to heaven". With the greater opportunities for a very few black scholars to head white colleges black college presidencies have become for far too many merely a stepping stone to more lucrative and, in their minds, more prestigious positions at a white school. In order to prove their qualification to lead a white institution these administrators must demonstrate in their leadership of a black school their commitment to the philosophy of the white world.

I heard a candidate for a black college presidency give a mind-blowing response to a question about what were the differences between the culture of a black college and a white one. His answer was that that he believed in a color-blind society and that there was no difference between black and white institutions of higher education. He went on to say further that nothing was going on on a black campus that was not also happening at the white college he was then presiding over. The irony is that having been hired anyway his first challenge was bomb threats to the black campus from the Klu Klux Klan.

During the golden years of black college education that I roughly locate at the first half of the twentieth century our schools were distinguished by the excellence of their leadership. Those leaders such as Mary McLeod Bethune, Benjamin Elijah Mays, Mordecai Johnson, and Vernon Johns were scholars, moralists and visionaries. They recognized that their challenge and mission was to recruit, raise and train generations of African-American freedom fighters who would continue to enlarge the vision of our ancestors in building "a nation within a nation". It was the spiritual aspect that stood out foremost amongst them. From the spirit comes the clarity of the vision and the power to be faithful to it.

This generation of intellectual and spiritual giants was

180

succeeded by a generation of scholars. These leaders did not have the unique spiritual qualities of their forbears but they were true scholars of African American history and culture and were committed to the ancient task of uplift and independence.

Today too many of the contemporary presidents of black schools have neither the spiritual genius nor academic mastery of their predecessors. They are neither visionaries nor scholars and many of them are not even competent spokespeople. They are a cohort of technicians. Their forte is not in any particular field of scholarship but rather in their know-how of the financial and political mechanics of running a school. The people I spoke of in the first generation were not only college presidents but leaders of the race. This current cohort of black college presidents are narrow in their scope of vision and activity. They are merely technicians of higher education administration and seldom express any ambition to provide us with leadership beyond the limited environs of their campuses. Worst of all their approach to teaching our young people is merely to prepare them to get good jobs in white corporations.

Too many black schools now see their primary responsibility as providing worker drones for Fortune 500 corporations rather than training a generation of authentic African American entrepreneurs to shape a new economy that will benefit our people as a whole. We have watched for the past thirty years independent business men and women from Korea, China, Puerto Rico, and the Arab world take over the retail outlets in the black community. We rant and rave and criticize but we do nothing to maintain or establish black-owned institutions. Historically this was not the case. The insurance company, funeral home, soul food restaurants, mom and pop grocery, beauty parlors, barber shops, dry-cleaners, Laundromats, shoe-shine stands and record stores were the economic cornerstones of every black community. But we also had our own hotels, hospitals, airports, professional baseball leagues, bus companies, at least one automobile factory, movie studios and theatres, to name only a few areas of black business endeavor. The only businesses we continue to control today are the church, the funeral parlor, the barber shop and the beauty parlor. Unbelievably enough, national conglomerates of white funeral homes have begun to make serious inroads into the monopoly of our funerals that black-owned funeral parlors have enjoyed for over a century. Our schools need to produce aggressive creative entrepreneurs dedicated to the proposition of developing black businesses which serve as the cornerstone for the uplift of our neighborhoods.

This nation has abandoned even the slightest concern about the condition of our people and the best they have to offer "the least of these" is time in jail as the new workers on post-modern chain gangs. It is up to us to come up with creative and courageous solutions to the dilemmas that our people face. We should be able to expect the members of our established intelligentsias on college campuses to do just that. The idea of college as an ivory tower fantasyland where uninvolved, detached scholars while away the years in sublime isolation from the everyday practicalities of real life has always been a false notion. Colleges and universities serve the important role of think tanks to apply the genius of a people to addressing the real issues and solving the real problems that those people must cope with in order to survive and prosper.

When I was working as an administrator and adjunct faculty member at Northern Illinois University some twenty years ago a white faculty member suggested in a meeting that it was not right for the university to be expected to address the problems of impoverished communities and powerless people because it was not the role of the academy to be involved in such mundane affairs as politics and economics. I corrected him by making it clear that the university has always served the interests of the wealthy. That if Mr. Rockefeller or Mr. Carnegie or

Mr. Mellon or Mr. Gates had a problem that they wanted the best minds at their chosen institution to address; it was done eagerly and enthusiastically. Poor people should have similar access to the best minds of this nation addressing their concerns.

Black colleges historically have understood their mission as being to utilize their resources for the uplift of the entire people. There is no better example of this than Dr. George Washington Carver's work at Tuskegee Institute when he dedicated his scientific genius to the innovative development of marketable products he derived from the crops of black farmers.

Our schools must become institutions of creative thought and tangible activity applying the measureless human resources of genius and vision to making our world a better place for both present and unborn generations. One thing we must consider is spin-off corporations. One of the great moves forward in this nation's economy for the past twenty years has been the transformation of America into an economy based on information rather than manufacturing. Factories were shipped overseas in a frantic search for cheap labor while white collar computing jobs became the basis of today's global prosperity of American business. This transformation was engineered in the graduate schools of this nation through a phenomenon known as "spin-off corporations". The computer firms that comprise high tech corridors of Northern California, Cambridge, Massachusetts, and High Point-Raleigh-Durham, North Carolina were originally conceptualized and organized out of graduate courses at Berkley, Stanford, Harvard, MIT, Duke University and the University of North Carolina.

We have no comparable practice in black schools. We are not producing entrepreneurs but Fortune 500 clones and drones who see as their purpose in life fitting in and getting along in a corporate culture that will also keep people of color in their place at the bottom or at best in the middle of their executive cultures. The lack of jobs for our people cannot mean other than the continued consignment of future generations to poverty, drugs and jail.

The ethnic groups that control the retail outlets in our communities did not come to where they are through standard American business practices. They did not initiate their businesses with start up loans from the Small Business Administration and then further financing from the local bank with an eye on going public with a stock offering on Wall Street. Most of these owners of small local businesses which employ tens of thousands of their people and provide a decent living for their families including sending children and grandchildren to colleges and universities have a unique manner of initial finance which is peculiar to the ethnic group involved. I have heard snatches of conversation of how both Korean and Arab stores are financed through cooperative groups of both fellow merchants and family. We are as capable of cooperative economics as anybody else. We proved that in Africa and in America after the Civil War. It is imperative that our schools begin to produce scholars with the skills of businesspeople but the innovative souls of artists and the aggressive courage of warriors.

We also need to reach out to other people. It is unworthy of us and an indication of a sense of inferiority that we act as if we have nothing to offer any students but our own children. Colleges and universities are supposed to be multicultural and international institutions. All great institutions aggressively recruit international student bodies. We have remained provincial in our approach to attracting and enrolling students from all over the world. Our schools should be problem solving think tanks that confront and engage the most critical issues that affect our condition as a people. Part of that condition involves our relations or rather lack of effective relationships with other ethnic and national groups. As millions of natives of Africa, the Caribbean, Central and South America and Asia change the demographic identity of this country we have not moved as a people to define and refine our relationships with these people.

We need coalitions with other non-white population groups. White schools use the education of foreign people as an inroad into the life of those people by tying generations of their new leaders to themselves in terms of the identification of former students as alumni and alumnae of these schools. Not to mention inculcating those students with the philosophy, world view and value system of white America. When these students return home and ascend to positions of power they see America as a friend and ally. We need to form our own alliances with other non-white groups whether they are from nations near this country's shores or from the faraway reaches of Asia.

There are all kinds of historical precedents for the internationalization of black colleges and universalities. Morehouse used to win swimming championships in the fifties and sixties because they recruited swimmers from Puerto Rico. The Afro-Caribbean enclave called Bluefield on the eastern coast of Nicaragua used to send students to [then] Tuskegee Institute back in the 1930's. Hampton Institute had a mission to educate Native Americans from its inception and had a significant Native American population during its first decades of existence. (Though it is true that as a white-run racist institution in its early days its approach to educating them was as racist and colonial as its education of its black students).

The reality is clear. It is possible for black institutions to reach out to, attract and recruit students from diverse populations all over the world. It should be done with a particular purpose in mind. To establish a basis for mutual identification with those people that we need to act in conjunction with as we struggle against the so-called New World Order that is just a new euphemism for continued international white supremacy.

The goal of the established powers of this nation is to

keep working class people separated on the basis of color and culture. The union movement in this country remained retarded and mostly ineffective as long as the white working class kept their unions lily-white and refused to allow black workers to join, thereby forcing our ancestors into the role of strike-breaking scabs. It has been a strategy for centuries of racist conquest to organize color stratified social systems that kept black or full-blooded native peoples at the bottom while lighter-skinned or so-called half-breeds were given a higher status. There never was a legally established mulatto class in America because of the one-drop rule which held that "one drop" of Negro blood rendered one as black as the most pure-blooded African that just got off the slave ship. In other places such as the Caribbean, particularly Haiti, in India, in South Africa with its "coloreds", lighter skinned or mixed people were encouraged to identify with the white ruling class over and against the black people at the bottom of the social structure through endowments of a little more privilege, status and opportunity.

The same thing portends to happen in this country if the other non-whites are convinced that it's to their advantage to accept having fewer opportunities than whites but more than that of black people. We can counter this racist strategy by forging life-long friendships and transgenerational alliances with other people when their children can identify with us because of our children's shared experiences as schoolmates. When our alumni groups meet they ought to be composed of diverse populations. For instance our seminaries ought to recruit ministers from the bourgeoning Protestant congregations of South and Central America, Korea and Japan. The churches of these people should fellowship with our own, individually and in our local, state and national conventions. We should be sharing the genius of our greatest theologians and preachers with the world and learning from theirs. We should not allow the major teachings of Christianity to remain the closed fiefdom of a failed and compromised European Christianity that has been unable to change the amoral course of European and American society as it continues to oppress and exploit the majority of the world's populations and resources.

Our schools should have international studies and international relations departments. Native American scholars ought to find a welcome haven on black college campuses just as the first Africans to escape slavery found refuge in the camps and villages of the Creek, the Choctaw, the Cherokee, the Chickasaw, the Arkansas, and the Natchez to name only a few. We should be the people who establish departments of Native American Studies. The alliance of Indians and Africans was the most effective counter force against slavery until the forced removal of the Southeast nations in the infamous Trail of Tears. We have forgotten that the Underground Railroad had branches that ran South and West to the Indian Nations as well as north to Canada. Anthropologists have estimated that as many of sixty percent of African American have some Native American ancestry.

There is no question that the only people in this nation in worse shape than black people are our former allies and kin people who are languishing in unimaginable poverty and deprivation on reservations that we as Buffalo Soldiers helped our common oppressors drive them to a hundred and more years ago. We cannot with integrity demand reparations from white people without considering what we owe Native Americans for our role in the robbery of their lands, the mass murder of entire populations, the slaughter of the buffalo, and their imprisonment in the wilderness ghettos we call reservations. Certainly, recruiting their students with scholarships, hiring Native American faculty, staff and administrator, and establishing departments of Native American Studies, and organizing branches of our schools on Indian reservations could all be forms of reparations.

The presence of international students, scholars and professors on our campuses ought to be forums of cross-cultural exchange and learning whereby we can forge a new era of understanding. We can learn from Asians and Arabs how they are able to put together business consortiums that have resulted in their controlling so many of the retail outlets in our own communities. We should be preparing our own ambassadors to go out to foreign countries to develop relationships based upon a more humane interaction with those peoples according to our own African and Christian-derived humane standards of diplomacy not tied to the corrupt practices of exploitative European capitalism.

The immortal words of Marcus Garvey continue to ring in our ears. "Where are the black man's businesses? Where are his shipping lines? Where are his factories? Where are his ambassadors? His men and women of great affairs?"

If the current schools cannot or will not do that then we need to create a new generation of black colleges and universities to meet the current challenges.

He who fills his head with other people's words will find that he has no place to put his own. **African Proverb**

VII. Fraternities and Sororities

Black fraternities and sororities are among the oldest and most honored social organizations in the black community. They have played a prominent role on college campuses, black and white, and in the lives of black alumni and alumnae since their inception in the early 1900's. Even the shortest list of some of their members constitutes an honor role of some of our greatest heroes and heroines. Paul Robeson, Shirley Chisholm, Martin Luther King, Jr., Debbie Allen, Thurgood Marshall, Zora Neale Hurston, Adam Clayton Powell, Jr., and Sarah Vaughn are just a few great African Americans who were members of fraternities and sororities.

Black fraternities and sororities began as a response to the organization of white fraternities and sororities. It was originally a defense mechanism but ended up being blind imitation whose long term consequences were not well thought out. Fraternities and sororities are social organizations based on socio-economic status. One thing that is clear about all of them is that you must be a college student in order to join. This renders them elite organizations which deny entrance to the vast majority of black youth who are not college students. White students organized fraternities in order to have social lives which would not be infiltrated by their inferiors. Until the development of land-grant colleges in the fourth quarter of the nineteenth century almost everyone on a college campus was upper-class, certainly no lower than upper middle class. Therefore the students could freely socialize with anyone and everyone on campus knowing that they were all of similar backgrounds. The organization of the land-grant state colleges and universities introduced people of working class backgrounds onto campuses. The

189

response on the part of the upper-class students in order to protect themselves from mistakenly associating with and being contaminated by their inferiors was to organize fraternities and sororities. People desiring membership had to first of all be invited, and then undergo a series of examinations to prove that they were the "right kind of people." If these groups did not want lower-class white people around them you know that they did not want any kind of black people as members.

The response on the part of black students was to organize their own fraternities. However they used the same criteria that the white sororities and fraternities used-- class background. The middle class or upper class of black people in those days was strongly based on skin color. It was the children of the slave master who emerged from slavery with a significantly greater amount of material resources in money, land, property and education. Many of these mixed people organized their societal lives around their supposed superiority to darker-skinned black people. There were "blue vein" societies in which membership was limited to people who were light enough for their veins to show through their skin. Others had the "paper bag test" wherein if you were darker than the standard brown paper bag you were too dark to get in. There were even churches that painted their front doors a certain shade of brown. Upon reaching the entrance, potential worshippers were to hold their hands up to the door, if their skin color was darker than the door they were to know that they were not welcome there. There was a clear color scheme behind the organization of the black fraternal orders so that they ended up practicing the same form of exclusionism on other black people that had been practiced on them.

However, all was not negative about them in their first fifty years of existence. They certainly provided a supportive, even nurturing, environment for their members, particularly on white campuses where the few black students were social outcasts and pariahs often not being allowed to live in dormitories with white students or being allowed to take their meals in the campus cafeterias. They also served as sources of positive peer pressure pushing their members toward academic excellence. I have listened to alumni of Lincoln University boast of how in their day in the forties and fifties the groups competed with one another for the highest cumulative grade point average and for leadership of campus organizations like student government.

Still they were not beyond criticism. The esteemed black scholar E. Franklin Frazier took fraternal and sororal life to task in his classic sociological study entitled *Black Bourgeoisie*. This book should be on the "must read" list of anyone interested in understanding the dynamics of life in the black middle class.

The advent of the civil rights movement caused the fraternities and sororities to lose their predominance as leaders of black campuses because these groups did not throw themselves with the full force of their national structures into the struggle. The heroes and heroines on black college campuses by the sixties were no longer the heartiest-partying, most fashionable and expensive clothes wearing, style-conscious, conspicuous consumption leaders of the fraternities but the men and women who were laying their lives on the line trying to forge a better world for the entire race. Fraternities and sororities lost their social cachet to the sit-inners, freedom-riders, and voter registration organizers who ventured into the bastions of Klan-led racism of the Deep South often to be rewarded with harassment, jailing, beatings, torture and murder. It was only after the movement died in the early seventies that they came back with a vengeance infected by the same premature sense of freedom that fueled the Me Generation's massive and unfortunate move into public hedonism.

Too many fraternities and sororities operate as little more than college gangs. Gang life has unfortunately

191

become the paradigm for social organization and interaction for far too many black youth. The "us against them" mentality and the willingness to fight over the most petty concerns has, primarily through the instrument of the media, immigrated from the most impoverished, deprived and uneducated neighborhoods onto college campuses and into groups that used to be characterized as the "elite".

While serving as chaplain at Lincoln University in Pennsylvania I witnessed on an almost daily basis fraternity and sorority violence serving the same role as gang violence in the most lawless sections of the ghetto.

Though hazing has been outlawed in practically every state in the nation it is so universally practiced that the laws against it, for all practical purposes, are not worth the paper they are printed on. Hazing or the practices of physical, psychological, sexual, mental and emotional exploitation and abuse of students who are pledging (in that trial period to determine whether or not they will be confirmed as members) is done in white and black fraternities and sororities. But there are significant differences based on race in the dynamics of the two groups. Both engage in practices so dangerous that literally scores of students have died over the past two decades as a result of being hazed. Hank Nuer, a white attorney specializing in issues surrounding hazing and the author of Wrongs Of Passage says that while white kids are killed as a result of binge drinking, black youth are beaten to death.

It is a common sight on black campuses to see both boys and girls who are "on line" show up in class or the cafeteria suffering from various kinds of injuries which they explain away the same way an abused wife, husband or child lies about the wounds suffered at the hands of violent family members. Everybody knows that the canes and paddles carried by the senior members have a much more serious function than that of public display. They are among the chief instruments used to beat the youngsters who are seeking acceptance in the group. It is only when someone is finally killed or hospitalized with life-threatening or career-ending injuries that the news media will give us a quick glance at the inner realities of fraternity and sorority life.

What we then see are young people lined up in isolated locales, sometimes dormitory rooms, sometimes off-campus apartments, sometimes secluded wilderness areas. Sometimes they are hooded so that they can't see their attackers, cannot defend themselves or even attempt to ward off blows. These beatings can go on for hours. They are proscribed only by the limits of the endurance of the attackers. This is done in the name of brotherhood. I don't know of any black family or white or Asian or Indian either in which the sons are taught to bond together as brothers through a process of having the older brothers humiliate, brutalize, torture, rape and even kill one another. If such goings on were to occur in a family it would be prosecuted as child abuse and domestic violence.

The fraternities and sororities use the neediness of those seeking belonging, value and social status as weapons against them. They take serious and sometimes fatal advantage of low self-esteem, loneliness and isolation to satisfy their sadistic lust to hurt, maim and kill. Practically every report of hazing incidents indicates that there are only a few super violent individuals who commit the greatest amount of damage on the pledges. They are enabled to do so by the majority of members who are prevented from acting in defense of the pledges by peer pressure.

I want to concentrate for a moment on the personalities of the ones most driven to commit violence and do physical damage to another human being, one who he or she will describe as "brother" or "sister." People who are capable of such cold blooded acts of conscienceless violence are diagnosed and labeled by mental health specialists as "sociopaths." These are individuals whose own history of child abuse has not been properly dealt with in therapy or some other healing experience and a result they are infused with such anger and desire for revenge that they lack all normal human sentiment for their victims. They are capable of the most extreme violence. Add to the mix the fact that their victims are helpless and are not allowed to defend themselves at all but must fully expose themselves to the most brutal treatment if they want to become "brothers" and "sisters". This strips away another possible source of constraint.

The rule in real life is: "You got to bring some to get some." Typically, in order for you engage in violence you must expose yourself to the same risks you are trying impose on others. Frederick Douglas taught us, on his occasion of being sent to a "professional Negro breaker" at sixteen because he was becoming a recalcitrant and rebellious slave, that the easier a person is whipped the more often they are whipped. When Douglass strove against the breaker for hours and finally fought him to a standstill he was never again beaten. When you remove the risk you enable the predator. All predators, even the most powerful lions, seek out the weak, the old, the newborn, the helpless and defenseless as their prey.

Then there is the assumed use of drugs and alcohol to further fuel the fire and lessen any sense of restraint. There is also the absence of elders. These activities are carried out by young men in their early to mid-twenties. They are not yet real men themselves since they seldom have wives and children for whom that they are responsible and to whom they are accountable. It is the role of the mature man in every human society to restrain the excesses of young males.

That which is most frightening to me is the role that self-hatred must play in these proceedings. We know that there is a powerful sub-stratum strain of self-hatred existing in our race. We know it because we are the most numerous targets of our own violence. We know it because the term "black" is still used more as a curse word than as a

194

compliment. We know it because the word "nigger" is used more often to preface an attack than it is used as a term of affection. We have to try to imagine what it means for a young, frightened, resentful, angry, wounded, insecure, immature, violence-prone, high or drunk, young man who hates himself and everybody like him to be allowed to take all of his frustrations out on some helpless, defenseless person while others cheer him on. This is a prescription for murder. It is only a testimony to the health and strength of these youngsters that more have them have not been killed.

Young people join these groups because of a need to belong. They obviously suffer from a terribly inadequate sense of self-value and an almost pathological lack of self-esteem, therefore they are motivated by an overwhelming need to belong to an organization that will give them, not only a sense of belonging, but also value and status. In order to achieve this belonging and status they sell their souls to the devil, completely surrendering their sense of right and wrong, embracing whatever the organization insists is right and rejecting whatever it regards as wrong. Thus the organization becomes a cult and functions as their religion.

Of what efficacy is a religion that practices torture and human sacrifice and engages in sexual orgies as their worship? Their high priests are power-mad, egomaniacal, immature, young people who have no wisdom to bring to these situations. Rather than serve those under their charge according to the Judeo-Christian concept of ministry, they demand to be served, often in the most egregious manner, designed to be utterly humiliating to the person trying to get into the organization. But it is the violence that is of the most concern. To lose a single human life to fraternity violence is unacceptable. To have had almost twenty young people killed in incidents of assault and torture is unthinkable. It is a form of human sacrifice. For the organizations it is an acceptable level of loss. It must be because they continue unabated the very same practices

195

that led to the deaths-- beating, branding, sleep-deprivation, verbal abuse, mental cruelty, humiliation, isolation, group sex, gang rape, blindfolding, bondage, denial of the free exercise of choice, no establishment of boundaries or the expression of individuality. These are the normal practices of the so-called "Greeks" among black college students.

Along with the violence of hazing, another prominent component of fraternal life is sexual promiscuity and sexual violence. One of the most important advantages of fraternity membership is access to sex. Rape is one of the most prevalent features of fraternity cultures. Most fraternity rapes seldom come to trial because they are covered up by administrators who are also fraternity members. Boys who don't have the personal confidence to approach girls on their own have to resort to doing so in groups. Fraternity rapes are very seldom solitary affairs. They are most likely group rapes called "running a train" in which any number of "brothers" will take advantage of the usually unwitting victim who may have been drugged, drunk or just too weak, isolated, frightened or incapacitated to successfully resist. The fraternities also have female auxiliaries whose primary purpose is to serve as sexual surrogates to the male members. These girls allow themselves to be used like that in order to obtain the social prestige of being identified with as belonging to the fraternity.

The primary reason that no progress will be made in changing these behaviors on black campuses is because an inordinate percentage of faculty members and administrators are themselves members of these organizations. Even the administrators specifically responsible for monitoring these organizations will, more likely than not, be members themselves. Thus you have a situation very much reminiscent of the police being allowed to investigate themselves in incidents of alleged police brutality. The older "black Greeks" serve in the role of protector for the younger members.

In a notorious incident at Lincoln University in February of 1999 a student on an Alpha line was sodomized with a baseball bat. His injuries were so severe that his intestines fell out of his distended rectum and it took two operations within a twenty-four hour period to stop the blood loss and repair the damage. The administration at first tried to exercise damage control when the president issued a gag order (Executive Order #001) stating that no employee of the university was allowed to discuss the incident with the press, a clear violation of the constitutional rights of free speech and academic freedom, and for a preacher like myself, the free exercise of religion. An unstoppable student uproar led to the administration taking some disciplinary steps against the identifiable fraternity members who had taken part in the incident. Fraternity members in retaliation provided the university community and the press with videotapes of the vice-president of student affairs engaging in hazing activities. However a faculty tribunal appointed by the president (also a member of the same fraternity) found the vice-president not guilty in spite of the videotaped record of his involvement. Hank Nuer in his book, Wrongs of Passage points out just such a scenario as one of the reasons hazing is so difficult to stop. He explains that crimes are supposed to be investigated by the police not by a committee of faculty members assigned to investigate the people who sign their paychecks.

Typically, however, the older fraternity members do their job and seldom do fraternities ever receive more than a slap on the wrist for the worst kinds of behaviors. One might well wonder what is going on that grown people in their thirties, forties, fifties and sixties identify so strongly with criminal behavior of young people in their teens and twenties. I suggest it is because these older people are also still living the fraternity life, albeit underground or as the young people put it on the "down low."

The preeminent black sociologist, E. Franklin Frazier, pointed out in his classic study Black Bourgeoisie that while white men and women end their fraternal activities upon graduation into the higher, more responsible realm of adult life, black people often remain active in these college-based groups for the rest of their lives. Much of hazing results from the fact that the everyday activities of fraternal groups on campuses are not being designed, led, directed, or monitored by the elders of the fraternities. Instead they allow young people at twenty to have total control of another young person 17, 18 or 19. This is a formula for disaster. As Jesus said: "If the blind lead the blind they both fall in a ditch."

It is not only the physical and psychic damage done to the fraternity members themselves that is at issue. It is also because these organizations are lifted up as the trendsetters and role models on our campuses. Just as athletics are so often over-emphasized, the perverted socializing of fraternities and sororities are given prominence all out of proportion to their real numbers on black college campuses.

The fact that so many administrators and faculty members are fraternity boys and sorority girls gives them the power to confer prominence on these organizations that do very little to contribute to the real reason for the existence of the school. I have not heard of such a study being done, but I am sure that we will find that fraternity and sorority members hold faculty and administrative positions on our campuses all out of proportion to their true numbers among black educators. There would be little to criticize if their disproportionate presence resulted in greater academic successes among the student bodies that they lead, guide, teach and instruct. The reality is that a decline in both academic performance and moral rectitude in black higher education has occurred on their watch and someone must be held responsible. I believe that the solution is to have mature men and women placed in charge of the pledge lines. People who are morally healthy and wise according to their years, who have no need to exploit young people's innocence and weaknesses and entertain no need to satisfy some perverse craving for power or for pleasure, should be the people in charge of taking these young people through such a major transitional period in their lives.

Fraternal and sororal pledging is supposed to be a kind of rite of passage into manhood and womanhood. What role does brutality play in teaching someone to be an adult? They are also supposed to be brotherhoods and sisterhoods. How does humiliating, objectifying, exploiting and dehumanizing people bind them to you as your brothers and sisters? It sounds more like a criminally dysfunction family engaged in a multiple forms of child abuse

VIII. DATING AND SEX

Sex is the source of the greatest power that exists in the human community. It is the channel through which new life is brought into being. Furthermore, it is the adhesive that binds men and women into the most intensive, satisfying and enduring relationships. There are few bonds between men and women greater than those of sharing the intimacies of penetration, conception, pregnancy, birth and the rearing of children. The contemporary terms "my baby daddy" and "my baby mama" trivialize and make a mockery of the sacred responsibilities and relationships of parents to one another and to their children. Even without children the bonds that sex creates between couples are so powerful that the pain resulting from misuse and breakdown often drives people insane. Emotional breakdowns, depression, alcoholism, child neglect and abuse, drug addiction, promiscuity, violence and murder are all classic consequences of not just divorce, but the end of any love relationship in which sex is involved. The emotional ties forged in the crucible of a loving intimate relationship are of such a nature that the human community has never fully been able to comprehend or control them.

One of the purposes of marriage is to organize a stable environment for sexual relationships. Given the common failure of marriage, which is an institution as old as the human community, it is easy to understand that relationships outside of matrimony are at even greater risk. Even in today's violence-ridden, gang, drug, and crime culture most murders are still hot-blooded crimes of passion involving the betrayal of love and the breakup of a relationship which one person refuses to let go of.

The European technological and sociological

imagination is convinced that we are able to reduce this awesome power to the purposes of mere recreation with no more consequences than riding a roller coaster at the amusement park. They have failed, but as in so many other areas of life, their arrogance and blindness won't allow them to admit to their failure. In attempting to reduce the profound to the trivial, an entire social system has been put at risk.

The breakdown of the American family in general and the black family in particular is directly traceable to the Sexual Revolution of the sixties. The consequences of uprooting and overturning the basic building blocks of human society which have been universally in place since time immemorial are being revealed more and more devastatingly with each passing day. The ravages of divorce is dramatized by the dysfunctional lives of the children, particularly the boys, who grow up without a male role model. While the revolution has been unable to displace mothers as indispensable to the production of children, fathers have in too many instances been reduced to the role of mere sperm donors. Black America is now the proving ground that answers the question: "What does a fatherless community look like and what are the consequences of its very existence?"

Reducing sex to recreation is a form of playing with fire. There are the wounds to the adult players when they discover that they have developed an illogical, impractical but an overwhelming, undeniable, emotional attachment to the person they thought they were only having fun with. Or the person who didn't develop an attachment being stalked by the one who did. How common is the headline: **"Man Kills Estranged Wife Then Self"**? Some people are so devastated by the searing wounds of unrequited love that they lose the capacity for true intimacy. Some become addicted to sexual promiscuity and thereby incapacitated from commitment to monogamous relationships. Others lose their sense of trust and are drained of the emotional energy required for a committed relationship. Another number cold-bloodedly masters the psychological splitting and emotional gymnastics required to engage in the most physically intimate activity yet deny to it the natural power to effect their emotions.

Understanding the power of sex for both good and evil, African elders have for millennia organized their societies to deny children access to information that they lacked the spiritual maturity and moral strength to handle properly. If grown people in their fifties and sixties still have problems dealing with the dangerous complexities of sexual relationships, how can anybody expect children to, even the big children that teenagers are. Our ancestors understood that the nature of the universe and the structure of the human personality demand that a high price be paid for sex. It is the chief physical pleasure an individual can experience but the cost is commensurate with the benefit. Not the cost of a theatre and dinner date. Not the cost of transportation, nor even the cost of a hotel room for the evening.

On the positive side the cost is commitment, marriage, accountability, half a lifetime of childrearing, the struggle to understand and make oneself understood, compromises, working out differences, defending the relationship from its attackers, especially among family members and friends. The price to be paid on the negative side of the ledger when things are not done right is heartbreak, loneliness, insanity, alcoholism, drug addiction, even suicide and murder. Science has given us myriad different forms of birth control but it has yet to produce a single palliative for the worst effects of broken relationships entered into prematurely and unadvisedly. There is no pill, no device, and no implant for a broken heart. As Bobby Blue Bland put it in his classic song:

"When you've got a headache, a little headache powder will see you through

When you've got a backache, a little rubbing will take care
of you
But when you've got a heartache, there ain't nothing you
can do."

It's difficult to get young people to project ahead and
envision what having a baby out of wedlock in one's teens
will look like five, ten and fifteen years into the future. The
sharing in the procreation of a child places the co-
conspirators in a relationship that will only become more
complicated with each passing year. The relationship
between those who share a child is a lifelong one. Even if
their relationship does not work out or last very long they
will continue to be a presence in each others lives affecting
every subsequent relationship they ever have usually for the
worse and not for the better. "My baby daddies" and "my
baby mamas" have an entree into each others lives which
cannot be denied or avoided. They can marry others but
still have the authority to call and demand to speak to
another woman's husband and some other man's wife
because he is the father and she is the mother of their child..

The African rule is that information is not to be shared
with anyone who does not possess the moral strength of
character to handle it correctly. When I was in seminary I
took a course under the great Dr. Charles Long, one of the
worlds foremost authorities in the field of history of
religions. Dr. Long taught us that while Africans were the
first people to invent writing, as we know from the
hieroglyphics written on papyrus parchment by our
Egyptian ancestors, they were also the first to understand
the limitations of writing. They came early to understand
that some things should never be reduced to writing.
Certain kinds of knowledge are so dangerous that they
should only be transmitted through face-to face, need-to-
know, your-eyes-only basis. They knew that anything
reduced to writing is available to anyone who knows how
to read. I wasn't able to get a handle on what he was
saying at the time. It was during my tenure as a chaplain at

Statesville Prison that I was given a first-hand illustration of this teaching.

Many of the inmates, in fact the overwhelming majority of them, had their wives and girlfriends send them nude pictures of themselves. Inmates who worked in the mailroom would often steal the envelopes that they could determine had pictures in them. They would then hang the nude pictures of somebody else's wife or girlfriend on their cell wall, sometime with disastrous consequences if the offended party found out. I realized then that there are some things you should not take pictures of because once such an image has been reproduced electronically anyone who has eyes to see with has access to it.

There are some things that most people do not want to share with any and everybody and the nakedness of their wife is one of them. We already have numerous situations where a couple who took nude pictures of one another later betrayed each other by making those pictures public. The Western custom of freely sharing all kinds of information with just anybody in general such as posting directions for bomb-making on internet sites is a perfect illustration. Africans would never share such dangerous information with anyone unless they first, through face-to-face interrogation and qualification assure themselves that the person had the moral fiber and strength to properly handle the information. Sex is glorious when used correctly and dangerous when used improperly. Children have historically been insulated from knowledge of such forces beyond their ability to handle correctly.

The crisis in black male female relationships has been a paramount concern in our community for the past thirty years. It has been the subject of books, plays and movies by the dozens. Books such as Crisis in Black Sexual Politics and The Endangered Black Family by Doctors Nathan and Julia Hare; Money Issues in Black Male/Female Relationships by George Subira; How To Find and Keep a BMW (Black Man Working) by Dr. Julia

Hare; <u>Anatomy of Female Power</u> by Chinweizu; <u>Sexual Life Between Black and Whites</u> by Beth Day. There are novels such as <u>Standing at the Scratch Line</u> and <u>Echoes From A Long Ago Summer</u> by Guy Johnson, <u>Gone Fishing</u> and <u>A Little Yellow Dog</u> by Walter Mosley; <u>The Color Purple</u> by Alice Walker; <u>Beento Blackbird</u> by Akosua Busia, and the short stories of J. California Cooper. There are any number of movies centering around this theme such as: <u>Waiting To Exhale, Brothers, Boomerang, The Best Man, Two Can Play That Game, Jason's Lyric, Poetic Justice</u> and <u>A Thin Line Between Love and Hate</u>.

The historical illiteracy of the black community in general and black youth in particular lies at the root of much of our current crisis in black male female relationships. In her book <u>Stolen Women</u>, Dr. Gail Wyatt locates the origin of black male/female relationship problems in slavery. Slavery's intent, she tells us, was to corrupt black men and women into a state of accepting even welcoming sexual perversion. Dr. Wyatt describes the traumas involved in our forced removal from our homeland, where sexual discipline was one of the cornerstones of the world's oldest civilizations and most stable family structures, to a land of moral chaos where sexual promiscuity was a way of life.

Africans did not separate sexuality from fertility. They understood sex as being the sacred channel through which the divine gift of new life was brought into the world. In almost all African societies virginity was required of both men and women until marriage. They had no concept of illegitimacy not only because so few children were born out of wedlock but also because they believed that all human life derives from a sacred source. As the proverb expresses it: **All people are children of God, no one is a child of the earth.** In Africa prostitution was non-existent and out-of-wedlock births practically unheard of.

She goes on to say that it was in chattel slavery that black women (and men) were reduced to being concubines

205

and sexual playthings not only for their so-called owners but for white folks in general. Our kidnapped, enslaved African ancestors had every form of sexual perversion forced upon them from rape (usually starting in late childhood or early adolescence), to incest, sexual child abuse, sadomasochism, exhibitionism, voyeurism, bondage and discipline, homosexuality, and bestiality.

For the most part these sexual practices did not continue after slavery as our ancestors used their spiritual strength to shake off the filth of slavery and moved to re-establish their families, find long-lost sold-away members, and maintain the integrity of their marriages. For many others however the perversions forced upon them had taken root in their own inner lives. No small number of individuals had become habituated to the perversities and passed them along within their own families. Incest, sexual child abuse, domestic abuse and homosexuality were among the sexual addictions most resistant to recovery. There was no science of addictionology to explain how these behaviors were passed along or psychoanalysts or psychotherapist specializing in individual or group therapy to help them to heal. The behaviors were for the most part covered up and kept in the closet. Perhaps it was the existence of these abominations that was at the core of much of our ancestors' reluctance to discuss slavery.

These forms of sexual acting out have endured to this day. Except that while for five generations these issues were hidden in the closets of shame and guilt now they are paraded in the open and celebrated as healthy "sexy" behavior. Rape, public stripping and fondling of black women, prostitution and the assumption and treatment of black women as prostitutes and sex objects, my baby daddy and my baby mama, calling black women b___'s and whores, calling black men niggers and dogs, the break up of the black family, disrespect for and abandonment of elders, the celebration of hedonism. These things were imposed on black people in slavery but resisted until the chains and shackles were finally thrown off. Today we surrender in freedom what they could not take from us in slavery.

Our young people do not understand that their insistence on calling themselves nigga's and b____'s and whores is a voluntary return to the imposed, enforced animalism of slavery. What the bible describes as: "As a dog returneth to his vomit..." Pr. 26:11KJV The use of black men as studs and black women as whores, prostitutes, concubines and breeders were two of the chief cornerstones of slavery. The great enduring hypocrisy of white America is their claim that Africans were a sexually promiscuous people who had no more control over their sexual urges than dogs. By doing so they sought to explain and excuse their own uncontrollable lust for black bodies, both male and female.

The opposite side of that construct is the cinematic depiction of the white male as the very apex of masculine attractiveness, supposedly supporting the idea that the black male is undesirable to the women of his own race and therefore unacceptable to any white women except the most degraded. Actually Black masculinity is the epitome of what it means to be a powerful attractive male. The stance, movement, voice quality, his walk, the aural projection of the undeniable power of his presence. For white men to be "cool" means imitating black men. Coolness is an African concept that basically means the ability to operate with grace under pressure. It is the ability to handle powerful spiritual and emotional forces without losing one's physical coordination or mental stability. It is seen most clearly in black musicians, athletes and dancers who handle the overwhelming powers of creativity and expression while "laying back in the cut". Elvis Presley who is called by white people the King of Rock and Roll was no more and no less than a palatable but pale imitation of black male singers, musicians and performers. This is not to discount Presley's musical talent which was outstanding within its own context. But his singing and performing abilities

207

could not ascend to the mid-range of the greatest black male performers.

The concept and existence of a legal state which deems a child to be "illegitimate" is a European creation. It derives from the Middle Ages or the Medieval period of their history when the so-called "nobility", the "blue-bloods", the knights, barons, dukes, princes, and kings had almost the same absolute sexual access to peasant women that white slave-owners had over their slaves, both male and female. The Europeans initiated legislation that proclaimed that the child borne of a noble father and a peasant mother had no "legitimate" claims upon the estate of the father. Illegitimacy then was not a moral concern for them but an economic one.

In their great hypocrisy white men have assigned to black men the image and role of irresponsible fathers when the term and practice is uniquely their own. The modern portrayal of black men as the quintessential irresponsible fathers flies in the face of historical truth. The term "my baby daddy" has been thrust on black males of this era but the original "my baby daddy" was the white slave master who raped our grandmothers and then not only denied the moral responsibilities of his parenthood but often sold his own children when he did not take them to be his concubines both male and female. In other words Thomas Jefferson was the original "my baby daddy".

Black women survived the systematic assaults on their bodies through the uses of a spiritual strategy that allowed her to say to herself and her husband: "He raped my body not my soul." For it was in fact the soul of the African woman that the white man lusted after as much as he desired the unique physical qualities of her unexcelled and inimitable feminine form. The white man saw the way that she treated her man. He observed her admiration for him. He saw the quality of her nurture of her husband, her father, her sons, her brothers and did not understand how she could continue to have such high regard for men who

208

had been defeated in battle, captured, chained, displayed, auctioned, sold like beasts and owned like property. It is a mystery he has yet to plumb.

He couldn't understand that the black woman looked beyond her man's current condition and focused her insights on his soul. She saw beyond his temporary state of enslavement. She remembered him in Africa as the builder of civilizations, farmer of thousand acre fields lush with yams, peanuts, cocoa, and herdsman to cattle as far as the eye could see. She remembered him as the most cunning of hunters, the bravest of warriors, the maintainers of order in society, the protectors of the weak, the heads of families of ten thirty forty sometimes fifty and more children. She remembered him as administrator and professor of universities. She saw him again from a prophetic viewpoint. She saw him through their sons and daughters, and as yet unborn generations, fighting and winning and the Civil War and then in Reconstruction building a "nation within a nation" in the midst of the howling wilderness of unrepentant unrestrained American racism. The white man wanted for himself what he saw the African woman give to her man. His own lack of spiritual depth allowed him to delude himself into believing that he could take by force that which could only be surrendered in love.

There are some people who are of the school of thought that black women resented their husbands, fathers and sons for their inability to protect them from the ravages of white men. I am of a different opinion, though it is undeniable that some small minority must have felt that way. For the most part I believe African women looked at the eye of the lion that blazed on their men's faces when they saw white men lay their hands on their wives, their mothers, their daughters, their sisters. They knew that their men were capable of killing that white man on their spot, gladly losing his own life in the next minute as the greater military and numerical forces of the plantation came down on him. I can hear those women silently pleading with the men as they were led away to the master's bedroom. "Don't kill the master. I know you can. I know you will. I know what a great warrior you are. But don't die for me". They were saying. "I don't need you to die for me; I need you to live for me. If I can live with it, you can live with it too and together we will produce the powers whether in this generation or the next or the one after that which will finally win our freedom". The men submitted en masse to the feminine genius of the women that they loved and together they lived out the African proverb "Where there's life there's hope".

The idea of the black woman as a whore who lusts after white men is a myth that has lost none of its seductive power over the past hundred and fifty years since the end of slavery. It's merely another plank in the platform of white supremacy. This spiritual, intellectual, and emotional structure was developed as a justification for slavery, conquest, genocide, population removal, ethnic cleansing and the so-called New World Order. It maintains that white people are superior in all things to all other people. Only in the past fifty or so years has it yielded that peoples of color overmatch Europeans in various schools of athletic endeavor. But in all other areas, even aesthetics, their international media continues to offer everyday high-tech proof that non-white women are irresistibly drawn to white men. One of the most dramatic evidences of this fact is Halle Berry's being conferred with an Academy Award for playing just such a role. There is practically no black woman past the age of twenty-five that has not been approached by some white man as though she were a prostitute regardless of age, venue, physical appearance or style of dress. Black women routinely avoid the lobbies of even the most exclusive hotels late at night because being approached by white men who mistake them for prostitutes is almost inevitable.

Today when our young people present themselves to the world as being sexually out-of-control and without any boundaries they don't have the historical knowledge to understand that such behaviors are not acts of freedom but a return to slavery. When our daughters refer to each other and entertain being addressed by our sons as b's and whores they need to understand that they didn't invent those terms and they are not a part of the golden legacy of our African past. These terms were not used in any African language and were not the way our ancestors addressed or referred to each other. These are the names that the slave masters called our great-great grandmothers and those generations never welcomed or accepted the degradation in their hearts.

Our sons need to know that "nigga" is not an African word. It's not an African American term. It's not proper Black English just because we pronounce it differently than white folks do. In the household we grew up in it was a curse word. Used only advisedly by elders around children and never spoken by a child in front of an elder. "Nigger" has one true meaning: "slave". It cannot be properly applied to white people because there were no white slaves in American and no matter what a white person dresses like, talks like, walks like or how many black friends they have they still are white and can never be brought down the level of powerlessness that only a slave can experience. "Nigger" is the story of our history in this country told from the perspective of the slave master, the slave trader and the slave breeder.

"Nigger" means: I stole you from Africa. I hunted you like beasts. Captured you like prey. Shipped you like cargo. Discarded your dead like garbage. Advertised you like commodities. Bid you at auction. Displayed you like wares. Worked the women like they were men and raped the men like they were women. I fed your children in troughs like you feed pigs or horses. I rode you like horses. Yoked you like oxen. Herded you like cattle. Castrated you like steers. Branded you like sheep. Drove you like mules. Bred you like pedigreed dogs. All in all, "nigger" means "less than human, more like animal". It means worth more than a cow and less than a horse. But they never reduced us to accepting the identity or status of "nigger" in our hearts because our ancestors knew that no matter how you treat a person they are still a human being. Nothing can make us less than human. How is it that while our ancestors held on to their humanity in slavery we have raised up a generation that threatens to give it away in freedom?

The other most popular name that young black men give each other is "dog". It is once again a break with our tradition. The great cats are the animals that our ancestors respected, revered, emulated and named themselves after both in Africa and since we've been in America. Black men referred to each other as "cats" and black women also. While white women use Cathy as the diminutive for the formal Catherine or Kathleen, black women will be called Cat. We admire the speed, strength, power, grace, courage, beauty, intelligence, and independence of the lion, the cheetah, the leopard and especially, the black panther. Both in African and in black America the dog has been a symbol of degradation. Nothing was lower than to be treated like a dog. You used to hear all the time the expression "He treated me like a dog". "She dogged me out". Then there is Billie Holidays classic lyric from her signature song, Billie's Blues:

I've been your slave, baby
Every since I've been your babe.
But before I'll be your dog
I'll see you buried in your grave

In Africa dogs were given little respect because they were the scavengers of the village who not only feasted on their own vomit but who also ate human feces. Even the Bible, lists the dog along with pigs as unsavory creatures when Jesus said "Cast not pearls before swine nor put what

212

is holy before the dogs. Lest they trample them underfoot and turn and rend you". An old lady once said to me "Only two things have sex in public, dogs and white people".

One of the most disturbing phenomena is the public gatherings in which our sons sexually assault our daughters by ripping off their clothes and sexually molesting them. The last time that black women were made a public spectacle of like this was during slavery when our foremothers were paraded naked on the auction block where white men could approach them and inspect them not only with their eyes but also with their hands. We now even hear of how black women in nightclubs are routinely fondled by any man who decides that he wants to touch what he can see and see if it feels as good as it looks. These mass public sexual assaults demean everyone who takes a part in them, men and women. The women who accept them without protest and the men who perpetrate them have no idea or perhaps are just so degraded that they could care less what the long term consequences are for themselves, the race in general and for the futures of unborn generations.

This kind of perverted, dog-like behavior is once again a legacy of slavery. It was on the auction block that the kidnapped queens of Africa were stripped naked and placed on display for audiences of potential buyers and lascivious onlookers to drink in their nakedness with salacious leers and then come forward to more closely "inspect the merchandise" with their hands. I believe that the modern day strip club has its origin on the auction block. What white people seem never to have understood is that evil fully entertained cannot be conveniently contained. As Lord Acton said: "Power corrupts. Absolute power corrupts absolutely." Once let loose from the leash the dogs of corruption run free, following their own course, rushing to meet their own demented destiny. The entirety of American culture is stained by the filth of the crime of slavery which is, even to this day, unrepented for. The ways in which the slaves were treated has found unforeseen and unexpected consequences in American life. The way capital has treated labor in America is so vastly less considerate than the way the working man and woman is treated in Europe because the American paradigm for owner-worker relationships is slavery.

No work caused more of a firestorm of controversy between black men and women than *The Black Man's Guide To Understanding The Black Woman* by Shaharazad Ali. I personally witnessed the anger, acrimony and animosity her book aroused among black women when I shared a forum with her at a church in Brooklyn, New York. The women in the crowd were so enraged that Ms. Ali had to be escorted from the sanctuary by a crew of bodyguards. The author had the nerve to criticize black women for their mistreatment of black men. Black men found the book to their liking and read it in droves. They recognized and appreciated the usually unspoken truths in it. Truths that so outraged black women that no sensible conversation about the book could take place in mixed company.

On an even more enlightening and instructive occasion I attended a forum sponsored by Spelman College at which the book and its author were the central topics of concern. It began with an impressive lineup of professors from Spelman and other institutions, both males and females, who as was to be expected, roundly and soundly condemned both the book and its author. Next came the female students, mostly from Spelman, but also representing other schools in the Atlanta University Center such as Morris Brown College and Clark College (now Clark-Atlanta University.) The female students, like the professors, unanimously agreed that the book had no merit and its very existence was a total disservice to the black community. Finally, the convener began to recognize young male students from Morehouse, Clark and Morris Brown. A strange thing happened that the predominantly female crowd initially reacted to with choruses of boos.

The male students stood one after another to speak in defense of the book and its besieged author. The crowd became quieter and quieter as each male speaker posited the same argument. They said that as much as they would like to be in agreement with the professors and female students in condemning the book and its author they could not do so with integrity because it would mean denying the witness of their own experiences. One after another they asserted that Ms. Ali's criticism of how black women treated their husbands was real and they knew it was real because they had seen it in their own homes, lived out exactly as the author described. They had seen and heard their mothers berating their fathers, shouting at them, cursing them, threatening them, even hitting them. Sometimes questioning, at other times denying and denouncing their manhood. They saw and heard these things with their own eyes and ears. They explained that they were intimately familiar with Ms. Ali's description of the mothers' rule: "Don't tell your father"; denying the supposed head of the household vital information needed by him to make intelligent decisions concerning the state of things in his own home. The forum ended in uncomfortable silence because no one seemed to be able to offer any kind of answer, much less an honest and forthright one, to the young brothers' questions.

I am afraid that we have made a serious mistake in following the white radical feminist (read: lesbian) strategy of making men the villains and women the victims in all male/female interactions. By demonizing black men and deifying black women we have left black men with no voice in what should be the give and take of conversations in which both sides concerns are accorded equal respect.

We have had no problems recognizing the black male contribution to the breakdown of the black family: the escalation of domestic violence, the use and sale of addictive drugs, organizations of gangs, and any number of other social pathologies. But it is unfair to label the man alone as the source of all problems in the black family and community. This placing of the complete onus on the man alone is made clear in almost all literature on domestic violence where the perpetrator is ubiquitously referred to as "he" and the victim as "she" as though women are not capable of abuse. Violence is not male or female. Violence is a spirit that women are as capable of entertaining as men. As the saying goes: "It's not the size of the dog in the fight, it's the size of the fight in the dog".

Violence is not necessarily the sole province of big men while little men tend to be pacifists. Some of the most violent men and worst killers I've ever known were men close to five feet in height, shorter than the average woman. Bill Russell contends that Wilt Chamberlain, AKA The Big Dipper dramatized that size had nothing to do with the potential for violence. In his prime Wilt was considered to be not only the best basketball player of all time and one of the world's greatest all-around athletes but was deemed by many to be perhaps the strongest man in the world. Russell is convinced that if Wilt had had a penchant for violence the Lakers would not have lost to the Knicks in the 1971 NBA championship 7th game deciding contest when an injured Willis Reed sparked the Knicks to victory. Russell says if it had been him he would have kicked Reed in his injured leg and put him out of the game. Wilt instead backed away from Reed refusing to take advantage of his infirmity. Wilt is the living embodiment of that legendary figure: the Gentle Giant. It is not size or gender that determine a propensity and capacity for violence but the spirit of an individual. Women are just as capable of violence as men. They are however more likely to express their violence verbally or seduce a man to do the physical damage to the target of their vindictiveness.

We even recognize verbal and emotional abuse as being forms of abuse in the same categories as physical and sexual abuse but then we act as though women cannot be as

216

verbally abusive as men or that men cannot be as emotionally devastated by such mistreatment as women. In doing so we deny men their humanity, while lifting all women to an angelic status that delivers them beyond the possibility of criticism, challenge and most importantly correction.

If we are able to give ready answers to how black male self-hatred is expressed in their violence, misogyny, predilection to marry white women, etc. How do we recognize black female self-hatred? Is it possible that black women express their own self-hatred in the ways that they treat their children, their men and one another? Remember, eighty percent of child abuse is committed by the mother's boyfriend, that is to say a male whom the mother introduces to and gives access to her children, which makes these women at least accessories before and accomplices after the fact.

Seldom do men raise children by different mothers, whereas the phenomenon of mothers raising children by different fathers is all-too-normal. In the movie <u>Boyz 'N the Hood</u> two themes predominated. One was how the character who had the least amount of courage, street smarts, charisma, sense of responsibility and leadership skills, Trey, ended up being the most successful boy in his neighborhood age group, principally because he had a father. The presence or absence of the father has a measurable effect on the outcome of the lives of boys. The second was how the boy who had the most heart, common sense, leadership gifts, sense of responsibility for others, street knowledge, and native intelligence, Dough Boy, ended up an habitual criminal and jailbird while his brother was the star athlete, although unfortunately also, like most black athletes a student at risk.

The difference between these two siblings raised in the same house by the same mother was that the mother favored one boy over the other. The reason she favored Ricky over Dough Boy was that she liked Ricky's father and for unexplained reasons had serious resentments and hostility towards Dough Boy's father. It was Trey who did not have the physical, athletic, intellectual or social gifts equal to either Ricky or Dough Boy who ended up at Morehouse College. Trey had a daddy in Furious Styles who taught him the real meaning of black manhood. The great flaw in the story was that Mr. Styles did not reach out to Dough Boy and Ricky making himself their godfather and giving them the same benefits that he gave to his biological son.

BET has a late night talk show called Oh Drama hosted by three black women. I watched one night as the topic of discussion was rappers use of the vulgar terms of "ho' and b---- 'sin addressing and describing black women. As their guests they had three gangster rappers who tried to defend their use of these misogynistic terms. The last one to try to defend this practice was asked by one of the women "Do you call your mama a 'b___?" He answered to a chorus of groans from the audience: "Yeah, that "b___" is a 'ho'! I tried to imagine how he could have come to this conclusion and it was pretty easy to figure out. We have failed to consider the effect of witnessing their mother's sexual acting out on the psyches of teenage boys and young men.

I have a friend who told me once how her fifteen year old son pointedly asked her never again to wear shorts in the presence of his friends. Boys do not like their mothers to be seen as sexual objects, particularly by their friends. Even less do they like seeing their mothers in sexual situations with men other than their fathers. The sexual freedom of the past two generations has made a single mother, sexually interacting with men other than their children's fathers, a regular occurrence. It is an all too-typical scenario for such women to entertain male company overnight in their bedrooms with their children at home. The women feel that because they are single they have the right to have that kind of company and will even explain this to their children. But explanations of adult realities do not ease the emotional states of perplexed and distressed children.

The mothers may see this as something that children just have to accept but they seem to have no consciousness and understanding of the short and long term effects on the children, particularly the boys, who will go out on the street filled with a rage that they cannot discuss, even with their closest friends. I am convinced that a major part of the use of these terms for black women has to do with the boys describing, not all women, but particularly their mothers since mother is the paradigm for womanhood.

Too many black mothers in particular and society in general have not taken into consideration the kind of emotional damage that's done to a boy to see his mother in situations that are unthinkable to him. This scene was played out an episode of the Sunday night legal drama <u>The Practice</u>. The black male lawyer in the show had a teenage son who was suspected by the police of murdering his divorced mother's boyfriend. The investigating officers explained to the attorney father that boys experience such rage at seeing their mothers being sexual with a man other than their father that they are automatic suspects in a murder of the mother's paramour.

One of the first and most important tasks of the race immediately following emancipation was the re-establishmentt of the black family.

One of the most beautiful and dramatic retellings of this era is found in the short story by Charles Chestnutt entitled 'Wife Of His Youth" I strongly recommend that every black family read this story aloud to each other as one of the most informative, heartfelt and moving expressions of who our ancestors truly were and who we could still become today.

But there is also a minority report. Those who were unable the break the bonds of addiction to sexual perversion were among us. Those most susceptible were the children who were molested at such a spiritually and emotionally vulnerable age that the practices they were forced into took root in their personalities. As the proverb says: "The way the twig is bent is the way that the tree will grow." Some of the people who had their personalities distorted and their behavior corrupted at such an early age did not know how to understand the real source of their behavior and usually ended up blaming themselves and living lives of great shame and guilt.

These were the prostitutes (even today sexual child abuse is found in the background of eighty percent of prostitutes), pedophiles, homosexuals, and various other sorts of sexual addiction. This was a hundred and forty years before the emergence of the recovery movement in modern psychology that popularized understanding the relationship between childhood trauma and adult disfunctionality. In the absence of a healing agency and knowing that these practices were instilled in them by evil men the black family and community for generations tried to treat these victims and the generations they produced and infected with their own illnesses as lovingly as they could. At the same time they tried to control the behavior by keeping it in the closet and taking steps to protect individual children. The sexual revolution opened the closet doors and bid the demons to stop hiding in shame come out and celebrate themselves.

And still, there is no healing. Major black churches for the past thirty or more years have been constructing multi-purpose facilities known universally as "family life centers." These centers ought to specialize in the healing and recovery of people who have been the victims of perverse sexual practices passed down from slavery. We ought to staff these centers with expert, qualified counselors who specialize in healing the victims and perpetrators of sexual abuse.

The relationships among black men and women have become increasingly sexual yet at the same time less loving and shorter lasting. What young people are looking for in life is actually not sex but love. Animals can be content with mere sex. Human beings need love. However in the absence of role models among their parents and community elders of loving, long-term, committed relationships they are driven by media and peer influences to mistake sex for love. Teen-age girls, in particular those without fathers, suffer from a tremendous need to have their budding womanhood endorsed, affirmed and encouraged by the healthy, non-sexual affections of their fathers. Where there is no father or other healthy older man, they end up settling for the expression of affections of their male peers and older predatory males who wait in line to take advantage of their youthful naiveté and unprotected status as fatherless girls. These immature young men by the very nature of male sexuality in its uninformed stage demand sex in exchange for their affection.

Boys and girls have to be taught how to properly relate to one another. As little children they functioned in same-sex communities with very little time shared with one another across the gender divide. Children have no sexual consciousness (unless they have been molested or otherwise inappropriately exposed to sexual themes). In fact they tend to look at one another with contempt bordering on disdain. Boys see little girls as being weak and scary. Girls see boys as being dirty, mean and uncouth. For years they have little interaction, each group operating within the distinct and separate environments governed by their own set of rules. Boys upon meeting grab, grope, grapple and wrestle with one another, rolling on the ground testing each other's strength. Girls play house and make nice and try to not to hurt each other's feelings. Boys establish rules. They will put anybody out of the game that won't play by the rules. Whatever rules girls have they will change if they hurts anybody's feelings.

Suddenly after a childhood of living in separate camps the biological imperative of puberty conspires to produce a revolution. What was just a few months ago detestable now becomes irresistible. The girls who were once like sticks have grown bodies with curves and swellings that the boys can't keep their eyes off of. The boys are now fascinated by the way girls talk, the way they walk, the way they smell. Girls who had been for so long turned off by the boys stupidity, weirdness, uncouth ways, their casual relationship with dirt, their loudness, obnoxiousness, meanness, and unnecessary violence are now drawn to the masculine energy of the deepening of their once boyish voices, the development of physiques, their superior height, their aggressiveness and athletic prowess.

Neither boys nor girls know how to handle the changes in themselves and the new objects of mutual interest. Boys in particular, compelled by their natural masculine rambunctiousness, will in early puberty tend to reach out and grab the new objects of fascination-- girls' breasts and behinds. Girls will experiment with their new-found power over boys and play with their emotions and excite them to distraction. It is the role of the elders, the parents, preachers, teachers, coaches, etc. to carefully and skillfully lead children through this exciting but dangerous period in their lives. They have to be taught social etiquette and sexual morality. They must be given boundaries on their behavior and treatment of each other. This is no mere game the breaking of whose rules can result in the loss of a down or the putting out of a player. This is life and death and time and eternity. When we fail to establish boundaries the result is the sexual chaos and family dissolution that reigns among our young people.

For this generation sexuality has been almost totally divorced from morality. This is a generation raised and educated by the sex education industry which glorifies sex for itself alone devoid of moral or relational concerns. Its message to our young people is that sex is a right which arrogant, stingy, close-minded grown people want to preserve for themselves; or it is biological necessity which they cannot control, as though they were lower animals in heat rather than rational human beings with the spiritual and intellectual powers to control themselves and others. They have been taught to major in erotic technique rather than mastering the subtle, complex nuances of committed relationships. The sex education industry itself is primarily controlled by homosexuals whose teaching and advocacy of total sexual freedom is just another way of promoting the homosexual agenda which is primarily based on promiscuity.

The teaching of androgyny which encourages our girls to act sexually the same as boys with a desire only to experience the tactile sensations and orgasmic release of sex without any consideration for the kinds of relationship commitments and responsibilities that ought to be part of the package leaves us a with a generation of girls who because they act like boys will be treated as such by their sexual partners.

Sex is intended to be a balance of male and female principles. The male drive for autonomy is balanced by the female need for intimacy. There must be both autonomy and intimacy in the dynamics of human existence. Either one, left to its own devices, is dysfunctional. Unchecked autonomy leaves men running wild without exercising any responsibility for the consequences of their behavior. The unrestrained intimacy of an all female relationship leaves women engaging in enmeshment, holding on so tight that they each lose sense of an individual identity.

Men teach women about autonomy which is why Daddy's girls are among the most successful personalities in the professional world where autonomy is so valued. Women teach men about intimacy so that men with healthy relationship with their mothers and sisters are among the best marital choices.

The caveat however is that there is a double standard which women across the board, and feminists in particular, tremendously resent. It's actually not so much a double standard as a separate reality. Women can in fact have sex

223

with the same reckless abandon as the most unfeeling and irresponsible of men. Women, in fact, are physically capable of much more sexual activity and greater physical satisfaction than men. Female sexuality is undeniably superior to that of males both quantitatively and qualitatively. The best men would have difficulty accommodating the demands of more than two or three women. A single women could accommodate scores of men. Women are capable of multiple orgasms. Men are thankful to have one every once in a while. Men have been described sexually as being like microwave ovens. Women one the other hand are like crock pots.

But only women get pregnant. Only women can experience carrying new life in their own bodies. Only they can birth new life into the world. Only they can feed those new lives from their breasts. Only they can know the ineffable intimacy with a baby that renders mother and child like one person and not two separate beings. The emotional ties between mother and child is something that men can only observe and often times envy but can never really know. "For unto whomsoever much is given, of him shall be much required..." Luke 12:28(KJV)

I am not arguing that boys should be given more sexual freedom than girls because they can't get pregnant. In communities with active fathers boys were restrained by the fathers' armed vigilance that stopped roaming predatory boys from violating their daughters and raiding their households then like the cuckoo bird laying their eggs in other birds' nests leaving their children to be taken care of by others. I am saying that we have to be, and teach our daughters to be, much more careful because they can and do get pregnant. Boys have the option of denying paternity or refusing to fulfill its moral demands. Girls cannot. The only option other than parenthood is abortion or various forms of abandonment. Two people have sex, only one gets pregnant. Two people can play with a gun. They both should both be careful of its danger. But the one that the weapon is pointed at ought to be the more careful of the two. The one who fired the weapon may or may not suffer the legal consequences of assault or murder but the one the barrel was pointed at will be injured or killed. Both car drivers and pedestrians ought to be careful how they conduct themselves in relationship to each other in order to avoid a collision. But it would behoove the pedestrian to be more careful than the driver. The consequences for the pedestrian are just greater.

The sex education industry has convinced now two generations that sex can be enjoyed freely without any consequences. They assure us of the superiority of technology over outdated questions and old-fogy concerns of morality, not to mention fertility. History has proven that their approach does not work. The larger the sex education industry has grown, the more popular it is in our schools, the more sophisticated the technologies of birth control have become and the cheaper and more available their products are; the out-of-wedlock and teenage mother's birth rate has gone higher and higher bringing us to a veritable crisis as we try to manage living in a society where so many babies are having babies. These premature parents lack the spiritual, practical, emotional, intellectual, and financial resources needed to provide their children with the kind of foundations they need to journey successfully through a world organized for their destruction.

Date rape and physical abuse are increasingly problems in teen dating. How a boy treats a girls will be determined primarily by three factors. 1. How he feels about her. 2.How she feels about herself. 3. Whether or not she has a father or other male protector to whom the boy must be accountable. In the sexual assault trial of Tupac Shakur he testified that he literally turned the young women who was visiting him over to his friends because if he had tried to protect her from them it would have meant that she was his girlfriend and that he cared about her. Gang rape or "running a train" has long been a feature of European male culture and too many black males have picked up the habit of abusing and exploiting women as a group activity. A man who loves a woman doesn't share her sexually. Each girl and woman sets her own standards for how she will be treated by a man. The more highly she values herself the more stringent boundaries and higher standards she will set on how she is to be spoken to, looked at, the places she will frequent and the activities she will participate in.

When it comes to dating there are two kinds of boys: the bad boy and the good boy.

The bad boy approaches girls disrespectfully from the get-go. His approach to her is at best casual, at worst abusive. He calls out to her to come to him. He addresses her not by her name but by a generic designation: "Slim", "Freak", "Baby" "Red", "Shorty" and of course worst of all: "'ho'" or "b****".

He is not interested in coming to her house or meeting her people. He has no good intentions towards the girl and doesn't want to be easily traceable once his damage is done. She has to meet him out on the street or at his place. His primary interest is sex. Without it there is no point to his being bothered with the girl. His conversations with her will center around her body. He is not interested in her academic performance in school, her dreams, ambitions and plans for the future. He will also insist on the girl giving or loaning him money.

He will share her with his friends. Among males it is clear that the only threat to the cohesiveness of the peer group is the presence of a woman that one of the members is in love with and committed to. When women marry they are encouraged and empowered to continue their intimate relationships with mothers, grandmothers, sisters, best friends. If the husband tries to interfere it is regarded even defined in literature as abusive. But when men get married and they insist on continuing their nights out with the boys it is often interpreted at best as immature and at worst as a

226

continuation of single male predatory behavior. The fellows therefore, in order to gauge a new girlfriend's threat to the group will ask the man to share her with them.

We see this clearly in the Tupac Shakur sexual assault conviction and in the movie <u>Jason's Lyric</u>.

If the girl gets pregnant he will deny paternity. He will even go so far as to scandalize her name and besmirch her reputation by accusing her of having sex with other men. He'll even have his friends insist that they had sex with her too. Or he may admit paternity as proof of his virility but he won't marry her or be a father to the baby in any real sense of providing emotional, financial, or spiritual support. He will be just be another "my baby daddy."

The good boy on the other hand is from the beginning a gentleman. He approaches a girl with respect and regard. He is eager to come to her house and meet her family members and undergo the classic interrogation of her parents. He enjoys and appreciates her family because the people that are important to her are important to him. Over the years his place in the family may well remain constant even after the romance is over. He and the girl will remain close friends for a lifetime, behaving towards one another as much like brother and sister as boyfriend and girlfriend.

He does not demand sex as a precondition for the continuation of a relationship. He understands the dangers to a girl's future attached to premarital sex and out-of-wedlock teenage pregnancies. He is interested in aiding, assisting and protecting her plans of future success, particularly in the area of higher education.

Lastly, and perhaps most importantly, if they do have sex and the girl gets pregnant, he will marry her. On any number of occasions girls will get pregnant by the irresponsible bad boy and the good boy who truly loves her will be the one to marry her. *"A boy won't take care of his own children. A real man will raise his own and somebody else's.*

There are a number of ways to take back control of the

227

dating process from teenagers. One is for parents to insist that they know not only the boy who's taking their daughter out but also his parents. The two sets of parents could through conversation agree on what their expectations are for how the young people will conduct themselves with one another. When I was courting in the sixties the girl and boy might make a date but only the parents could confirm it. As fellows we had to present ourselves to the girl's parents, undergo interrogation and wait to see if we passed muster and were allowed to escort their daughter out of their house.

Another approach is to simply insist that young men have to ask the girl's father for permission to take his daughter out. Boys don't like to bother too much with fathers. But when he's serious about the girl he will meet whatever challenge is presented to him. As teenage boys seeking a relationship with the opposite sex we learn early that you can not only get past the mother but you can even enlist her as an ally in your campaign for her daughter's affection. Just court the mother the same as you do the daughter. Pay her compliments, bring her flowers and candy, ask her about herself and sit with rapt attention as she answers your questions.

You can't do Daddy like that. He is not interested in your flattery. Don't bring Daddy no flowers or candy. With Daddy you got to come correct every time. That's because most fathers take their role of protector very seriously. Boys know this. That's why one of their first questions to a new romantic interest is: "Who you stay with?" If the word "my Daddy" is part of the answer his entire strategy for progress or conquest must change. He knows he cannot approach a father-protected home the way he would a single mother home.

For girls who do not have fathers at home a godfather will do, or an older brother, uncle or cousin. The idea is that the boy must know that there is a man to whom he must be accountable for his treatment of the girl he takes out.

This approach could even work before the question of an actual date comes up. Some boys are known for putting girls under the kind of tremendous pressure that would be defined as sexual harassment in a corporate or adult environment would. If a boy persistently demands a girl's phone number for instance she could tell him: "I'm not allowed to give out my number. In my family any boy that wants my number has to go to my father (grandfather, uncle, older cousin, godfather, pastor) and get the number from him."

What is most dangerous and yet generally ignored about promiscuity is that it is the very beginning of child abuse. The same sex education industry that convinces our children that sexual activity is their right, which oppressive adults are trying to deny them, also convinces them that because of the blessings of birth control technology there are no consequences to their promiscuity. Young people are convinced that they also have a right not to be burdened by the birth of children just because they have chosen to engage in pre-marital sex. The reality is of course that there is no one hundred per cent effective, fool-proof method of birth control. The closest science can get is to that goal is abortion which from a moral perspective is not birth control but child murder. Moreover, in later term abortions it is common for the fetus to be removed from the womb while yet alive. Then it must be killed through starvation or strangulation. In partial birth abortion the fetus is partially removed from the birth canal and then killed by thrusting a sharp instrument through the skull and into the brain.

The sex education industry rails against the unfairness and oppressiveness of what they call unplanned or unwanted pregnancies. They do not have a godly perspective to inform them that human beings seldom successfully "plan" pregnancies or births. Only God controls that process. It is the task of human beings to rise to the challenge of properly receiving the new life that God blesses us with.

It is the perspective with which one views babies that determines how they are received and how they are treated. Former generations believed with all their hearts that every new birth was a gift from God. They believed that every child sent to this earth was a deliberate, intentional act on the part of an all-wise God to bless humanity and the earth we live upon through the inestimable gift of new life. The African proverb states: "Children are the reward of life". Another says: "He that has money is not rich. It is he that has children that is truly wealthy". Therefore when we were born despite the relatively deprived material circumstances that obtained in the lives of our parents we were received with joy as evidence of God's continued favor. The mathematical logic that concludes that black people only had many children while living in the rural South because that meant more hands to work the fields is not borne out in our Northern and urban experience.

In my neighborhood in Chicago there was, on practically every block, at least one family with ten or more children. Larger families were looked upon admiringly if not enviously. My family of six children was medium-sized. Families with only one or two children were pitied. The larger the number of children, the greater the resources for fellowship and material and emotional support that exists among brothers and sisters. Not to mention the more allies one had in the event of a dispute with other kids.

That's why child abuse was so rare in the black community prior to the 1970's. Whenever we heard or read about incidents of child abuse in the local newspapers we knew it was taking place in somebody else's community and not ours. The elders of our families had the authority to place the children in the family in the home that was deemed best for their well-being and well-raising. Government agencies had no part in child placement until the post civil rights, pseudo-integration era. Historically,

230

our grandparents and great-grandparents exercised complete authority regarding the well-being of the children no matter who the individual parents were. If there was a case of abuse or neglect those elders could and often did mandate the removal of a child to a better place. Grandparents often arbitrarily took their grandchildren from the parents if they concluded that those homes were not the best places for them and raised them themselves until they were convinced that the parents had matured enough to be responsible for the proper care of those children. When there were cases of juvenile delinquency the elders often sent the offending, at-risk youth Down South to spend time on the farm in the bosom of the very center of traditional African American values and isolated from the dangers of urban existence.

The proverb: "It takes a village to raise a child" was not mere words back then. Our community wide commitment to the care of children was such that the elders could put a four or five year old child alone on a train or bus for a two or three day trip Down South with a shoebox of fried chicken and biscuits to eat and a note pinned to the front of their clothes indicating the child's name and destination. Every black adult that came into contact with that child would demonstrate care and concern and see to it that the child arrived safely at his or her destination.

The old people and past generations saw babies as gifts from God and treated them as such. They did not subscribe to the modern-day notion that babies should only be brought into the world if they can enjoy a certain so called "quality of life". This term, "quality of life" is so inaccurate as to be a misnomer. It is actually a synonym for "standard of living". There is no such thing as a measurable "quality of life" because quality is abstract and intangible. It cannot be seen, felt, tasted, touched, smelled, counted, or measured. What they really mean is "standard of living" which is based on the material lives of middle-class white Americans.

With their materialistic mind-sets all too many Europeans believe that life is not worth living unless one can enjoy all the material advantages of middle-class American society. If our parents and ancestors subscribed to such a notion: that is, that children should not be brought into the world unless they could have their own bed, or their own room, or new clothes every season, or a different pair of shoes for each outfit, or to be able to wear new clothes without a repetition for at least two weeks in a row, until daddy had a better job and a higher income, most of us in my generation would not be here.

Furthermore, if our slave ancestors had subscribed to the quality of life theory infanticide would have been a wholesale practice amongst them. Who could have been born into a worst set of circumstances than slaves, defined as property and treated worse than horses and dogs? Yet their parents saw them as gifts from God with unlimited possibilities in a future that was in God's hands and not the slave masters. Therefore they had their children, insisting that they represented the greatest value this side of eternity: life and that where there was life there was hope.

The greatest and supposedly, at least on the surface, most convincing argument for abortion is in the case of rape. Our slave ancestors dealt with that argument in a most transcendent and convincing fashion. Many of their children resulted from the systematic rape of our women by the white masters. Our daughters were oftentimes taken to the slave owner's bed before they reached puberty. Many of them were used as long term concubines. Others were handed out to guests as part of the hospitality of the plantation culture. Many were sold at auction to be employed in the brothels of the big cities like New Orleans, Charleston, Mobile, and Savannah. The white master was the original pimp. But he was also the original "my baby daddy."

We know that mixed race children in the slave community did not come about from relationships between

232

black men and white women because such unions were typically punished by the murder of the black father and the light-skinned baby, and at least the exile if not murder of the white mother. The babies of white men by black women were held in the same state of slavery as the mother. Black men often had to raise up the child of the master's rape of his wife or daughter in his own house. How amazing the love of these Africans for children that they could overlook the sordid circumstances by which they arrived in this world and instead receive them as precious gifts from God with limitless potential to be a blessing to their families and communities! They understood in the most profound and dramatic manner what Joseph meant in the Bible meant when he said: "...ye thought evil against me; but God meant it unto good..."Gen. 50:20

If our ancestors had employed abortion to destroy babies born of rape we would never have been blessed by the magnificent lives of such people as Frederick Douglass, W.E.B. DuBois, Booker T. Washington and Adam Clayton Powell to name just a few of the our people who descended down a genealogical line polluted by rape and incest.

The parents of today however who subscribe to the values of the post-modern, technology-worshipping American standard do not see children as gifts from God but as unwanted accidents and unintended mistakes. Is there such a thing as an unwanted diamond? Does anyone reject receiving an unplanned economic windfall? Too many of us truly believe, along with Planned Parenthood, that all babies must be planned, that there should be no unintentional births or as they like to put it "unplanned pregnancies". This goes against the common sense understanding that some of the greatest blessings in life often come as surprises.

There is no greater indicator of the dangerous state of social behavior among our young people than the public gatherings they are involved in known by various names:

Freaknik, Greek Picnic, Puerto Rican Day Festival. When the controversy about our young people's public gatherings first arose around a Spring Break gathering in the city of Virginia Beach, VA the city's reaction to their presence was to call out National Guardsmen armed with wooden batons the size of baseball bats for crowd control. Our college students were only emulating the riotous Spring Break gatherings of white students that had been going in places like Daytona Beach, Florida for decades. Like most black adults I was outraged at this military response. A few months later however I was sitting next to a young couple who had been there. They said to me: "The boys were stripping the clothes off the girls in the middle of the street"! I lost all anger towards the National Guardsmen and turned it on the rapacious young men who would strip our daughters naked in public. This behavior had not been seen since they stripped us on the auction blocks for public display. We did not struggle for all these centuries so that our children could be free to adapt the worse behavior of the slave masters.

We, the elders of our people must take back control of dating from our children. We must reinstitute controls over their sexual practices which will insure for them better marriages and for our grandchildren more stable environments to grow up in. We cannot surrender to the idea that we are all victims of the changing times and the clock of human progress can't be turned back. As human beings we are not the objects of history but he subjects of history. History doesn't make human beings. Human beings make history. There is no question that we have the power. The greater question is: do we have the courage and the wisdom to use it?

There is no correlation between homosexuality and the civil rights movement. The Civil Rights Movement seeks a positive freedom, the freedom "to" rise to the highest levels of our capacities. The homosexuals seek a negative freedom: the freedom "from" all moral restraint. **Author**

IX. HOMOSEXUALITY: THE FATAL INTEGRATION

In 1973 groups of homosexual activists produced the greatest victory in their campaign to have their lifestyle accepted as normal behavior when they engineered a series of attacks on the American Psychiatric Association (APA) that resulted in the APA dropping homosexuality from its list of mental disorders. A major part of their public campaign consisted of adopting the slogans and rhetoric of the Civil Rights Movement as white feminists had already been doing successfully for over a hundred years. They labeled themselves an "oppressed minority". Liberals, especially in academia, the white mainstream churches and in the press, accepted their creation of these and other rhetorical devices such as naming themselves "gay" to create a false image of themselves as healthy normal people living positive and happy lives. They further claimed that anyone that opposes their full acceptance is the one who is really mentally ill and suffering from a made-up condition they called "homophobia." Another aspect of their campaign for acceptance was to claim that fully ten percent of the population was homosexual; thus appealing strongly to political interests whose only way of evaluating any situation is by counting the votes that it represents.

Flying in the face of over a hundred years of medical findings in the field of psychology, they argued that they were born that way and therefore could not change their condition. And even more astoundingly they challenged thousands of years of moral standards and insisted that having been born that way it was the will of God that they be homosexuals despite the clear condemnations of their sexual practices in the Bible and in the ancient traditions of African people both on the continent and in the Diaspora.

The reason that the American Psychological Association voted to remove homosexuality from its list of mental disorder was that their campaign was based on the disruption of APA events. The most effective course of action they took in their attacks on the APA was to threaten to "out" (expose as homosexuals) a number of the organization's top leadership.

Another one of their most effective tactics was to claim common cause with the Civil Rights Movement. Dr. Jeffrey Satinover, psychiatrist and psychoanalyst specializing in reparative therapy for homosexuals describes one such episode in his book <u>Homosexuality</u> and the <u>Politics</u> of <u>Truth</u>:

At the 1970 meetings, Irving Bieber, an eminent psychoanalysts and psychiatrist, was presenting a paper on "homosexuality and transsexualism". He was abruptly challenged. Bieber's efforts to explain his position …were met with derisive laughter. One protester called to him: 'I've read your book , Dr. Bieber, and if that book talked about black people the way it talks about homosexuals, you'd be drawn and quartered and you'd deserve it."

Many of the most prominent black leaders have fully accepted this self-serving identification with our struggle. The Rev. Jesse Jackson, Sr. when he lists the constituency of his Rainbow Collection describes them as: "blacks, whites, gays and lesbians". Dr. King's widow Correta Scott King embraces their cause and misrepresents Dr. King by claiming he did also. The NAACP wages a campaign against "homophobia". The Rev. Al Sharpton endorses same-sex marriage

While the homosexual activists pay lip service to the liberation struggles of black people and, for purposes of public consumption, identify themselves as liberals and political progressives there is another side which we as black people need to be aware of:

Eric Pollard formerly belonged to the prominent homosexual organization ACT-UP and founded its Washington, D.C. chapter. In an interview with the *Washington Blade*, a major homosexual newspaper, he stated that he and other group learned to apply " subversive tactics, drawn from the voluminous *Mein Kampf*, which some of us studied as a working model."

Mein Kampf was, of course, written by Adolph Hitler and is still the bible of the Nazi Party world-wide.

In support of the argument that they were "born like that" the homosexual movement has publicized so-called scientific studies that declare the discovery of a "homosexual gene." The media was quick to give major publicity to these claims, producing front page headlines and magazine cover stories that proclaimed the scientific proof of homosexuality as an inborn condition. Numerous subsequent studies have proven the falsity of these claims, but the same news outlets have gave practically no coverage to the exposure . Thus the idea of homosexuals as some kind of "third gender" exists in the mind of the American public as a reality though it is just a myth that many people believe in because they read it in the newspapers or saw it on TV. Unfortunately the American public is notoriously anti-intellectual and prefers to receive most of the information they base their opinions on from ninety-second fragments on shallow, entertainment-driven news programs, neglecting to spend the time required to seriously investigate crucial issues by reading well-researched, fact-based books and/or scholarly journals.

Because of the academic, religious, media and political support of homosexual liberation this cause has made tremendous strides in the life of this nation. They have truly come out of the closet and are now acceptable on Main Street as part of the politically correct crowd. Bill

Clinton made them a major segment of his political apparatus in both his presidential campaigns and his administrations. In the entertainment worlds they are practically inescapable. They are featured on prime-timeTV sit-coms and in Hollywood movies. Any public figure that makes a critical statement about them is forced by media pressure to apologize and beg their pardon. Preachers who take a moral position against their practices are denounced and ridiculed as being ignorant, backwards, unsophisticated, and worst of all, bigoted. Homosexual parades are annual events in major cities attended by tens of thousands of homosexuals on display especially in the cities identified as having large homosexual populations such as San Francisco, Atlanta, GA, Washington, D.C. and New Orleans, LA. On college campuses, annual "coming out" days are celebrated by the homosexuals who urge everybody to show their support by wearing a certain color or article of clothing with administrations gently pressuring faculty and staff to fully participate.

Finally, the homosexual argument for acceptance includes the notion that they are no different from anybody else. They contend that they are just everyday, normal human beings who have a different sexual orientation. They claim to want the same things everybody wants, to do the same things everybody else does and that they have the same values everybody else has. They want, therefore, full acceptance into the mainstream of the life of this nation, and they especially want their relationships to be sanctified in holy matrimony and the right to adopt children. While they have yet to find a state that will sanction their unions as legal marriages there are a number of states that allow them to adopt children whether singly or as a homosexual couple.

The momentum of the movement for the popular acceptance of homosexuality suffered from a major setback with the discovery of AIDS in 1979. The original designation the medical community gave this still-incurable, fatal venereal disease, first diagnosed in a homosexual flight attendant named Gaetan Dugas, was GRID (Gay-Related Immune Deficiency). But once again popular politics intervened and the name was changed to AIDS (Acquired Immune Deficiency) so as to remove the stigma of the disease from homosexuals. It was clear in almost all the original diagnoses that AIDS resulted from the peculiar sexual lifestyle of homosexuals.

However, within a few years it crossed over into the heterosexual community. First, through intravenous drug abuse when infected homosexuals shared needles with other drug abusers. Then through sex by infected homosexuals (they would describe themselves as "bisexuals") with heterosexual females. At that point when a significant number of people who were not homosexuals had contracted the disease, the homosexuals waged a campaign to convince the world that everybody was at equal risk of infection. The Centers for Disease Control and Prevention (CDC) in Atlanta was in the forefront of a multi-million dollar ad campaign that tried to prove that no particular group of people was more at risk to contract AIDS than any other group. There were dire predictions of a heterosexual AIDS epidemic that threatened to wipe put the majority of youth of this nation.

Dr. Jeffrey Satinover in his Homosexuality: The Politics of Truth explains why AIDS and any number of other illnesses, diseases and disorders are peculiar to the homosexual's uniquely at-risk lifestyle:

Even if condoms are used, anal intercourse is harmful primarily to the receptive partner. Because the rectal sphincter is designed to stretch only minimally, penile-anal thrusting can damage it severely. The introduction of larger items, as in the relatively common practice of 'fisting', causes even worse damage...Thus gay males have a disproportionate incidence of acute rectal trauma as well as of rectal incontinence (the ability to control the passing of feces) and anal cancer...Furthermore, anal intercourse, penile or otherwise, traumatizes the soft tissues of the rectal lining. These tissues are meant to accommodate the relatively soft fecal mass as it is prepared for expulsion by the slow contractions of the bowel and are nowhere near as sturdy as vaginal tissue. As a consequence, the lining of the rectum is almost always traumatized to some degree by any act of anal intercourse. Even in the absence of major trauma, minor microscopic tears in the rectal lining allow for the immediate contamination and the entry of germs into the bloodstream. Although relatively monogamous gay couples are at lower risk for AIDS, they tend to engage in unprotected anal intercourse more frequently than do highly polygamous single homosexuals. As a result, they are at higher risk for non-AIDS conditions—if all other factors are equal, which is usually not the case because of the clustering of risk factors.

Because receptive anal intercourse is so much more frequent among homosexual men than among women, the dangers of this kind of sex are amplified among homosexuals. Furthermore, comparable tears in the vagina are not only infrequent because of the relative toughness of the vaginal lining, but the environment of the vagina is vastly cleaner than that of the rectum. Indeed, we are designed with a nearly impenetrable barrier between the bloodstream and the extraordinarily toxic and infectious contents of the bowel. Anal intercourse creates a breach in this barrier for the receptive partner, *whether or not the insertive partner is wearing a condom.* (emphasis mine.)

As a result, homosexual men are disproportionately vulnerable to a host of serious and sometimes fatal infections by the entry of feces into the bloodstream. These include hepatitis B and the cluster of otherwise rare conditions, such as shigellosis and Giardia lambia infection, which together have been known as 'Gay Bowel Syndrome'.

Dr. Charles Socarides in his definitive work entitled: Homosexuality: A Freedom Too Far says this about why homosexuals are and will continue to be the group most at risk to contract AIDS:

"The walls of the vagina are elastic and several layers thick, and they have glands that produce natural lubrication during intercourse. This prevents quantities of sperm from entering the bloodstream. But the lining of the rectum is made of a single layer of columnar epithelium. Unlike the vaginal epithelium, the rectum is not only incapable of protecting against any abrasive effect. It also promotes the absorption of sperm antigens, thus enhancing their exposure to the immune apparatus in the lymphatic and blood circulation. During anal intercourse, then the biological design of the rectum, combined with the aggressive properties of sperm, expedite entry into the bloodstream. When this occurs repeatedly, antibodies to sperm circulate throughout the bloodstream and impair the immune system. This happens both apart from and along with infection by the AIDS virus."

But AIDS is not the only medical indication that the homosexual lifestyle is unhealthy: To quote Dr. Socarides again:

They plunged into traumatic sex--promiscuous, abusive, violent, brutal, vicious, ramming sex, using poppers and speed to enhance the thrills, they were exchanging semen and blood and feces with hundreds of partners, thousands. Most of them started coming down with hepatitis. They picked up venereal warts, and herpes. They got intestinal diseases, like amebiasis and giardiasis. In the late 1970's at the New York Gay Men's Health Project, 30 percent of the patients suffered from gastrointestinal parasites. Randy Shilts reported that, between 1976 and 1980 shigellosis in San Francisco increased 700 percent among young men in their thirties. Incidence of "Gay Bowel Syndrome" had increased by 8,ooo percent after 1973. As Shilts told the story in his book on AIDS, AND THE BAND PLAYED ON, 'Gay doctors had long recognized that parasitic diseases...were simply a health hazard of being gay. The problem grew with the popularity of anal sex, in the late 1960's and early 1970's, because it was nearly impossible to avoid contact with fecal matter during that act. As sexual tastes grew more exotic and rimming [i.e. anal-oral sex] became fashionable, the problem exploded. There wasn't a much more efficient way to get a dose of parasite spoor than by such direct ingestion'.

Another researcher and author, Harris L. Coulter gives us a similar look at the conditions that are part and parcel of the homosexual lifestyle. His concern is that the readers understand that AIDS is not the result of any random one-time sexual encounter but the end product of years of profligate living. In his book, AIDS And Syphilis: The Hidden Link, he takes a broader look at the true lifestyle of homosexuals and the incredible amount of disease that is a necessary consequence of its behaviors.

"...in tracking the genesis of AIDS we are interested in the whole way of life of those who are particularly vulnerable. Joan McKenna and her coworkers in Berkeley, California, described as follows the medical histories of a group of 100 homosexual men interviewed by them:

Among the most presentations we have found are the following:

Gonorrhea: multiple incidents with treatment by antibiotic therapies; twenty incidents per year for two or more years were not uncommon.

Hepatitis: high incidence of known hepatitis or positive antigen tests; 10 percent had chronic hepatitis of five years or longer duration.

Non-specific urethritis: multiple presentations, sometimes chronic in that an individual will report 6 or 7 episodes per years for up to 8 years; higher doses and longer duration of antibiotics as condition became to chemical intervention.

Dermatological eruptions: specific, palliative, and prophylactic use of antibiotics, tetracycline, and corticosteroids for skin eruptions; reports of prescribed tetracycline for 5 to 18 years continuously.

Sedatives, tranquilizers, and mood drugs: for psychological conditions; prescribed or used without prescription.

Chronic sore throat: more than 50 percent report frequent episodes [requiring] antibiotic medications.

Herpes simplex: 25 percent report chronic herpes; 90 percent herpes within the past 10 years.

Allergies: high incidence of history of chronic and severe allergies, allergy medications, and symptomatic suppressants.

Lymphadenopathy: frequent to chronic swollen lymph glands in 40 percent of sample for up to 25 years preceding survey.

Diarrhea: high incidence of known and unknown etiologies; frequent parasites suspected, and parasitic with and without confirmation of actual organisms in nearly 30 percent of our study.

Recreational drugs: nearly universal use of marijuana; a multiple and complex use of LSD, MDA, PCP, heroin, cocaine, amyl and butyl nitrites, amphetamines, barbiturates, ethyl chloride, opium, mushrooms, and what are referred to as "designer drugs".

Since this description probably characterizes a large portion of those whose pursue the gay (sic) lifestyle, it can be seen that this lifestyle involves a very heavy concentration of medications."

...all of these medications add a further burden of immunosuppression

242

to the systems of those who may already suffer from syphilis or some other venereal disease.

In order to cut through the prevarications, myths and untruths that abound around the question of AIDS we need to be clear on what it is. It is primarily a venereal disease that derives from the peculiarly homosexual practice of anal sex. The homosexual lobby argues that we are all equally at risk for AIDS but they know that that is not true. AIDS began in the homosexual community, was passed from there to intravenous drug users, women, recipients of contaminated blood and newborn infants of AIDS infected mothers. The group with the least risk for AIDS is lesbians. That's because this group has the least amount of contact with infected males who are the main transmitters of the disease and because lesbian sex does not involve the kinds of fluid-exchanging, blood-vessel bursting penetration that are the province of male homosexuals. The fact that so many of our daughters suffer from the disease does not mean it is equally a heterosexual disease. It means that many of our young women have been seduced, convinced or forced into a sexual practice that is homosexual. AIDS can be contracted through genital sex, but only if there is already a sore, lesion, bruise or some other opening on the penis or in the vagina through which the virus can find its way into the blood stream. This typically happens when a person already has a venereal disease that provides the virus with the opportunity for infection.

AIDS and other diseases are only the tip of the iceberg when it comes to beginning to understand the overall unhealthiness of the homosexual lifestyle. Again we quote Dr. Satinover:

In April 1993 three researchers presented a paper to the Eastern Psychological Association in which they analyzed the age of death for nearly seven thousand homosexuals and heterosexuals by obituary notices in a large number of gay and a smaller number of large non-gay newspapers. They found that the gay male life span, *even apart from AIDS* and *with* a long-term partner, is significantly shorter than that of married men in general *by more than three decades*. AIDS further shortens the life span of homosexual men by more than 7 percent.

It was and is the reality of AIDS, all these other diseases and an acutely shortened life span that provides us with the most dramatic indication that homosexuals are not like everybody else and that we are not all equally at risk to contract the disease. It is not only in their specific sexual practices that we find homosexuals to be different from the general population. In his book SECOND COMING author E. Lagard Smith gives us an indication of what the overall agenda of the homosexual liberation movement consists of:

For over two decades, much-behind-the-scenes maneuvering has been going on. Consider, for example, the 1972 Gay Rights Platform drawn up by the National Coalition of Gay Organizations. Among the Coalition's goals were the following:

Repeal of all laws prohibiting private sexual acts involving consenting persons. (Remember that the animal rights groups say that animals are people)

Repeal of all laws prohibiting prostitution, both male and female.

Repeal of all laws governing the age of sexual consent.(emphasis mine.)

Repeal of all legislative provisions that the sex or number of persons entering into a marriage unit; and the extension of legal benefits to all persons who cohabit, regardless of sex or numbers.

Enactment of legislation so that child custody, adoption, visitation rights, fosters parenting, and the like shall not be denied because of sexual orientation or marital status.

Encouragement and support for sex-education courses, prepared and taught by gay women and men, presenting homosexuality as a valid, healthy preference and lifestyle and as a viable alternative to heterosexuality.

The sex-education plank has had growing success in some parts of the country, as has the plank relating to homosexual parenting and adoption. That is why it is so important that we examine the strategy and tactics of the movement. If gay-rights advocates are successful, then two decades from now we could be facing legalized prostitution, both male and female; the complete legalization of homosexual relations even with children; legal marriages for gays; parents losing custody of their children for disapproving of homosexual behavior; and even churches convicted of 'hate crimes' for preaching that homosexual behavior is a sin.

The ways in which homosexuals differ most from the general population is not just in their specific sexual practices but in their overall philosophy of revolutionizing human society as we have known it for thousands of years. Their disdain for marriage and family and their insistence that children be used for the sexual satisfaction of adults can only be described as perverse. This would mean the legalization, institutionalization and sanctification of sexual child abuse.

Authors George Grant and Mark A. Horne in Legislating Immorality describe some of the books used in the propaganda campaign to legalize pedophilia:

Alyson [Publishers] has other books on children and homosexuality with a slightly different angle. In books such as Pedophilia: The Radical Case, Gay Sex: A Manual for Men Who Love Boys, and one of Alyson's earlier works, THE AGE TABOO: Gay Male Sexuality, Power and Consent, the intended audience is child molesters, those who would like to be child molesters, and those who wish to rationalize child molestation. GAY SEX goes so far as to provide recommendations from NAMBLA to advise pedophiles on how to avoid outraged parents and police.

Additionally, THE ALYSON ALMANAC, a book of homosexual trivia, directs readers interested in pederasty to contact NAMBLA (North American Man Boy Love Association) ; The Spartacus International Gay Guide, 1992-1993 is a homosexual travel guide that tells readers where to find boy prostitutes in other countries; MACHO SLUTS is a collection of Pat Califia's allegedly erotic short stories, in one of which a lesbian protagonist 'performs sadomasochistic' sex on her daughter, whipping the girl until she bleeds; ONE TEENAGER IN 10: Writings by Gay and Lesbian Youth is a pedophile anthology...

Dr. Satinover talks about how much progress they have already made in their campaign to make pedophilia as acceptable tomorrow as homosexuality in general is today. The groundwork for the acceptance of homosexuality was first laid in the world of psychology because that discipline enjoys near religious status in this nation's popular culture. Psychologists and psychiatrists often play the role in American society that ministers and priests fulfill in traditional cultures. They are the arbiters of right and wrong. Many otherwise intelligent people depend on them to explain how the world works and how the universe functions. Already the AAP has removed pedophilia from the list of mental disorders and declared that having sex with children is just another sexual preference:

...Careful studies show that pedophilia is far more common among homosexuals than heterosexuals. The greater absolute number of

245

heterosexual cases reflects the fact that heterosexual males outnumber homosexual males by approximately thirty-six to one. Heterosexual child molestation cases outnumber homosexual cases by only eleven to one, implying that pedophilia is more than three times more common among homosexuals....the American Psychiatric Association normalized homosexuality in two steps: At first it only removed from its list of disorders homosexuality that was 'ego-syntonic,' comfortable and acceptable to the individual leaving only; 'ego-dystonic'—unwanted—homosexuality as a disorder; later it removed 'ego-dystonic' as well.

In a step strikingly reminiscent of what occurred in the seventies with respect to homosexuality, the 1994 edition of the DSM(DSM-IV) has quietly altered its long-standing definitions of all the 'paraphilias' (sexual perversions). Now, in order for an individual to be considered to have a paraphilia—these include sado-masochism, voyeurism, exhibitionism, and among others, pedophilia—the DSM requires that in addition to having or even acting on his impulses, 'fantasies, sexual urges or behaviors' must 'cause clinically significant distress or impairment in social, occupational or other important areas of functioning'. In other words, a man who routinely and compulsively has sex with children, and does so without pangs of conscience and without impairing his functioning otherwise, is not necessarily a pedophile and in need of treatment.

While they claim to be enjoying a "sexual orientation" which they were born with, the real causes of homosexuality have not changed over the past thirty years just because the homosexual liberation movement insists that it is not an illness. Psychologists long ago traced much of the genesis of this illness to family dysfunction, particularly to unhealthy relationships among parents and children. Homosexuality in men is predominantly the result of hostile and/or absent fathers (physically or emotionally) and overbearing, smothering, controlling and often seductive mothers. In other words, the absence of a healthy male role model and the overwhelming presence of a controlling mother who works hard at suppressing and destroying the masculine impulses in her son is the most common cause of homosexuality, along with sexual child abuse.

There is a significant opposition to homosexuality as

healthy behavior that comes not just from the ranks of conservative white Christianity but from such groups as the American Association of Psychoanalysts. The homosexual lobby was able through political pressures to force the American Association of Psychiatrists to remove homosexuality from its list of mental illnesses. There remained, however, a number of therapists who never bowed to the pressure to allow popular politics to determine a medical diagnosis. Many *psychoanalysts*, those psychiatrists who specialize in discovering through therapy the underlying kinds and sources of trauma that lead to a particular form of aberrant behavior, continue to recognize homosexuality as form of sexual perversion and addiction stemming from certain types of. We know that sexual addictions are more powerful than those of any manmade drug but they are still treatable. A number of psychoanalysts continue to treat homosexuals who want to be released from the powerful grip of this disorder and they have an excellent recovery rate for individuals who are sufficiently motivated to change. They have also produced a body of scientific studies documenting their work with homosexuals and their consistent success in treating them. The National Association for Research and Treatment of Homosexuality was formed by therapists of this persuasion. Their website www.narth.com is an excellent resource for those interested in a viewpoint on homosexuality that is not merely politically correct.

As far as I'm concerned, the homosexual liberation movement is a family problem among white parents and children. White parents are notorious for coddling their children and lacking the intestinal fortitude or moral strength to hold them to higher standards of behavior. White children have a long and well documented history of being traumatized by the abuse and neglect which is normative to the European family. Our enslaved ancestors recognized the built-in dysfunctionalities of the Euro-American family long before sociologists and psychiatrists began taking critical looks at its structure and function. Its operating philosophy of individualism; its narrow, stingy, exclusivistic nuclear construction that limits itself by definition to mother, father, sister, and brother; its history of alcoholism, that is so often at the root of domestic violence; and its bunker mentality expressed in the European proverb: "A man's home is his castle". All of these are at the root of a family system often given to institutionalized neglect and abuse.

Many white children, so negatively affected by these childhood problems, end up becoming habituated to a lifestyle of acting out based on addictive compulsive sexual encounters with people of the same sex. As in most addictive behavior they are searching for a source of pleasure which will give them some respite from the unending pain of not having been sufficiently loved by their parents. In their anger and frustration at their parents, who they correctly understand to be the root of the problem, they decide to rub their parents' noses in the difficulties they are responsible for. While on the one hand there is a certain lightweight poetic justice in this approach it is not true righteousness nor is it the way of healing. It is a vengeful spirit on the part of the originators of the idea that; we are going to declare that "Our sickness is no sickness, our sin no sin, and we are going to make everybody else accept our behavior by acting out outrageously in public until they accept us as we are and stop criticizing us and trying to heal us". The parents feel inadequate to the task of calling their children to correction and healing because they know they that they are at fault in the first place and to deal forthrightly with the child's conditions means to confront their own behavior which gave rise to it. We are all familiar with white parents' pattern of surrender to their children's demands when those children engage in emotional blackmail by acting out in public arguing, screaming, cursing at them, calling them names, telling them that they hate them, wishing them dead, accusing them of not loving them, throwing tantrums. Our elders have always maintained that: "The actions of the child reflect on the parent". This is what the homosexual liberation movement boils down to. Or what Dr. Joseph Nicolosi, calls the "gay deception", in a chapter by that title published in HOMOSEXUALITY AND AMERICAN LIFE edited by Christopher Wolfe:

"Gay is, I believe, a self-deceptive identity. It has been brilliantly marketed and bought without question by the most influential institutions—professional psychology and psychiatry, churches, educators, and the media—of American society...the gay-*identified* person –[is]a person who is personally identified with the idea that homosexual behavior is as normal and natural as heterosexual behavior. A man who recognizes that he has a homosexual problem and struggles to overcome it is not 'gay . He is simply, 'homosexual.'

...there is no such thing as a gay person. Gay is a fictitious identity seized upon by an individual to resolve painful emotional challenges. To consider that the concept of a gay identity is valid, a person must necessarily deny significant aspects of human nature.

I propose a three-step, psycho-social model for the development of a gay identity—first we see the gender distortion of the pre-homosexual child; second, his eventual assimilation into the gay counterculture, reinforcing those same distortions; and finally, we see the expansion of the gay community's successful self-deception into the further deception of a large portion of society.

The person who accepts the gay label in adulthood, has typically spent much of his childhood emotionally disconnected from people, particularly his male peers and his father. He also has likely assumed a false, rigid, 'good little boy' role within the family.

The emotionally disconnected reveal themselves in their view of their family life: 'I was a non-entity I didn't have a place to feel'; 'I always acted out other people's scripts for me. I was an actor in other people's plays' ; 'My parents watched me grow up'; 'I watched myself grow up.' No wonder the pre-homosexual boy is often interested in theatre and acting. Life is theatre. We are all actors. Reality is what we wish it to be'. In the absence of an authentic identity, it is easy to self-reinvent.

Freud claimed that "The father is the reality principle". The father represents the transition from the blissful, mother-child symbiosis to harsh reality. But the pre-homosexual boy says to himself, "If my father makes me unimportant, I make him unimportant. If he rejects me, I reject him and all that he represents'. Here we see the infantile power of 'no'.—'My father has nothing to teach me. His power to procreate and affect the world are nothing compared to my fantasy world. What he accomplishes, I can dream. Dream and reality are the same' Rather than striving to discover his own masculine, procreative power, he chooses, instead to stay in the dreamy, good-little-boy role. Detached, not, only from father and other boys, but from his maleness and his own male body—including the first symbol of masculinity, his own penis—he will later try to find healing through another man's penis. That exactly is what homosexual behavior is: the search for the lost masculine self.

Since anatomically-grounded gender is a core feature of individual identity, the homosexual has not so much a sexual problem as an identity problem. It follows that narcissism and preoccupation with self are commonly observed in male homosexuals. In his early teenage years, unconscious drives to fill this emotional vacuum—to want to connect with his maleness—are felt as homoerotic desires. The next stage will be entry into the gay world.

Then for the first time in his life, this lonely, alienated young man meets (through gay romance novels, television personalities, or internet chat rooms) people who share the same feelings. But he gets more than empathy. Along with the empathy comes an entire package of new ides and concepts about sex, gender, human relationships, anatomical relationships, and personal destiny.

Next he experiences that heady, euphoric, pseudo-rite-of –passage called 'coming out of the closet' It is just one more constructed role to distract him from the deeper, more painful issue of self-identity. Gay is not 'discovered' as if it existed *a priori* as a natural trait. Rather, it is a culturally approved process of *self-reinvention* by a group of people in order to mask their collective hurts. This false claim to have finally found one's authentic identity through gayness is perhaps the most dangerous of all the false roles attempted by the young person seeking identity and belonging. At this point, he has gone from compliant, 'good little boy' of childhood, to sexual outlaw. One of the benefits of membership in the gay subculture is the support and reinforcement he receives for reverting to fantasy as a method of problem solving.

He is now able to do collectively what he did alone as a child. When reality is painful, he chooses the fantasy option: 'I have merely to redefine myself and redefine the world. If others won't play my game, Ill charm and manipulate them. If that doesn't work, I'll have a temper tantrum'.

The lonely child receives awesome benefits of membership by assuming the gay self-label. He receives unlimited sex and unlimited power by turning reality on its head. He enjoys vindication of early childhood hurts. Plus as an added bonus, he gets to reject his rejecting father and similarly, the Judeo-Christian Father-God who separated good from bad, right from wrong, truth from deception. Oscar Wilde said, 'morality is simply an attitude we adopt toward people who we personally dislike.' ...But historically although the gay rights movement followed along the coattails of the civil-rights movement, it continues to draw its ideological power from the sexual liberation movement....Chasseguet-Smirgel claims that the 'pervert' (in the traditional psychoanalytic sense of the term) confuses two essential human realities: the distinction between the generations and the distinction between the sexes. In gay ideology, we see just this sort of obliteration of differences. Midge Decter observes, for example, that we treat our children like adults(we have only to look at sex education in elementary school), at the same time that adults are acting like children. A number of contemporary movements, including the animal rights movement (with its idea that man is no higher animals), also exemplify the confusion. As animal liberationist and founder of PETA Ingrid Newkirk says, 'a rat...is a pig...is a dog...is a boy.' There are movements to break down the barriers between generations: Witness the recent change in the definition of pedophilia and the publishing of the double *Journal of Homosexuality* issue, 'Male intergenerational Love' (an apologia for pedophilia). Thus we see animal confused with human, sacred confused with profane, adult with child, male confused with female, and life confused with death—all of these *traditionally the most profound of distinctions and separations, are now under siege*...Gay is a counter-identity, a negative. By that I mean it gets its psychic energy by *'what I am not,'* and is an infantile refusal to accept reality. It is a compromise identity seized upon by an individual, and increasingly supported by our society, to resolve emotional conflicts. It is a collective illusion; truly, I believe, 'the gay deception'.'

The Christian churches in the white community have confronted the issue of homosexuality head-on. One of the most common features in the institutional life of the white church over the past thirty years has been their grappling with this issue. They have in their national bodies researched, reported on, debated and voted for or against the acceptance of homosexuality on the terms of the homosexual liberation movement or rejected it on the basis of the moral authority of scripture. So-called progressive churches and self identified liberal denominations like the Unitarian-Universalists, the United Church of Christ (U.C.C.), the Episcopal Church and the Society of Friends (Quakers) have fully embraced homosexuality. These churches perform ceremonies celebrating homosexual "marriage", ordain homosexuals as ministers, and even appoint homosexual couples as co-pastors of their churches. There is even a national network of homosexual congregations known as the Metropolitan Community Churches. The United Methodists and the Presbyterians continue in discussion and debate over this issue.

The churches that regard themselves as fundamentalist, evangelical or conservative, such as the Southern Baptists, Pentecostal and Holiness churches adhere to the biblical teaching that homosexuality is not only sin but "abomination" held in the same light as incest and bestiality. The Southern Baptist Convention will disaffiliate congregations that affirm or promote homosexuality. But most importantly the conservative churches have organized scores of ministries dedicated to the recovery of homosexuals from this deadly lifestyle.

The greatest killer of this generation of black youth is now AIDS. The fight against AIDS unfortunately has been captured by the homosexual lobby that has successfully in the public eye defined being against AIDS as being for homosexuality. That's the moral equivalent of being against syphilis but in favor of promiscuity. This is the uniqueness of the persuasive powers of the homosexual lobby. There are no parades for sufferers of syphilis celebrating their martyrdom to the cause of promiscuity. There is no demand that the government invest billions of dollars in medical research to find a vaccine for syphilis so that fornicators and adulterers can be made safe from the consequences of their behavior. There is no Syphilis Quilt for those who have died of syphilis as a result of choices they made about their sexual behavior.

Our daughters are particularly at risk from infection because we have not addressed the dangers of homosexuality and bisexuality caused on the one hand by incarceration in jails where homosexual practices are epidemic and on the other hand by drug addiction which leads male drug addicts to engage in acts of homosexual prostitution to support their habit. In both these situations the men maintain that they are not homosexuals according to the common law of the streets and the prisons which hold that the male playing the role of the aggressor (penetrator) is not the homosexual, only the one acting the role of the female (penetratee). Someone must cry out to this confused generation that when two men have sex together, both of them are homosexuals. Furthermore, for men coming out of prison there is no program to assist them in overcoming the habits of homosexual encounter and when they are released they almost immediately search for a woman to be become involved with. These women are then put at the twin risks of contraction of both AIDS and the other forms of abuse that go along with being intimately tied to a man that is unsure of his sexuality.

At greatest risk are those women who are connected to men who were involved in prison rapes. The neglect of the sexual abuse of boys and men is one of the most prominent features of this nation's discrimination against males. Our guarantees of protections for women is present in the very marrow of the law, whether written statutes or customary behavior. One of the most outstanding features in American jurisprudence over the last thirty years has been the intensification of the role of the law in the protection of women, especially from sexual crimes, exploitation and harassment.

There has been no such concern expressed for men. Over a million men are raped every year in America, the overwhelming majority in prisons. Yet such rapes, for obvious reasons are the least reported and least prosecuted crimes in America. While countless studies have been done on both the frequency of male rape of females and its consequences to the victim in terms of mental and emotional states and subsequent patterns of behavior, no such studies have been done for the male victims of homosexual rape. There is a critical need for us to understand the state of mind of men who have been subjected to rape in prison and how the resultant trauma affects their interaction with men, women and children upon their release. But further it behooves us to use this information to develop recovery programs for these victims.

At the same time we must be even more concerned about the men who committed the rapes. My good friend and esteemed pastor, the Rev. P.M. Smith of the Huber Memorial Church of Baltimore, MD raised this critically insightful question to me: "In the case of male on male rape which person is truly the homosexual, the one who was raped or the one who committed the rape". The question relates back the moral condition of our foremothers who were raped in slavery and then labeled as whores by their rapists the white slavers. Who in fact was the whore? The woman who did not desire or will to participant in the sexual act or the predator who forced sex upon her? Who is the true homosexual, the man who had the act forced upon him through intimidation or brutality or the man who desired the act so much that he forced himself upon an unwilling victim? It is the homosexual rapist who is most likely to refuse to accept or identify his own homosexuality and insists that as long as he plays the male role of the aggressor he is not a homosexual. It is this sort of hyper-masculine male that populates the new sub-culture of the "down low brother".

In an article published in the New York Times on August 3, 2003, the author, Benoit Denizet-Lewis writes about spending weeks hanging out with black men on the "down-low", that is brothers who habitually, but secretly, have sex with other men . By their public presentation these men would never be suspected of homosexuality. They are athletes, body-builders, weight-lifters, even self-described "thugs". They all have girlfriends or wives and children. But they are active in a homosexual underground that includes the most dangerous features of the sub-culture

254

that gave rise to AIDS. They even have their own bathhouses which homosexual activists agree were the original incubation centers of AIDS when it was first labeled Gay-Related Immune Deficiency. Yet they incredibly insist that they are not homosexuals. These men are the spearhead of the spread of AIDS among black women and children. They are psychologically and emotionally incapable of admitting their homosexuality to the women in their lives because they can't even admit it to themselves. The degree of their self-deception rivals that afore-treated "gay' movement in the power of its denial of an obvious reality. Such denial is an unmistakable indication of a serious mental disorder, the very thing that the American Psychological Association by fiat declared did not exist among homosexuals.

We, as black people, must look at this issue from every possible perspective, come to our own assessment of what it means for our community and develop our own response to it. Black church bodies need to convene conferences, workshops, debates and referendums in which there can be full and open conversation on this matter. Our silence has left an entire generation unarmed and defenseless against a phenomenon that is highly contagious, almost always fatal and has no cure. It is as though former President Bill Clinton got his strategy of "don't ask, don't tell" from the black church. We have certainly been practicing this strategy for at least a hundred years. We can no longer afford to bury our heads in the sands of denial and must confront this controversy head on. Since 68% of women with AIDS are our daughters and since fully 1/3 of all men who engage in the homosexual lifestyle will die prematurely of AIDS, it behooves us out of the common-sense logic of self defense to provide our children and coming generations with weapons of truth to confront and defeat this threat to the well-being of our communities.

As Christians we ought to be providing our members in particular and the black community in general with a view of homosexuality that is based on traditions of truth older that the fads of the latest headlines. We need to provide them with them profound wisdom from the three deep sources which have guided our people for countless millennia, the Bible, African traditions and African-American history. To do otherwise is to consign ourselves to a continued second-class Christianity in which we suffer from a sense of unworthiness and incapacity to think for ourselves. We wait for others to teach us how to be real Christians and define for us how to live.

The approach of the homosexual liberation community has been that AIDS must be defeated through the development of drugs that will cure it and a vaccine that will prevent it thus leaving them free to practice their life-style without consequence. The primary weapon they wield against contracting AIDS now is advising people to use a latex condom when engaging in homosexual sex. However, anyone who understands anything about the realities of homosexual behavior know that not only is this approach unworkable because of the failure rate of condoms but also because use of a condom does not prevent the diseases that result from the introduction of fecal matter into the bloodstream as a result of anal sex. This approach reduces a serious moral and medical question to one of mere technology, just as Planned Parenthood and the sex education industry have reduced the complex question of relationships, fertility, and family to just using birth control.

The issue of homosexuality is too crucial for us as a community to accept the unproven and simplistic arguments of the homosexual liberation movement and their supporters in the liberal media which maintains "God made them that way" and that they are like black people, an oppressed minority. By doing so they reduce anyone who disagrees with them to being a bigot.

On the web site dealing with the church and homosexuality there is a list of over 44 churches mostly located in the United States but with a few from Europe, Africa and Asia that explains each denominations stance on homosexuality. There is not a single black American denomination represented. The only black church listed is the Coptic Church of Egypt. No black church in America has taken a stand for or against. We have not discussed, debated, researched, held conferences, issued press statements, written position papers, debated or voted on this critical issue. Yet at the same time Black Christians are crying out for direction from their moral and spiritual leaders.

This has to be one of the greatest tragedies of this age. We as a people have not engaged in the kind of moral and intellectual conversation that will help us to understand the short-term and long-range ramifications of the acceptance and popularization of homosexuality in our communities. No black church body has officially considered the question of whether homosexuality is morally right or wrong. We continue to stand as mute and helpless spectators on the sidelines of history while others of a less lofty and profound moral tradition than our own wrestle with this question that will have much to do with deciding the future moral landscape of this nation. The great Morehouse thinker, scholar, visionary and writer Lerone Bennett, better known as the Senior Editor of Ebony Magazine, anticipated such an hour as this when he wrote in his book the Negro Mood: "Future generation of black youth will indict their elders, not for the battles they lost but for the battles they refused to fight"

Where do we find homosexuality playing a part in our history? Are there legends about it in the classic recitations of the griots of our homelands in West Africa? Are there any African proverbs that refer to it as an acceptable form of human interaction? Is it mentioned in any of the voluminous collections of slave narratives? Did our grandmothers and grandfathers from Down South teach us that it was an acceptable part of the traditional behavior of their generation and the generations of their elders?

Homosexuality was introduced into the community of the kidnapped ones by homosexual slave-owners. Just as those ancestors were oppressed by any number of other sexual perversions at the hands of people so corrupted by their power that they refused to recognize any restraints upon their behavior. Perhaps the real reason that many black people don't like to discuss slavery is the natural sexual modesty of African people which is a prominent feature amongst our people wherever they are found. Perhaps they didn't like to talk about slavery because it would have meant discussing the horrid ways that they were sexually exploited. It would have meant talking about rape, child molestation, incest, prostitution, breeding, and other such abominable and disgusting homosexual sexual practices such as urinating (the homosexuals of today call this a "golden shower") and defecating on people.

When the captured men of that era were forced into penetrating the master they defended their manhood by declaring, once back in the slave quarters: "He the homosexual, not me. He didn't do it me. I did it to him." That same peculiar explanation and specious justification is still popular in street and prison culture to this day. The idea being that only the man being penetrated is a homosexual. Of course common sense tells us that if two men are having sex with each other they are both homosexuals. Just like in the New Testament story of the "woman being caught in the act of adultery", despite the accusers relating of the incident, the woman was not the only adulterer in the situation. It takes two to tango.

Little boys, or for that matter grown men, who were forced to become the receptive partner in the slave owners' sexual outlawry were not shunned by the black community but received and accepted in the spirit of understanding, love and forgiveness. (Though people later would learn that some of them were threats to the sexual safety of black children if they became truly addicted to homosexual

258

behavior.) They would say of these often effeminate men and boys: "They can't help they self". And of course they couldn't. They were the victims of physical brutalities to themselves and threats to their family members that made their physical surrender a matter of a common sense strategy of survival.

What will be the long term effect on the black family when millions of men are given a carte blanche supposedly "scientifically valid" excuse for abandoning their critical roles as husbands and fathers? Haven't we seen enough of the consequences of fatherlessness with the current generation of almost two million black men locked up in jail all over this nation? Are we to accept bi-sexuality and encourage our daughters to marry men that identify themselves as such and expect them to be able to build a strong healthy family with open adultery as a standard component? Do we really want to give pedophiles easy and open access to introduce little boys and girls to sexual activity at grammar school age or earlier? If we do what will be the long-term consequences to those children and their ability to form committed relationships once they have been long acclimated from their most formative years to a lifestyle of sexual licentiousness?

How ought a man to respond to a request from another man that he have sex with him? Do we teach our boys to entertain the sexual overtures of homosexuals as though it were really possible that they could be convinced to try it? Already there are a number of cases around country that involve big boys and young men responding violently to aggressive overtures by homosexuals. Women and girls have historically used sophisticated non-violent feminine strategies for deflecting the unwanted advances of strange men. They will even go so far as to pretend to enjoy the conversation and then extricate themselves by giving the man a false name and number or even make a date they have no intentions of keeping.

Do we really expect that our boys and men will act coy

and coquettish under the physical and verbal pressure of a homosexual, bat their eyes and pitch their voices demurely, claiming to be interested in a homosexual liaison only to give the homosexual a false name and number? We would be insisting that men accommodate the gender bending of the homosexual who would make them sexual objects by switching their own response from typical masculine direct rebuffs into a feminine strategy of pretense and indirection. That would constitute men acting like women and the possibility of that happening on any large scale is unthinkable.

How should a man respond to a question from someone as to whether or not he is interested in having sex with his own mother, his sister, or his daughter? How should a man respond to someone who insists on engaging him in conversation about having sex with a child or with an animal? Should we really expect people to be liberal and philosophical enough to engage in extended conversation on these unthinkable matters? For people whose spiritual and moral values are based on biblical and African principles all of these above activities exist in the category of taboo and abomination--that which is not only not done but that which is not discussed and not even thought about. There are things that exist in our culture which from prehistory are considered unthinkable. To violate or desecrate sacred space. To curse God. To curse or strike an elder. Murder. Rape. Sex with children, animals or the dead. But we live in the midst of a pagan people who hold nothing sacred and to whom the most perverted behaviors are a matter of public performance. Do we integrate with these people, throw away our own ancient standards of what constitutes right and wrong and embrace their philosophy of "anything goes"?

What political reasons are there for us to make common cause with the homosexual liberation movement? Are they less racist than other white people? They do have a higher standard of living and more disposable income even than other white people. Have they used their financial resources to aid or assist our community in any measurable way? Should we even be discussing whether to accept or reject this dangerous lifestyle based on monetary gain? Does money have a place in a moral discussion? Or are we now all for sale? Can our manhood and womanhood be bought and sold in freedom in a way that our ancestors refused in slavery? What black causes do they support other than wanting to have sexual access to ourselves and our children? Haven't we learned anything from our historical experiences with other white groups who wanted us as allies until they didn't need us anymore then discarded us like used up paper towels?

The black community's response to homosexuality has been almost entirely controlled by white people. Our own leaders, especially our religious leadership, rather than articulating and advancing a perspective based upon the ancient spiritual principles and moral standards of our ancestors instead have allowed themselves, like children, to be led by other people as if they have no independent minds of their own. Since when have white people earned the right to instruct us in morality? Since when have they become the dependable beacon light of righteousness that is able to direct us in discerning right from wrong?

We daily are forced to witness the incredible sight of some our most respected leaders making common cause with the homosexual liberation movement declaring it to be another wing of the civil rights movement. Not since the 1920's when the black leadership establishment which included W.E. DuBois, A. Phillip Randolph, Walter White and others conspired with the federal government to jail and then deport Marcus Garvey has black leadership been so out of touch with its followship. Garvey at that time until now was the most popular black leader that Black America has yet seen. His Universal Negro Improvement Association had over six million members world-wide at its height of popularity and power during the early 1920's.

Out of professional jealousy, class bias and color-struckness, these so-called "responsible" black leaders collaborated with a young J. Edgar Hoover, in direct opposition to Garvey's embrace by the vast majority of our people. The black leaders who endorse and promote homosexuality are out of step with the moral traditions of our people.

While the black church as a whole in its denominational bodies have not dealt with the issue of homosexuality there are individual ministers who have taken up the banner of being the champions of the acceptance of homosexuality in the black church and community. Some of the most highly educated, erudite, eloquent, popular and sophisticated black preachers in the country are traveling this nation day and night most of the weeks of the year on a preaching mission to bring about the acceptance of homosexuality in the black church. The Rev. Dr. Jeremiah Wright, pastor of the Trinity United Church of Christ of Chicago, preaches a sermon entitled "Good News for the Homosexual" as though the gospel of Christ endorses their sin. The Reverend Dr. James Forbes of New York City, pastor of Riverside Church, one of the historical bastions of white theological liberalism in the country, writes guidelines for black preachers to use in preparing sermons on homosexuality but is at least honest enough to admit that the bible is of no use in constructing such sermons so that the preacher will have to find other authoritative sources. The Rev. Dr. Joseph Ratliff senior pastor of the Brentwood Baptist Church of Houston, TX defends homosexuality and sits on the board of the ministry Balm in Gilead which supports the behavior but claims that he is no homosexual himself. However, Dr. Ratliff's homosexuality was publicly exposed by audiotapes produced by a man who successfully sued him and his church for Ratliff's sexual assault upon him. The tapes so clearly proved Dr. Ratliff's homosexuality that he and the church settled out of court with the plaintiff. In the meantime Dr. Ratliff was retained

262

as pastor of the church despite the preponderance of evidence indicating his attempt to perform a homosexual act in his office at the church. Dr. Ratliff also serves as chairman of the board of the Interdenominational Theological Center in Atlanta, one of the largest and most prominent of the few accredited black seminaries in the country. This same school which is composed of denominational seminaries representing four different major black denominations had a lesbian wedding performed in its chapel in the early 1990's.

The message to the world, when neither his church nor the seminary nor the leading black pastors in this country censure his behavior, is that black America has descended to a popular acceptance of white immorality and can no longer claim a higher standard of righteousness than the people we live among. For some people this is the best news of all, that we have finally become like these people all together and now await confirmation of our acceptance in the mainstream. For others it is the beginning of the end. One of the classic ways we have seen ourselves theologically throughout our history here is as a salvific remnant that stayed the hand of God from destroying America for its unrestrained sinfulness by our faithfulness. We are becoming the salt that has lost its savor.

The positioning of these great religious leaders as spokespeople for a foreign philosophy goes against the very purpose for which our ancestors made provisions for them to obtain higher education in the first place. Almost every black college started out as a seminary because of our ancestors' understanding of our need for an educated clergy. Since our moral and spiritual leadership was our predominant leadership the ancestors wanted those men and women to have the very best academic preparation available.

One of the roles of the educated leader is to keep the black community abreast of the moves by white academia which mean us harm. To debunk the racist mythologies and intellectual constructions of the morally challenged people that we live amongst. The educated are the people we depend on to as the bible says "rightly divide the words of truth" and equip us to defend ourselves against the next racist assault. Racist campaigns and attacks are always preceded and under girded by some set of pseudoscientific half-truths and outrageous whole lies. We depend on the most educated of the race to keep us abreast of what's going on in the white world and interpret them for so that we can make the most intelligent response to them. The response we are looking to make is not merely scientific, nor is it based on sheer popularity. Has anyone ever heard of "scientific racism"? Or does anybody remember when slavery was popular and lynching was the #1 form of entertainment in this country?

I am still waiting to hear one of these men of God declare a truly authoritative source for their support of homosexuality. All I hear them saying is: "The APA says". Since when does psychology dictate to religion? Particularly when psychology is such a culture specific field that has so little regard for the religiosity of black people. Basically then they end up saying "The white man told me to tell you". They do not appeal to any of the truly authoritative honored sources of wisdom out of our own traditions. They can't appeal to the Bible except to deny it means what it says. They don't appeal to African traditions because homosexuality is a universal taboo in classical African civilizations Africa as is incest and beastialism. They can't even appeal to the ancestors or elders and declare "My granddaddy told me". They certainly do not use the most authoritative source, which is spiritual revelation. They do not say: "God told me that He formed these people as homosexuals in the womb and that He endorses their life-style as co-equal to that of heterosexuals" The multiple dangers of the homosexual lifestyle cry out for a response based on the deepest sources truth.

264

We, as a community, already suffer from a serious deficit of functional, productive men. We can hardly afford to write off tens if not hundreds of thousands of men who are distressed by a treatable mental and emotional disorder. Our faith teaches us that with God all things are possible. The church therefore should not be a haven providing excuses and justification for sinful, unhealthy and dangerous behavior but a hospital for the healing of sin-sick souls. There are a number of successful ministries dedicated to the healing of homosexuals among various white denominations and churches. I know of very few such ministries sponsored by black churches.

Dr. Jeremiah Wright argues that fornicators and adulterers do more damage in the black church community than homosexuals. He seems not to understand that these committers of heterosexual transgressions are not engaging in a whore-monger liberation movement in which they demand that the church accept their behavior as morally legitimate despite the bible's injunctions against them. Prostitutes are not coming to the church demanding that they be not only welcomed but also affirmed. Adulterers are not insisting that they were born like that and that God loves them just as they are and thus the church must embrace and encourage their behavior.

In one article in a Balm in Gilead publication the author argues that homosexuals are critical in the church in leading us in worship and providing the enthusiasm that heightens the spiritual level of the service as though homosexuals have a deeper form of spirituality than others. Mistaking enthusiasm for spirituality is nothing new in the black church. Dr. King in his classic sermon "A Knock at Midnight", talked about black congregations that "burn up", where the people "have more religion in their hands and feet than in their hearts and souls". The Apostle Paul in the 1st chapter of Romans described such people as having a "zeal of God but not according to knowledge". It is undeniable that homosexuals have had a major presence

265

in the music ministry of the black church for generations and now have a prominent presence in the ministry though the overwhelming majority of homosexual ministers remain on the down-low. But we ought to be spiritually discerning enough to understand that just because someone is loud does not mean that they are profound. Or that just because someone has the audacity to project themselves to the forefront that they are qualified to be a leader.

These days of moral confusion and spiritual ambiguity call for men and women of God of discernment. Everybody that 's been baptized ain't saved. The old folks say: "Some people go into the baptismal waters a dry devil and come up a wet devil but they still a devil." Everybody that preaches has not been called. Every sermon is not the truth. Everybody that shout ain't happy. Every spirit that evidences itself in the sanctuary is not the Holy Spirit. The church is a spiritual battlefield. It is always has been and it always will be. There is acting out sometimes in worship that has to do with people struggling with powerful emotional and spiritual issues. Some people act out for all kinds of reasons that are neither holy nor righteous. We have witnessed the hypocrisy of the white church for hundreds of years as they perform supposedly sacred acts while their hands are covered with the blood of the innocent.

The question becomes will your blackness define your Christianity or will your embrace of white Christianity define your blackness? The black church decided over two hundred years ago that they would not define themselves according to white Christian presuppositions. Over and against black Christians who insisted on remaining in the white church and allowing their Christianity and thus their blackness to be defined by white people. When I speak of blackness defining Christianity I return to the beginnings of Christianity as being originally African. The perversion of Christianity by Europeans stands as one of the great challenges to our people who identify themselves as

266

Christians. Our ancestors critiqued white Christianity based on ancient African values which were in line with the teachings of the bible. They recognized the error in the Christianity espoused by the white people who claimed that they were Christians yet at the same time treated them in ways that were in horrendous contradiction to the teachings of both the Old Testament about justice and the New Testament about love. The seeming inability of so many black Christian leaders to establish independent moral ground outside of the teaching of their white Christian leaders and mentors has put us as a people in general and the church in particular in a dangerous place.

The Bible mandates that we both hate sin and love the sinner. We can accomplish this responsibility by continuing to, on the one hand declaring through the unique power of our preaching and teaching that homosexuality is sin. While on the other hand, opening our arms and the doors of our churches to *receive the sinner in the spirit of recovery.*

It is a spiritual travesty and an abomination to entertain sin and treat it as though it were no sin. We preachers are constrained by the gospel to serve, like the prophet Ezekiel, as watchmen. We stand on the high towers of prophetic farsightedness to overlook the moral landscape of this world, responsible for warning God's people of the dangers of sin that approaches the camp. If we are true to our calling and warn the people, even if they will not heed the warning, even if they decide that they want to commune with evil for a season, even if they refuse to receive our report, the bible says then that their blood is on their own hands. However, if we forbear to carry the word, if we decide that its not worth risking the people's disfavor, if we decide like some that "where ignorance is bliss, 'tis folly to be wise", if we decide that the loss of our pulpits or some other plum of an ecclesiastical office or lucrative, prominent appointment is too much to suffer for the sake of warning the people of their transgressions, then the bible

267

says: "his blood I will require at the watchman's hands".
EZ 33:6 KJV

We have already witnessed the disruptions to society caused by the sexual revolution of the sixties and seventies. We have seen the tragic increase of the divorce rate and the horrors of child abuse. All because we decided that we would, like Adam and Eve in eating the forbidden fruit, be like God and decide good an evil for ourselves. Any time moral markers are moved, there will be tragic results. The bible is still right: "the wages of sin is death." Rom. 6:23 KJV In the sixties heterosexual couples and the liberal church concluded that calling fornication and adultery sin was old-fashioned and therefore decided that the moral markers for sexual intercourse would no longer be marriage but rather love. Anybody who was "in love" therefore had the right in their eyes to engage in sex. I don't know why they overlooked the commonsense reality that the male of the species especially young ones will tell almost any lie to convince a woman to surrender her virtue and her charms. The result was millions of babies conceived in what the women were convinced was love only to find out when it was time to shoulder the consequences of sex, which is babies, their partners were not interested. Or as Billie Holiday put it in song:

Love is just like a faucet.
It turns off and on.
Just when you think you got love.
It's done turned off and gone

Thus we have reaped a bitter harvest of disillusioned mothers and unwanted, fatherless children.

But where does the moving of moral markers stop Are the homosexuals the last group that will lay claim to the right to engage in that which we have for thousands of years recognized as not just sin but as abomination? Of course not, because one of the chief characteristics of evil is aggressiveness. Evil never says: "Enough, I'm satisfied". The old people say that: "evil is long-legged and

268

loves to travel". They tell also tell us: "Don't let the devil ride. If you let him ride, he'll want to drive".

It is already a common practice in hundreds of high schools across this nation that when teen-agers express a sense of sexual confusion that they are referred to homosexual support groups within their schools headed up by adult homosexual authority figures to counsel them. These adult authority figures use these opportunities to convince these young people that they are in fact homosexuals and to give themselves up entirely to the lifestyle. In some instances they seduce these children into the behavior themselves. But they don't warn them of the real physical not to mention spiritual and psychological dangers inherent in that behavior. Homosexual behavior cuts short the life span of those that engage in it.

Another concern is the number of homosexuals in the would-be Pan-Africanist community. The homosexual community have made African American Studies Departments on college campuses a special target for co-option. They insist on linking their "gay" studies to our discipline claiming that we are both oppressed minorities. These are brothers and sisters who have African names, African hairdos, wear African clothes and African jewelry and insist that their homosexuality is authentically African. This is unfortunately not a new phenomenon. During the sixties we had people that we described as "talking black and sleeping white". These were men and women who in their public performance staunchly declared their unlimited, undying, total and complete love for their people. They claimed to love and appreciate everything black. They were militants and activists. They marched, sung, shouted and demonstrated their commitment to black people in every way except romantically. These people would inevitably be found with a white person on their arm, at their sides, and in their beds. We saw their behavior as being oxymoronic and self-contradictory, as is the behavior of this new generation of, to here them tell it "super-black" black people, but who engage in a European behavior as their preferred form of sexual expression. They are like their counterparts in the sixties, "talking black but sleeping white".

We already have a young man, Aaron Price, a Morehouse College student and C.M.E. pastor's son charged with a hate crime but convicted of aggravated assault and now doing ten years in jail because of his violent rebuff of an act of sexual harassment by a homosexual schoolmate. Brother Price was interrupted while taking a shower by another student who pulled back his shower curtain and leered at him. He became so enraged at the assault (the legal definition of such an act had it been committed against a woman would have been "peeping tom") became so outraged that he left out of the shower got a baseball bat came back and beat his transgressor with it.

The homosexual community in Atlanta reacted with outrage and publicly excoriated Morehouse College as being an unsafe environment for homosexuals. The campaign of highly publicized denouncement was so effective that the president of Morehouse within weeks of the incident issued the astounding statement that "sexual orientation has nothing to do with being a man and a brother". The president, Dr. Walter Massey, then commissioned a Committee on Tolerance and Diversity for the purpose of proposing steps that the school should take in dealing with the presence of homosexuals at Morehouse. The commission invited as its most prominent guest member Dr. Peter Gomes, dean of the chapel at Harvard University, an avowed homosexual and notorious apologist for the behavior.

Thus the committee decided the direction it was going in before it held its first meeting. There was no allowance for a differing viewpoint that reflects the moral traditions of our people. It was a concession to political correctness based, I believe, on two primary considerations. The first being the considerable presence of homosexuals at

270

Morehouse, though mostly on the down low, among students, faculty and administrators. Rampant homosexuality has been an open secret at Morehouse for at least a generation. The second being Morehouse' desire to continue being a prominent producer of executives for corporate America where "diversity" means the acceptance of homosexuality as we can see from the number of corporations who offer benefits to same-sex couples that used to be reserved for married couple.

In the school's response to this crisis the president went along with the homosexual community and local press campaign to portray Morehouse as an "unsafe environment for homosexuals" using the beating as prima facie evidence that such was the case. They shamelessly promoted the idea that homosexuals at Morehouse were being constantly harassed and mistreated by the majority of the student body. The fact is just the opposite. Morehouse has had a significant homosexual population since at least my student days in the early seventies. The acts of harassment that I am familiar with have not been those foisted upon homosexuals by heterosexuals but just he opposite. Aggressive approaches by homosexuals to straight students are legend at Morehouse.

A former student related to me an incident that took place only two or three years ago when a student went to an administrator to confess that he had run out of funds and would have to leave school. The administrator told the young man that he would provide for his expensive if the student would enter into a homosexual relationship with him. The student did so and as a result suffered a nervous breakdown and spent the rest of the school year walking around in an obvious state of emotional and mental distress. In considering the case of the young man who defended himself from an extremely aggressive homosexual approach by beating the aggressor, one must factor in the pressure involved in having witnessed the possible dire consequences of engaging in homosexual practices.

This country, pressured by feminist activists, has become tremendously sensitive to the effects of sexual harassment of women by men. Even to the point of using a history of such harassment or abuse as credible defense of women who use violence against such men. The battered woman's syndrome is a standard defense of women, for instance, who kill their husbands. Had it been a Spelman student who had been approached in the privacy of her shower by a man who pulled back her shower curtain to expose her nakedness, the response of authorities would have been entirely different. The uncovering of a woman's nakedness by a man is an egregious assault that stands as a prelude to rape. They would not have accepted the man's specious explanation that he thought it was his girlfriend in the shower but since he didn't have his glasses on he had to pull back the curtain to look. Common sense tells us that the correct thing to would have been simply to open one's mouth and ask. Whatever the girl put her hands on and attacked her assailant with would have been acceptable in the eyes of college administrators, law enforcement officials, members of the student body and the public at large. If she had run out of the shower to her father, brother, or boyfriend and they came in and caught the miscreant and beat him as we say "like he stole something" or "went upside his head 'til it roped like okra" it would have been understandable and acceptable. Yet we deny the same privilege to young males to defend themselves from homosexual assault.

We don't know how many times the young man in question had been subject to advances from homosexuals at Morehouse, in particular from the one who pulled back his shower curtain. We do know that a pattern of such harassment would have produced a heightened concern on his part to protect himself. This should have been a credible defense for the young man. Instead Morehouse stood by and sacrificed this young man on the altar of political correctness, even going so far as to accept the

272

transgressor's claim that he was not a homosexual and that the beating was an irrational reaction to an imagined threat or what homosexual activists term "gay panic". The article on down low brothers in the New York Times had a revealing comment on the incident. The author describes a conversation he had with three down low black men:

...I ask them if they have heard about what happened recently about an incident at Morehouse College, where one black student beat another with a baseball supposedly for looking at him the wrong way in a dormitory shower.

'I'm surprised that kind of thing doesn't happen more often,' William says. 'The only reason it doesn't is because most black gays are sly enough about it that they aren't going to get themselves beaten up.'

The atmosphere at Morehouse is such that the homosexual brother felt no need to be "sly" or in any way disguise his intentions. We have through our moral cowardice created a situation in which innocent black boys are doubly victimized by homosexuals. First, by their extremely aggressive approaches; secondly by our punishing the victims for trying to protect themselves in the best way that they know how. A storm is looming on the moral horizon that we have not properly prepared for. We have empowered homosexuals to loose any bounds to their campaign to convert straight people to their ways. But we have not considered what a moral outrage it is for a heterosexual to be forced into a conversation about violating moral boundaries and engaging in behavior described in the bible as abominable an thus threaten the very standing of his soul in the corridors of eternity.

The standard European amoral approach of "anything goes" has unleashed energies in the universe which we cannot fully account for. We do know that evil has its consequences. It always has and it always will. This cannot be changed by vote, plebiscite or referendum. God is not subject to us. We always have and always will be subject to him. Slavery had its consequences in the Civil War when white men engaged in a four year orgy of slaughter over black people that both of them hated and despised. They killed and died for us despite themselves. Political common sense should have prevented the Civil War. But there are other forces at work in the universe. As one of Dr. King's favorite quotations expressed: "The arc of the universe is long but it bends toward justice". Promiscuity produces venereal disease, fatherless children and abandoned, lonely, and desperate men and women. Gluttony produces obesity. Anger produces violence and hatred gives birth to murder. Homosexuality has produced the warning of AIDS but because we will not pay attention a further reckoning awaits us all.

X. ENTERTAINMENT

   Sex and pain are both themes that should be dealt with
in private. Sex at best should take place within the confines
of a sacred relationship whose chief characteristics are
respect, love and commitment but even at its worst it still
should be an intimate activity carried out in private
between two consenting adults. People in pain ought to go
the hospital or at least to a doctor. If the pain is emotional,
spiritual, psychological, they ought to go to a minister or
therapist. The idea of using a public forum to exhibit your
psychic distress is at best childish and immature. At its
worst it's demonic. There is no period in history that the
state of contemporary entertainment can be more likened to
than that of Imperial Rome in the days of the spectacles of
the circus. The entertainments of the circus were based on
public displays of sex and violence or a combination of the
two. The freak shows on television which are called talk
shows by their producers, the so-called songs of the
gangster and hard-core rappers, and the r-rated movies are
all, like the Roman circus, based on the obscenities of
unrestrained exhibitionistic sex and unlimited sadistic
violence. It is a testimony to the moral degradation of any
human society when the worst kinds of morally deficit
behavior become a matter of entertainment, when the most
painful kinds of human experience becomes a running joke
to be played out before live audiences.
   The Jerry Springer show and others specialize in having
the most intimate family dramas and traumas displayed
before audiences whose members howl like hyenas as

husbands and wives, parents and children, brothers and sisters tear out each others hearts with open, proud, contemptuous and boastful confessions of betrayal and abandonment. To find enjoyment in the display of inflicting the kinds of wounds that drive people to drink, drugs, murder and suicide is an indication of the moral bankruptcy of American society in the entertainment industry. These are the kinds of behaviors that past generations would have termed unthinkable. The kinds of things that grown people would have sent children out of the room before discussing them in hushed tones.

Our young people, according to every study I've read, watch TV and go to movies twice as much as their white counterparts. They also take what they see on TV and at the movies more seriously and imitate it more faithfully. One of the worst examples of this phenomenon is found in the movie New Jack City, a story of black dope dealers starring Wesley Snipes as the founder of a crack-cocaine empire, replete with glorifying the so-called gangster lifestyle. In one scene there is a drive by shooting at a wedding. One of the black gangsters grabs a little black girl toddler and uses her to shield him from the gunfire of his attackers. This is the sort of scene of child-abuse that could only have been dreamed up by some racist Hollywood screen-writer high on alcohol, cocaine, LSD and maybe PCP who imagines that black people have so little regard for the life of a child that they would use an innocent baby in such a horrendously unthinkable fashion. The worst part of all of this is that numbers of black youth took the scene in New Jack City to heart. I am familiar with at least two occasions, one in Chicago and the other in Atlanta, where black gangsters engaged in gun play grabbed black children and used them as shields. In the Atlanta incident a thirteen year old girl was shot to death and in Chicago a two year old boy was killed.

TV watching is one of the greatest impediments to academic success among black youth. In the book The

Plug-in Drug the author, Marie Winn, cited a scientific study that measured brain-wave activity among TV watchers. The study concluded that when people are watching TV their brains function below the level of consciousness and above the level of sleep. In other words, we watch TV in a semi-hypnotic state in which our brains take in information without reacting critically to it. Our young people need to be more critical in their thinking than others because so much of what they are presented with is designed for their destruction. They need to be able to recognize stereotypes, myths, half-truths and out-right lies when they see them.

Also, TV watching is destructive of social interaction. People sit in the dark watching images on a techno-color screen with a minimum of conversation between them. Or people sit at the dinner table in front of a TV with no interchange among the generations. The tradition of meal time as family ritual in which the goings on of the day at school and at work are reported, described, discussed and evaluated is lost. The opportunity for the elders to hand down wisdom to the youngsters in the family is surrendered to the dysfunctional practice of everybody watching some inane program, that has little value other than to fill up the time before going to bed.

Television programs and movies rob their watchers of the continuing development of the imaginal capacity of the brain. When reading books or listening to stories or the radio the brain must translate the words into images. When watching TV and movies this crucial work is done for the watcher and encourages laziness in the viewers. One of the most important gifts that young people bring to the world is that of imagination. All human progress is dependent upon imagination, which is chiefly a gift of the young. The continuing disappointments of time and circumstance teach older people to stick with the tried and true which are the gift of memory which is the child of experience. It is up to young people who are not yet convinced of the futility of the untried to venture into the unknown through the inspiration of imagination. TV and movie watching erodes and atrophies these powers and renders young people old before their time and unable to imagine a new thing that has never been done before.

In a classic experiment a teacher scratched two dots in chalk on a blackboard and asked a classroom full of eighteen year old high school seniors what they were. The entire class agreed that they were just "two dots." Next the same thing was done for a class of thirty-two five year-old kindergartners. Those little children came up with thirty-two different ideas as to what those two dots represented such as: two stars, two diamonds, two gold rings, two moons. The kindergartners were still in the prime of their childhoods and gloried in the powers of their imaginations. The older kids were already so afraid of the embarrassment of being wrong they did the obvious thing and came up with the safest solution which was to accept a thing on its face value only without extrapolating to greater, wider, deeper or grander possibilities.

We are surrounded by and immersed in immorality, outright evil, even demonism in music that promotes and encourages selfishness, unrestrained hedonism, violence, drug use, orgies, rape, murder, torture, and dismemberment. Everywhere in the world but Europe art is considered a divine gift to be used to uplift human life. Martha Bayles, the author of *A Hole in Our Soul*, one of the five best books I've ever read on music, states that:

"It is ironic that, in this age of multiculturalism, so many people seem intent upon ignoring the fact that the West is the only civilization to have created a form of art whose sole purpose is to attack morality…(emphasis mine)*Now by morality…I mean simply the difference between good and evil as understood by most human beings Too often artistic modernism has sought just such a repeal of morality-in the name of the radical freedom needed to create a radical new culture… without any of the old culture's imperfections. Here too the West*

is unique, because no other culture asks human beings to live without cultural continuity. Art is timeless when it touches aspects of human life that do not change. But modernism has dreamed of the most disruptive possible change, the greatest discontinuity between past, present and future."

Music among African peoples the world over thru the 1960's served the traditional role of music and art among all the world's peoples, uplifting traditional moral standards. One of the hallmarks of our four-hundred-year sojourn in this country has been the fact that practically every generation of black folk has produced a new body of music and dance. We have given this country and its culture lining hymns, the spirituals, work songs and field hollers, prison songs, jubilees, the blues, ragtime, gospel, jazz, swing, jump, bebop, doo-wop, soul. Up until the seventies the most popular black music for parties, dinners, dancing, basketball and football games and easy listening was music that promoted the traditional values of our people. Our love songs were about fidelity, marriage, family and children. There were even songs celebrating the wisdom and authority of the elders such as "Yakety-Yak (Don't Talk Back)", "Night Owl", "Shop Around", and "Mama Said".

The seventies gave us the first songs that were about sex rather than love. A man's pitch to the woman of his desire and affection was no longer "let's get married" but "let's spend the night together." There were even outright challenges to morality such as "If Loving You Is Wrong I Don't Want To Do Right". And even more devastating and scary was "Whatever It Is Do It 'Til You're Satisfied". These kinds of songs were merely the headwinds of a hurricane of musical obscenity that was just around the corner.

The consistency of black music's moral message was unbroken until seventies disco and rap music of the eighties and nineties and now the new millennium. At first rap was an infectious form, full of rhythm and fun, as is becoming the artistic offering of young people yet with a not inconsiderable amount of wisdom thrown in for good measure.

The Sugar Hill Gang in the first rap hit "Rappers Delight" had all of the elements in one song which would later on split off into different schools. For those interested in wisdom they declared:

The best advice I ever had
I got from my wise dear old dad
From six to sixty to this very day
I never forgot what he had to say
He said sit down son I want to talk to you
And don't say a word 'til I get thru
There's a time to laugh and a time to cry
A time to live and a time to die
A time to bake and a time to chill
To act civilized and act real ill.

The Fat Boys entertained and instructed with their "Jailhouse Rap:"

In jail because we failed

I used to drive around in my big car
Now I look and all I see is bars
I used to think that I was better
Now I'm a little boy just waiting on a letter

In jail because we failed.

Or Whodini doing a dissertation on friendship:

How many of us have them let's be friends
Some you grew up with around the way
And you're still friends 'til this very day
Some you like to be around because they're funny

Some you don't see 'til they need some money
I'll say this to again and again
The dictionary doesn't know the meaning of friends

Or Grandmaster Flash with their apocalyptic nightmare
entitled "New York, New York":

What you look at on TV tells you what life is supposed to
be
But when you go outside what you see is the poverty-
stricken reality
Abandoned places, angry faces
Much hate and anger throughout the races
So you sit at home talking on the phone
Doing a hundred miles an hour in the fifty mile zone
You say I'm grown and on my own
So why don't everybody just leave me alone
They didn't take the time to teach you 'bout sex
So you had to learn it in the discotheques
Nine months later the baby is here
And the "boy" that did it said
I don't care!
You don't have enough money to help feed two
So you have to choose between the baby and you
The sky was crying, rain and hail
When you put your baby in a garbage pail
Then you kissed the kid and put down the lid
And tried to forget what you just did
But the muffled screams of a dying baby
Was enough to drive the young mother crazy
So she ran through the rain trying to end the pain
But ended up driving herself insane.
New York, New York big city of dreams
But everything in New York ain't always what it seems
You might get fooled if you come from out of town
But I'm down by law and I know my way around.

Hardcore and gangster rap made its appearance in the late eighties and early nineties. As much as I was a lover of rap music and an admirer of the creativity of the hip-hop generation, this new edition of the music made me stop, pause, think, reconsider and reject it absolutely. The very names indicated it should not be consumed by the public at large. "Hardcore" meant cursing and the graphic depiction of sexual activity. "Gangster" means celebrating the criminal lifestyle. A criminality imposed on one's own people. What is there to celebrate about black men terrorizing their own neighborhoods with drive-by shooting that often kill innocent little children? Who would want to praise the rape of our own daughters by their brothers? What is there to applaud in our young people drinking themselves into stupors while turning our neighborhoods into de facto gambling dens?

Here are a few examples of this music, gleaned from Mwalimu Bomani Baruti's excellent critique of modern – day sexual practices entitled The Sex Imperative:

Adina Howard's "Do You Wanna Ride?"; R. Kelly's "Bump and Grind"; Dog Pound's "Bomb P***y"; Eightball and MJG's "Pimp a B**** College"; Snoop Dog's "Pay for the P***y; Tupac's "Me and My Girlfriend"; Master P's "Killer P***y and Freeck Hose"; Luke Skywalker's "Me So Horny"; Sisqo's "What Those B***** Want From A N******? and "Pop That Coochie"; Notorious B.I.G's "Nasty Boy";Camaflauge's "Let's Be F*** Friends"; DMX's "F***ing All Day and F****ing All Night"; Lil Kim's Queen B*** and Someone To F*** You; Old Dirty B*****rd's " Girls Ain't Nothing But Hoes and Tricks"; Dr. Dre's "F*** SH**"; La Cjat's "Slob On My Cat"; Three 6 Mafia's " Sob On My Knob"; D12's "B**** Pimpin'" to name only a very few of the best-selling records of the past few years.

These kinds of songs and poems were not unknown in black America. Black males have been engaging in hardcore recitations of poems about bad men and fast women for a hundred years and more. Not to mention the obscenity-laced tirades of playing the dozens. The laws of traditional decency, however, provided boundaries for these performances and the rhymes were never recited around children, decent women, or elders. There is a tradition of the "blue" performance among even the best black comedians like Red Fox and Moms Mabley but it was understood that this was "grown folks' conversation" and it took place in night clubs where consenting adults came specifically to enjoy x-rated entertainment.

The obscenities of hard-core rap put them beyond the pale of anything that could possibly be acceptable among decent people. When parents try to provide their children with a decent home life, doing their best to shield them from the amoral denizens of the streets, people we know as "alley Negroes", the children should not be allowed to bring the messages of the dope dealers, pimps, prostitutes, con men, junkies, thieves and murderers into their homes.

Hardcore rap was bad enough with its curse words and graphic depictions of sexual situations. It's breakout song and anthem was probably I Want Some P**** by Two Live Crew. Then came so-called "gangster" rap. I use the term "so-called" because even though its messengers purport to be acting in the tradition of the master criminals of the past and present even naming themselves after Mafia leaders like Capone, Gotti, and the like. The fact of the matter is that gangsters don't "rap". True Mafioso upon becoming "made men" take a blood oath called "omerta", the code of silence, vowing upon the pain of death never to reveal their criminal activities or to squeal like a rat on those who participated with them. They don't boast and brag openly about their crimes and lifestyles, to do so would amount to a public confession of criminal deeds that could be used in court against them.

Gangster rap took hardcore to a new and lower level as it glorified drug dealing, gun-running, drive-by shooting, car-jacking, robbery, theft, murder. People, who signify, play the dozens, call each other names in their recordings and then shoot at each other out on the street because they were dissed, sound and look too much like the blackface minstrel shows of the 19th century. In these shows black people, but more often white people in blackface, dressed up in ridiculous outfits with insane names like Jim Dandy, Rastus and Zip Coon, insulted each other and then fought with razors and guns to the delight of an overwhelmingly white audience who loved to see black people portrayed so childishly, stupidly and most of all non-threateningly. It soothes the tortured conscience and frightened sensibilities of white people to see us portraying ourselves as clowns and buffoons dangerous only to each other. There is nothing white America fears more than a strong intelligent black person. It allays their fears and feeds their fondest fantasies about us to see us portraying ourselves as the sex-crazed, childish, violence-prone, drug-ridden, alcohol-soaked, forties-guzzling, "real nigguhs" that they have been claiming we were to justify slavery for over three hundred years.

The image of the black male as an inherent criminal was one of the cornerstones of the justification of slavery. This process of criminalization began with the portrayal of Africans as barbaric savages in need of civilizing through the agency of chattel slavery and African colonization. Throughout slavery itself a multiplicity of ultra-violent devices and strategies such as chains, shackles, tortures, brutal beatings, branding, mutilation, and burning were employed to restrain the supposed criminal tendencies of the African male. The "nigger" is an invention of racist white society. Our people understood the true nature of these distortions as a means to control and exploit us and devised their own counter-strategies to deflect them as much as possible. This current trend on the part of young black males to buy totally into these stereotypes is a dangerous surrender to other people's attempt to impose an identity upon us which is totally to their advantage and

284

completely against our own.

This portrayal of a themselves as thugs is in fact partly do to the immaturity of a male generation that is still play-acting the games of childhood and the result of their being raised by immature mothers who are fascinated with the "bad-boy" " outlaw" persona. The moral and political immaturity of boys pretending to be dangerous criminals does not take into consideration the long term consequences of their behavior.

True criminals like the Mafia and members of the CIA go to great lengths to disguise themselves. They don't want anyone to know who and what they really are because they understand the consequences of being found out. For the Mafia to be found out means jail. For the CIA operative to be discovered means death or imprisonment in foreign jails. (Note the current national scandal in the Bush administration over the exposure of a female undercover agent). In both cases the real criminals don elaborate disguises and cover stories to hide their true identities and purposes. Mafia soldiers don't wear camouflage clothing or distribute pictures of themselves carrying automatic weapons. CIA operatives work under the cover of being diplomats, scholars, businessmen, students, even Christian missionaries. The African proverb says: "The roaring lion catches no game."

A major reason for the ease with which the police and other repressive agencies like the FBI and CIA destroyed the Black Panther Party was due to the fact that those young men and women, though to be much respected for their boldness and courage, did not understand the concept of the roaring lion and gave their positions away by announcing at press conferences and other public forums that they were out to "off the pig." You don't announce to your enemies that you are dangerous to him because: "Forewarned is fore-armed." The Viet Cong did not parade around in daytime in their black pajamas waving AK-47 assault rifles hollering out: "Kill the Yankees!"

The black boys and men who go around displaying themselves as criminals set themselves up for the special attention of the police and make suspecting, stopping, searching, harassing, accusing, arresting, convicting and jailing them all too easy. The idea of being a petty criminal as the most authentic expression of black manhood goes against the most ancient logic that the true role of men in any human society is that of husbands and fathers. Drunken, drug-ridden, robbing, stealing, fussing, cussing, fighting, cutting, shooting, jail-bound thugs don't make good husbands or fathers. Boys who commit themselves to the code of this criminal culture to being "thugs for life" are totally lacking in a long-range perspective that demands that they mature into spiritually, academically, professionally, emotionally, proficient men able to assume the leadership of our families, institutions, communities and nations

This kind of play-acting is attractive and cute to the immature husbandless women who are raising many of these boys. These immature mothers delight in dressing their boys as early as two and three years old like miniature thugs and encourage outrageous behavior in them. Too many black women do not comprehend the nature of the danger that they put these boys in. Black women seldom if ever encounter the kind of racism that their boys will be confronted with because white society does not fear black women. When an army of barbaric men conquer a nation they kill off or try to neuter its men. They rape the women and make babies from them. The challenge that our foremothers met so incredibly well was how they took these babies made from the master and raised them into great men and women of their own people. White men do not look at black women as dangerous foes. They look at them as potential sex partners.

What is most sickening and frightening about this so-called gangster rap music are lyrics that are so graphic and the details of violence so horrific that it begins to sound like the insane ranting of homicidal maniacs or demons set loose from hell. The boasts of killing sound like episodes of sexual pleasure. Many of the most typical sexual encounters are rapes and other forms of sado-masochistic encounters. Tales of dismemberment and mutilation abound in this so-called music. The themes of horror have become so prevalent that black rap is about to enter into a confluence with white heavy metal music. Heavy metal music has always been about unabashed Satanism. The number one social problem among white youth for the past thirty years has been devil-worship. All of the young white boys involved in the recent phenomenon of mass murders at schools were allegedly devil worshippers. Gangster rap is already intrinsically demonic in its celebration of horrific scenes of assaults, rapes, murder. One of the most popular rappers today, a white male named Eminem, has a hit song in which he exults in raping and killing his mother.

Too many of our children are being raised in a set of social circumstances that almost mandates not only academic failure but moral disaster. They live in a media driven world of supposed, but actually only the shallowest kind of, surface integration in which they are convinced that they can do what the white kids do. But continuing racism in every sphere of life even more assures that they will, if caught, suffer penalties unthinkable for a white child. Every study of court proceedings both juvenile and adult show that black people accused of a crime will more likely be found guilty and suffer penalties at least twice those of a white person found guilty of the same infraction.

Hardcore rap is based on the idea that our young people in order to be authentic African Americans must remain "real nigguhs." That is they must continue to live the gangster lifestyle of drug use and sale, brandishing weapons, raping women, fighting each other over the most petty perceived acts of disrespect. The idea that social pathology is the normative condition of black life in this country is a racist concept and construct and the only black people that could spout that kind of idiocy are those that either truly don't know any better 'cause they haven't seen any better (because they haven't had any home-training at all) or because they've been paid what they consider to be reasonable restitution to sell-out their people. It makes no sense for people who live materially upper middle-class lifestyles to continue to behave as if they live in the most impoverished and violent corner of the projects.

One of the new frontiers of immorality for rap music is "pimpin". The pimp has historically been considered a low-life person and a member of a degraded group of men so unmanly as to live off the earnings of women whom they willfully and hatefully expose to the most dangerous set of circumstances. Most serial killers murder prostitutes. They are easy prey not only because they put themselves in dangerous situations by driving off into the night with strange men but also because they have so little social capital. Among the people most despised, least-valued, and most looked-down upon, prostitutes are to be numbered along with the homeless and prison inmates. The pulp fiction of Ice Berg Slim, particularly his auto-biographical novel Pimp, and blaxploitation movies like Sweet Sweetback's Bad*** Song and The Mack glamorized the life of pimps and prostitutes and lifted them to the level of honored representatives of true blackness in the minds of many of our young people.

Now there is a revival of pimping with the HBO documentary Pimps Up and Ho's Down leading the way. Next came Jay Z with Big Pimping; Fifty Cent with P.I.M.P and to top it off Snoop Dog's declaration that he was getting out of the gangster business and turning to pimping because he explained: "Pimps live longer." It's bad enough people with limited exposure to education or religion so they lack the tools to do the simplest moral critique of this kind of corrupt conduct. It's even worse when the members of the so-called intelligentsia sign off on the same deranged behavior and give it the imprimatur of what passes in their minds for scholarship . One would-be scholar, Beth Coleman, author of "Pimp Notes on Autonomy", writes that pimping is a liberation strategy that was developed by brothers in slavery. She describes pimping as having its beginning when a brother said to a sister who had received a command to make an appearance in the master's bedroom: "He gon offer you a pork chop. Tell him you want two and bring the other one to me". This is specious reasoning and perverted thinking that has no basis in historical reality. The fact is that there were no pimps in slavery because white men had total access to the bodies of black women, men and children and took them whenever and wherever they got the notion, whether it was in the fields in front of the other workers or in her home in the presence of her husband and children.

Pimping is a post-slavery invention. Immediately after black men took their freedom by fighting in the Union army and destroying by force of arms the Southern rebellion we moved to restore the integrity of our families. This meant not just legitimating marriages through church weddings and obtaining marriage certificates from the state. It also meant black men denying white men the opportunity to rape their mothers, sisters, daughters and wives, turn them into their concubines or make prostitutes of them. This was a tremendous blow to the psyche of white men. They had become addicted to black flesh and needed it like a junkie needs a fix and like a crackhead needs a rock. Endangered by the armed vigilance of black husbands, fathers, brothers and sons, white men needed someone to procure black women for them. Thus the invention of the pimp. He was and is a specialized category of Uncle Tom with a specific portfolio, to give white men access to black women. His function was so important then and now that he was and continues to be afforded almost complete exemption from investigation or prosecution by law enforcement officials.

We are all familiar with the brutal treatment of black

men by white people in general and the police in particular but pimps have been dramatically spared any mistreatment by white people, police or otherwise. Yet they are among the most notoriously flamboyant of the criminal class flaunting themselves publicly with complete immunity. I'm certain that this public display is a twenty-first century urban phenomenon. The original generation of pimps in the country down south would have had to operate in a most carefully clandestine and seriously surreptitious manner. They would not have dared announce themselves and publicize their mission to a community of armed and vigilant black men who would have recognized them for what they were- flesh peddlers and would have dealt with them according to their deserts. .

I will give white people credit for their take on pimps. When I was going to St. Ignatius College Preparatory High School on the West Side of Chicago the white students used the word "pimp" as an insult. They would put each other down by spitting at one another "You f****ing pimp!" Look at the way the white pimp is portrayed in such movies as The Godfather and Casino as an object of scorn and contempt and a one of the lowest people on the totem pole of the gangster hierarchy. But they lift up pimps for us until we lose sight of the common sense fact that firstly, pimps are immature little boys who like all boys want a woman to take care of them. And secondly, are two steps from a sissy because a pimp is in it for the money and will unashamedly have sex with a man if the price is right.

Who could ever have imagined a time when the lowest people in our society, the criminal element, would be promoted as the truest representatives of what black people are about and even more astonishingly be accepted as such by a major part of our population even by college students who are supposed to be among the most intelligent individuals that the race has produced? No one is startled when the sister on the street corner living a dead-end existence tries to convince us that she is proud of being called a whore or a b****. But when our privileged daughters who live a favored existence on college campuses, that we lift up as role models for their younger sisters, also refer to themselves and address each other in these same vulgar terms then we know that we have reached a watershed moment in our moral history.

The negative aspects of the hip-hop movement encourages our young people to define themselves at the lowest levels of moral existence. It is a negativistic and nihilistic philosophy that maintains that money is the sole measure of life. "Getting paid" is what life is all about and it does not matter at all what people do to get that money. As the saying goes "It's all about the "Benjamin's." People caught up in such an approach to life will find it difficult to rise to the high levels of moral behavior which are necessary for true success in life for individuals, families, or communities.

Rap music, hip-hop culture and the media that drives them threaten the future of the black family. Family is based on marriage and marriage is holy matrimony. The promiscuity that is promoted by hip hop culture is a direct threat to marriage. During the height of the sexual revolution in the early and mid-seventies the idea of "open marriage" was strongly advocated in a number of counter culture and avant garde circles. It never worked because marriage by definition is a closed system. Even today, in this most modernistic of times the old-fashioned virtue of fidelity is the indispensable element in any marriage. Most divorces are still the result of infidelity. *Young people who practice promiscuity during courtship will not be prepared to perfect faithfulness in marriage.*

Sex as recreation is, like any other drug, easily perverted into addiction. Very few junkies started out with the idea that using heroin or cocaine recreationally would result in a destructive habit that would drag them down the pathway to destruction. The same thing goes for promiscuous sex. Most of these young people expect to get

291

married and raise families. They see their engagement in sexual promiscuity as mere youthful recreation that like a faucet, can be turned off and on. They believe that upon the occasion of marriage the promiscuity habit will disappear upon command. Like the naïve user of deadly addictive drugs and like social drinkers, who are in fact alcoholics in denial, they declare: "I can stop whenever I get ready."

They are in for a rude awakening when they discover that they are addicted to multiple partners, one-night stands, orgies, and other forms of non-intimate sex that is so easy to get into and so hard to get out of. The proverb "Practice makes perfect" is as accurate and true about social relationships as it is about athletic prowess. These young people think that they can practice promiscuity and perfect fidelity but it just doesn't work like that. A successful marriage demands hard work, dedication, sacrifice, selflessness, and denial of individual urges for the greater sake of the relationship.

A second danger and perhaps an even greater one is child sexual abuse. My generation and those which preceded us were never confronted with the kind of situations that we too often read about in today's new stories where little children are the perpetrators of criminal sexual offenses. We have incidents weekly detailing stories of ten and twelve year old boys raping even killing girls and boys four and five years of age. In the fall of 2004 the Philadelphia Inquirer printed a story about an incident in a local middle school where an eleven year old boy beat up a twelve year old fellow student and then raped him. The sexual activity of children is of primary concern because children who are prematurely introduced to and addicted to sex typically carry these perversions for the rest of their lives. The exposure of children to sex is itself the beginning of sexual child abuse. But a child once exposed to adult themes, which they cannot begin to understand the consequences of, much less control their impulses to be involved in, cannot keep this knowledge or behavior to themselves. Children tell and show everything that they know. An exposed or abused child naturally introduces their playmates to their forbidden knowledge. To that extent sexual child abuse can be described as a form of "vampirism". Like the vampires of literature and film once bitten themselves they then turn around and bite somebody else, infecting them with their ungodly disease and initiating them into their deadly way of life.

Earlier generations of black youth did not have to worry about being sexually active because children can only do what they see. The African proverb states: "What a child says he heard at home". Little children are imitators. The old folks warned us against the foibles of uncritical imitation with the statement: "Monkey see. Monkey do." We did not and could not become sexually involved because *we had not seen sex*. We could not even name it much less describe it, explain it or participate in it. We were, of course, curious about what grown people did in their beds at night while sleeping together. But we did not know because grown people zealously protected us from knowledge that we could not have handled properly. There was no such things as "r" and "x"-rated movies played in people's homes on TV. There were no songs on the radio filled with vulgar terms and salacious images. Grown people made sure that we did not see sex. I have received testimonies from witnesses all over the country concerning the frightening sexual behavior of children as young as two and three years old. For example two year olds in day-care centers having to be treated for injured penises the result of episodes of mutual fellatio gone bad.

Grown people protected our childhood innocence to the extent that we were not allowed to project ourselves even conversationally into dating and courting much less sexuality. If a little boy in grammar school described a little girl as his "girlfriend" he would quickly be told: "You too young to have a girlfriend. What you have is a 'friend girl' not a 'girlfriend'. "

Today little children while yet in the cradle are exposed to the rawest forms of sexual behavior. Children have access to cable TV without parental oversight and watch everything from HBO, to BET to the Playboy Channel.

Not long a ago a seven year old girl told me that she was a lesbian, confessing that she and her girl cousins watched <u>Girls</u> <u>Gone</u> <u>Wild</u> and imitated the lesbian behavior they saw. Children are taken to R-rated movies by immature parents and watch scenes that will rob them of their innocence and introduce a premature sexual consciousness which will be dangerous to them and other children that they come into contact with. They are taken to these totally inappropriate venues and exposed to these dangerous behaviors by their own parents.

Its always young parents in their teens and twenties that expose their children like that. I have never seen grown people in their forties or even thirties as far as I can tell doing something so horrendous. It constitutes sexual child abuse to allow a child to watch this kind of performance. Mature adults understand the dangers to children of exposing them to behaviors that if imitated could cause them serious problems for the rest of their lives. Young parents in their immaturity are still smarting from that which they were not allowed to do as children and rather than identifying with the mature long-term perspective of their parents who had sense enough to shield their children from behaviors that were unhealthy today's parents say aloud: "I'm not gon do my kids like my parents did me"!

If you can talk you can sing. If you can walk you can dance. **African Proverb**

When the drum changes, the dance must change. **African Proverb**

XI. DANCE

We have no theology, philosophy or even commonsense approach relating to dance. We have no way of measuring, determining or evaluating whether a particular form of dance is good or bad, healthy or unhealthy, positive or negative. Therefore we give our children no guidance concerning one of the most important aspects of their lives. To black youth dancing is like breathing, they do both continuously and unselfconsciously. In traditional black child-rearing teenage parties were held under adult supervision. But we didn't wait for parties to dance. We danced in our homes in front of our parents on a daily basis. Whenever our favorite song came on the radio, the record player or the juke box we cut our step and did our dance. The elders were there to give us direction and instruction as to what dances were acceptable or unacceptable. For instance in my house we weren't allowed to do "the Dog", today's equivalent of the dog would be "the Butterfly."

Black people always have danced, and as long as we are black, we always will dance. We dance in church. Our choirs rock in a side-to-side two-step as they sing. The choirs and the ushers have their own step as they promenade down the center aisle for their offering. The preachers who use their entire body to tell the story do so in rhythmic movements that can only described as a kind of dance.

The question for parents is what kinds of dancing will our children be encouraged to do and what kind will they be prohibited from doing. In all things moral guidance must be the key. In order to determine the nature of that guidance we must have a systematic approach to the dance. We must have a theology of the dance. We do have a theology of song to some extent. It is not as profound as it ought to be but it does allow us to examine songs from a moral perspective and decide what is sinkable, playable or listenable in our homes, churches and classrooms.

But when it comes to dance the voice of the church is peculiarly silent. We accept European dances with no problem. Even the preachers' daughters will take ballet, jazz, modern dance or tap. When it comes to the everyday dances of the people, it is a different question. In fact there is no question. They are all roundly and soundly condemned out of hand or completely ignored as though they did not exist nor had no moral aspect to their existence that the church needed to be bothered with. One of the oldest rules of successful child-rearing is that you can't just tell young people what they can't do. You have got to tell them what that they can do. We cannot just tell young people that they can't dance or all, or point out to them what dances they can't do. We have to provide them with positive alternatives in the form of dances that we encourage then to do.

Dance is too significant an aspect, not only in the lives our youth, but of black culture as a whole, for our moral leaders to ignore. We are a dancing people. Dance exists in all human cultures as an extension of song. The African genius for dance is universally recognized. Not only does the whole world sing our songs but it also does our dances.

All dance is basically a combination of two primary

elements: 1. A conversation between the parts of the body and the beats of the music. You don't dance to the melody or the harmony. You dance to the beat. European dance is relatively lifeless, static and stiff compared to ours because historically, before the introduction of African rhythmic elements into the European sensibility, their music was primarily melody-based and had one, at the most, two rhythms to enable the dancers to move in conversation with. Therefore Europeans danced with the upper body held rigid while just the feet moved.

African music has not one or two or even three beats but such a multiplicity that they are almost beyond counting. There is a primary beat, a beat before the beat, a beat after the beat and countless beats between the beats. Therefore when we dance we experience so many beats that every part of the body can converse with a different rhythm. Our dances consist of beautifully coordinated movements of a multiplicity of body parts. There is a beat for the feet, a beat for the knees, a beat for the arms, a beat for the head, a beat for the shoulders, a beat for the derriere and so on and so forth. Like the fox in Aesop's fable who called the grapes sour because he could not reach them, European labeled our dances barbaric and uncivilized because they could not do them.

The second part of why we dance is the most important. It is to celebrate some aspect of life. In Africa we danced to celebrate the birth of babies, marriages, rites of passage, funerals, and the coronations of kings and queens, to mention a few. We danced to celebrate the harvest, the changing of the seasons, the coming in of a new year. We also danced to celebrate the marvels of God's natural order. We did animal dances. These dances unlike the other aforementioned ones carried over into the New World. Europeans have no animal dances. But every black generation no matter how far removed from Africa have done animal dances. The Buzzard Lope, the Funky Chicken, the Camel Walk, the Elephant Walk, the Monkey, the Gorilla. This present generation's alienation from nature has prevented them from developing an animal dance. The closest the hip-hop generation has come to a nature dance was Morris Day and the Tymes "Oak Tree."

When I was pastor of the Abyssinian Baptist Church in Rockford, Illinois I decided to have my teenagers hold their parties in the church. I had become distressed over their accounts of house parties where there were no adults present and all kinds of drug use, fighting, and sexual misbehavior took place. I decided that it was better for them to party in a controlled environment where I determined the music that would be played and the dances that would be performed. That way I could ensure that they would not celebrate an inappropriate theme in their dancing. My presence also meant that nobody would come in high or drunk, disrespecting people, molesting females or looking for a fight.

One of the popular dances at that time was the Punk. I told my young people that they couldn't do the Punk and backed it up with scripture. I explained the two meanings of the word. 1. A coward. 2. A homosexual. I instructed them that they could not celebrate cowardice because the bible says: "God has not given us the spirit of fear but of love and of a sound mind." and "Perfect love casteth out fear." And the gospel song that maintains: "God don't want and he can't use no coward soldier". I told them that they could not celebrate homosexuality because the Bible teaches that: "For man to lie with man as with woman is an abomination". Lev. 18:22(KJV)

It is now common for young people while dancing to not only openly rub their own private parts in masturbatory frenzies but to put their hands under the clothes of their dance partners. Dancing for past generations was contest, coordinated movement, exercise, and just good clean fun. For too many in this generation dancing is only sex. One practice on the part of boys is particularly onerous. That is the custom of two or more boys surrounding a girl locking

298

arms to trap her in the circle of their male strength and simultaneously humping like aroused dogs on her body. This constitutes sexual assault and if anyone ever brought the charge I have no doubt that they would stand in a court of law. Our young men practice it with impunity and it lays the foundation for other more recognizably criminal assaults in the future. It is a dangerous thing for young men to believe that they are entitled to force sexual contact upon a female. These young males conduct themselves in such a manner because they are receiving no guidance from their elders about how to properly treat our daughters and their sisters.

The key to developing a theology of dance is not to condemn dancing out of hand but to control, direct and guide it by insisting that dancing be done to celebrate positive themes. I had not advanced far enough in my thinking back in those days. I wish I had known enough then to encourage my youth to develop steps to celebrate academic success, virginity, marriage, family unity, respect for elders, love of wisdom. But this is our challenge today. Rather than allow our young people to be exposed to what amounts to sexual assault on the dance floor we can inspire and instruct them in the use of one of our most creative artistic gifts to uplift that which is most important in their lives and the life of our people.

We can challenge them to choreograph an Honor Roll step that only students with a B average or above can get on the floor to do. We can have a perfect attendance dance. There can be a virgin dance. A grandmother dance. A dance for fathers and sons and another for mothers and daughters. There can be a baptismal dance, a graduation dance. The possibilities are unlimited but I hope I have made the point clear. This most precious aspect of our culture has been kidnapped and hijacked by amoral forces of evil and ignorance and is being used to degrade our young people. As adults we should have the wisdom and the power to recapture that which is lost, to repair the breach and establish something wonderful for the lives of our young people.

"It does not no good to pray to God that you will win the race, if you don't intend to run as fast as you can."
African Proverb

XII. ATHLETICS

Sports, as with music and dance, is an area of life that black people in this country have been afforded an unusual license to excel in. In the worlds of amateur and professional sports the black athlete has achieved exceptional prominence. From boxing to baseball, from soccer to sprinting, from football to long-distance running, and most especially in the game of basketball. The black athlete is at center stage at every level of competition, amateur, professional and Olympian, leading the field in amazing feats of strength, speed, grit, quickness, agility, stamina, creativity, exuberance and determination. Their prominence in athletics and the relative wealth it earns them places athletes, as a class, among the most celebrated, influential and resourceful members of our race. However, the commanding presence that they present on the field of play has seldom been reduplicated in the boardrooms of ownership or the conference rooms of decision-making. The race has not yet received the fullest benefits from our investment in athletics because the athletes themselves have such a limited sense of their wider capabilities and responsibilities.

I was on a radio talk show with a member of the Dallas Cowboys Super Bowl Champion team some years back. It was a call-in show and one caller was an older black male who said to the player: "You know y'all black Cowboys lost a lot of respect in the community when y'all played up under that Confederate flag." He did not respond to the caller but said to me off the air: "We let them know how we felt, but that's all we could do." I later on asked myself the question:

"How do people who are millionaires and the best in the world at what they do feel powerless?"

Did the black players really believe that had they refused to take the field until that offensive symbol of slavery, mass murder, systematic rape and institutionalized dehumanization was removed, that corporate America would have risked the loss of the greatest one-day spectacle in the world of sport in order to stand on the principles symbolized by the Confederate flag? Had the brothers stood their ground and refused to take the field under the flag, I'm sure it would not have been taken five minutes of argumentation and negotiation before the flag would have been hastily, unceremoniously lowered. Fortune 500 corporations had already paid their tens of millions of dollars for commercial advertising. How long would it have been before Mr. General Motors was on the hotline to Mr. ABC wanting to know what was holding up the game? Does anybody really believe any Fortune 500 corporation that has such a strong commitment to the Confederate flag and the racist legacy it represents that they would risk losing billions of dollars in profits just to fly it in the face of stern opposition. Had the black players been more steadfast in their collective resolve they would have experienced a deeper sense of their enormous political, economic and spiritual power.

In another conversation with a black professional athlete the brother said to me: "Whenever a black athlete signs a multi-million dollar contract the entire black community benefits." This is the scurrilous logic of the irrational "law of vicarious benefits". Its most classic example is the black leader who is supposed to have boasted: "When I sit at the banquet table all of black

America gets fed".

Somebody needs to say to that brother and all others who think like him: "If the black athlete with the multi-million dollar contract does not live in the black community and contribute to the community economy how can the black community benefit from his millions? If he does not put his money in a black bank; does not retain a black lawyer or agent to advise him in handling his business; if he is not a member of or does not to contribute to a Black church; does not donate money to black colleges or universities or scholarship funds for African-American youth; does not help to finance black think tanks; does not support the candidacy of black politicians; does not eat in or have his working lunches catered by black restaurants; does not buy his fleet of automobiles from a black car dealership; does not have his home designed by a black architect and built by a black construction firm; does not have a black secretary and other black employees in his office; if he does not have his travel itinerary arranged by a black travel agency; then how could the Black community possibly profit from his multi-millions? The African-American proverb says: "It ain't what you got it's how you use it that counts."

There are many people both black and white, athletes and spectators, fans and critics who question why the black athlete should even be challenged to give something back. They wonder what is it that the black community believes our athletes owe us. In order to answer their question we need to examine for a moment the real source of the black athlete's prowess and competitive success. The search for the source of black athletic domination has commanded an unusual amount of time, thought and energy from fans, writers, sociologists, geneticists and physical anthropologists.

There are three prevailing theories. Firstly, the evolutionary theory maintains that Africans are lower on the evolutionary scale than all the other races. Supposedly

302

this leaves us more animalistic, less developed cerebrally than other races. Thus we have certain physical advantages. Our leg muscles are supposed to be longer and looser. Our bodies are, according to this school of thought, naturally configured in such a manner as to make us superior runners and jumpers. We are considered to be reflexive and reactive but not reflective and contemplative.

The newest term for this system of thought is "athleticism" It was originally coined by racist sportswriters to indicate the physical advantage of the black athlete but now is in universal use even by black athletes and coaches. Common sense of course tells us that all athletes are athletic and therefore have "athleticism" so that the use of the term is to say the least "redundant". It's the equivalent of saying a soldier is "soldierly", or a college professor is "intellectual". Or that a bibliophile is "bookish".

Secondly, there is the genetic argument that in slavery we were originally chosen by the slave catchers for our size and strength. Then we were bred for those same physical characteristics during hundreds of years of slavery. Moreover, we had to survive a brutal environment according to whose laws, only the strong survive.

The third argument is part economics, part sociology, part psychology. From this perspective the black athlete's greatness lies in the power of his determination to escape from the horrors of the Ghetto. Those who posit this idea are convinced that the desire to get away from his own kin and kind provides the black athlete with the incentive to engage their chosen sport at its highest levels.

There is a fourth and neglected rationale in which lies the real truth of the matter. I call it the Black Athletic Philosophy (BAP). The black athlete's first love is competition. When young brothers get together and start talking about finding a game of basketball their chief question is: "Where is the comp'?" They are not primarily concerned with what courts have the sturdiest rims or the most level playing surface or the best stores for snacks in the near vicinity. Or even where the best looking young ladies congregate to watch the game. The brothers want competition. The insistence on one-on-one, strength-on-strength confrontation is the essence of the Black Athletic Philosophy and the foundation for our success in sports. It begins with an understanding that competition raises the level of everybody's game, that competition drives excellence. For the Black athlete there is no glory in defeating a weak opponent or in overcoming inferior opposition. The competition is the thing. It is in the furious intensity of head-on collisions between evenly matched contestants that inspires and compels players to take their game to a higher level. It is the drama created by such fierce rivalry that makes the game interesting, attractive, exciting, and at its very best, compelling, and spellbinding-- when the proverbial irresistible force meets the fabled immovable object.

Strength comes from struggle. The greater the struggle, the greater the strength. My Daddy used to say: "Weak men hang around men weaker than themselves so that they can seem strong by comparison. Strong men associate with men even stronger than themselves so that they can grow even stronger through the interaction. Because association breeds assimilation." The black athlete therefore is not interested in winning for winning sake alone. Winning is not the chief thing to him, the challenge is. For him or her it's better to get your shot blocked by a champion than to slam dunk on a chump. Better to lose to a master than to walk over a novice. The confrontation with the champion provides us a challenge that is an opportunity for growth. There is no betterment in doing what is easy and safe.

The standard American approach to organized and even impromptu sport is best expressed in the oft-quoted dictum of Vince Lombardi, the legendary coach of the Green Packers during their first championship years in the sixties, when he said: "Winning is not the main thing. It's the only thing." In this approach to the game, winning is an end unto itself. There is therefore no such thing as a bad win. No matter how the win was achieved even if it was through a clever ruse or even blatant violation of the rules of the game. As their saying goes: "A win is a win". There is little understanding and no sympathy for or acceptance of The Black Athletic Philosophy in the community of thought that adheres to this principle of winning at any cost. In the hit movie White Men Can't Jump the Woody Harrelson character said to his teammate, running partner and hustling buddy played by Wesley Snipes: "The difference between a white and black player is that the white player would rather look bad winning and the black player would rather look good losing". He got only the first part right.

There is an honored tradition among white athletes and coaches called "winning ugly". But for the brother it's not so much that he wants to "look good". That would reduce the game to mere cosmetics. The brother does not just want to look good he wants to play good because when you play good you can't help but look good.

The White Athletic Philosophy might well be described as strength-on-weakness, that is, maneuvering the players in such as way as to produce a "mismatch". They consistently organize their strategy to produce a situation in which a stronger or better player is matched against a weaker or inferior opponent. It is in actuality a form of refusing to compete. We see this best in a number of standard strategies by white coaches.

Firstly, in basketball where the tactic involves running an offensive player through a number of picks in order to free him up for an open jump shot or put a big man in a situation where he is guarded by a smaller one. Or when the coach puts on a stall when his team achieves a lead and he has his players pass the ball around and refuse to attempt a shot, thereby playing it safe and refusing to compete while waiting for the game to end. The great Phi Slamma Jamma

University of Houston team led by All-Americas and later
All Pro's Clyde Drexler and Hakeem Olajuwan lost in the
NAACP championship game when their coach had them
stop playing their fast break game and stall in the second
half. As a result they lost momentum and were beaten by a
decidedly less-talented squad from North Carolina State
University in one of the greatest upsets in the history of
basketball. The tremendously negative fan reaction to the
stall finally caused it to be legislated against by the
initiation of a rule that required a team shoot the ball within
thirty seconds or lose possession it.

Secondly, in baseball when the pitcher issues an
intentional walk to a stronger hitter in order to pitch to a
weaker one. One of the scandals of modern day baseball is
the refusal of white managers to allow even their best
hurlers to pitch to Barry Bonds. White baseball denigrates
and dishonors Bond's greatness and impugns the integrity
of the game when they refuse to compete against him by
walking him so often intentionally that he has set records
for walks the past three seasons. This strategy was not used
against Babe Ruth when he was setting home run records or
against Mickey Mantle, Roger Maris or Mark McGwire
when they were having their banner years. Bonds 73 home
runs in one season broke Mark McGwire's standard and
shattered Babe Ruth's record, making him the greatest
hitter of this era and the most dangerous slugger since Josh
Gibson of the Negro Leagues. Gibson during his prime in
the twenties and thirties regularly hit seventy and more
home runs in a season and was the only man to ever hit a
ball out of Yankee Stadium. In Negro League Baseball it
was not uncommon for the pitchers to intentionally walk a
weaker hitter in order to face a stronger, more dangerous
batsman.

In black basketball we continuously drive to the basket
seeking to avoid and defeat the defensive efforts of not just
one but two or three or more defenders. The three point rule
in basketball pays homage to the white athletic philosophy

and down plays the black approach. It awards three points for a successful long-distance shot supposedly in recognition of the degree of difficulty involved. But isn't the truly more difficult play to go the hole where in the close quarters of the paint a player is pushed, grabbed, bumped and hit with hands, elbows and fists and still score with an imaginative lay-up or a powerful slam dunk? If a long-distance jump shot often made without a defender being in the vicinity is worth three points then a dunk against multiple opposition ought to be worth four or five.

For us the level of competitiveness determines the aesthetic quality of the game. Competition is to the Black sporting world what winning is to the white athletic community. The Black athlete would rather lose in a closely contested, glorious struggle in which the final outcome is in doubt until the very last shot or play or pitch and legendary feats of unprecedented prowess are performed that will become part of the eternal lore of the game, than to win big by fifty points in a boring blowout.

The breathtaking skills of the black athlete has thrilled spectators, won championships, created legends, established dynasties, filled stadiums, generated multi-billion dollar media deals. But it has not had an appreciable effect on the overall economic condition of the black community. It has been a doorway that a precious few have passed through and entered the mansions of youthful success and lifelong prosperity. It has not been all that it could have been and still can be in terms of generating resources for the black community as a whole. Like every other aspect of our culture our gift in sports is a communal project. The community therefore ought to benefit from the coming to fruition of abilities that it fostered and nurtured.

There are many black athletes who are convinced that they don't owe their community anything. They are absolutely certain that they have succeeded not because of us but in spite of us. They see the odds against them that they had to overcome in their journey to success as being chiefly composed of the pathologies of our community. Yes, it is true that there is a multiplicity of problems endemic to our community that makes it particularly difficult to rise above the poverty and powerlessness that pervades our lives like some miasma of poison gas. But that is hardly the whole story. Our successes are as much the product of our community as are our failures. The foundation for these young men's success stands alongside the difficulties as a continuing testimony to the positives of black society as well as the negatives. The Black Athletic Philosophy of strength-on- strength competition is not the only thing that they derive from their people.

The very rhythms that they play to are ours. We are a rhythmic people. Black athletes' movements are in response to rhythms that they didn't create. They were bequeathed to them by their culture. The way the brothers move on the basketball court, on the football and soccer field, on the baseball diamond and in the boxing ring are a dance-like response to the ancient rhythms of African people. Everything Africans do is rhythmic. We walk to the beat, talk to beat, drive our cars to the beat. That's why the brothers set out a boom-box on the side of the court to play to the rhythms of rap, jazz, reggae, and R&B music. Despite the lying promotions of the NBA that claim so don't no brothers play ball to Frank Sinatra or the Rolling Stones.

The trash-talking that lends such a playful and entertaining quality to the game when it is done right is just another form of signifying, one of the most ancient of African social customs of dynamic, creative speech. The support they received as boys and young men came not just from their parents but from innumerable personalities such as coaches, neighbors, pastors, teachers, the proprietors of the mom and pop grocery store around the corner, past stars and players on their high school teams whose traditions have been passed on to them. The very moves that they make are nothing new.

The philosophy, the flavor, the full-court press, the fast-break, the cross-over dribble, going to the hole hanging in the air making up new moves while waiting for the defensive player to go back to the ground, the no-look pass, dribbling behind the back and between the legs, the essential elements that make our players and teams so great were handed down to them by their ancestors, however unknown they may be to the present generation. There is an African proverb that says: "No matter how far the river flows it never forgets its source". Our athletes ought to honor the culture that handed them the gifts that empower and enable them to rise so far above the ordinary. They can demonstrate that honor by contributing to the continuation of our greatness as a people by supporting the essential institutions of our community-- the family, the church, schools and businesses.

Our lack of consciousness of the very existence of a Black Athletic Philosophy, much less familiarity with the details of how it operates, has led us to consistently make huge mistakes in the business of sports. For instance we still celebrate Jackie Robinson's entrance into the white leagues as a red-letter day in black history as though it was an indication of the tremendous progress we were making as a people. We still fail to realize that that day should be cloaked in the deep purple of mourning because it sounded the death-knell of the one of the most prosperous black-owned industries. One that was not only nationally prominent and profitable but that had international status and influence. The Negro baseball leagues were a black-owned industry and a major source of employment for our people. We even mistakenly describe Mr. Robinson's playing for the white leagues as being our entrance into "major league" or "big league baseball" making an erroneous self-admission that the quality of baseball played in the Negro Leagues was inferior.

The Negro Leagues did not practice discrimination so

all of the best players in this hemisphere, which meant the players from Puerto Rico, Cuba, the Dominican Republic, Venezuela, Panama, Mexico and everywhere else in the Caribbean and South and Central America played with us. The term "major league" can only honestly and accurately be ascribed to the league that plays ball at the highest competitive and artistic level. If we reconstituted the Negro Leagues today it would mean removing all of the great black, Caribbean, Central and South American players from Major League Baseball and leave them only their white players. Now imagine a team composed of those players arrayed against an all-star team of the only the best white players. If you remove Barry Bonds, Sammy Sosa, Alex Rodriguez, Rafael Palmeiro, Pedro Martinez, Andruw Jones, Mariano Riviera, Kenny Lofton, Frank Thomas, Vladamir Gurerro, Nomar Garciaparo, etc., from white-owned American baseball and have them play in the Cuban League, which one is the "major league?"

The reason white baseball integrated had nothing to do with liberalism or altruism. It was a simple business decision. The Negro leagues were playing a superior brand of baseball that was filling the stands in white ballparks that the white teams were losing money in. Not only were the black teams composed of legendary international stars which all fans both black and white longed to see, but they played a style of ball more entertaining than white baseball. They would for instance intentionally walk a strong hitter in order to get to weak one. Their most typical offensive scheme was based on the hope of a home run. Their philosophy was to" play it safe" by "playing by the numbers" and "playing the percentages". The black leagues intentionally walked weak hitters in order to get to strong ones thereby maintaining a high level of intensive drama by featuring constant head-on confrontations between the best pitchers and the most fearsome hitters.

The black players played what I call "fast break baseball". Whenever a runner got on base he tried to steal the next base. Or when there was a bunt the base runner on first wasn't just trying to make to second he was trying to get to third. Nowadays a spectator will be lucky to see one stolen base in the course of an entire game. A double steal is almost unheard of. One of the most daring and dramatic plays in baseball is the theft of home plate. I saw the highlight of game not long ago in which the announcer described a theft of home plate as the first one since 1997. When Jackie Robinson came into white baseball he virtually discombobulated pitchers and catchers and electrified the fans with his bold attempts to steal home plate whenever he got on third base. In doing so he was continuing an every day practice in black baseball.

When integration occurred it meant the destruction of the Negro Leagues. This ought to be a matter of consideration as an area of reparations because the white leagues seldom compensated the black team owners for any of the players that they signed. Rather than true integration which would have meant bringing in entire teams, the white leagues instead, dismantled the black leagues by taking all of their best players. The white owners refused to admit the black owners because that would have meant a form of social equality.

This is to be contrasted with the treatment of the American Football League and the American Basketball Association. When these new leagues were organized to compete with the existing National Football League and the National Basketball Association the old leagues incorporated the new leagues, wholesale in the case of the AFL. The NBA took in the strongest franchises of the ABA. When competition escalated with the black leagues the white leagues destroyed them. This was an act of racism. Had things been done right the Renaissance Big Five and the Harlem Globetrotters would be franchises in the NBA and the Kansas City Monarchs, Pittsburgh Crawfords, the Philadelphia Stars, The Chicago American Giants would be teams in today's Major League Baseball.

We look forward to the day when the Black athlete will regain his sense of independence, autonomy, imagination, creativity and courage in his business dealings off the field in such a way as to parallel his athletic feats on the field. When that day comes we will witness a new era of economic growth fueled by the dramatic entry of a generation of bold and innovative young black entrepreneurs who will turn the millions they make off their bodies into billions they generate from their minds.

Let me offer a couple of suggestions on things black athletes could do to give back to the people that produced them. First, the black athlete could build a great neighborhood. Most professional black athletes live twenty, thirty, or more miles from the inner-city black communities where they grew up or at least where the nearest black community is located. One of the most popular questions asked of them by reporters and interviewers upon the signing of their first contract is: "How does it feel to get out of the ghetto?" We black people are the only people for whom escaping from ourselves is a measurement, even a requirement, of success. You never hear this question put to people of any other ethnic origin.

Nobody asks a young successful Italian: "How does it feel to get out of the Italian community?' Nobody asks a successful Jewish person: "How does it feel to get away from the rest of your people and be the only Jew in your neighborhood? Why? Because these people are not trying to escape from themselves. The Chinese are not trying to get out of Chinatown. They are trying to make Chinatown the best town in town! Our acceptance of the idea that we must get away from our own people and own communities holds the same moral weight and comes out of the same sense of racist illogic that says slavery was good because at least it got us out of Africa. Our best and brightest and wealthiest young people do not have to have to leave their communities in order to enjoy lives lived at the highest possible level. There is a more excellent way.

Why don't they come back to the ghetto and build a new neighborhood that meets their standards for housing quality and living conditions. In traditional Africa when there was a dispute over succession to kingship of a particular village, in other words if there were two brothers in consideration to succeed their father as king, the response of the one that lost the election, would not be to wage a fratricidal warfare against the winner as was usually the case with such situations in European history. Rather the loser would just take the people who insisted on having him as their leader and move a few miles down the road and build a new village where he would be the king. He would demonstrate his qualifications by trying to build a better village rather than by trying to kill somebody. We use the same spirit in the black church. When a congregation rejects a pastor, he will often take the people who are committed to his leadership and find a place for them and organize a new congregation. We call this process: "multiplying by division".

Our young athletes could use this same spirit of initiation and origination and build a new neighborhood for themselves on the same spot or not that far from where their old one stood. Most of these fellows, upon signing a multi-million dollar contract, also buy their mothers a new house. However, in order to enjoy it their mothers must move out of their old neighborhoods where they have been living long years if not most of their lives. They must leave behind all the social capital they accumulated over those years. They must forsake family members, best friends, and caring dependable neighbors. They have to completely unravel their entire social network, leaving behind the culture that they are so much a part of, that is so much a part of them and relocate to a distant, cold, sterile, unwelcoming, alien suburban environment in which they will probably never have as sense of true belonging.

Why can't these millionaires instead purchase four or

five square blocks in the ghetto, build their own mansion and one for their mother, grandparents, brothers, sisters, aunties uncles, cousins, and best friends ? Convince their business partners to do the same-- their lawyers, their financial advisors, their agents. Then rehab or build some affordable housing for the people in the neighborhood that they don't want to leave behind. Their mother's best friend. Their best friend. Their best friend's mother, brother and sister. They could cooperate with banks and savings and loans to provide financing for people who might not be able to meet the traditional criteria for housing loans but whom they know for themselves to be good, hardworking, responsible people who have been prevented from attaining home ownership because of institutionalized racism in the employment and commercial sectors. Or even start their own bank. A million dollars initial capitalization is all that is needed and that's chump change to the biggest stars.

Perhaps they could develop a criteria through the local churches in which tithers would be considered good credit risks. Anybody who has consistently paid tithes over the years ought to be seen as someone who is financially responsible. Using the ancient African model of a neighborhood as a miniature village composed of people who are related both by blood and by spirit. Just as we lived in the South with entire sets of brothers and sisters building houses on the same plot of land so that all the first cousins were within hollerin' distance of each other.

This is what our mothers and fathers did when we first moved up North. First, living in the same crowded apartments, sleeping on pallets on the floor until one by one we could move out and get our own place. But even then we tried to stay on the same block. That wonderful style of living could be recreated and become a role model and example for others to reduplicate. The multi-millions of dollars generated by these talented young men whose skills came out of their people can give back to their communities in the most tangible way by creating a living testimony that would continue to be there and bear fruit long after they are gone. These young brothers need to stamp their names on something more lasting than a gym shoe, because the best made gym shoe won't last longer than a season.

This leads me into the next possibility. Why won't these young brothers build their own gym shoe factories and companies? Right now they are just a shill for the white-owned companies who use them up while they have a baddest game and the biggest name but discard them like yesterday's styles when they are no longer at the top of their game. Gym shoes are sold according to the name of the star player embossed on them. Whoever the best, most famous, most successful, most unique, most stylish, most dominant player is, his name sells the most gym shoes just as it sells the most tickets to games so people can see him play.

However, when that star's career is on the downside, when he is over the hill of his athletic and therefore commercial life, he loses the multi-million dollar endorsements. Just like his name on the gym shoe, his relationship with the company except for a very few exceptions like Michael Jordan, will only have lasted during the seasons of his success. He will not be given a senior vice-presidency that will continue to pay him in the seven figures so that he can maintain the life-style to which he and his family have become accustomed. He will probably not even be given a seat on the board of directors which can pay as much as $25,000.00 just for attending a single meeting. Instead he will be discarded and the white owners, executives and decision-makers will send out scouts, recruiters and agents to find the next generation of black stars, pay them for the temporary use of their names, ride them while their at the top of their games and the peak of their fame.

They won't have to look very far for them because in their long-term planning they will already have developed a relationship with them in junior high school, stuck with them thru high school, financed summer experiences at their luxurious camps, had them travel nationally and internationally at no expense, steered them to colleges where the coaches are on the gym shoe company payroll, sometimes making more from the gym shoe company than from the school where they coach. Signing them to a minor deal when they ink their first pro contract. As the player's star rises so does his place in the company. If he makes all-pro, is in the top ten in scoring, has an unstoppable move like an ankle-breaking cross-over, a dominating presence, a unique style, an entertaining, likable charming personality, or makes it deep into the play-offs he will get his own shoe. Not really his own shoe. A shoe the company pays him to let them put his name on as long his name sells shoes.

But if he gets traded, has a disagreement or a personality clash with the coach or the owner, doesn't smile enough, is not friendly, patient and gregarious enough to racist sportswriters and sportscasters who bombard him with degrading and demeaning questions, is seen as not being properly respectful or appreciative of the opportunity to play ball and make millions while making billions for the people he is working for. Or finally, when gets old, loses his starting position to a youngster, suffers a career ending injury, loses his zest for the game, wants to get off the road and spend more time with his growing children and cultivate a deeper relationship with his wife; in a twinkling of an eye becomes past tense. He declines into yesterday's news and the cycle starts all over again.

But what if a group of players decided to build their own gym shoe factory? It wouldn't be like building a steel plant, or a airplane or automobile factory. Gym shoes are just not that high tech. The same shoes our children pay up to a hundred fifty dollars a pair for cost about $2.50 per unit to manufacture in sweat shops in Asia.. The factories could be built in the ghetto neighborhoods so that the people who will buy the shoes the most will have a means of producing the income to purchase the product. That was part of the genius of original Ford automobile factory. Its workers were paid a wage that allowed them to purchase the product their labor produced.

The brothers would be the owners, the board of directors, the chief executive officers. They could go out and recruit the new young stars and sign them to contracts that stipulate that when their playing career is over they will come into the company in some significant position and help produce the next generation of gyms shoes by recruiting the next generation of superstars and offering them the same lifetime deal.

Finally, black athletes should be aggressive enough to move globally to develop the basketball talent and capitalize on the potential markets in Africa and Asia. We have allowed ourselves to be consigned to the roles of perpetual workers, never owners. Always following, refusing to make a move for the lead. Were it not for racism in the sports industry most of the coaches at least in basketball would be black. Since the mid-sixties black players have dominated the game at every level from high school through the pros. The first generation of those dominators are long since retired and should by now all be in senior positions in the industry as coaches, referees, executives, commissioners, administrators and owners. Instead we see the decision making areas of sports still dominated by white men.

Racism is alive and well in pro sports. Witness the travesty of Kareem Abdul-Jabbar having to beg for a coaching position in the NBA. It has been painful to watch him undergo the humiliation of having to be the voluntary coach of a high school team because the industry will not give him his just reward for having been one the greatest players of all time. This is all just revenge for Abdul-Jabbar's leadership role in the black athlete's boycott of the 1968 Olympics in Mexico City. Because Kareem was such a powerful force, being the legitimate successor to both Wilt Chamberlain and Bill Russell as the dominant player and most marketable asset of his era, they dared not touch him while he was filling stadiums, winning championships and generating billions in profits for the owners. But now in the twilight of his athletic days they serve him up a cold dish of revenge. One would think that some black college could at least give the brother a head coaching position. Or have we all forgotten how proud he made us from his days at Power Memorial High School in New York, to his unprecedented, never-reduplicated, three consecutive NCAA championships at UCLA, to his championship with the Milwaukee and his dynasty with the Lakers? For all the credit we give Magic Johnson for the Lakers successes we should remember that he never won another championship after Abdul-Jabbar retired.

To the Black Athlete:

We know you can outthink your opponent on the field but can you out-negotiate him in the business meeting? We know you can fake him out with your move to the hoop but can you outmaneuver him on a development project? We know you can stop your opponent, stand him straight up and drive him back when he tries to cross your goal line but can you stop him from controlling all the retail outlets in your community when you don't have a single one in his? We know you got enough ambition and determination to be the star of a team, but do you have enough intelligence and stick-to-it-tiveness to be the owner? We know you can endorse a product, but can you produce one? We know you can put your name on a gym shoe but can you put your name on a gym shoe company? We know you can generate multi-millions of dollars for yourself but can you produce multi-billions, maybe even trillions, for your people? We know you can give out turkeys for Thanksgiving and Christmas to the hungry and homeless but can you run a turkey farm or own a meat packing company and give those

318

people jobs so they won't have to be beggars.

The ball is in your hands.

XIII. PRISON

My first job when I finished seminary was Protestant Chaplain at the notorious Stateville Maximum Security Correctional Center near Joliet, IL., some twenty-five miles southwest of Chicago. The most consistent theme of my teaching, preaching and counseling ministry was a comparison of prison life to slavery. The difference was that slavery was actually a more positive experience than jail. During slavery our ancestors were driven in the field like beasts from before the sun came up 'til long after it went down. They were subjected to a never-ending stream of the foulest language and called the most vulgar names. They were beaten, raped, humiliated, constantly reminded of their worthlessness and powerlessness by the white people who claimed to own them. But in the evening of the day when the sun had gone down, when they came back to the slave quarters, they returned to an African community of their own making where people loved one another, looked out for one another, extended to each other helping hands and healing arts.

But in the prison community the oppression doesn't end when the inmates get a break from the intense, uncaring, often brutal supervision of the guards and return to their cells. When they go back to the small spaces that they share with one another the environment is, if anything, perhaps more dangerous than their interaction with the guards. The prisoners have constructed for themselves a way of life that is a re-creation of most of the worst aspects of gangster life on the streets. In many ways it actually gets worse. Prison as a rehabilitation or correctional center is a cruel joke. Prisons are, in way we would rather not be aware of, criminal enterprises in which every racket out on the street has its counterpart in the jailhouse. They rob each another, rape one another, fight and kill each other both individually and in gangs. Prison is no respite from street life. Drugs, gambling, prostitution, robbery, extortion, even protection rackets are all there. Any number of inmates' families pay protection money to keep their incarcerated relatives from being beaten, raped or killed. Every drug available on the street can be found in prison. It's possible for a person with an addiction to heroin, cocaine, PCP, crack or amphetamines to maintain that addiction during their entire sentence as long as they have the money to pay.

The route to prison begins with our young people, particularly our young males and their everyday contact with the police. The continuing presence of white racism as one of the most powerful sources of values in this country ensures that our children will be treated vastly different than white youth. A white teenage-boy can be stopped by the police for a traffic violation, get out of the car reeking of alcohol, act belligerent, curse out and threaten the police. What will the response of the police be? It will be sympathetic. They will identify with the white youngster in a number of ways. One will be seeing in him their own teenage sons. Another way will be seeing themselves at the same age.

It is interesting that despite the well-known proclivity of white males to drink to access with all of the negative behaviors that drunkenness induces there is no tradition of policemen killing out-of-control, drunken white youth, not even in the midst of riots on college campuses or at venues like the Mardi Gras riots in Philadelphia's South Street tourist area. The white policemen will think to themselves: "Boys will be boys." It is understood amongst them that white people have a right to "blow off steam". Or they may see the boy as the son of a superior, some wealthy and powerful white person who could cause them all kinds of problems if they mistreat their child. And on the opposite end reward them if they go out of their way to protect that child.

The role of the police in the white community is as it is stated on many of their squad cars : "to serve and protect." That is not the role and function of the police in the black community. It more like to "to control and oppress". I have seen policemen in the white community help people change tires, give them jumps when their batteries are dead, push them out of snow banks. I have seen just the opposite in the black community with white police using any incidental contact with black people as a justification to look for something wrong so that they could arrest us.

The rape of an eleven year old black girl by three sixteen year old white boys in Philadelphia at the Philly's baseball stadium is a case in point. It is a story that reads so much like the famous novel and movie, A Time To Kill that it seems almost like a copycat crime. The three white boys lured the little girl away from her aunt and brutally raped her. They were soon caught and arrested but in court they received the most minor of sentences.

In the book by Grisham and the Hollywood movie a little eleven year old black girl in Mississippi was beaten and raped and almost killed by three grown white criminals. When the procedures in court indicated that the men would be exonerated the father, played by Samuel Jackson, machine gunned them to death on the courthouse stairway with an AK-47. He was subsequently tried for murder and his defense attorney in the climactic scene asked the jury to imagine that the victim had a been a little eleven year old blonde-haired, blue- eyed white girl and her rapists three black males of any description. Can anyone sensibly imagine that black males guilty of raping a white female would face anything less than the maximum penalty?

Then, even more amazingly and a tack that was not

taken in the novel, the black judge found the girl at fault for her assault by describing her conduct as being "flirty." It harkens back to slavery time when African women were blamed for the assaults on them by white men because their animal-like sexuality and jungle-natured sensuality was more than any "civilized" white man could be expected to resist. This is just one of a thousand incidents that occur every day in the courtrooms of this country that demonstrate that there is little justice for black people in the so-called criminal justice system.

If there is one area of ministry in our churches weaker than the ministry to youth it is ministry to the young men and women in prison. The United States today has more people locked up in prison than did apartheid South Africa at the height of its oppression. The drug laws are the main reason for the outrageous number of young black men and women behind prison bars. These laws are written so that the possession of powder cocaine, which is the drug of choice among white people, is punished with a slap on the wrist. Those caught with crack cocaine, which is the cheap by-product of powder cocaine marketed in the black community, get long-term mandatory sentences.

What is called the War on Drugs is in actuality a war on the black community. There never has been a true war against the drug trade in the history of this country. The international trade in addictive drugs has been a part of this country's geopolitical and commercial strategy for well over a hundred years, partly as a profit producer and partly as chemical warfare against peoples of color.

The modern drug trade started in 1839 when Great Britain conducted the Opium Wars against Imperial China to force the Chinese to allow them to import opium from India into China. The Chinese had banned the importation of this addictive poison since 1800. The British recognized the kind of profits that the drug trade would produce and upon the refusal of their request by the Chinese emperor, sailed warships up the Yangtze and Yellow Rivers and bombarded Chinese cities until the deaths of tens of thousands of civilians caused the emperor to relent.

The United States became involved in drug trafficking contemporaneous with the importation of Chinese labor in the 1870's and 1880's to work the plantations of California and the western expansion of the railroads. They brought opium to sell to the Chinese men who were not allowed to bring their wives with them. Opium dens were a prominent feature of frontier life and their clienteles included not only Chinese laborers but any number of cowboys from among the local populations. Clipper ships owned by the old money shipping lines of the Northeastern Brahmin families were heavily involved in the importation of opium to supply the trade.

The modern trade in heroin, which has been such an affliction to the black community since the 1940s, was directly sponsored and organized by the CIA. The movie Godfather I portrays part of the scene but does not tell the whole story. In one of most pivotal scenes of the entire film, leaders of various Mafia families have a summit meeting and decide to engage in the heroin trade but to limit it the black community. One of them explains with the notorious remark: "We'll sell it to only to the colored. They're animals anyway. Let them lose their souls".

What was left out was the role that the CIA played. At the end of World War II the socialist movement threatened to control unions of workers for American firms that produced super profits by rebuilding the war-torn nations of Europe. The socialists were a powerful presence in the union movements of Europe. (This is why even to this day European workers enjoy higher wages, better working conditions, longer vacations, better health care and other perquisites far beyond those of American workers.)

In order to destroy or at least control the socialist unions in Italy the CIA struck a deal with the Mafia. The crime syndicate families weakened unions through assassinations of their leaders and other acts of terrorism. In return the

323

CIA gave them access to the fertile fields of the Golden Triangle where the borders of Laos, Myanmar(Burma) and Thailand meet. Most of worlds poppy harvests are found in this mountainous region of Southeast Asia. The CIA also gave them protection for their laboratories in Italy and France where the raw opium would be chemically transformed into heroin then safe transport of the finished product to the streets of the black communities of America.

Late in the 1980's revelations were made in a number of newspapers about the cocaine and crack trade being organized by CIA interests in Central and South America, some of it as part of the drugs for guns interchanges of the Reagan administration's illegal support of the right-wing Contra's war against the popularly elected socialist government of Nicaragua. What we do know is that chemical warfare through the introduction of addictive poisonous substances has historically been a major plank in Europe's platform of conquest, control and exploitation of peoples of color the world over.

Opium was used against the Chinese and the traffic was not halted until the freeing of China through the revolution led by Mao Zedong. Alcohol was used against the Native American so much so that the drunken Indian is a classic stereotypical character in Hollywood's distorted portrayal of those great people. Against the black community they've used variously and in combination, alcohol, heroin, and crack.

The only illegal substance that is domestically grown is marijuana which is now second only to corn as an American-grown agricultural product. Most of the world's heroin starts out as poppy plants grown in Southeast Asia.. The coca plant is grown in the highlands of Central and South America and its derivatives of power cocaine and crack have their strongest world markets among white people in the United States. Yet in the so-called war on drugs we don't see tens of thousands of the white farmers who are growing marijuana in the heartlands of America

324

going to jail.

Black people are only the lowest level dealers of cocaine and heroin. We don't own any shipping lines that transport these drugs by the tens of thousands of tons into this nation. Nor do we own airplanes that fly it in under the radar screens of the military and commercial aviation. Every publicized report and study indicate that white people use more drugs than black people, including crack cocaine. But it is black people who go to jail for the sale and possession of drugs. The war on drugs is a war against black people in general and young black males in particular. Rather than fighting the war with addiction as the target and using drug rehabilitation programs as the primary weapon, instead the United States chooses to make addicted people the target and rather than treat their addiction punishes the addicts with imprisonment.

Now the prison industry is in the midst of a privatization campaign which promises to be the new slavery. Private companies running prisons for profit need people to fill up their cells like hotel owners need guests renting their rooms and like airlines need travelers occupying the seats on their planes. Through racial profiling our young people are the easiest people to put in prison. They are the easiest people to suspect, follow, stop, search, accuse, arrest, hold, try, convict and finally incarcerate for lengthy sentences. The prison privatizers want them as cheap labor. Prisons are becoming manufacturing plants that turn obscene profits on investment because they have a wonderful source of cheap, captive labor.

The inmates will be paid pennies a day to manufacture products to be sold on the open market. They are the kind of cheap labor that American manufacturers have been moving their plants overseas to find for the past thirty years. Incarcerated men and women cannot organize unions, engage in job actions, strike or picket and they can be beaten and even killed with a minimum of fuss. Most of the civilian population believes they deserve whatever they get. This constitutes the final, truest, and most dramatic measure of a return to slavery- a captive population of workers who can be beaten like beasts of burden if they do not produce in absolute obedience to the commands of their overseers.

The practitioners and students of the so-called science of penology talk sanctimoniously about being engaged in the business of reform. But while the penal system preaches education and rehabilitation what they really do is isolate, degrade, dehumanize, brutalize, torture, rape, drive mad, and kill their inmates. Far too many men and women come out of prison much worse criminals than they went in. Many of them went in as innocent victims of a system where justice is an expensive commodity only available to those who can afford the most high-priced teams of big-name defense attorneys.

Too many will return to our communities bruised, scarred, mean, angry, hardened, unemployable misfits who have no job skills other than those of the predator that they learned from master criminals who were the only people who cared enough to take the time to teach them anything. When they return home they will not prey on the white community. Residential segregation and racial profiling based upon making sure black people are not in the wrong neighborhood insures that white people will have little to fear from the ex-convicts. It will be to their own communities that these men and women will return. They will come back to our homes, our churches, our businesses, our schools. If we have no positive alternative to a life of crime to offer them we will inevitably become the victims of their desperation.

We need prison ministries that will go the heart of the matter. Historically and presently, our prison ministries consist of teams of singers and preachers and maybe a few Sunday School teachers going to the prison to conduct a worship service. This is good but it's not enough. The inmates need from us what many of the white denominations provide--full-time ministers independently paid by their denominations to serve as chaplains in prisons. We need them to be on our pay rolls rather than the state's because "he who pays the piper calls the tune." I found in my work as a state-employed chaplain that I was expected to be just a sanctified security guard whose first responsibility was not service or salvation but restraint and control. Independent, denominationally-employed chaplains would be free to develop the kinds of counseling and educational programs that will prepare inmates for a positive future on release as people gainfully employed who know how to be functional family members, husbands, wives and parents.

Furthermore, we need vehicles in place to provide these people with the necessities of life upon their release. The recidivism rate among black inmates is ridiculously high because all too often they return to a community that has no support structure in place for them. When faced with hunger, nakedness, and homelessness it is difficult to resist the urge to do whatever one has to and what one knows best to survive.

The black church is the one institution that has both a theological mandate and the human and financial resources to meet the challenge of effectively addressing the needs of both inmates and those lately released from prison. These men and women just released need not only the basic necessities of food, shelter and clothing. They need jobs and incomes. And they need counseling. There are no studies of the effects of prison life on the minds, personalities and spirits of the inmates because no one cares enough to finance and produce one. But I contend that the prison experience has got to be likened to that of combat. The everyday traumas of incarceration, with its continual violence, brutality, and exploitation, is like living in a war zone. These are the kinds of conditions that cause Post Traumatic Stress Disorder (PTSD) in combat troops.

The Armed Forces of this country has yet to fully meet its responsibilities to its troops that return from wars, distorted in their spirits and dangerous in their behavior, in terms of providing them with an effective support system of counseling to aid them in being delivered from this dangerous syndrome. But even less has society attempted to attend to the wounds to the personalities of men and women locked in cages like animals and brutalized like beasts for years and years.

The church's theological mandate is found in the words of Jesus who instructed His followers that the outer expression of the inward condition of being born again in the spirit required them to minister to the least of these your brethren. Who are the least of these?--the hungry, the homeless, the naked, the sick, the oppressed and the imprisoned.

We need a prison reform movement. It must be a grass-roots movement organized principally by the families of the incarcerated ones. The brutal mistreatment of inmates must stop. There need to be conjugal visits. Prisons are a hothouse for AIDS. Homosexuality is the dominant form of sexuality practiced there and I have no doubt that rather than bear the expense of treating someone diagnosed with AIDS at tremendous expense to the state or federal government it is much more cost-effective to give them early release into the general population. A prison movement would demand conjugal visits to help break the grip of homosexual behavior among inmates. The movement might have to consist of coordinated efforts of demonstrations by camped out protestors on the outside of prison complexes with simultaneous general strikes by inmates on the inside.

One of the unaddressed consequences of imprisonment is the fact that prisons are homosexual communities. Because inmates are denied access to their wives in conjugal visitations, the vast majority meet their sexual needs in encounters and relationships with other

328

incarcerated men. These relationships are often of a forced nature with the physically and spiritually weaker men being raped by those who are stronger, more aggressive and more brutal. One of the reasons for the proliferation of gangs in prison was to provide protection from homosexual rape. Men who have lived in that culture and become habituated to its practices leave prison with the idea of immediately returning to heterosexuality. However, sexual addictions are perhaps the most difficult to overcome. Much of the transference of AIDS to black women has been accomplished by the insistence of former inmates on engaging in anal sex with their wives and girlfriends. Anal sex being the primary method by which AIDS is contracted.

We know what the consequences are rape are for its female victims. The books written on this topic number in the hundreds. Despite the fact that homosexual rape is endemic to certain same-sex communities such as the armed forces, same-sex boarding schools, fraternities and sororities and, of course prisons, there are no studies of the short and long term effects of rape on male victims. We can only imagine what kinds of problems men bring back to their wives, children, families and communities when they have been the victims of rape while in prison.

One of the most brilliant and respected ministers that I know, The Reverend P.M. Smith, senior pastor of the Huber Memorial Church in Baltimore, Maryland and the organizer of the one the most effective men's ministries that I have worked with, raised this issue to me: "Why do believe men who have been raped have thereby been reduced to being homosexuals. When we hear of a man being raped the most common and immediate response is: 'He got punked.' But when our foremothers were being raped in slavery did that make them whores? So why when a man is raped do we conclude that he has been turned into a homosexual?"

The more important question is: in the case of rape who

is the true sexual outlaw? When a woman is raped which of the people involved in the encounter has a sexual disorder. Which one is the whore? Is it the woman who had the sexual contact forced upon her but never desired it? Or is the real whore the rapist who wanted the sexual contact so badly he was willing to commit a crime to have it?

In the case of homosexual rape, who is the real homosexual? Is it the man who was victimized? Is it the one who had no desire for such an interaction but was forced into by a brutal assault? Or is the true homosexual the man who wanted sex with a man so badly that he was driven to attack the man and intimidate, threaten and in many instances beat him into insensibility to achieve his objective? Both the victim and rapist are in need of long-term therapeutic care to effectuate their healing. But it is the rapist who is in denial about his true condition that represents the greater threat to the safety of our daughters, grandchildren and the wider community. Predators always seek out the weak, the small, the old, the infirm as their victims.

The ultimate strategy for prison reform would be for the Black Church to go into the private prison business. If there is one group in the world that believes in and practices redemption, transformation, recovery and restoration it is the Black Church. We in the black church are supposed to specialize in healing, rehabilitation, and recovery. If we can't rehabilitate hundreds of thousands of lost, thrown away and rejected, men, women, boys and girls that society has given up on then we need to get out of the soul-saving business. As the sermon title says: "If You've Gone Out Of Business, You Ought To Take Down Your Sign." Our faith gives us a mandate to save to the utmost. If our sense of Christianity was able to deliver our people from a worse slavery over a hundred years ago it ought to still be able to deliver brothers and sisters from this lesser slavery today.

330

A church-run prison would provide a world-wide model for true rehabilitation. The church could provide the kinds of support systems that a released inmate could depend on for jobs, housing, clothes, food, and various forms of counseling. We should be able to provide inmates with the kind of love they need in order to engage in radical, fundamental, positive change. If we can build multi-million dollar show-piece worship palaces with funds that were collected from working class and poor people who intended those monies to build up the kingdom of God in this world then we can take a percentage of those funds and do real ministry to the downtrodden and the oppressed. We need scholarship money to train ministers and counselors to specialize in treatment of incarcerated people. We need Christian halfway-house for ex-offenders to live in as they try to meet the daunting challenge of returning to normal life. We need training programs to teach people a skill so that they can be gainfully employed because history has taught us that men in need would rather steal than beg. It is now standard psychological truth that no addict kicks their habit except in the presence of unconditional love. Our faith mandates that kind of love and it is a denial of the faith if we can't provide it to those Jesus commanded us to serve as the true test and measurement of our faith. Those he described as "the least of these, your brethren". Not to address this most critical issue through the power of our faith would be fulfilling what the Apostle Paul described as: "… having a form of godliness but denying the power thereof…"II Tim. 3:5KJV

Whosoever will be chief amongst you let him be your servant. Matt. 20:27KJV

The one nearest the enemy, in pursuit, is the real leader.
African Proverb

Where there is no bull, a castrated ox will lead the herd.
African Proverb

XIV. LEADERSHIP

In a recent edition of *Savoy* magazine there was a list of people the magazine described as the 100 most powerful black people in America. The most startling aspect of the list was that the overwhelming majority of the people chosen were not heads of black organizations, or people known for their commitment to uplifting the race. Rather they were individuals who either worked for powerful white firms and institutions; were wealthy no matter where they got their money from; or were merely famous, so they were not even true leaders just celebrities, people known for being known.

Savoy's list differed radically from the similar annual list compiled by Ebony Magazine, whose listing is composed primarily of the heads of the most significant black organizations, institutions and businesses. One's relationship to white people or their institutions had never previously been the criterion for the rank of "black leader". Just because a black man or woman is CEO of a Fortune 500 corporation does not mean that they will leverage their power to bring in more black workers. Nor does it mean that they will institute an affirmative action plan that will

332

give more contracts to black owned suppliers. Or that the company will make serious contributions to black colleges and universities or deposit funds in black banks. Or in any other way redirect the massive resources of their corporations for the good of the black community. In fact one of the most often observed and commented upon features of corporate life is the refusal many black employees to even acknowledge each others presence around white people for fear of being seen as being race-conscious or, God forbid, "militant".

One of the most outstanding and peculiar virtues of African American life has been the moral and spiritual quality of our leadership. It stands in stark contrast to the nature of the leaders of the people that we have been forced to live among. One way to look at the difference is to take note of the membership of the boards of directors of Fortune 500 corporations. These individuals will be members of the most respected and feared occupations in Euro-American society: businessmen (thieves), lawyers and politicians (liars) and soldiers (murderers).

Hardly ever will a minister, priest, schoolteacher or even a social worker or anyone else who represents a moral principle or profession be found there. Contrast this with the board of directors of any number of typical black institutions and you will find an inordinate, disproportionate number of ministers as members. Until this present dispensation our leaders have been most uniquely characterized by their outstanding moral and spiritual qualities.

In the European community religious leaders are secondary, if not tertiary, to the true centers of power. Ministers in white America are only called in after important decisions have already been made by the businessmen, soldiers and politicians. They are brought in as an afterthought to offer God's blessings over the decisions concerning war or peace, prosperity or poverty, slavery or freedom, life or death.

This is just a continuation of the role of the priest in European society established during the Medieval Era of so-called chivalry, the days of knights errant and damsels in distress. Europeans in those days had one law of inheritance known as "primogeniture", it meant the first son got everything. The subsequent sons of the estate had to become knights errant and win their fortune by force of arms. They had to go out and make camp at some busy intersection and challenge each knight that passed by to a contest of arms. The winner got the loser's armor and warhorse, if not also his castle lands and lady. Enough such victories and the knights who won more than they lost could amass a workable fortune. But if a son had no inclination to fight and kill for his living he was retired to the monastery, where he could find refuge from the hard knocks of the world. Thus have priests and ministers among Europeans been the retiring, passive, non-aggressive, non-threatening types.

A good illustration of this tradition is found in cowboy movies. There is a standard scene played out in these movies set in the local church. Someone bursts into the service and shouts: "The bad guys are coming!" The fighting men organize themselves to meet the threat while the pastor is told: "Reverend, you stay here with the women and children." With a look of relief on his face he demurely obeys.

Replay the same kind of scenario in black life and when the person comes in and cries out: "The Klan is coming!" It is likely to be the pastor who will draw his pistol first, brandish it over his head and declare: "Come on men let's cut 'em off at the pass!"

We have never purposely or knowingly chosen leaders who we knew were corrupt individuals. (Of course there are exceptions to every rule but the existence of the exception does not invalidate the rule, it dramatizes it). A striking example of this phenomenon was seen a few years ago when Mrs. Coretta Scott King named General Colin

334

Powell as the chairman of the Martin Luther King, Jr. Holiday celebration held annually in Atlanta. Of course, General Powell was a big man by this time, being the first person of African descent to be named the Chairman of the Joint Chiefs of Staff, the premier soldier in this nation's military apparatus. The black community raised such an uproar of protest that Mrs. King was forced to rescind the appointment.

Popularity, fame, wealth and power were not enough in and of themselves for us to render to General Powell a position of such leadership and recognition. The common people recognized General Powell for what he was and who he is, a servant of white interests, not someone committed to the welfare of black people world-wide and therefore willing, like Dr. King to take a stance against European oppression of peoples of color. He never protested the unjust and illegal military incursions into such black nations as Grenada, Panama, Somalia and the Sudan. As Secretary of State he did not even have the courage to defy President Bush, when Bush told him that he was not allowed to attend the international conference on racism being held in South Africa. A real leader would have boldly disobeyed his boss, even given up his job, to be in a place where the most crucial issues affecting his people were being discussed and deliberated. He then went on to further damage his credibility here and abroad when he appeared before the United Nations making a case for Bush's war against Iraq by citing data and statistics whose accuracy and veracity he doubted.

American society and its European antecedents founded their wealth and power upon the four great crimes of the human experience: murder, kidnap, theft and rape. Its leadership must be composed of individuals and classes of people who are experts and past masters in carrying out these atrocities on a massive scale. Europeans have historically chosen for their leaders warrior-kings and killer-queens, men and women who are distinguished by their ability and propensity to kill. Africans have on the other hand chose as their leaders priest-kings and priestess-queens, people celebrated for their ability to heal.

There is a reason that there has never been a pacifist president of the United States. No one can ascend to the Oval Office who cannot convince the American people that he or she has the emotional wherewithal to push the red button and rain down nuclear destruction if it is deemed to be in the best interest of American foreign policy. One of the most interesting and instructive features of Rev. Jesse Jackson's campaigns for the presidency was a trip to Germany in which he had pictures taken of himself riding in an American tank. He had to pay homage to American military might in order to be taken seriously by the white electorate. He had to demonstrate his willingness to use America's awesomely and obscenely destructive military power for the furtherance of this nation's geopolitical agenda.

America pays surface homage to the idea of its leaders as people of some at least ritually religious, if not truly deep moral qualities, so that all of its presidents have had some seeming membership in a church. This cultivation of an image has only been for purposes of public relations. The real nature of so-called American morality is found in their overriding philosophical and constitutional principle of the " separation of church of state" which for all practical purposes works out to being a "separation of politics from morality." What is more important than right or wrong to them are hard-headed matters of self-interest in which they dispense with questions of good and evil in favor of what they call the "realpolitik". They do what they have to do to further their financial and political interests no matter what that ends up looking like from a moral perspective. While America loves to describe itself as a Christian nation the two most profound institutions that it developed and which continue to define it are slavery and capitalism. Neither of these ways of life can be considered

336

Christian by anyone with the most cursory understanding of the principles of the Bible.

One of the most troubling aspects of black leadership today is that of celebrity leaders. The classic rule for black leaders has for centuries been captured in the proverbial expression "walk among kings but keep the common touch". Or another: "never get so high that you get above your color". While intense classism and being color-struck has been a feature of black middle-class culture since slavery no one could become a popular leader while expressing contempt for the dark-skinned masses. (With, of course, the few inevitable exceptions such as the younger W.E.B. DuBois.) This new phenomenon of celebrity leadership however does exactly that.

When I attended the March on Washington in 2000 organized by Martin Luther King, III and Rev. Al Sharpton, I was astounded to find the demonstration organized along class lines. There was a VIP tent in which the leaders gathered prior to and after the proceedings. These black VIP's, modeled after the European elites, held themselves aloof from the masses of the people and surrounded themselves with entourages of paid bodyguards and voluntary sycophants whose responsibility it was to protect them from contact with common people. There were three different color badges given out to the participants to indicate to the police what level of access the individual with the badge could have to the leaders, with ropes at varying intervals to keep people without badges away from the center of things.

During the sixties at the height of the Civil Rights Movement, while participating in scores of marches and demonstrations, I never witnessed those events being organized along class lines. I watched people come up to Dr. King, greet him with a handshake and words of encouragement without any sense from anyone that the availability of and accessibility to this premier leader was somehow inappropriate. Anybody could approach the biggest names and most famous and powerful people without the fear of being rebuffed because you were not somebody important yourself. The movement as Dr. King was wont to put it was for the Ph.D.'s and the no D's or as it is expressed in the black church "No big I's and little u's."

If there is one person that black people ought to have ready access to it is the preacher. When the average one of us lacks the social, economic, or political clout to obtain an audience with the mayor, city councilman, state legislator, senator, congressman or president we ought to be able to see the preacher, the man of God. If Jesus had operated the way these celebrity preachers do, the legendary woman with the "issue of blood" would never have been able to "touch the hem of his garment" and been "made whole.'" While the primary lesson to be learned from this story was about healing the secondary lesson was about access.

This kind of behavior, founded upon the European notion that some people because they have money, education, status and power are inherently better than other people, is anathema to the African principle of "I am because we are." Dr. King consistently instructed us that the relationship between leaders and followers is a symbiotic relationship, a reciprocal relationship between indispensable equals. He taught us that neither can exist without the other. By precept and example he made it clear to us that there are no leaders without followers and no followers without leaders. A leader without followers is a cruel joke and followers without leaders are directionless people going nowhere in particular. Mutual respect and concern are the watchwords of the leader-follower relationship. The biblical principle goes even deeper, making it clear that it is the leaders who exist to serve the people and not the people who exist to serve leaders.

Another present day phenomenon of black leadership that is out of step with the best of our traditions and values is leaders who cannot be challenged, criticized or called into account for their performance on the job. From Africa days black people have congregated in open forums to have public discussions about matters important to the community at large. Whether they were village meetings or councils of the elders or the meetings of the men's or women's secret society, we organized our societies based on democratic principles that held that everybody had a voice and a right to be heard. Even in hierarchical societies led by kings and queens the leaders were never little gods who could not be challenged, criticized or questioned. When leaders are treated in that fashion the organizations that give them such exalted god-like status are known as cults.

Cults will invariably exist among smaller grouping in any population because there will always be individuals so lacking in self esteem that they will make themselves subject to some megalomaniac's domination, trying to obtain vicariously, through slavish dedication to the leader, a sense of value they lack within themselves. But the idea of an entire race operating like a cult; being led by leaders we cannot touch, talk to, shake hands with, question, or criticize is worse than ridiculous, it's dangerous.

One of the most outstanding features of black leadership during slavery was the national meetings of the Colored Conventions held from 1830 through the 1850's when representatives assembled from all over the country to engage in public discussion about the course the race should take and the strategies to be employed for our liberation. During these meeting debate was an everyday occurrence. Rev. Henry Highland Garnett, Rev. Frederick Douglass, Sojourner Truth, Martin Delany, Harriet Tubman and their contemporaries engaged each other daily over the question of whether an immediate violent revolt should be called for among the slaves. The question of emigration was always on the agenda. Both sides of the issue of the white racist American Colonization Society's campaign to return free black people to Africa were discussed. Some insisted on going back home. Others took the position that free black people must stay in America and continue to struggle for the liberation of our enslaved brothers and sisters.

During Reconstruction as we laid the foundation for the institutions that made us "a nation in a nation" . Conversations, discussions, disputes and disagreements about the direction our people should move in were constantly taking place. For instance, black Baptists debated for almost thirty years whether to accept the competing invitations from white Baptists in the Southern Baptist Convention and the Northern Baptist Convention to join their fellowships or to organize their own independent national body. The debate culminated with the formation of the independent National Baptist Convention in 1895.

The turn of the 19th century into the twentieth was highlighted by the continuing challenge to Booker T. Washington's accomodationism by W.E.B. DuBois, Ida B. Wells and Monroe Trotter's insistence on full political rights. What would the twenties have been like without the intellectual ferment of opposing ideas among Marcus Garvey, Ida B. Wells, DuBois, A. Phillip Randolph, Mary Church Terrell, Chandler Owens, Mary McLeod Bethune and the Noble Drew Ali? Some of the most riveting scenes of Ralph Ellison's Invisible Man are his descriptions of impromptu debates between black nationalists and Negro communist orators on the street corners of Harlem. During the Civil Rights/Black Power I witnessed great debates between proponents of non-violence from SCLC and advocates of armed self-defense from the Deacons for Defense and the Revolutionary Action Movement (RAM).

One of my most unforgettable moments in the sixties was at a civil rights rally of the Chicago Freedom Movement held at the Liberty Baptist Church on 49th and South Park (now Martin Luther King, Jr. Boulevard) pastured by Rev. A.P. Jackson , a Morehouse classmate of Dr, King's and one of his closest friends. When Dr. King was interrupted in the middle of his message by a heckler in the crowd he responded in an amazing fashion. Rather than directing us young bloods to remove brother by force, which we would have gladly done, instead Dr. King taught us a lesson in democracy, generosity, humility, respect and nobility. The heckler was Monroe Sharp, the leader of the SNCC chapter located on the South Side. Dr. King addressed the young brother and said to him: "Monroe, don't stand out there in the crowd hollering like that. Come up to the podium and use the mike. You are too important a leader for the people not to be able to hear what you have to say." You can imagine what would happen to anyone who tried to interrupt a speech by most of today's leaders whose bodyguards stand at the ready to protect them from any form of interference, question, challenge, or criticism.

In the leadership of both Rev. Jesse Jackson and Minister Louis Farrakhan we find an absence of discussion, debate and accountability. Rev. Jackson has never provided us with an explanation for his activities before, during and after the assassination of Dr. King. Why did he so virulently oppose the Poor People's Campaign that Dr. King once walked out of a meeting so disgusted by his filibustering that he told him with uncharacteristic anger: "Why don't you get your own kingdom and leave mine alone!" Why (according to King family attorney, William Pepper, in his book, An Act of State) did he give the order for the Memphis Invaders (a group of local young black men who advocated like the Black Panthers armed self – defense) to be ejected from the Lorraine Hotel an hour before Dr. King was shot, further removing from the grounds the possible protection of an armed black presence? Why did he leave Memphis to return to Chicago when every SCLC staff member that was able made their way to Memphis to stand vigil over the body of our fallen leader and accompany it to Atlanta for burial? Why did he stand in the chambers of the City Council of Chicago and claim that he held Dr. King in his arms as he died and bore

341

Dr. King's martyred blood on is shirt when he was in fact standing on the ground beneath the balcony when the fatal shot was fired. It was Ralph Abernathy and Andy Young who were on the balcony holding the leader as he breathed out his last. Why has he never denounced the false image portrayed on the front pages of newspaper's world-wide showing himself standing at Dr. King's right hand and Rev. Ralph Abernathy at his left bearing the erroneous caption that the picture had been taken moments before the fatal shot was fired? Why did he so eagerly thrust himself into the leadership of the Poor People's Campaign after Dr. King's death when he had so aggressively opposed it when Dr. King was alive? Why has he given no account for the abysmal failure of the Poor People's Campaign that Dr. King envisioned as the most radical use of civil disobedience and direct action in the history of the Civil Rights Movement?

Rev. Jackson's ascendancy to national prominence and leadership is linked to one event and one event alone—the assassination of Dr. King. It was not attained through long years of paying dues by building an organization by member and block-by-block through fits and starts and ups and downs. The week before Dr. King's murder Rev. Jackson met with the hundred or so people who came to his Saturday morning Operation Breadbasket meeting held in the cafeteria of McGiffert Hall, the married student dormitory of the Chicago Theological Seminary on the corner of 57th St, and Woodlawn in the Hyde Park neighborhood on the South Side of Chicago.

One week later, two days after Dr. King's murder, over four thousand people showed up, convinced by media portrayals that Rev. Jackson was Dr. King's true successor. All the false images: Rev. Jackson standing at Dr. King's right hand "moments" before he was shot; Rev. Jackson claiming to have held Dr. King in his arms and being the last one Dr. King spoke to before he died; his shirt supposedly covered with Dr. King's blood because he was

342

standing so close to him as the bullet struck that the blood spattered on him; resonated in the black biblical consciousness. It was to us a familiar and prophetic replaying of the Old Testament story, recorded in the second chapter of II Kings, of Elijah the old prophet who promised his protégé Elisha that if Elisha remained loyal to the old man, when he was translated into the heavenly realm, his mantle of prophecy would be conferred upon Elisha, making him his successor.

Countless millions accepted Rev. Jackson as Dr. King's legitimate successor, despite Rev. Ralph David Abernathy having been Dr. King's best friend since the days of the Montgomery Bus Boycott, a co-founder of SCLC and its senior vice-president, named in its constitution as Dr. King's successor. The media-fed public relations campaign was unquestionably one of the successful attempts on the part of white America to determine who would be our most significant leader. Nor has it ever been examined or explained what Rev. Jackson's special attributes were that made him so attractive to the white establishment that he was their popular choice to be promoted as our leader.

Minister Louis Farrakhan has never fully accounted for his role in the assassination of Malcolm X. He has never even apologized for his defamatory and inflammatory rhetoric when he repeatedly called for Malcolm's head to be cut off because Minister Shabazz left the nation of Islam and formed his own political organization and Muslim denomination. Nor has he ever accounted for his role and the Nation's in the foul murder of the daughters, sons and infant grandchildren of Imam Hamaas Abdul Khaalis as a result of the imam's criticism of the Nation.

Imam Khaalis was originally one of the Nation's highest ranking officials, having served as its first national secretary before being ousted in the late 1950's. His name then was Ernest 2X McGee. After his ouster he became so embittered toward the Messenger and the Nation that he waged a campaign of condemnatory poison pen letter-writing to people within and without the Nation, accusing the Honorable Elijah Muhammad of deception and fraud. As a consequence Lieutenant John 38X Clark of Muhammad's Mosque #12 in Philadelphia orchestrated one of the first mass murders attributable to black people when on January 17, 1973 he led an assassination squad of 8 men to Imam Khaalis' home, a mansion on 16th Street in Northwest Washington D.C. The multi-storied brick building was bought for the Imam by his most famous convert, basketball immortal Lewis Alcindor, whom he renamed Kareem Abdul-Jabbar. It was an orgy of killing that was unmatched in the black community until 7 people were murdered in a crack house in Philadelphia at the turn of the new century almost twenty years later. The imam was not at home so the men wreaked their vengeance on the members of his family that were there.

Eight people were killed. Only one survived. Daud Khaalis, twenty-five year old son, was shot to death. Amina, twenty-two year old daughter and mother of nine-day old Khadyja was shot eight times but miraculously survived to testify against the murderers. Bibi, one of the imam's two wives, was shot eight times and died in a pool of blood. Rahman, a son, eleven years old was shot twice in the head and died instantly. Abdullah, two-year old son, was shot three times in the head but was killed by the first bullet. Abdul Nut, an adult male member of the Khaalis congregation stopped by unexpectedly and was killed with two bullets to the head. The crowning achievement of this group of killers and what put them in the same demonic territory inhabited by the Klu Klux Klan was that they took the two babies in the house, Bibi's one year old daughter also named Bibi and Amina's nine day old daughter Khadyja and drowned them in a bathtub as if they were unwanted puppies or despised rodents.

It can never be right to murder a child. There is only one kind of entity, power or force in the known universe that requires the hurting, molesting or killing of a child to curry its favor. These being are known to the spiritually aware as demons. Anyone who attacks children seeks favor from the devil and puts themselves beyond the pale of human mercy. Even peace-loving Jesus said "It were better for him that a millstone were hanged about his neck and he cast into the sea than that he should offend one of these little ones." Lu 17:2KJV The madness of child abuse, a distinguishing characteristic of American life in both the white and black community, is something for which this nation must one day give an account. A madness which was only further fed by that day's murder of innocents in the name of religion.

Because there have been no public discussions around these concerns, we as a people, have been left in a state of information deprivation. People need accurate information to make intelligent decisions.

Most black people think that Minister Malcolm X left the Nation because of the Honorable Elijah Muhammad's fathering a number of children out of wedlock with younger women. This is not a credible reason because Muslims are allowed to have as many as four wives and a number of concubines. Since the legal machinery of this country defines multiple marriages as the crime of polygamy numerous Muslims in America, like many Mormons, continue to practice polygamy privately, beneath the radar screen of the legal establishment.

Author Taylor Branch, in the second volume of his notable trilogy of Dr. King and the Civil Rights Movement, Pillar of Fire, offers his own remarkable and eye-opening account of the true nature Imam Malik El Shabazz' disagreement with the Honorable Elijah Muhammad. Branch contends that the roots of the conflict lay in the murder of Charles Stokes, a member of the Los Angeles Nation of Islam congregation by Los Angeles city policemen in 1961. The policeman not only shot and killed the unarmed Mr. Stokes and shot a number of other Muslims, but then entered the mosque and brutalized many other members, both male and female.

Branch reports that when Minister Malcolm got the news he booked the first flight he could get into Los Angeles with the intention of retaliating against the police. Malcolm X had been berating activists in the Civil Rights Movement for years, inveighing against and insulting them for their non-violent philosophy. He called them weaklings and cowards. And he insisted that if any white person laid their hands on a Muslim, retaliation would be swift and powerful. But when he got to L.A. and spoke to The Messenger he was instructed to take no revenge. In fact Branch reports that his orders were just the opposite. That he was to present the members of the Nation as non-threatening and peace-loving black people. Even to the extent of having injured witnesses testify that they were not even *angry* at the policemen who killed their brother, insulted their wives, sisters and daughters and defiled their place of worship.

Malcolm as a result felt betrayed and embarrassed. All his vaunted boasting of the manliness of the Muslims and his threats of physical reprisal for any attack against them turned out in the end to be just empty posturing. He felt exposed as being no more than what the Chinese would call "a paper tiger". The position of respect, even fear that Muslims maintain in the eyes of the black community derive from the image they have assiduously cultivated of being black nationalist militant practitioners of armed self-defense. The truth of the matter, however, is what Malcolm finally had to admit to himself, that whatever violent potential the Nation possessed, it was only directed towards white people as rhetoric. Their truly violent behavior was and is only used against dissident Muslims and other members of the black community that disagree with them or criticize them.

I heard economist, college professor, author and nationally syndicated columnist Dr. Julienne Malveaux give a speech at Lincoln University in which she described how she received threatening, middle-of-the night phone calls and had the tires on her car slashed as a consequence of taking a critical position against both the Million Man and the Million Woman March.

The most visible symbols of black progress in the past twenty years have unquestionably been Rev. Jackson's campaigns for the American presidency and Minister Farakhan's Million Man March.

What did these campaigns and events actually accomplish on behalf of the black community? Rev. Jackson's presidential campaigns resulted in his being given a prime time slot to address the nation live on network TV; an honor and an opportunity that no black person has ever been afforded in the history of this nation. That kind of exposure and popularity translates into the perquisites of kings and five figure fees for speaking engagements. Rev. Jackson's exponential increase in his personal wealth did not even translate into the kind of political capital for black people that would have purchased us some consideration in the halls of decision making in the Democratic Party. Rev. Jackson's Rainbow Coalition was not allowed to aid a single plank to the Democratic Platform. Not only did it not prevent a rightward move in the party but it helped to precipitate one by inspiring Bill Clinton and Al Gore to organize the "moderate" Democratic Leadership Council which distanced itself from the concerns of black people in order to appeal to racist white voters.

Despite all the ridiculous and sad jokes about Bill Clinton being the first "black" president. If Bill Clinton can be described as being black it is only in the same sense that Elvis Presley and Eminem are black. While playing black in public performances Clinton proved to be among the whitest of whites in his conservative actions such as the dismantling of welfare, ignoring the genocide in Rwanda, sending troops to Somalia, bombing a pharmaceutical company in the Sudan and establishing the North American

347

Free Trade Agreement (NAFTA) as the law of the land thereby further removing factory jobs from this country in search of cheaper labor in Mexico.

What was the result of the Million Man March? Minister Farrakhan eclipsed Rev. Jackson in popularity and came to be recognized by many as the premier black leader of this day. It is interesting to note the similarities between the Million Man March and the March on Washington of 1963. Nation of Islam spokesmen in 1963 denounced and ridiculed the march and its organizers. They lambasted the march as being the puppet of white political leaders like the Kennedy's and ridiculed the marchers for having been told when to arrive in town and when to leave—on somebody else's schedule. They derided the march because it was non-violent and non-threatening.

Forty years later the Nation of Islam organizes its own march. Was it, as we should expect from their denouncement of the first march, significantly different? Amazingly enough there were few actual differences. The men came in town with a non-violent agenda. It wasn't even so much non-violent as "non-confrontational". The purpose of the march as stated by Minister Farrakhan was not to confront this nation's white racism but rather for black men to come together to "atone" for our failings as husbands, fathers, and brothers, and sons. Instead of protesting white racism, it protested black male irresponsibility

How did the black community as a whole benefit from the March? At least the first march ended with people having received a challenge from Dr. King's immortal address to go back to their localities and continue to wage the fight for justice. And they did just that. The March on Washington was followed by one of the most activist periods in our history in this country. After the March came the movement in Birmingham, the Mississippi Freedom Summer of 1964, the organization of the Mississippi Democratic Freedom Party, and the march from
348

Selma, Alabama to the capitol in Montgomery and the passing of three Civil Rights Acts-- in public accommodations, voting and housing.

The Million Man March's, (what many people are now calling the Million Man Picnic's), most tangible effect was the pouring of countless millions of black people's dollars into the pockets and bank accounts of white merchants. Total the economic consequences of a million black men traveling to Washington, D.C. for a day-long trip and for many an overnight stay. They flew on white people's airplanes; or drove cars, vans, and buses rented from white-owned car rental companies; bought most of their gas from white owned filling stations; ate in white-owned restaurants; and slept in white-owned hotels. The Million Man March was a boon for the white economy and added little to the economic well-being of black people locally or nationally. It was followed by—not much of anything. The monies that were collected were never reported on or accounted for and they had to have been in the millions. Since not only did the members of the Nation of Islam pass garbage cans around for the collection but people had to pay a thirty five dollar registration fee in order to attend.

The past thirty years since the death of Dr. King and the end of the movement can only be accurately described as a period of great decline. We have lost almost all of the spiritual momentum and many of the measurable gains of the civil rights/black power era. Nor have we arrived at any definite conclusions about the next stage of struggle (except for the reparations movement which bears great promise as the headwinds of a new dispensation of struggle). Yet as the fortunes of the race as a whole have declined we have at the same time produced leadership whose individual fortunes have increased all out of proportion to the condition of our people. Along with the celebrity leader, we have the millionaire civil rights leaders, and the mega-church pastors who revel in the conspicuous consumption of their sumptuous lifestyles. It parallels the phenomena among Fortune 500 corporations like Enron and MCI where, while the corporations go bankrupt, ordinary workers lose their jobs and pensions and working class investors lose the value of their stocks, senior executive pay themselves multi-million dollar bonuses and walk away with golden parachutes untouched by the tragedy they have inflicted on others.

Never before has civil rights leadership been an entrepreneurial endeavor in which individuals became wealthy from their supposed efforts on behalf of the race. In his exhaustive work on the life of Malcolm X and the history of the Nation of Islam entitled The Messenger: The Rise and Fall of Elijah Muhammed, author Karl Evanzz arrives at an arresting conclusion concerning our current leadership's status and philosophy. He says that among many other parallels in the lives of Dr. King and Malcolm X there are these significant four: 1. They were both sons of Baptist preachers. 2. They were both assassinated at the age of 39. 3. They were both faithful to vows of poverty, having pledged not to seek financial reward for their service to the cause of the liberation of their people. Fourthly, finally and most importantly, both had chief protégés who ascended to significant leadership positions and became multi-millionaires. Never before has leadership supposedly threatening to and subversive of America's racist treatment of black people led to such outstanding financial rewards. If anything the history of our leadership shows just he opposite.

Toussaint L'Ouvature was kidnapped, exiled, imprisoned and starved to death. Denmark Vesey, Gabriel Prosser, and Nat Turner were executed by hanging. Harriet Tubman had a warrant out for her arrest and fifty thousand dollar bounty on her head. She died in virtual poverty when the U. S. refused her a pension for her military duties as a spy and a scout during the Civil War. Marcus Garvey was fraudulently charged, jailed and deported. Paul Robeson lost his millions once he dedicated himself to full-time leadership and the espousal of unpopular causes. W.E.B. DuBois always lead a precarious pecuniary existence, being fired from significant positions both with the NAACP and at Atlanta University because of his insistence on sticking to principles rather than popularity. The Reverend Adam Clayton Powell, Jr. was wrongly found guilty of libel for exposing police corruption and driven out of Congress. When the Supreme Court ruled that the members of Congress could not decide who sat there Powell was reinstated but stripped of his seniority and his chairmanship of the powerful House Committee on Education and Labor. He died a few short years later; many say of a broken heart.

If Dr. King didn't become a millionaire for all of his brilliance, giftedness, dedication and courage then who should? Leadership of the race for over two hundred years has guaranteed those people not wealth but hard times and trouble, persecution and victimization of myriad sorts including assassination. How then do we account for the multi-millionaire status and opulent life-styles of the two men who are most widely accepted as the premier leaders of the past thirty years?

Neither Rev. Jackson nor Minister Farrakhan, unlike black leaders of the past, have been a target of Cointelpro type attacks. Neither have been investigated by the IRS. Rev. Jackson has been jailed hundreds of times but only by appointment. Minister Farrakhan has never seen the inside of a jail despite his fiery rhetoric calling for people's heads and his curious relationship with Colonel Ghaddafy of Libya, who the United States hated and feared enough to bomb his home and kill his infant daughter. Yet Minister Farrakhan has led a charmed life in which none of the standard procedures of white repression have been applied to him. Neither man has ever been the victim of police brutality.

When even popular and powerful white political candidates like Gary Hart were being driven off the campaign trail by revelations of sexual indiscretions Rev. Jackson was given a free pass. Only when information was needed to blunt his ability to mount a significant protest of the 2000 stolen election were details about his outside child released, knowledge of whom had been the talk of Washington, D.C. insiders for over a year.

"Lifting as we climb" is a motto popularized by the black women's movement as the 19th century turned into the twentieth. It was a derivative of its predecessor, the classic statement of our national purpose "uplifting the race". If this philosophy was being applied today it would mean that the phenomenon of millionaire leadership would at least be attended by many of the most significant followers of the millionaire leaders sharing in their wealth. Furthermore, it ought to mean some kind of trickle-down dynamics where the wealth of these individuals would be shared with the wider community in some significant way. Instead we have individuals who have achieved exalted financial status along with members of their families but no sharing of their personal fortunes with other members of their organizations. This kind of radical individualism based upon the European anti-ethic of "me first and everybody else a poor second" is the very anti-thesis of what our struggle has been about for the past four hundred years.

Rev. Jackson and Minister Farrakhan did not invent the phenomenon of civil rights entrepreneurs though they may have profited from it more than anyone else. The reality is that the ethos of profit-making has penetrated to the marrow of the bone of every aspect of black culture, most disappointingly to those heretofore most careful about not being seduced by fortune and fame. The millionaire preacher is an everyday feature of black religious life and for far too many young ministers success in ministry does not mean to service to" the least of these, your brethren" but rather garnering the trappings and accoutrements of conspicuous consumption.

Even our intellectuals have not been exempt from the desire to make money at the cost of their integrity. Men and women like W.E. B. DuBois, Horace Mann Bond, Mordecai Johnson, Benjamin Elijah Mays, Carter G. Woodson, Mary McLeod Bethune dedicated their intellectual powers to the uplift of the race at the expense of their possibilities to amass personal fortunes. Today some of our most brilliant intellectuals are more concerned about appealing to the popular taste in order to make money than adhering to the rigorous task of challenging scholarship concerning profound matters.

No one is a better example of the phenomenon of the intellectual entrepreneur than the Reverend Doctor Michael Eric Dyson, who styles himself "the Hip-Hop Preacher". We ought to be able to expect that such a sobriquet means he is the preacher *to* the hip-hop generation. In other words that he has a unique message to reach the hearts and minds of so many of young people caught up in the tragic delusions and deadly behavior of the so-called gangster life-style. But that is not who Dr. Dyson is. He is not the preacher to the hips hop generation. He is the preacher *of* the hip-hop generation. He doesn't have a message to rescue them from their headlong plunge into self and other destruction. Instead he preaches their message. They don't recite his words of wisdom. He recites theirs. Dr. Dyson is a devotee of Hip-Hop culture. He offers no critique to any of its even most lurid aspects and expressions. His critique is of us old people who just don't appreciate the genius of the younger generation. Dr. Dyson does. He regales his audiences with recitations of the rhymes of Tupac, Biggie, JayZ, Nas, Too Short, Fifty Cent, Lil Kim and a continuing list longer than I have the patience to list. In his mind, these young people who my generation's grandparents would have called "heathens" because of their lack of respect and regard for themselves, their elders, their mothers, sisters, daughters and the mothers of their children or their entire community, are brilliant beyond measure.

His outsized ego takes him further into self-delusion and empowers him to boasts to audiences that he is our "intellectual warrior" --everyday on the frontlines of great rhetorical battles where figurative blood is being shed protecting us from the vicious attacks of tongue-lashing racists . He is a self-appointed, self-promoting leader whose worship of all things new puts him in a new category of black leadership never been seen before. He does not walk in the moral tradition of the best of black preachers, parents and teachers because he has no moral vision. As easy as a moral vision is to come by since they are found on practically every page of the bible. As a rabid supporter of homosexuality based upon the specious argumentations of the white homosexuals he does not stand on any familiar moral ground that represents any of our traditions. As an intellectual his grandest weapon is his rapid-fire delivery of five and six syllable words. His rhetorical pyrotechnics pass for intelligence on his part and the part of many of his listeners who our fascinated by the hype.

But he has missed the mark of the true black Christian intellectual. Back in the early 1990's s I received a phone call from one of my godsons, then a student at Morehouse College. He excitedly told me: "Uncle Clarence, a great doctor spoke at the Chapel (Martin Luther King, Jr. International Chapel) this morning at convocation. That man is so heavy, I couldn't hardly understand nothing he was saying"! I replied: "In that case he ain't heavy." I told him: "Son, you one of the most brilliant young people I've ever known. If he couldn't make himself understandable to you, he ain't heavy." (Think about it a--black teacher that leaves a student with a prodigious intellect feeling not so intelligent. Hasn't that been the role of the racist white intellectual and common man throughout our history here.)

This young man went on to prove my case by accepting his call to the ministry, graduating with honors from Morehouse, earning a Master of Divinity at Harvard, working on a PhD and being appointed Dean of the Chapel at an elite black university.)

I explained to him that white people and black people have different approaches to knowledge and its dissemination. White people use knowledge as a closely held weapon of oppression and exploitation. They share it with as few other people as possible. They use their "superior" knowledge to justify keeping "less informed and less intelligent" people powerless and helpless as they abuse them in numerous ways. Their approach can be summed up as "rendering the simple complex" so as to convince the vast majority of people that they are incapable of accumulating profound information and must depend on the educated classes to make their decisions for them.

The black approach on the other hand is to use knowledge and wisdom as instruments of liberation. The black thinker understands his and her intellectual powers are gifts from God so that they have a moral obligation to share freely with their brothers and sisters not as fortunate as they to have attained the blessings of higher education. They see their job as being to "render the complex simple". That's why two of the most classic responses to a black speaker is "make it plain" and "break it down".

But Dr. Dyson's ugliest doings concern his treatment of Dr. Martin Luther King, Jr. In a book entitled arrogantly enough: I May Not Get There With You: The True Martin Luther King, Jr. I say arrogantly because we should be able to suppose that the only person who could present the "true Dr. King" would be someone who knew him. It is not enough that Dr. Dyson compares Tupac Shakur and Biggie Smalls to Dr. King as though they were kindred spirits. His first comparison being that all three of them smoked cigarettes, drank liquor and chased women. He then went onto a more lengthy and detailed comparison of Dr. King and Tupac alone in which he states:

"Although it may seem blasphemous to say so there is a great deal of similarity between Martin Luther King, Jr.

and a figure like Tupac Shakur. They both smoked and drank, worked hard ,and with their insomnia waged a 'war on sleep'. King and Shakur cursed, told lewd jokes, affectionately referred to at least some of their friends as 'nigger'. Had fierce rivals, grew up in public at the height of their fame, shared women with their friends, were sexually reckless, wanted to be number one in their fields, occasionally hung out with women of ill-repute, as youth liked nice clothes and cars,

Brilliant but unfortunately vulgar comedian, Chris Rock pointed out one of the differences between Dr. King , Tupac and Biggie when said: "People need to stop talking about Tupac and Biggie got assassinated. Dr. King got assassinated. Them two n****rs got shot". If Chris Rock can see the difference between Dr. King, Tupac Shakur and Biggie Small why can't a man as erudite and scholarly as Dr. Michael Eric Dyson?

The greatest blow he aimed at Dr. King's reputation is one that bounced off Dr. King and landed back on Dr. Dyson as a tragic commentary on his own lack of character and integrity.. He actually wrote these words:

*"It has been said that when Dr. King was having sex he would say' I'm f***ing for God.' "*

I think I am still as much in shock as I repeat these words today as I was when I first read them. My outrage comes from a number of sources of which I will try to enumerate just a few. One is: What kind of person concerns themselves with what people say when they are having sex? What kind of person puts their eye to the keyhole and their ear to a crack in a wall to not only ascertain someone's behavior during their most private moments but then does not just go out in the alley (which is the only place I know of where such behavior is entertained, among crack heads and drunkards,) but actually publishes such foolishness in a book? The old folks call it "getting under somebody's clothes" and it is considered among the most low-life forms of anti-social

356

behavior. Africans recognized that some topics were taboo. They were not even discussed.

There is a lyric of a gospel song taken from proverbs that says

When you dig one ditch
You better dig two
The trap you set
Just may be for you.

Dr. Dyson's lurid interest in another mans' sexual performance is most curious. This kind of interest in a man's most private moments can only be described as "prurient" and is an area of concern for not only his moral and intellectual health but for his mental and emotional well-being. What kind of man sits up and imagines what another man says or does in such an intimate setting? What kind of mind invites itself into someone else's bedroom activities? And then runs out to tell everybody what he imagines he saw and heard? The act of hiding oneself in order to surreptitiously observe someone's nakedness or sexual behavior is called "voyeurism". The individuals who do it are called "Peeping Toms". Morally it's a sin, legally it's a crime and psychologically it's a mental illness.

Who here is the one with the problem? Is it Dr. King who, whatever his sins were, committed them behind closed doors so that none of us really know what he did or didn't do. We do know that he never suffered from a moral lapse that left him calling right wrong and wrong right. His moral vision was never clouded. He always pointed us to the straight way. Whatever may have been his failings he observed the rule that sin-sick people should quarantine themselves and not spread their sin throughout their families and the general population. He wrestled with them in the recesses of his soul and in the privacy provided by closed doors and shuttered windows.

Dr. King is being victimized by people searching through his garbage for filth. Who of us from the highest to the lowest can stand such a search? The bible is clear:

"All have sinned and come short of the glory of God". One of the most childish and immature behaviors is the outrage of children who, having discovered a parental peccadillo, now declare that the parents, because of their sin, have forfeited their moral authority. If that were the case nobody would have any authority in any situation because we are all sinners.

It only becomes worse when there is no one that he cites as a source for this information which means he either made it up or his source is just not credible. His source is "it is said". That's the same as "I heard it on the grapevine". It's one thing to hear something filthy and salacious. It's another thing to repeat it.

In a public confrontation with Dr. Dyson, when I challenged him upon what authority he said these things about Dr. King, he admitted that the basis of his allegations was the FBI campaign to discredit Dr. King and drive him to commit suicide. But he insisted that they were a believable source. We know now that when that course of action didn't work they killed him on the balcony of the Lorraine Hotel in Memphis TN. How a man's murderers can be a conceivable, much less plausible, source of information about that person is beyond my limited imagination to comprehend. Is Cain a person we would go to better understand Abel? Could David have had a speaking part at Uriah the Hittite's funeral after he had him murdered to cover up his adultery with his wife, Bathsheba? Does Herod or Salome have anything worthwhile to tell us about John the Baptist? Do we go to the members of the Sanhedrin Council to explain to us who Jesus really was? The FBI is all the more corrupt to have the nerve to let Dr. King's name come out of their mouth after stalking him like a beast and slaying him in cold blood. In the movie, The Five Heartbeats, the wife of the group's murdered manager did the right thing when she slapped her husband's killer in the face for having the unmitigated audacity to show up at his funeral crying

358

crocodile tears.

I wonder if Dr. Dyson is willing to apply the same standards of disclosure to himself that he has imposed on Dr. King in his absence. Is he willing to tell us the details of his adulterous liaisons and what words he calls out when he is having sex? But whether he is or not is beside the point. Even if he wanted to tell us, like Eminem insisted on retelling his fantasies about raping and killing his mother. That kind of information is way more than we want to know about anybody, even as great a man as Dr. Michael Eric Dyson.

Dr. Dyson like too many others of our so-called leaders is a media creation. He is a darling of TV talk show producers, both black and white, because he has advanced degrees from major universities, a gift of gab, an intimidating (and obfuscating) vocabulary and a flair for showmanship. A good friend of mine who is the chairman of the trustee board in one of Black America's greatest churches describes him as: "the greatest showman in the African American pulpit." What he has done is taken the sacred art of preaching and turned it into a sophisticated minstrel show full of heat but no light, what the Apostle Paul described as a "zeal of God but not according to knowledge."(Rom. 10:1)KJV

Shame on you Dr. Dyson! But the shame is not his alone. He belongs to us. We birthed him and we raised him. He attended our churches and listened to our sermons. If he didn't get anymore out of them than what he has so far displayed then his moral failures are also our own. We buy his books, seek out his autograph, laugh at his misplaced priorities and salacious frivolities. We pay big money to hear his self-described: "riffin' and pontificatin'." Shame on all of us that we come to a point that we honor this kind of behavior. What will our children and grandchildren do who take this behavior as their role model? I shudder to think.

The standard for leadership in the bible is based on

servant hood. In traditional African society it is based on family. These two notions are not distinct from or unrelated to one another. In a sermon entitled, *You Got To Pay The Cost To Be The Boss*, I point out that the authority of parents over their children derives from the parents' role as servants to their children. There are no greater servants than parents. We carry, feed, clean, our children with assiduous care. We go out and work and bring home our money and spend the majority of it to meet their needs. We house, clothe, feed and educate them until at least the age of eighteen and if they go to college or graduate school we extend that care into their middle or late twenties. The exercise of our responsibility for them gives us unusual authority over them. It is in the meeting of people's needs that the authority of leadership is derived.

In the European tradition the people serve the king. In African culture the leaders serve the people. In one of his most profound teachings about leadership Jesus said: "Who would be greatest among you must be you servant". I can remember hearing elders say to me "as long as I am telling you to do right you have to obey me. I'm not teaching you to lie, cheat, steal, rob or rape." The authority to lead rests upon a moral foundation. We have the responsibility to continue to insist on morality from our leaders. We have historically produced a more excellent class of leaders than European American because our morality bas has been consistent with the foundational African proverb: "What goes around comes around". This proverb is an expression of African people's unshakeable sense of the eternal, unchangeable, immutable moral order of the universe. The European counterpart which continues this day as the most succinct expression of how they view the world as working is: "Might makes right".

This present hour cries out for the emergence of new leadership based on the ancient African and biblical standards of moral excellence, spiritual maturity and humble servant hood. But such leaders must be raised up from among our people. They must be taught, trained and seasoned by their elders. The entire race and our children in particular are left with a leadership vacuum because we have allowed other people to tell us who our leaders are based upon popularity, entertainment value, non-threatening strategies and acceptance by the mainstream. Our leadership has declined to too large a degree into a bunch of black Tweedlee-dees to their white Tweedlee-dums, differing only in the colors of their skin rather than in the content and substance of their values, visions, standards, philosophies, behaviors, strategies and tactics.

Marcus Garvey's ability to organize six million black people world wide based upon the philosophy of black independence gives confirmation to the historic desire within the minds and spirits of black people to have our own. One of the major reasons for the emergence of the philosophy of Black Power was discontent within black activist communities with white people who came, supposedly to serve, but ended up trying to lead. SNCC repudiated the role of white students as leaders in their organization as a part of the process of evolving into a Pan African organization instead of an integrationist one when in 1966 they changed their name from Student Non-Violent Coordinating Committee to Student National Coordinating Committee.

Our ancestors recognized that a white person labeling themselves liberal instead of conservative did not mean that they were not racists. While white conservative Christians enslaved us insisting on our divine-sanctioned inferiority, white liberal abolitionist Christians segregated us in their churches because while they were anti-slavery they still did not believe in the full humanity and social equality of black people.

Little has changed over the years. Politically we have been attacked, insulted and spurned by the conservative Republicans who maintain that we are genetically inferior. Consequently, we have yoked ourselves to the liberal

Democrats who insist that we can become just like them. True freedom is the freedom to be one's own best self not a dark-skinned imitation of a supposedly superior white standard-setter. The Democrats have held us back just as the Republicans have.

Neither conservatism nor liberalism can be the guiding philosophy that empowers us to move to the next rung on the ladder of continued struggle. They are both white and are both fatally flawed by their racist, Eurocentric, amoral presuppositions. We must learn to recognize the little good that each has to offer and adapt it to our needs as it fits our circumstances. To that extent we need to be the best of both conservative and liberal but then seek higher ground beyond where neither of these preceding has dared to climb. We need to be our authentic, unlimited, creative, audacious, independent thinking selves. We are engaging in self-destructive behavior by tying ourselves to ways of thinking and behaving that our not in our own best interests.

We cannot find a solution in either conservatism or liberalism in and of themselves but we find some parts of truth in each. White people tend to limit themselves by these self-definitions seemingly bereft of the power to think beyond the self-imposed boundaries of their labels. White conservative Christians for instance are conservative straight down the line. They are conservative theologically and conservative politically. There are certain aspects of their conservatism that we can sympathize with such as taking the bible seriously as the word of God and their espousal of family values as seen in their opposition to divorce, abortion, and homosexuality. Yet they are hypocritical in their championing of family values. They act as though they invented the concept of "family values" and are its chief proponents. Nobody has had to fight against greater assaults on family than black people. It is our ancestors who have been the examples to the world of what it means to struggle successfully to maintain families

362

in the face of the attempt of an entire culture to destroy them.

The conservatives act as though black people and our root culture are the great enemies of family values. It was in fact their own ancestors that they honor so highly that warred against family integrity. The Southern Baptist Convention was born as the theological and ecclesiastical justification and support of slavery. Was there any greater threat to the family than chattel slavery? Yet I've never heard the Southern Baptists honor the successful struggle of black people to maintain our families. I've never heard them refer to the slaves as the greatest examples of a people's commitment to the highest Christian principles and dynamics of family life. While we can agree with the conservatives in their support of family values, we cannot embrace their political conservatism which is by definition anti-black, pro-wealth, anti-labor, pro-war, and anti-immigration.

We can agree with the liberals inasmuch as they have supported our struggles at various times including abolitionism, desegregation, open housing, equal opportunity and affirmative action in employment, and the campaign against the war in Viet Nam, to mention a few. But just as they are politically liberal they are also theologically liberal. Even those that are Christians do not take the Bible seriously and wherever its moral proscriptions disagree with their personal proclivities they choose what they want over what the bible demands. Therefore liberals are, to an unacceptable degree, without moral boundaries.

We need to do the historical research that will reveal to us the nature of the roots of modern liberalism in the writings and teachings of the Enlightenment philosophers who were not only racists but atheists who believed in the supremacy of each individual to be free to establish his or her own sense of right and wrong. We have to break ranks with the liberals when they embrace homosexuality, pedophilia, and government intrusion into and interference with the way we raise and educate our children. Here is another aspect of white supremacy in the liberal mind. These people who have raised the most violent, greedy, rude, unmannerly, selfish, uncharitable people on the face of the earth have the nerve to try to tell us how to raise our children.

Black leadership at its best stands in spiritually, morally and intellectually creative places which incorporate the best of liberal and conservative thought but goes beyond them to areas of excellence that the former two have not considered. These areas are located in the best of our own traditions in the teachings of the Bible, the principles of ancient African traditions and the ways of our own African American ancestors whose legacy of courage and power should be held high as our guiding light never to be dimmed by the obfuscations of modernism and false integration.

Today even our religious leaders appear to have no independent ground of their own to stand on. Imam El Hajj Malik El Shabazz broke with the Nation of Islam but did not become a client of Arab Muslims. He organized an independent body which was committed to addressing the issues of black people in America. Dr. King could never be defined or controlled by the white-generated labels of "conservative" or "liberal". He had the freedom of thought to be conservative on some issues and liberal on others dependent upon values and thought processes anchored in the moral traditions of his people. Therefore he was too radical for the conservative black leaders in the NAACP and the Urban League but too "conservative" for the militants in SNCC and CORE.

We don't need mainstream leaders. We don't need leaders who are struggling to become acceptable to mainstream America so that they can get on the talk show circuit and eventually have their own TV programs. We have already produced too many recreational preachers, religious entertainers, ecclesiastical clown, and congregational con-men. The greatest of our thinkers and leaders of the past did not see getting in the mainstream as the solution to our dilemma. They understood the mainstream of European thought and behavior as being the continuing source of our problems. They recognized that out of the mainstream came and continues to come racism, classism, the conquest and exploitation of indigenous peoples and resources (now called the New World Order), colonialism, imperialism, two world wars, the genocide of the Indians, the slaughter of the buffalo, the ravaging of nature, the pollution of the environment, the enslavement of Africans, the Middle Passage, de jure and de facto segregation, lynch law, mob rule, chain gang, convict leasing, share-cropping, block-busting, red-lining, profiling, police brutality, inequitable race-based drug laws, capital punishment that officially sanctions the ritualistic murder of disproportionate numbers of black men, the poisoning of the air and the fouling of the streams, rivers, lakes, and oceans.

We have historically consistently produced leadership that was not interested in getting into the mainstream but was dedicated to the courageous proposition of cutting a new stream, their own stream, a unique stream, an African stream, a truly Christian course way, a mighty river of righteous blackness flowing from its headwaters in the seats of the worlds oldest civilizations and diverging into tributaries that feed the far-flung nations carried off into bondage in the Diaspora.

If Harriet Tubman had stayed in the mainstream, she would have remained a nameless field hand on a southern plantation instead of the leading engineer on the Underground Railroad, able to boast in the face a $50,000 reward on her head: "I have made over thirty trips back into Egyptland to set my people free, over 300 enslaved peoples have rode on this train. I have never lost a passenger and never ran my train off the track".

If Frederick Douglas had stayed in the mainstream he would have been an anonymous cotton-picker on a Maryland farm instead of the most powerful and eloquent voice for black liberation in the 19th century. We would not now still be reciting his immortal words: " Power concedes nothing without a demand. He who wants progress without agitation is like a man who wants crops without plowing up the ground. Like those who want rain without thunder and lightning. Like someone who wants the ocean without the awful roar of its many waters. We may not get everything that we pay for in this life but we shall certainly pay for everything that we get".

If W.E.B. DuBois had stayed in the mainstream he would have been a low-paid clerk in Great Barrington, Mass. Instead of an honors graduate of black Fisk U, in Nashville, TN; earner of Masters and Doctoral degrees from Harvard U., co-founder of the NAACP; one of the twentieth century fathers of Pan-Africanism, author of a score of books equally scholarly and artistic, all of them masterpieces, some of them classics. DuBois was physically diminutive and slight of stature but a giant in terms of his courage and independence of thought. He was never afraid to stand alone whether against individuals like Booker T. Washington or systems like the United States military in his protest against black involvement in the Korean War.

If Paul Robeson had stayed in the mainstream, he may well have been a champion athlete earning fifteen letters in four sports while a student at Rutgers University. He may well have used his six four inch 225 pound muscle-bound frame of powerful, electric, elusive grace to be named the greatest end that ever played football and to perform his legendary athletic feats in both professional football and basketball. The mainstream always has and always will have a place for our athletes to run, jump, catch and throw things. But if he had remained in the mainstream he would not have graduated from Rutgers University after four years

366

of magnificent matriculation as valedictorian of the class of 1919 and a member of the most exclusive fraternity in this nation's academic history- Phi Beta Kappa. If he had remained in the mainstream he would not have set a standard, still unmatched over a hundred years after his birth and almost thirty years after his death, for the consummate combination of and balance between athletics and academics. If he had remained in the mainstream he would not have earned a law degree from prestigious Columbia University. Nor would he have gone to Hollywood and made movies distinguished by the nobility of his portrayal of intelligent, heroic, noble black characters when standard Hollywood fare gave us stereotypical "coons" like Stepin' Fetchit and Mantan Moreland.. Nor would he have become a international sensation on the concert stage, even today still heralded as the greatest bass voice in the history of recorded music. He would not have walked onto the Shakespearean stage and justly earned the title of "the greatest Othello of the twentieth century". He would not have been a self-taught ethno-musicologist who made himself fluent in *thirty-one* foreign languages. Including thirteen African tongues so he could better understand the link between African and African-American music. He certainly would not have defied the power of the Unite States Congress' House on Un-American Activities Committee in person and in his book, <u>Here</u> <u>I</u> <u>Stand</u> Unquestionably Paul Robeson was the greatest Renaissance Man of the twentieth century. This is the man of whom Jackie Robinson, also a multi-talented star performer in basketball, football, track and of course baseball, and a graduate of UCLA would declare: "I'm not worthy to unlace Paul Robeson's gym shoes".

If the Mighty Marcus Mosiah Garvey had stayed in the mainstream he would have been a banana picker on a Panama plantation instead of the leader of the most popular and powerful international African organizations since the reign of Menelik II, King of Kings of Abyssinia whose army destroyed the Italian invaders at the battle of Adowa in 1894 sending shock waves through every colonial office in Europe. Marcus Garvey's United Negro Improvement Association's six million followers in 54 countries and their motto of "Africa for African's, at home and abroad" sent shivers down the spines of European colonists from the North of Belgium to the beaches of South Africa.

If Mary McLeod Bethune had stayed in the mainstream she would have been a laundrywoman and seamstress in the low country of South Carolina instead of the founder and president of numerous schools including, most famously Bethune-Cookman College in Daytona, Florida; organizer and president of the National Council of Negro Women and one of the most visionary leaders our people have ever produced.

If Malcolm Little, Martin Luther King, Jr. Septima Clark, Albert Luthuli, Ella Baker, Fannie Lou Hamer, Jomo Kenyatta, Kwame Nkrumah, Julius Nyrere and Nelson Mandela had stayed in the mainstream, where would we be as a people today?

We as elders are required to teach our young people how to become leaders. First of all, instructing them that each and every one of them is a leader to the extent that they must at least lead themselves and their children. We must design and organize formal and informal activities that teach our young people how to choose leaders, how to recognize leaders, how to place individuals in leadership positions and how to remove them and how to recognize when its time to do which. We have to teach them how to support leaders and then how to hold them accountable for their stewardship. They must be taught to look beyond appearance and a slick conversation for true leadership qualities, to search beyond extensive, fashionable wardrobes, pretty smiles and winning, charming personalities. They have to know how to organize and run meetings, exchange ideas, disagree without being disagreeable, communicate to and through various aspects of the media, write press releases and responses to editorials in newspapers and magazines, raise funds, manage them and account for them. How to develop and structure organizations of every type from ad hoc committees, to single-issue movements, to permanent associations to transgenerational institutions and to recognize and understand the peculiar functions of each differing sort. How to negotiate with their enemies and how to cooperate with their allies. All of these things are best taught through active mentoring relationships with their elders who are already fulfilling these functions in their everyday lives.

Every generation is sent into the world to deal with the challenges of their time. A generation that fails to cope with its challenges leaves them for the next generation thereby bequeathing to their children a double burden and if their children fail to cope with those challenges then the grandchildren are left with the weight of three unanswered questions hanging around their necks. Every generation of our people since the first group of kidnapped Africans landed on these shores over 500 years ago has stood up to confront the challenges unique unto itself. History tells the story of how our ancestors conquered slavery, put an end to white race riots and public lynching as community entertainments, purchased land by the millions of acres, organized systems of public and private grammar schools, colleges and universities, built businesses, patented inventions, advanced technology, brought an end to the everyday humiliations of American apartheid, outlasted and escaped from share-cropping and tenant farming, and brought an end to the chain gang and the leasing of convict labor.

Every generation can boast of its triumphs and lament its failures. All were not successful but all tried. This generation must define its issues, determine its priorities, understand its predicaments, analyze its situation, choose its battlegrounds, develop its strategies, forge its weapons,

369

put in place its logistics, identify its friends, negotiate its alliances, recognize its enemies, do long term planning, maximize its strengths, marshal its resources, leave its mark and carve out its legacy.

Each and every human generation owes a debt to the past which it must pay to the future. All of us when we arrived here found a world in place designed and equipped for our sustenance and growth. Fields had been plowed, crops had been harvested, fruit trees had been planted, schools had been established, families had been organized, institutions had been maintained, and economies were being administered. We all owe a debt to our elders and ancestors who put this world in place for us. The debt we owe to the past we must pay to the future. What we owe to those who came before we pay to those who will come after. What our parents and grandparents did for us we are obligated by the workings of the machinery of the universe to do for our children and grandchildren and unborn generations.

Where are the leaders of this generation? Who are the leaders of this generation? Who are its representatives? Who speaks for them? Who represents their best selves? Who are their standard-setters? Who are their role models? Who embodies their beliefs? Who sets their goals. Who manifests their collective sense of purpose? Who articulates their vision?

He who starts the race of life from behind must run faster to catch up. The Rev. Dr. Benjamin Elijah Mays

Ije on oremi imuommo ise ise.
Competition and reward induce a child to work. African Proverb (Yoruba of Nigeria)

XV. BLACK YOUTH RENAISSANCE

This generation of young black folk at risk require rescue and restoration. The job obviously belongs to the two centrally located, inseparably intertwined institutions that have always been our source of strength, power, wisdom and direction-- the black church and the black family. However they both must first undergo a serious restructuring and retuning in order to properly prepare for the job.

The black family must be resurrected to its previous levels of integrity and power. The black church must face its own demons of neglect and misdirection. Both of them are victims of the disruptions, confusions, and corruptions of the sixties and seventies. They both lost a major part of their direction as millions of our people bought into the notion of being "true Americans". In our search to become more like the people who brought us here we lost our way. We forgot the wisdom of our ancestors who built independent institutions based on their own values and standards. They did not want to have what white people had because they saw close up the kind of things white people did to attain their status in life. They saw the inner sickness of the white nuclear family that operated like a

371

military camp where a man's home was his castle, rank had its privileges and to the victor went the spoils. They were not interested in being like white people because they saw them at their worst. Not the white people of the newspapers and the magazines and books, but the real human beings who as a matter of course treated other human beings, especially black people, but even the poor and powerless of their own kind, like animals. They were not willing to pay the price white folks paid for their earthly superiority because they knew that one day there would be a reckoning. They knew that: "What goes around comes around". They were not willing to risk their immortal souls and great eternal reunion with the ancestors in the land of God for the opportunity to lord it over their brothers and sisters for a season in a world that they knew would soon be no more.

The black family must be repaired, rebuilt and revitalized from the ground up. The knowledge and wisdom of how to move through the world that was taught in the oral traditions of the black family have been replaced by the silly and sick offering of the popular media. We must move to recover everyday behaviors that kept our families intact through all the historical assaults that were intended to destroy them. The homes of the black family must be rebuilt brick by brick. The extended family that used to be the black community must be reconstructed block by block.

The elders of our families must once again convene in councils to determine the destiny of present and future generations. They must, first of all, remember their ancestors and the strength and power that brought us thus far. They must write family law. Determine the mission of the family. Define childhood, adulthood, and elderhood. Draw boundaries of behavior appropriate to each age group. Design rituals to celebrate the family. Compose family songs and choreograph family dances. Insist on standards of academic excellence. Raise scholarships for

372

the best of our students. Place children in only the healthiest of environments regardless of the individual parents' or social workers' wishes.

Children don't belong to individuals, nor even to individual parents. They are the most precious assets of the extended family in particular and to the human community in general. They should live with and be raised by those who will do the job most effectively, which means, most lovingly.

One of the first ways this can be done is by returning to eating family meals together. The first formal gatherings children attend are family meals. This is one of the activities where initial instruction in mannerly behavior is given. I have witnessed college students who would not sit all the way through a convocation and wait to be formally dismissed because they have never sat at the dinner table and waited until the elders gave them permission to leave the table. Family meal time is a spiritual, emotional, and educational learning ground. It is at the dinner table that stories are told about the family history and the heroes of the extended family are made known to the children. Prayers of thanksgiving are prayed over the food. Politeness is insisted on and everyone must be on the best behavior. It is a special time carved out from the rest of the day that brings out the best in everybody at the table. Sharing a meal is not just a nutritional exercise it is an intimate experience. Soul food is not just about the various dishes that are served but the spiritual fullness of the accompanying ritual. The spirit of hospitality, generosity, communication, recognition, fellowship and love that are involved in the preparation, serving and consuming of the food is one of the bedrock experiences that molded us into the great people that we once were.

At the dinner table the family practices the art of conversation. The littlest child enjoys their first formal audience to perform in front of as they are as full participants as the oldest person present. Long before children go to church and recite bible verses and poetic couplets for the annual rituals of Christmas and Easter programs they learn to recite a bible verse after the elder blesses the food. We can extend children's presentations beyond bible verses to the recitation of African proverbs even in their original tongues helping them take their first steps toward an appreciation of African culture and an introduction to multi-linguality. At the dinner table reports should be rendered of the events of the day, plans made, dreams shared, and problems hashed out. One of the hallmarks of any healthy family is the sharing of family meals.

We can reestablish family meals in at least these two ways. Firstly, each individual family should strive to eat at least one meal together, preferably dinner, every day. Secondly, the elders should convene meals for the extended family at least once a month if not once a week for instance on Sundays. So that the children who are not participating in family meals in their individual homes will do so at the extended family gathering.

We must develop rituals that guide and support our family members through every developmental stage of life as we once did in Africa. We have to do this to check the perversity of the modern-day blurring of roles. We face a crisis of hitherto unthinkable dimensions when we cannot tell by dress, language and behavior whether a child is six, sixteen or twenty-six years old. The daylong celebrations of graduation from pre-schools to colleges are not enough. Our children achieve the technical prerequisites that allow them walk across a stage, receive a diploma and go to the next stage of formal education. But they are not being prepared for the crucial roles they must play in the wider world of family and community. We have to stop leaving the education of our children to academic systems that don't know or appreciate us. They can only prepare our children to move through their world. They cannot help them to function in a world they know nothing about- our world.

Foremost among these rites of passage must be the creation of a system to prepare adults to become elders. We must give special recognition and place to the elders who live lives of intelligence, dignity, wisdom, nobility and power. These are the people we must learn to once again depend on to lead us with the special gifts of the aged, principal among which are wisdom, discernment, forbearance, forgiveness, farsightedness, patience, balance, prudence. But we must first have a means of educating and preparing those who aspire to such positions to able to fulfill them. We must define what an elder is, what an elder does, how elders carries themselves. We must relearn and reestablish the authority, responsibility of our grandparents, great-grandparents, great-aunts and great –uncles. These are the people our brothers and sisters on the continent call "the living ancestors". The old people of our families must gather in counsel and remember the lives of their own elders that lived their lives well. Retelling their tales, passing on their stories, making their greatness live again in us. Recalling the proverbs they spoke, the wisdom they dispensed and the lessons they left. They must once again be honored with titles attached to their name. It is an abomination when four year old children address someone old enough to be their parent or even grandparent by their first names the way white people did us in years past.

Those who aspire to the position of elder must like, preachers and deacons, undergo training. When it is completed there must be celebrations like such as are held at all other forms of graduation, ordination and installation. If at all possible these ceremonies should take place outdoors and be accompanied by a parade so that no one in the entire community can escape from the power of their message. We are an outdoor people. It is an essential part of our identity that our leaders always organized rituals and celebrations that came to the people and pulled them in instead of waiting for the people to come in and pull them out.

Because elderhood is a learned position and not one that is attained just through length of years, a poorly lived younger life does not have to consign an older person to perpetual disregard. Anyone blessed with long life yet has the possibility to rise above the mistakes and missteps of their youth and become role models for newer generations. The key to the reconstruction of the black family and community is in the hands of the elders who will use their spiritual powers to dream dreams and see visions of a brighter future and use those dreams and visions to make family and community law. Then black men must step forward and be responsible for protecting and enforcing the peace and the prosperity that they bring.

The elders of the family must begin to do long-term planning. They must engage in the spiritual discipline of seeking for and working out a vision for the family's future. Our enslaved ancestors were long term planners. In the most dark and dire days of slavery they had visions of yet unborn generations of free people. Those that fought their way out of slavery did not emerge without a plan. The vision of "a nation within a nation" had been nurtured for a hundred years and more while they still wore their chains and scars. Our families need five-year, ten-year, twenty-year and fifty-year plans in which we envision and work toward what kind of lives we want our children and grandchildren to have. This includes not only what kinds of professions we want represented in the family, but also such concerns as where the family should live.

Many of our families are so fragmented by educational, occupational and marital dislocation that we have entire generations of first cousins that see each other as infrequently as every five years or even less. Some first cousins, if they bumped into each other, would not know each other by name or by face. The strength that comes from the support system of the extended family is lost when families are geographically fragmented. The residential patterns of Africa and the South were reduplicated in our first generations in the North when families relocated to the same block, or at least neighborhood. The support system for child-rearing, illness, elder-care was always near at hand.

Millions of black families are at the mercy of a corporate system that cares little for family concerns, dislodging and relocating families at regular intervals with no concern for the disrupted lives and relationships left in the wake. We must begin to act out of a sense of our own needs because to be black and a stranger is a much worse phenomenon than to be white and a new arrival. Because the problems we face are greater, the solutions we construct must also be stronger and more intelligent than those of the people we live amongst. We need family more than they do because only family has been able to protect us from the unimaginable horrors of life lived among people that hate us.

Every family ought to have certain skills and professions. Every family needs a doctor, a lawyer, and accountant, an auto mechanic, and a carpenter, etc. Long - term planning will assess the interests of young people and assign them to these critical roles that help families become units of production and not just bodies of consumers. A debt-ridden body of consumers who are dependent on outside sources for all of their basic necessities is like a country that suffers from a trade deficit with other countries. In other words having to purchase from others more than others purchase from them. Our ancestors strove to be as independent as possible by producing goods and generating services through their own resources. They grew gardens, preserved fruits and vegetables, sewed clothes, repaired their own cars, patched their own cement and plaster.

I have vivid memories of the day that the front porch on the little cottage we rented from an absentee landlord collapsed. A few days later on a Saturday my father assembled a crew of his friends and relatives and before the day we over they had built a new porch. He did not have to hire a construction crew and pay exorbitant labor costs with credit arrangements. They acted out of the great African tradition of cooperative labor. It was not that long ago when a moving company couldn't make money in the black community because helping one's family and friends to move was a universal obligation owed by black men to one another. What fosters independence is the ability to do for oneself.

We must envision what kind of housing we want our grandchildren to live in. What kind of schools they will attend. How many new black colleges, universities, seminaries, law schools, medical schools must be built. We must envision what kind of fund-raising and money-management systems we need to build these institutions. Our ancestors, during and after Reconstruction when white local authorities would return them insufficient resources from their taxes to adequately fund their schools, taxed themselves again to build and maintain schools and pay teachers and principals. We cannot afford to sit around and bemoan the injustice of white governments that render us inadequate funding for our children's education. If we can't find the heart to make them give us our due then we must require it of ourselves rather than allow our children's and our own futures to be place at risk.

Black men can and must be put to work. I call this concept: **The Black Man' Action Plan**. The idleness of men in any community is a harbinger of disorder. Federal and state governments refuse to invest in the massive kinds of make-work programs that were organized during the Depression to rescue white males from the dangers of unemployment and resulting poverty and the inevitable predations of men made dangerous by being backed into corners of desperation. Idle young men are a threat to order in any society. In their unstructured, unguided search for affirmation as men they will either make something, take

378

something or break something.

The one institution that has both the financial resources and the moral mandate to address the problems of black unemployment is the church. The church can issue a general call to mobilize black men to report for volunteer duty of service to the community. Individual neighborhood churches will be recruitment and sign-up stations where the men and boys can report for duty and be given their assignments. The nature of a man drives him to respond to calls to duty. Black men have known from the most ancient of days how to respond to the collective voice of the community that calls them to service when the nation is in danger or is dedicated to the critical task of some great building project.

Who can doubt the collective power of black men? History bears witness to his love for family, clan, tribe and nation. He built the pyramids of Egypt. He designed and constructed the mountain-top cathedrals of Ethiopia. He changed the face of Islamic slavery with the Zanj revolt. He constructed the agricultural systems of West and Central Africa and made them breadbaskets for the world. Almost two hundred thousand of them responded to the call to join the Union forces, run the rebels to cover on land and on sea, break the back of the Confederate conspiracy and strike the deathblow to slavery. Our fathers rose up by the hundreds of thousand marching against the walls of Apartheid and tore down that fortress of oppression brick-by-brick and sign-by-sign. The kind of men they were in their day we can be in ours.

Men can be assigned various roles as guardians of public safety. They can be assigned to stand on post on busy corners to help children and old people cross dangerous intersections. They can be appointed to escort older people to and from banks and on shopping errands. They can be posted inside and outside of schools to prevent the fighting that is so prevalent among our children who don't seem to know how to manage conflicts. They can be sent to stand around crack houses and on drug corners. Armed with video cameras they can be dispatched to record every encounter between police and black citizens to prevent police brutality. Teams of trained observers can be present in every courtroom where a black person is on trial to monitor the proceedings and when necessary intervene as "amicus curiae"(friends of the court) or as assistants to the overworked, under-resourced public defenders who handle most of the legal cases of black defendants. These ideas only skim the surface of the enormous range of possibilities for harnessing the underutilized energies of black men for the uplift of the entire community.

Shelters need to be established for homeless individuals and for families. The scandal of homeless people living on city streets, searching for food in garbage cans and dumpsters, sleeping in alleys, on sidewalks and park benches is the shame of this entire nation. Churches can address the issue of homelessness by obtaining through purchase or donation dilapidated and/or abandoned housing. The repairs to these structures can be done by crews of homeless men and women supervised by skilled craftsmen. Men and women can be housed in single sex facilities dormitory style. Separate facilities for families with children would also be made available. Many of the homeless are employed but underpaid or have been thrown into the midst of a financial crisis by unforeseen circumstances. Those who are unemployed can be assigned to make-work responsibilities in the community. They can clean streets, vacant lots, alleys and shopping centers. We should not be satisfied living in filth and wading through garbage as we move through our neighborhoods, communities and shopping areas.

Neighborhood gardens can be tended and the produce used to feed the hungry. Donald B. Freeman, the author of City of Gardens: Informal Urban Agriculture in the Open Spaces of Nairobi, Kenya, reports that in that East African capital city thirty per cent of the food consumed by the

380

population is grown in vegetable gardens located within the city limits. The food prepared for communal meals can be cooked by the homeless themselves supervised by the master chefs of the sponsoring churches. The homeless should be made a part of the solution and not mere receivers of charity.

Unemployed people can be compensated in the receipt of housing, food and clothing but also with subsistence wages. They can be paid enough so that they can have some money in their pockets. I know that any number of people will find this idea ridiculous. Their modern day sensibilities based on the bling-bling, conspicuous consumption philosophy of this age would insist that people would rather sell dope than sweep streets, labor in gardens, or guard street corners for far less than minimum wage.

But I remember that back in the sixties SNCC staff members and field organizers were paid as little as thirteen dollars a week. What made it possible for them to survive and have a sense a self-worth while being paid such miserable wages? It was not only that the community would feed and house them but even more importantly that they were honored and celebrated as heroes and heroines selflessly struggling for the betterment of their people. I believe that our young people today would be willing to accept lesser pay to engage in work that will earn them the priceless positions of community heroes looked up to by young and old alike. We must provide for our young people opportunities to contribute to a noble cause that makes them significant contributors to the betterment of their individual lives and to the improvement of the quality of life in their community.

The church must return to its original mission as the chief education institution in the black community. Dr. Diana P. Slaughter then of Northwestern University now at the University of Pennsylvania wrote a critically acclaimed monograph in the 1970's entitled: The Education of Black

<u>Youth</u> <u>as</u> <u>a</u> <u>Moral</u> <u>Problem</u>. She indicated that for African people the most important aspect of education is teaching young people right from wrong, instructing them in the difference between good and evil and equipping them to make the correct choice between the two. American education has become value- free, which translates into being "free of value" from an African perspective because it leaves its students unprotected from the social and personal disasters that result from moral chaos. Traditional African societies were built on the foundations of love, justice, peace, communal obligation, cooperative efforts, and the absolute necessity of treating people right. The church carries the responsibility to continue this tradition of making moral instruction paramount in the curricula of the schools that our children attend.

As the old folks taught us: "It ain't what you got its how you use it that counts." Jesus said the same thing in a different way when he taught: "For what shall it profit a man if he should gain the whole world, and lose his soul. Or what shall a man give in exchange for his soul?" Mk 8:36&37   Isn't this what the people of Europe have done? They have conquered the whole world and control most of the world's peoples and resources, yet their lives are a living hell full of violence, crime, serial killers, mass murderers, divorce, depression, loneliness, drug addiction, alcoholism, suicide, child abuse, homelessness, homosexuality, and insanity. The church must provide the educational community with its blueprint for operation. We in the Kingdom of God know the real value and worth of His children and we cannot afford to let an uncaring world consign them to a lower place in creation than He intended for them.

Parenting classes need to be an essential part of the Christian Education curricula of our churches. They should be taught in Sunday Schools and in Bible Classes. They should be made a part of the New Members Classes where mothers, fathers and guardians can be further prepared for their proper role as the primary educators of their children. A major reason for our children's academic failure is that we have surrendered the role of chief educator to the university-trained, Eurocentric, so-called specialists who in most instances do not believe in our children's real abilities and do not appreciate the deepest and most powerful aspects of our culture. Our parents need to be reminded that the parent is the first and most important teacher that the child will ever have and that the home is the first and most important school that they will ever attend. Parents don't have to have college degrees or even high school diplomas in order to do this job. They need only be dedicated diligent watchers over their children's homework. Making sure that the TV is turned off and homework assignments completed neatly even if they can't read or understand what's written or computed on the page.

The parent is responsible for order in the classroom. Only when the student knows that the parent will back up the demands of the teacher for respect and discipline in the classroom will they submit to proper classroom behavior. The minimal standard for our children's conduct in any learning situation must be that expressed in the classic spiritual: "If You Don't Go, Don't Hinder Me". The song is both about escaping to freedom in the North and in the Indian Nations to the South and the West and about living a righteous life as one prepares for the final journey into the land of the ancestors in the home of God. The songwriter is saying: "I if you are not going to try to do better for yourself; if you refuse to run from the plantation because your wife and children or your mother and sisters are on another plantation and you refuse to leave them; alright. But if you don't go, don't get in my way as I leave. Don't disrupt my move, don't reveal my plan. In fact help me on my journey. Give me piece a cornbread to eat. Draw me a map of places you know of but I'm not familiar with. Give me the name of a trustworthy friend or relative that lives along my escape route."

In today's classrooms the same motto must be put into effect. Parents need to let their children know that if they don't want to learn anything they had better not stand in the way of those who do want to learn. Somebody must learn. One day this generation in its adult stage must look to itself for the critical skills that make life livable. They must be able to locate among themselves, doctors, lawyers, teachers, counselors, and bankers. Those of our generation will have gone on to our appointment with eternity. They must be able to rely upon themselves for the fulfillment of their needs. They must therefore not hinder those among themselves who are dedicated to excellence, determined to achieve, and committed to learning.

We must encourage the recruitment and commitment of male teachers through both preaching and practice. The preaching is the easiest part. Black men can be convinced of their importance in the lives of both little boys and girls. It is the practice that requires us to move to unfamiliar ground and develop innovative tactics to accomplish this objective. One approach is to fund college and graduate scholarships for black males who will major in education and make a commitment to teach in our local schools for a minimum number of years following graduation. The state of North Carolina instituted such a scholarship program for black males almost ten years ago. This concept needs to be extended throughout all forty-nine other states and it needs to be funded not just by public funds but by private scholarship programs in our churches and other institutions.

Every church can organize an educational committee responsible for monitoring, encouraging and assisting the academic progress of its members, young and old. This committee should register all of the students in the church from pre-school to post-graduate levels. It should know the student's school, teacher, major, and aspirations. It should visit the schools its students attend and develop a working relationship throughout the entire staff from janitors to principals. The parents should sign a release form giving

384

member's access to students' records so that they can intervene with authority on the part of the student when there are problems at school. When report cards come out they should be brought not only to the students' homes but then to the education committee. Rewards should be given based upon performance. In my churches and with my children our formula was as follows: In grammar school $1.00 for each A, $.50 for each B; high Schools $2.00 for A's, $1.00 for B's, colleges $10.00 for A's, $5.00 for B's. This formula, I'm sure could use adjusting for it is over fifteen years old. Somebody may ask: "What do we get for C's?" The answer is "nothing"! Why nothing? I ask children all the time. What does a C stand for? Sooner or later they get around to the answer: "C" means average". I then ask: "What kind of the shape is the average black person in this country?" Bad shape! We can't afford to be average. *We have to be twice as good to get half as far.* This is the standard of excellence that our ancestors held themselves to that empowered them to survive and even prosper in the midst of the worst oppression that any people has been subjected to in the history of the world.

The Education Committees' reward programs should be held each time report cards come out, not just at the church but also at the schools. Children should not just be rewarded individually, instead, using the African concept of communalism, rewards should be given to everyone in their support system, this includes parents, siblings, godparents, best friends, study partners, other family members, teachers, counselors, and classmates. By doing so we can deflect and defeat the jealous resentment that fuels the strain of anti-intellectualism and anti-successism that afflicts the cultures of too many of our youth, particularly black boys. Providing rewards for classmates will encourage them to support successful students as heroes who bring good things to everybody around them.

We can also offer encouraging recognition to our educators using parents, students, and fellow teachers, administrators and staff to nominate one another for recognition and rewards by the week, month, semester and year. These awards can be offered at various levels from the local school to district, state and national levels. It is a means of countering the pervasive sense of collective despair that affects our educators as they feel so unappreciated, given their relatively low pay. The teacher in the black community has always had a higher social status than those in the white community because our teachers were seen not merely as technicians but as moral agents with a crucial social portfolio almost co-equal to that of the preacher.

These reward programs can be held jointly by numbers of churches so that their impact can be not only community wide, but city-wide and state-wide. They can be forums to celebrate positive success and give our children the kind of role models they both need and deserve. We adults must assume the responsibility for providing our children with positive role models to counter the negative personalities foisted upon them by the media industry. The media gives them and us so-called gangster rappers, out-and-out criminals, outlandish movie stars, freaks-of-the-week and multi-million dollar athletes who abandon their communities surrounding themselves with white people as their best friends and chief advisors, returning to the black community only at Thanksgiving, Christmas and Easter to hand out free turkeys and gym shoes.

Our children need to see scholars and leaders rewarded and recognized in mass gatherings and in the local and national media. They need to see everyday young people like themselves not just people with extraordinary physical gifts or artistic talents being lifted up before them as role models that they can emulate. They need to be able to aspire to successful lives based upon their own common abilities that consist of hard work, high standards, respect for themselves and their communities. We should demand that the media and white and black cover these events.

They never fail to show up when our children are involved in destructive behavior. They need to cover the events that demonstrate the power of the black community to produce success-driven young people who are well on their way to making this world a better place for everybody. But we should not just rely on them. We need to increase the presence of our own media that serves the purpose of uplifting that which is best amongst us and not just exposing and sensationalizing that which is worst. If they won't then we must produce those instruments and institutions of mass communications for ourselves.

Through organizing massive and continuing intensive and extensive interaction among the home, church and school we can reinstitute and revitalize the sense of community that was lost in the move north. In these mass meetings in the church and similar gatherings in schools with the participation of the churches we can introduce and reintroduce the principal players in the developmental lives of our children. In the South all black people lived in the same communities. Parents and teachers ran into each other on a regular basis in the everyday life of the community: in grocery stores, beauty parlors and barber shops not to mention in church.

Moreover, we should instill within our youth an aggressive entrepreneurial spirit that will move them to use their skills and proficiencies beyond mere employment into the realm of developing a network of service industries.

Our ancestors, with less formal education and exposure to standard business philosophy and practices, were independent minded enough to have their own commercial infrastructure as does every people who came here from someplace else. In our rush to integrate we abandoned and dismantled tens if not hundreds of millions of dollars worth of black-owned businesses. However small they might have been and however narrow their profit margin they were ours and each one represented a triumph over and an alternative to the amoral practices of racist employment.

Each one provided a safe haven for at least two or three black people from the everyday exploitation and humiliation of working for people who kept us as the last hired and the first fired --the hardest workers at the lowest pay.

What is missing in much of commercial America is not skill but morals. An honest mechanic is a much sought after commodity in any community, especially among working class, budget-conscious people who need to keep older cars running. Such a mechanic is a rarity. In the parlance of the ghetto he is something "often spoken of but seldom seen". Dishonesty, exploitation, lying, downright cheating are cornerstones of American capitalism. So much of this amoral approach to doing business has seeped into our own community that honest black businesspeople are becoming as increasingly hard to find as white ones. We can change this trend by raising up a generation committed to a work ethic based on integrity as their bottom line, not just profit. Such people will operate from the understanding of our ancestors that short-term profit is not be preferred to long-term relationships. Too many people would rather beat somebody out of a few hundred dollars on the front end of what could be a long-germ relationship that would profit them in the tens of thousands of dollars over the years. They discount good will as one the most important assets to anyone in business. We need to produce a generation of merchants, artisans, professionals and skilled workers that understand and are committed to integrity as the most important aspect of doing business.

In the North our communities are massive in terms of space and numbers of people but are fragmented by geography and social class. People just don't know each other. Most of the time the contact between parents and teachers is limited to the negatively- charged atmosphere of a parent being called to the school because of their child's misbehavior. In these situations too many parents come to the school to defend their child rather than to participate

388

with the teachers in correcting him or her. They suffer from a lack of confidence that the teachers truly have the best interests of their child at heart.

This belief derives from the fact that the parents themselves were mostly raised in the urban North and attended public schools. While they were students they thought that they were receiving an excellent education. They childishly believed that the most popular teachers, the ones who coddled them, played with them, let them have fun in the classroom, overlooked their failings, made excuses for their misbehavior and entertained low expectations for their abilities were the best teachers. But when they went to college and into the work world they found out that they had received a less-than-first-class education and preparation.

Their parents spent little time in the alien atmosphere of a school environment staffed by mostly white teachers or strange black people who treated them as interlopers and interferers rather than as partners in their children's education as they were treated in the South. Feeling betrayed by their own experiences they now visit the sins of their teachers upon the teachers of their children. The only way to combat this syndrome of failed confidence is to bring parents and teachers into social contact that is not strained by the stresses of fault-finding and finger-pointing. Another way to do this is for the churches to organize forums for parents and teachers to come together and work on a shared agenda to anticipate and ensure the academic success of the children.

The church must project itself into the entire scope of education including meeting with the various teacher groups, and educational organizations and forums, particularly the black groups such as the National Association of Black School Educators (NABSE). We can encourage and motivate teachers and administrators as well as students and parents. In fact we must be the fulcrum whose leverage brings back together the ancient coalition of parent, church and school which is essential for our young people's maximum development.

An old man said to me not too many years ago: *"If you have a skill people ask you how much you charge. If you don't have a skill people tell you how much they pay."* Minimum wage in this country is not a living wage. Anyone who does not possess some form of marketable skill is left in the position of working on jobs which do not pay them sufficiently to enable them to survive alone; much less enough so that they can take care of a family. The high schools are not doing the job of preparing young people for the job market. Somebody must step in the breach and give our youth an opportunity to successfully enter and compete in the employment sector.

Part of the church's renewed mission as an educational institution would be in the area of job preparation. We invest more money in the church than in any other sector of our social and institutional lives. Therefore the church constitutes the most prosperous businesses in the black community. The church is not just an ecclesiastical organization. It has important business functions. That makes every active member a part-owner of a business. Every intelligent business owner prepares his children to take over the business by teaching them the business "from the ground up". We need to initiate formal programs in which our young people are taught the entire function of the church from the foundation in the basement to the tiles on the rooftop, from the mechanical maintenance to money management, from electronic installation to program design.

Most of our homes do not have computers but our churches do. We can combat the digital divide by making sure that our children learn computer literacy in the church. Most of our churches have vans and even buses. Every child ought to be taught basic auto mechanics. Every church has heating and air conditioning. The young people who learn installation, maintenance and repair of these systems can make a living for themselves with those skills.

Our young people ought to be able to go out looking for a job with a certificate of training in some specialized area from their church. That document ought to mean more to local employers than a high school diploma from the local school system. The reputation of our churches as institutions of excellence and the performance of our children on jobs ought to make a human resources director's face light up with a welcoming smile when they see that this young person has been prepared for the work world by the most outstanding institutions in our community.

If the church has money in stocks and bonds, treasury notes then the children of the church should know what these instruments are and how they are used. Jews have for centuries used their synagogues as educational vehicles to provide their children with tools for uplift that they were not receiving in the local public schools. We must do the same with our children. On the one hand we must continue to fight to see to it that the local schools do their job. Yet while we struggle for justice in that arena, we must in our own way, with our own resources, which are under our control, prepare our young people for a future of success. In fact we are not just preparing them for their future, we are preparing them for our future. Our lives will be in their hands in just another ten or twenty years and while those numbers are just an incomprehensible statistic to young people, we who have lived those numbers two and three and four times know that they are just the blinking of an eye. We are the one who can say "It seems like only yesterday" and we are talking about thirty years ago.

Our children particularly, boys, know as early as five and six years old that the three ways for them to receive recognition and reward is by being an entertainer, an athlete or a criminal. Seldom do they see black people, particularly young black people, being feted and celebrated for their scholarly achievements. It is our responsibility to change this scenario. When young people know that studying can lead to positive attention from society in the form of rewards and recognition they will, out of their own incentive, prepare themselves to earn those rewards.

You don't see black mothers and fathers dragging their boys and now girls to the basketball court. Those children are out there on their own, some of them from before the sun comes up and they stay until long after it goes down. Some in the North will shovel away snow in the depths of a frigid winter to get out on the court and shoot some ball. Why? Because they know there are rewards that await them if they become masters of the game. The know about college scholarships that give four years of free higher education and about professional contracts worth millions and millions of dollars.

We have consistently over the entire extent of the twentieth century replaced and replenished our stock of athletic and entertainment genius. Annually, monthly, almost daily, if not hourly, we find emerging into the limelight new champions in various sports, new gold medal winners, new world record setters, new singers of hit songs, new chart-busters, new gold and platinum record makers and new winners of Grammy awards.

We have dominated the heavyweight division is boxing since 1908 when Jack Johnson took the title from Tommy Burns and thereby began the campaign for one of the most notorious characters in American culture: The Great White Hope. For the next twenty-five years not another black man was allowed to fight for the heavyweight title until Joe Louis in 1937. Since Joe Louis there has been Ezzard Charles, "the Cincinnati Cobra", "Jersey" Joe Walcott, Floyd Patterson, Sonny Liston, Muhammad Ali, Smokey Joe Frazier, Big George Foreman, Larry Holmes, Mike Tyson, Evander Holyfield and Lennox Lewis. White people haven't had a heavyweight champion in so long that Hollywood had to resort to creating a cinematic caricature named Rocky Balboa so that they could have a heavyweight champion.

But where are our new leaders, scholars, scientists, builders, inventors? Why have we not produced another leader of the stature of Frederick Douglass, Paul Cuffee, Harriet Tubman, Ida B. Wells, Paul Robeson, and Martin Luther King, Jr.? Where are our new college champions of higher education like Mary McLeod Bethune to initiate a new cycle of school-founding and college-building of black educational institutions whose graduates will be prepared to meet the current crises and do the long-germ planning required to prevent future catastrophes? Where are our new Elijah McCoys, Daniel Hale Williams, George Washington Carvers whose scientific genius presents us with high-tech inventions, industrial innovations and medical cures that put us the forefront of human progress?

Why don't we have any black-owned automobile factories since a combination of our unique aesthetic style, superior engineering ability and Christian integrity in manufacturing and sales ought to enable us to produce super-bad automobiles that could compete on the world market with cars manufactured anybody else. Where are our Pan-African commercial structures that Marcus Garvey tried to teach us to build in the nineteen twenties in order to link the wealth in human and mineral resources of the hundreds of millions of black people in Africa, the Caribbean, Central and South America and the United States?

The reason athletic and entertainment genius is replenished on such a consistent basis is because the white people who dominate these fields spend tens of millions of dollars each and every year on Research and Development (R&D). They have their talent scouts scouring every nook and cranny of every black neighborhood in this country daily for our most talented and gifted young people. They look in high schools, churches, nightclubs, on playgrounds and on street corners to find the most extraordinarily creative and hardworking, dedicated young people who demonstrate an outstanding ability in sports, singing, dancing, fashion, and rapping. They recruit these young people with tangible inducements of monetary rewards, media attention and public recognition. They place them under coaches, put them on teams and enter them in competitions to hone their gifts.

Young athletes in junior high school are recruited by talent scouts from the major gym shoe companies, paid in the form of free shoes and athletic wear that they can sell for thousands of dollars, recruited onto traveling squads that tour the United States even overseas during the summers. Young singers, dancers and rappers have a thousand opportunities to compete with other aspiring artists in all kinds of venues all over this country. It is impossible to get a group of young people together in any kind of overnight conference or convention without somebody organizing a talent show.

I believe that we can use the same system to reproduce and replenish our stock of leaders and scholars. We neglect the intellectual abilities of our young people just as other people do. I often ask high school teachers why is it that no black boy over six feet tall or who weighs over two hundred pounds can walk the hallways of a high school without being approached by the basketball or football coach, yet a young brother or sister that demonstrates verbal skills and oratorical giftedness in rapping and rhyming is not sought after, inquired about, chased down or aggressively recruited by the debate coach or the sponsor of student government.

We can and must produce a *Black Youth Renaissance.* We must organize and bring about a new flowering of spirituality, leadership, scholarship, creativity and productivity among our young. We must devise the conditions to produce a great harvest like that of the Harlem Renaissance. We are the same people who built "a nation within a nation" in the midst of our enslavers deep in the land of bondage. We must recapture the spirit of our ancestors who committed all of their spiritual, organizational, financial, and intellectual powers to the task of redefining themselves as independent people while the scars of slavery yet stood out on their bodies. It was to a great extent the fresh memory and the still standing symbols of slavery which drove them on. They did their great work in the shadow of the big house and within sight of the auction block. They were able finally to proclaim aloud in the brightness of day that which had to be whispered in the silence of dark nights of slavery: that we were a great people whose enemy had yet to figure out how to destroy. We must produce the conditions that will lead us back into the same spiritual territory that our ancestors occupied in their times of their most daunting challenge.

The church must lead the way. It is still the most powerful, the most populous, and the wealthiest institution in the black community. Of whom much is given, much is still required. It can begin as simply as sponsoring competitions among youth groups around bible quizzes and it can expand to black history contests, debates, oratorical contests, essay contests, spelling bees, mock trials, geography bees, science fairs, and product fairs.

Something as simple as a Bible quiz will help our young people develop intellectually and spiritually. They must first of all read those parts of the bible out of which the questions come. That will improve their study skills. They will have to concentrate on memorizing materials which will improve their power of recollection which is a neglected area of cognitive development in this era of intellectual laziness. They will learn the critical moral lessons that are embedded and concentrated in that cornerstone of our faith. They will facilitate the reinforcement of high standards of academic achievement by bringing together like-minded young people who are determined to do something positive with their lives but are all too often isolated as iconoclasts and derided by naïve peers and shallow-minded adults as nerds. And they will be so busy being dedicated to something positive they won't have time to get in trouble wandering the streets with nothing to do. The old folks were right: "An idle mind is the devil's workshop."

I am not claiming the idea of intellectual competition as new idea for the black community. The NAACP to their credit and through the inspiration of the great black journalist Vernon Jarret initiated their ACT-SO competitions years ago. However, this program has been limited in the scope of its involvement to the elite students recognized for their accomplishments in their local schools and already identified as promising young scholars. I am calling for a radical expansion of this concept until it becomes a mass movement reaching into the depths of our youth population, reaching those who have been overlooked, unthought-of and unconsidered.

What I'm calling for is a program that will be a missionary movement, a recruitment campaign and teaching device to convince young people of their untapped potential and provide them with the training they need to transform hidden potential into tangible reality. The church has the ability to touch young people everywhere from the playground to the prison, from the library to the foster home. Some of our greatest minds and talents are locked up behind prison bars as we are reminded in this phrase from the classic black prayer: "Bless the men and women, boys and girls locked up behind prison bars, some are there for crimes that they have committed but some are there who have committed no crime."

The National Spelling Bee is a world famous event that begins in local competition in grammar schools all over this country and culminates in the finals held in Washington D.C. in the spring of the year and carries a ten thousand dollar first prize. In 1998 a little twelve year old black girl from Jamaica named Jodey-Anne Maxwell won. It was the first time in history that a black child or a student from outside the United States won. Two months after her victory the board of directors of this event amended their rules in such a way as to disqualifying the Jamaicans from further competition.

Interestingly, the students from Jamaica had been making better and better showings each year since their Jason Edward James took eighth place in 1997. They made a remarkable showing in 1998 when not only did little Jodey-Anne win first place but her teammate Bettina McLean finished sixth.

There is nothing unusual about the administrators' response. It is a classic racist reaction to "change the rules when we start winning the game". But I have but a greater question. Where are "our" National and International Pan-African Spelling Bees? Where is the National Black Spelling Bee that galvanizes tens of thousands of our pre-adolescents to reading encyclopedias and studying dictionaries, and tracing the etymological roots of esoteric multi-syllable words? Where is the Pan-African Spelling Bee that brings together young scholars from North America, Central and South America, the Caribbean Islands and the all the nations of Africa?

Another time I was surfing TV channels at about 2:00 AM and ran into the National Geography Bee. Here was a contest among fourth to eight graders for a twenty-five thousand dollar college scholarship as the top prize. A young East Indian boy won but there was not a black face to be seen anywhere in the vicinity. There is an entire hundred million dollar industry of academic-based competitions from which young black people are virtually excluded because most of us don't even know it exists. Competitions exist in mock court, drama, architecture, engineering, marine biology, aeronautics, chemistry, poetry, that motivate young people to the highest levels of development and performance. They serve as vehicles for college scholarships, professional internships, and national and international travel and educational opportunities. But even more than these, they lay the foundation of a skilled generation that can change the course of our current state in this nation from victims to victors, from consumers to producers, from spectators to activists.

We can sponsor local and national competitions in developing business plans and in the marketing and sale of new and innovative products. We can have product fairs where our young people can display, sell or even auction art, products or even inventions of their own design and manufacture. There is no limit to how highly developed or how internationally expansive this renaissance can become. What is sure is that it must be done. The future of our people both here and abroad is at stake. We must address this current crisis with creative thinking, hard cash investment, adult involvement and institutional support.

We must finance a flowering of the immense, immeasurable natural genius of our young people for the present and future betterment of our people. The blessings of one generation are inevitably visited upon their parents and their children.

Scholarship and leadership rather than sports teams and fashion shows must become the major priority of our people for the foreseeable future. We must have a new Civil Rights/Black Power movement based on rescuing our youth from the dead-end streets of the negativism and self-destructiveness offered them by the popular media. We have to show them that it makes sense to be good people, committed students, and helpful members of the community. We need to have more money in our scholarship funds than in our building funds. Not only for churches, the entire black community must be persuaded and recruited to invest in our young people. Every black organization and institution from block clubs to mom and pop grocery stores, from barber shops and shoe shine parlors to hair care manufacturers and black newspapers, from soul food restaurants to black radio stations, from black magazines to insurance companies must all not only initiate scholarship programs but those that have them need to exponentially multiply their funds by ten and twenty and a hundred times what they are today.

Many of our brightest young minds cannot afford to attend college because as a race we still rely on government support for higher education to the same degree we did in the sixties. Those monies became insufficient decades ago as the costs of higher education rose at twice the rate of inflation but government grant and loan programs did not keep up. Nor did black institution step in to take up the slack and fill in the vacuum. As the government support for black higher education diminished, black support did not increase. As a result we became increasingly dependent on the government to pay for our young peoples' education and now that they have gotten out of the business of paying for the children of poor people's higher education we find ourselves in a crisis where the number of black college students especially males has been steadily declining for the past twenty years.

I envision these competitions as being team competitions among church and /or community youth group. We always have and always will have extraordinarily gifted individuals who will super-achieve in spite of the most unpromising circumstances. We are not trying to merely make a place for those individuals who will make a place for themselves regardless of what we do. We need to produce a mass movement that will touch the lives of our young people in such a way as to change their collective sense of who they are as a generation. Our current crisis began when the Civil Rights/Black Power generation changed into the ME Generation. We need to help this generation change from the LOST/LEFT Generation into *The New Black Youth Renaissance Generation.* We need to help them change not only their name but also their mission and their destiny

We must reclaim our culture and refashion it for our own development. When they enslaved our ancestors they did not just capture strong bodied individuals. They captured our culture and put it the use of development and profit for their purposes. Our culture is the world's oldest and most sophisticated. They took our agricultural genius and used it grow the cash crops they didn't know how to plant, cultivate, harvest or process. We grew the cotton, indigo, rice and sugar that provided the enormous profits that financed their industrial revolution that lifted Europe out of the Dark Ages and gave them the highest material standard of living in the world. They took our music and dance and made them the centers of their entertainment industry. All popular music and dance since the minstrel shows that started in the 1830's to this day are based on our melodies, harmonies, rhythms and dance steps. They used our building and metallurgical skills to construct their grand mansions. They took our athletic skills and used them to dominate sport world-wide from the Olympics, to boxing, to football, baseball and basketball. We need to take back our culture from its exploitation for their profit and use it for our own benefit.

We must return purpose to our culture. In traditional African culture everything has purpose and meaning. Names, clothing, jewelry, hairstyles, music and dances all tell a story, teach a lesson, and express a value. We have in a real since lost our minds over the past thirty years. Too many of us live lives and engage in behaviors that are devoid of meaning. One of the most popular statements on the part of black people young and old is: "It doesn't mean anything". Our ancestor understood that everything that exists has a purpose and a meaning. Many young people respond to criticisms about the lyrics of their music by saying: "It doesn't mean anything". How can a word not have a meaning? Even moans and groans have meaning. The cries of inarticulate infants have meaning that the sensitive parent can interpret. Meaninglessness is beneath being animalistic for even animal behavior has meaning. Meaninglessness is demonic for it is a denial of the human. We are challenged by the divine purpose of our very existence to connect with the meaning of our very presence on this earth. The negativity and nihilism of so much our behavior is in direct correlation to our inability to ascertain the ultimate meaning of our actions.

We must infuse meaning back into our lives and the lives of our children. We can do this by reclaiming our culture and using it to express and invest in noble purposes. We have a massive investment in athletics to the extent that boys and girls as young as seven and eight years old are playing team sports in organized leagues. We need the same kinds of involvement of young scholars in academic based competitions. Team competitions will mean not only the production of individual superstars but the construction of an intellectual and academic culture for our youth as a whole. The best scholars tell us that classrooms composed of children of unequal ability does not mean that the slower students will hold back the more precocious ones, rather just the opposite, that the more advanced students will inspire acceleration in the slower ones.

We have allowed the public school systems to segregate our children on the basis of demonstrated ability and supposed intelligence. In doing so we have denied the children with the least exposure to excellence access to those who have had greater exposure. It means not only have the slower students not been blessed by the example of the better students, it also means that the better students have not learned their responsibility to the less advanced ones. God produces heterogeneous generations of differing gifts and abilities but He intended for them to operate as brothers and sisters as our ancestors did. When they organized their children into age groups it was to teach them a sense of obligation toward and cooperation with one another so that they could all collectively benefit from their various gifts and abilities. As my pastor, The Rev. Dr. Shelvin Jerome Hall of the great Friendship Baptist Church on the West Side of Chicago, loves to proclaim: "Individuals rise with their generation".

I was doing a workshop a group of grammar school students in Chicago years ago. I asked the children to stand and declare what they intended to be when they grew up. A disappointing percentage of the boys wanted to be professional athletes and too many of the girls' highest aspirations was to be secretaries and models. Finally a little skinny, long-headed, dark-chocolate-complexioned boy stood up straight and with great determination in his voice declared: "I'ma be a congressman". The rest of the class burst out in laughter. I immediately quieted them and began to teach. I told them that when one of their number expresses a great goal which is the result of a wonderful dream they should not make fun of it. They should find their own place in his dream. If he's going to be a congressman then he needs a team. He can't do this by himself. He needs organizers, administrators, lawyers, accountants, fund-raisers, office managers, public relations people, van and bus drivers, printers, researchers, airplane pilots, etc. Our children must be taught how to lift each other up and not just tear each other down.

It means that in a spelling bee every team member must participate, which means every member of the team has to study their spelling. The competition being organized through church means that the young people who have been untouched by the mission and ministry of the local church will be exposed to the gospel not just as mere words but as a living transformative force in their lives. We have raised an unchurched generation who are unacquainted with the fundamentals of our faith. We must bring these young people into the light of the belief system that was our ancestors' saving grace.

We need to organize debates in which our young people will hone their skills of logic, oratory, analysis, and problem-solving. Therein they can deal with both the classic issues of past times and the burning controversies of this day. By doing so they prepare themselves for that time when they will be this nation's and the world's problem-solvers, law-makers and standard-setters.

We need mock trials so that our children will begin to learn at an early age the role of law in human society and the complex dynamics of applying the principles of justice to human affairs. They can reenact the great trials like Dred Scott, Plessy vs. Ferguson and Brown v. the Topeka, Kansas Board of Education. They will learn to stand in courtrooms as lawyers, sit on juries and act as experts and witnesses. They need to learn to meet the challenge of a system of jurisprudence which has been an enemy to our people since we have arrived on these shores. One day very soon they will, as adults, prosecute the accused, defend the innocent, and weigh the lives of human beings in the balance between justice and mercy.

We would be challenging our young people to put their imaginations to work helping us to envision a new world. For instance we need a competition in architecture to design new housing and neighborhoods to suit the life style and world-view of our people. We are an extended family, multi-generational, village-minded, outreaching, horticultural, outdoor people. Housing designed for Europeans are for people who are nuclear in their family structure. They don't take into consideration, grandparents, great aunts and uncles, cousins, godparents, play sisters and play brothers, when they design their housing. We love to entertain our people overnight. The weekend sleepovers when your cousins and best friends stay over and you roll out the sofa bed or the rollaway bed or make a pallet on the floor are always among the fondest memories of our childhoods.

We need to be able to keep our elders comfortably in our homes. That means constructing housing that is elder-friendly with bedrooms and bathrooms on the first floor in mother-in-law suites. When our young people first leave home, especially girls, trying out their wings from up under mama and daddy's supervisory eyes who are yet unable to view them as being grown and their own persons; they would rather move in with other family members. The same can go for boys. We need space in our homes for the older cousin or aunt who is single or widowed who would like to live in community with family. These people have traditionally served as babysitters in the home so that we would not have to send our children out to strangers. We need housing that would maximize our interaction with our neighbors on front porches where people sit and face each other rather than this new phenomenon of backyard decks that fosters increased isolation. We need living space that will bring us outdoors, particularly to garden. This is a multigenerational activity that will bring elders in contact with youngsters to teach them one of the most ancient skills of African people.

We can have science fairs, art fairs, fashion fairs, inventors' fairs, and product fairs where young people can bring that which they have discovered, designed, made, constructed and display them not only for competition but for sale, even for auction. Out of these competitions will come the new generations of scientists, doctors, furniture-makers, chemists, inventors that will provide us with a cure for sickle cell anemia, a means of defeating high-blood pressure, new inventions for manufacture that will allow us to compete on the global market.

We need competitions in the publication of newsletters, newspapers and magazines to encourage a new generation of writers, reporters, editorialists, journalists, and publishers. Competitions in playwriting and filmmaking to generate a cohort of actors, directors, choreographers, producers who will give us the plays and movies that Hollywood is determined never to produce. There has yet to be a movie made about the greatest people, most important themes, most glorious accomplishments and most critical issues in our history. No one has made a feature film about the ancient civilizations of Africa, such as Monomatopa (ancient Zimbabwe), Ethiopia and Egypt. (Instead we have Hollywood racist epics with white actors portraying Moses, Pharaoh, and Cleopatra as though Egypt was a peninsula off the coast of Europe instead of being an African country.) There are no cinematic rendering of the glories of the great empires and everyday life of the people of Mali, Ghana and Songhai. Hollywood, neither black or white, has done a movie on Toussaint L'Ouverture, Paul Cuffee, Benjamin Banneker, Frederick Douglass, Nat Turner, Harriet Tubman, W.E.B. DuBois, Ida B. Wells, Marcus Garvey, Paul Robeson, Zora Neale Hurston, Mary McLeod Bethune, Jomo Kenyatta, Adam Clayton Powell, Jr., Katherine Dunham, Kwame Nkrumah, Louis Armstrong, Duke Ellington, to name only a very few of our greatest leaders, scholars, and artists.

Every form of organized competition will also achieve that necessary purpose of linking the elders to the youngsters. In order for the youngsters to learn, to compete and to win the elders must be their teachers, instructors, consultants and coaches. There is no champion in any sport absent the presence of the old man and old woman guiding and directing the movements of the young. No boxer no matter how skilled, determined, resourceful, courageous, and powerful ever wins a championship without the old trainer in his corner advising of things inexperienced eyes cannot see. No group of basketball players no matter how high they can jump, how fast they can run, how accurately they can shoot will ever carry the championship trophy off the court unless they have the wisdom and experience of the coach to coordinate their individual abilities and forge them into a winning team.

Is there any better example of this truth than those fantastic champions of the women's tennis, Venus and Serena Williams? This is the genius of black people exhibited on the world stage. Their father, Mr. Richard Williams, a man with limited formal education and no first-hand exposure to tennis taught himself the game, historically the province of upper class and middle white people. He then taught his daughters, amazingly through a novel approach of his own design, refusing to employ the strategies of the tennis world that often burned out their daughters by immersing them in the professional tennis culture while in their early teens denying them the usual broadening experience of regular adolescence. Instead he insisted on their having a normal life and maturing into poised, intelligent, commonsensical, well-rounded, multi-faceted, broad-minded, multi-lingual, evenly balanced personable and articulate young women who are champions in more ways than one. In the end he produced two of the greatest players the game will have ever seen.

If he were a white man he would be known as the greatest tennis coach in the world if not the greatest of all-time, being father, mentor, coach and manager of the world's two greatest players of their era. Instead he is derided by the racist tennis establishment for his novel approach of refusing to play the game by their rules. Because he is a man of his people, he employed the classic strategies of African people to reach his goals. He worked hard, was disciplined and focused. He refused to be discouraged by the incredible obstacles that were placed in his way. He used analytical thinking and creative approaches to make a way out of now way. The incredible successes of the Williams family are not theirs alone. They are example of who we are as a people when we are at our best, being truly ourselves.

We need dance contests where our young people can be challenged to develop dances that will lift them and us up. We need dances that will bring out and celebrate the best in our culture and society. We need songs that will teach manners, songs that will teach respect for elders and love for babies, songs that will increase our enthusiasm for going to school, songs that will teach us to respect and revere our teachers, songs that will put wings on our feet and hurry us to school to experience with awe the precious gift and opportunity of education, songs that will make us love learning, songs to carry books by, songs to sing on the way to the library, songs to keep us virgins, songs that extol discipline, songs that help young women respect themselves, songs that help young brothers be patient and forgiving with one another instead of songs that cry out for blood at the most petty offenses. We need songs that teach algebra, trigonometry and calculus. We need songs that build vocabularies. Songs that boost confidence. Songs that raise standards. Songs that make little girls who have been called "black but pretty" see themselves in the full beauty of their blackness. Songs that elaborate on the theme: The blacker the berry the sweeter the juice." Songs that stop boys and men from assaulting and raping their sisters, but will teach them respect love and reverence for their very gift of womanhood which the scriptures tells us it is not good for men to be without. Songs that stop girls and women from selling their bodies. Songs that help mothers love their babies. Songs that inspire us to take care of and raise not only our own children but even somebody else's. Songs that give instruction in the key values of life. Deep songs to help us to contemplate that which is most profound in the universe and silly songs to help make life fun. Songs to help a carpenter hit a nail straight, songs to help a worker find the right tool for the job. Songs to help teachers prepare their lessons. Songs to help a principal organize her school.

We must as the elders entertain a positive vision for our children's future to counter the destructive plans that the racism of this nation harbors for them. This nation has a plan for our children. It is a plan of failure, leading to continuing poverty for our youth and increasing wealth for the planners. They envision our young people being in jail and they put their money where their mouth is. They continue to invest millions and billions into hiring more police, training more prosecutors, manufacturing more weapons, building more prisons, and employing more guards.

We need to lovingly compel our young people to engage

407

their spiritual and intellectual powers to rise to the highest level of their greatest possibilities so that they can become all that the Creator sent them here to be and to insure the health, safety and prosperity of their children and their children's children and for as yet unseen generations.

It is our responsibility as the elders and the living ancestors to organize our communities to bring out the best in our young people. We must construct a world that rewards them for being a positive person, for being helpful, polite, mannerable, encouraging and supportive. That convinces them being an optimistic progressive member of one's community and a benevolent force in the neighborhood is not just for squares, chumps, lames, and weaklings but it is the stuff out of which heroes are made. And everybody wants to be a hero. Somewhere deep down inside I believe that there exists in all human beings not only the capacity but the desire to do that which is good, and right, even noble. Too many older people have lost hold of the dreams of their youth and have surrendered to the shallow popular notion that "We can't win for losing or that "you can't fight city hall". We have to appeal to the same spirits of power in our young people that energized and directed the lives of past generations that have carried the names of African people all over this world and caused us to be known as a great people.

I believe in our young people. I believe in them because I am convinced that it is in the nature of every human being to strive for that which is noble. Not the nobility of Europeans based upon some people being better than others based on socioeconomic status but the real nobility of our ancestors. The kind of nobility that even in the darkest hours caused them to look upward toward a light not yet visible. This nobility has always been best expressed in our hopes for our children.

Even the prostitute dreams of her daughter being a secretary. The burglar prays that his son will be a lawyer. We must appeal to the best in our young people not to the worst. Commercial interests have made fortunes appealing to the worst in our youth. Somebody must care enough about them and believe enough in them to appeal to their best. No matter how deeply it may be hidden by crusted-over layers of neglect and mistreatment the human desire for goodness has not been extinguished in them. I am convinced that given a believable choice our young people will choose good over evil.

I was there when Dr. King received a visit from a delegation of the Vice Lords. The Vice Lords and their rivals, the Egpytian Cobras were the two largest and most feared gangs in Chicago. These young brothers came to Dr. King's third floor walk-up apartment at 1550 S. Hamlin Ave, around the corner from their headquarters on 16th Street known, as Vice Lord City. I was awed by their reverential approach to that great leader of our people. The same young men who were the terrors of the neighborhood and as named in one sociological study the "warriors of the streets". Yet they came before Dr. King humbly and seekingly. They drank in his words as those that are dying of thirst take cool waters into their mouths.

Dr. King told them he wanted them stop fighting and killing there brother, stop wreaking havoc in the neighborhood and to go back to school. I'm not talking about what I heard, or even what I read. I was there. Dr. King's presence in their neighborhood wrought a difference in many of those young brothers' lives. A few short years later many of them returned to school attending along with myself the Central YMCA Community College whose campus now long closed was located at 211 W. Wacker Dr. across the street from the world-famous Merchandise Mart. Even more amazingly a number of those gang-bangers attended Dartmouth College sponsored by the same program that recruited me to Harvard. Those of us who are willing to invest in our young people can make the same kind of difference today.

It is not enough that our young people are the world's

greatest athletes and entertainers. We cannot be satisfied until they restore us to our place as world leaders in law, science, technology, agriculture, engineering, architecture. We know what it means when somebody says a black boxer. The image that comes to mind is one of power, grace and dominance. We know that to say black dancer means fantastic moves and breathtaking extemporaneous choreography. When someone says black runner it means silky smoothness combined with raw power and unmatchable speed and stamina. When we say black singer it conjures up in our minds voices with sounds that surpass the music of instruments, sweetness, virtuosity, lilting altos and soaring sopranos that cause mockingbirds and nightingales to fall silent in awe and admiration. When we say black basketball player we are talking about those whose traditions have lifted the game to a state of unrivaled performance, unimagined artistry and unparalleled creativity that so exceeds the vision of its inventor that he would not recognize it if he saw it played today. But that's not enough.

There are races of people that have set universal standards of excellence in their fields such as German scientists, Portuguese fishermen, Japanese engineers, and Jewish lawyers We must lay before our children the challenge to produce a tradition of such excellence that black lawyers carries the same expectation of excellence as black boxer. Until they plant their standard of achievement and productivity alongside those of the best in the world in every meaningful field of endeavor. Until the adjective "black" represents preeminence in every field of endeavor. Black business man. Black mechanic. Black diplomatic. Black restaraunteur. Black executive. Black professor. Black oceanographer. Black astronomer. Black pilot.

We cannot be satisfied until our children invest the same kind of dedication in studying their lessons as they do in practicing their sport. Until only the kind of superlatives used to describe black athletes are used to point out black

410

scholars and scientists. Until we dominate inventions like we dominate the sprints. Until the moral excellence of our sons and daughters are as recognized as their entertainment expertise. Until it becomes a watchword that if you need a great thinker, a profound analyst, a visionary, an innovator, or a problem solver, you need to go to the ghetto and seek that person out among the sons and daughters of Africa.

Lastly, I believe in our young people because I know the One who sent them here to dwell amongst us. He did not send them as a mockery or a joke. He didn't send them as a testimony of the lostness of His cause for His cause can never lose. He did not send them here to oppress their parents or to molest their children. The purpose He had in mind could only have been of the most exalted nature because that's who He is and how He operates. It is the nature of His creation that truth and justice always prevail at the end .This generation may not be able to win the ultimate battle against the ancient evils that have oppressed our people in this land for the past five hundred years. They may not be destined to be the last generation to be beset on every side by the forces of racism. They may not be the last cohort of our children to be wounded by the weapons of hatred, viciousness and cruelty. But they are intended like every generation of their forbears, to as the Apostle Paul put it to: "fight the good fight, to finish their course, to keep the faith" and then to pass on the baton of our cherished values to the generations that follow after them.

History awaits our response.

BIBLIOGRAPHY

Bayles, Martha; **HOLE IN OUR SOUL: The Loss of Beauty and Meaning in American Popular Music**; The Free Press; New York; 1994

Blankhenhorn, David; **FATHERLESS AMERICA; Confronting Our Most Urgent Social Problem**; BasicBooks; New York; 1995

Boswell, John; **THE KINDNESS OF STRANGERS: The Abandonment of Children in Western Europe from Late Antiquity to the Renaissance**; Pantheon Books; New York; 1988

Bowman, J. Wilson; **AMERICA'S BLACK AND TRIBAL COLLEGES:A Comprehensive Guide to Historically & Predominantly Black and American Indian Colleges and Universities**; Sandcastle Publishing; South Pasadena, CA.;1994

Breggin, Peter R. and Breggin, Ginger Ross; **THE WAR AGAINST CHILDREN OF COLOR: Psychiatry Targets Inner City Youth**; Common Courage Press; Monroe, ME; 1998

Brint, Steven and Karabel, Jerome; **THE DIVERTED DREAM: Community Colleges and the Promise of Educational Opportunity in America, 1900-1985**; Oxford University Press; New York; 1989

Carnes, Patrick; **DON'T CALL IT LOVE: Recovery From Sexual Addiction**; Bantam Books; New York; 1991

Clark, Reginald M.; **FAMILY LIFE AND SCHOOL ACHIEVEMENT: Why Poor Black Children Succeed or Fail**; The University of Chicago Press; Chicago, IL. 1983

Cosby, Bill; **FATHERHOOD**; Doubleday & Company, Inc.; Garden City, NY; 1986

Coulter, Harris L.; **AIDS AND SYPHILIS: The Hidden Link**; North Atlantic Books; Berkeley, CA; 1987

Dash, Leon; **WHEN CHILDREN WANT CHILDREN: The Urban Crisis of Teenage Childbearing**; William Morrow and Company, Inc.; New York; 1989

Davis, Anthony and Jackson Jeffrey; **"YO, LITTLE BROTHER...": Basic Rules of Survival for Young African American Males**; African American Images; Chicago, IL; 1998

Dobson, James and Bauer, Gary L.; **CHILDREN AT RISK: The Battle for the Hearts and Minds of Our Kids**; World Publishers; Dallas, TX.; 1990

Emecheta, Buchi; **THE WRESTLING MATCH**; George Braziller, Inc.; New York, NY; 1984

Farrell, Warren; **THE MYTH OF MALE POWER: Why Men Are The Disposable Sex**; Simon&Schuster; New York; 1993

Farrell, Warren; **FATHER AND CHILD REUNION: How to Bring the Dads We Need to the Children We Love**; Penguin Putnam Inc.; New York; 2001

Fleischer, Arthur A.; Goff, Brian L.; and Tollison, Robert D.; **THE NATIONAL COLLEGIATE ATHLETIC ASSOCIATION: A Study in Cartel Behavior**; The University of Chicago Press; Chicago, IL; 1992

Fleming, Jacqueline; **BLACKS IN COLLEGE: A Comparative Study of Students' Success in Black and in White Institutions**; Jossey-Bass Publishers; San Francisco, CA.;1984

Fumento, Michael; **THE MYTH OF HETERSEXUAL AIDS: How a Tragedy Has Been Distorted by the Media and Partisan Politics**; Regnery Gateway; Washington, D.C.; 1993

Gabriel, Richard R.; **NO MORE HEROES: Madness and Psychiatry in War**; Hill and Wang; New York; 1987

Gilder, George; **MEN AND MARRIAGE**; Pelican Publishing Company; Gretna, LA. 1986

Gilmore, David D.; **MANHOOD IN THE MAKING: Cultural Concepts of Masculinity**; Yale University Press; New Haven, CT; 1990

Grossman, Lt. Col. Dave; **ON KILLING: The Psychological Cost of Learning to Kill in War and Society**; Little, Brown and Company, Boston, MA;1995

Gurin, Patricia and Epps, Edgar G ; **BLACK CONSCIOUSNESS, IDENTITY AND ACHIEVEMENT: A Study of Students in Historically Black Colleges**; John Wiley & Sons; New York; 1975

Hagedorn, John; **PEOPLE AND FOLKS: Gang, Crime, and the Underclass in A Rustbelt City**; Lake View Press, Chicago, IL; 1988

Haight, Wendy L.; **AFRICAN-AMERICAN CHILDREN AT CHURCH: A Sociological Perspective**; Cambridge University Press; Cambridge, UK

Hale, Janice E.; **UNBANK THE FIRE: Visions for the Education of African American Children**; The Johns Hopkins University Press; Baltimore, MD; 1994

Hale, Janice E.; **BLACK CHILDREN: Their Roots, Culture, and Learning Styles**; Brigham Young University Press, Provo, Utah; 1982

Hare, Nathan and Julia; **THE MISEDUCATION OF THE BLACK CHILD: The Hare Plan: Educate Every Black Man, Woman and Child**; The Black Think Tank; San Francisco, CA. 1991

Hare, Nathan and Julia; **CRISIS IN BLACK SEXUAL POLITICS**; Black Think Tank; San Francisco, CA. 1989

Hester, Jimmy; CHRISTIAN SEX EDUCATION; Family Touch; Nashville, TN.; 1993

Hilliard, Asa G. III; **TESTING AFRICAN AMERICAN STUDENTS: Special Re-Issue of The Negro Educational Review**; Aaron Press; Morristown,

N.J.; 1991

Hunter, Mic; **ABUSED BOYS: The Neglected Victims of Sexual Child Abuse**; Fawcett Columbine; New York; 1990

Hudson-Weems, Clenora; **AFRICANA WOMANISM: RECLAIMING OURSELVES**; Bedford Publishers, Inc.; Troy MI; 1993

Hymowitz, Kay S.; **READY OR NOT: Why Treating Children as Small Adults Endangers Their Future— and Ours**; The Free Press; New York; 1999

Janus, Sam; **THE DEATH OF INNOCENCE: How Our Children Are Endangered By The New Sexual Freedom**; William Morrow And Company, Inc.; New York; 1981

Jewell, K. Sue; **SURVIVAL OF THE BLACK FAMILY: The Institutional Impact of Social Policy**; Praeger; New York; 1988

Johnson, Guy; **STANDING AT THE SCRATCH LINE: A Novel**; Striver's Row; New York; 1998

Judkins, David; **STUDY ABROAD: The Astute Student's Guide**: Williamson Publishing; Charlotte, VT. 1989

Kimbrough, Andrew Kimbrell; **THE MASCULINE MYSTIQUE: The Politics of Masculinity**; Ballantine Books; New York; 1995

Kochman, Thomas; **BLACK AND WHITE: STYLES IN CONFLICT**; The University of Chicago Press; Chicago, IL 1981

Levin, Shirley; **SUMMER ON CAMPUS: College Experiences for High School Students**;College Entrance Examination Board; New York; 1989

Lynn, David B.; **THE FATHER: His Role in Child Development**; Brookes/Cole Publishing Company; Monterey, CA; 1974

Margo, Robert A.; **RACE AND SCHOOLING IN THE SOUTH, 1880-1950: An Economic History**; The

University of Chicago Press; Chicago, IL; 1990

McCray, Rev. Walter; **THE BLACK YOUNG ADULT TEST: How Mature Are You?**; Black Light Fellowship; Chicago, IL.; 1994

McDowell, Josh; **THE MYTHS OF SEX EDUCATION: Josh McDowell's Open Letter to His School Board**; Here's Life Publishers; San Bernardino, CA. 1990

Meade, Michael; **MEN AND THE WATER OF LIFE: The Initiation and the Tempering of Men**; HaperCollins Publishers; New York; 1993

Medinger, Alan; **GROWTH INTO MANHOOD**; Waterbrook Press; Colorado Springs, CO; 2000

Medved, Michael and Diane; **SAVING CHILDHOOD: Protecting Our Children from the National Assault on Innocence**; HarperPerennial; New York; 1998

Medved, Michael**; HOLLYWOOD VS. AMERICA**; HarperCollins Publishers; New York; 1992

Mincy, Ronald B.; **NURTURING YOUNG BLACK MALES: Challenges to Agencies, Programs and Social Policies**; The Urban Institute Press; Washington. D.C.; 1994

Nuwer, Hank; **WRONGS OF PASSAGE: Fraternities, Sororities, Hazing, and Binge Drinking**; Indiana University Press; Bloomington, IN. 1999

…**HIGH SCHOOL HAZING: When Rites Go Wrong**; Grolier Publishing; Danbury, CT; 1990

Oakes, Jeannie; **KEEPING TRACK: How Schools Structure Inequality**; Yale University; New Haven. CT.; 1985

Olivas, Michael A ; **THE DILEMMA OF ACCESS: Minorities in Two Year Colleges**; Howard University Press; Washington, D.C.;1979

Pattilo-McCoy; **BLACK PICKET FENCES: Privilege and Peril among the Black Middle Class**; The University of Chicago Press; Chicago, IL; 1999

416

Perkins, Useni Eugene; **HARVESTING NEW GENERATIONS: The Positive Development of Black Youth**; Third World Press; Chicago, IL; 1986

Perkins, Useni Eugene; **EXPLOSION OF CHICAGO'S BLACK STREET GANG: 1900 to Present**; Third World Press; Chicago, IL. 1990

Pinar, William F.; **THE GENDER of RACIAL POLITICS and VIOLENCE in AMERICA: Lynching, Prison Rape, & The Crisis Of Masculinity;** Peter Lang; New York, NY; 2001

Ro, Ronin; **HAVE GUN WILL TRAVEL: The Spectacular Rise and Violent Fall of Death Row Records**; Doubleday; New York; 1998

Robeson, Paul Jr.; **THE UNDISCOVERED PAUL ROBESON: An Artist's Journey 1898-1939**; John Wiley & Sons, Inc.; New York; 2001

Rotello, Gabriel; **SEXUAL ECOLOGY: AIDS and the Destiny of Gay Men**; A Plume Book; Penguin Putnam; 1998

Sacks, Peter; **GENERATION X GOES TO COLLEGE: An Eye-Opening Account of Teaching In Postmodern America**; Open Court Publishing Company; Chicago, IL; 1997

Sanday, Peggy Reaves; **FRATERNITY GANG RAPE: Sex, Brotherhood. And Privilege on Campus**; New York University Press; New York;1990

Satinover, Jeffrey; **HOMOSEXUALITY AND THE POLITICS OF TRUTH**; Baker Books; Grand Rapids, MI; 1996

Schmierer, Don; **AN OUNCE OF PREVENTION: Preventing The Homosexual Condition in Today's Youth**; Word Publishing; Nashville, TN; 1998

Scarce, Michael; **MALE ON MALE RAPE: The Hidden Toll Of Stigma And Shame**; Insight Books; New York; 1997

Shilts, Randy: **AND THE BAND PLAYED ON: Politics, People and the AIDS Epidemic**; St. Martin's

Press; New York; 1987

Snarey, John; **HOW FATHERS CARE FOR THE NEXT GENERATION: A Four-Decade Study**; Harvard University Press; 1993

Socarides, Charles, W.; **HOMOSEXUALITY: A FREEDOM TOO FAR**; Adam Margrave Books; Phoenix, AZ; 1995

Some, Patrice Malidoma; **THE HEALING WISDOM OF AFRICA: Finding Life Purpose Through Nature, Ritual and Community**; Jeremy P. Tarcher/Putnam; 1999

Sommers, Christina Hoff; **THE WAR AGAINST BOYS: How Misguided Feminism Is Harming Our Young Men;** Simon & Schuster; New York; 2000

Stanley, Lawrence A.(ed.) **RAP THE LYRICS: The Words to Rap's Greatest Hits**; Penguin Books; New York; 1992

Subira, George; **MONEY ISSUES IN BLACK MALE/FEMALE RELATIONSHIPS**; Very Serious Business Enterprises; New York, NJ; 1994

Tzu, Sun (Translated by Samuel B. Griffin); **THE ART OF WAR**; Oxford University Press; New York; 1982

Wade-Gayles, Gloria (ed.); **FATHER SONGS: Testimonies By African-American Sons and Daughters**; Beacon Press; Boston, MA; 1997

Washington, Valora; **BLACK CHILDREN AND AMERICAN INSTITUTIONS: An Ecological Review and Resource Guide**; Garland Publishing Inc.; New York; 1988

Wetzel, Dan and Don Yeager; **SOLE INFLUENCE: Basketball, Corporate Greed, and the Corruption of America's Youth**; Warner Books; 2000

Wheelock, Anne; **CROSSING THE TRACKS: How "Untracking Can Save America's Schools"**; The New Press; New York; 1992

White, Vibert L. Jr.; **INSIDE THE NATION OF ISLAM: A Historical and Personal Testimony by a Black Muslim**; University of Florida Press; Gainesville,

FL; 2001

Whiting, Ernestine; **THE BLACK STUDENT'S GUIDE TO SCHOLARSHIPS**; Beckham House Publishers, Inc.; Silver Spring, MD; 1993

Wilmore, Gayraud; **BLACK RELIGION AND BLACK RADICALISM: An Interpretation of the Religious History of African Americans**; Orbis Books; Maryknoll, New York; 1998

Wilmore, Gayraud (ed.); **BLACK MEN IN PRISON: The Response of the African American Church**; THE ITC PRESS; Atlanta, GA; 1990

Wimberly, Ann Streaty(ed); **HONORING AFRICAN AMERICAN ELDERS: A Ministry in the Soul Community**; Jossey-Bass Publishers; San Francisco, CA; 1997

Wilson, Amos N.; **AWAKENING THE NATURAL GENIUS OF BLACK CHILDREN**; Afrikan World InfoSystems; New York; 1992

Wilson, Amos N.; **BLACK-ON-BLACK VIOLENCE: The Psychodynamics Of Black Self-Annihilation In Service Of White Domination**; Afrikan World Infosystems; New York; 1990

Winn, Marie; **CHILDREN WITHOUT CHILDHOOD: Growing Up Too Fast In the World of Sex and Drugs**; Penguin Books; New York; 1984

Wyatt, Gale; **STOLEN WOMEN: Reclaiming Our Sexuality, Taking Back Our Lives**; John Wiley & Sons, Inc.; New York; 1997

Youniss, James and Smollar, Jacqueline; **ADOLESCENT RELATIONS WITH MOTHERS, FATHERS, AND FRIENDS**; The University of Chicago Press; Chicago, IL1985

The Reverend Clarence Lumumba James, Sr. was born and raised on the West Side of Chicago. As a high school student he came under the tutelage of Dr. Martin Luther King, Jr. and became a member of his Southern Christian Leadership Conference Staff. He was involved in most of the major Civil Rights/Black Power initiatives of those days including organizing tenant unions, the Open Housing Drive, the student movement, the Meredith March, the Poor Peoples' Campaign and the National Mobilization to End the War in Vietnam. As an undergraduate he sat on the Standing Committee to Develop the Afro-American Studies Dept. at Harvard University. He ended his undergraduate studies at Morehouse College.

He has been a Baptist preacher for 35 years and the founder and president of Youth Leadership Development Programs since 1984. He has also served as Director of Recruitment for Morehouse College, Administrative Dean and CEO of Morehouse School of Religion and the chaplain of Lincoln University. He has taught at Northern Illinois University, the Interdenominational Theological Center (ITC), Temple University and Eastern Baptist Theological Center.